The Grace of Christ and the Grace of God in Augustine of Hippo

Christocentrism or Theocentrism?

Basil Studer, O.S.B.

Translated by
Matthew J. O'Connell

A Michael Glazier Book
THE LITURGICAL PRESS
Collegeville, Minnesota

A Michael Glazier Book published by The Liturgical Press

Cover design by David Manahan, O.S.B. Fragment of a floor mosaic, Hinton St. Mary, Dorset, 4th century, The British Museum.

1	2	3	4	5	6	7	8

Library of Congress Cataloging-in-Publication Data

Studer, Basil, 1925–
    [Gratia Christi, gratia Dei bei Augustinus von Hippo. English]
    The grace of Christ and the grace of God in Augustine of Hippo :
Christocentrism or theocentrism? / Basil Studer ; translated by
Matthew J. O'Connell.
       p.   cm.
    Includes bibliographical references and indexes.
    ISBN 0-8146-5855-5
    1. Augustine, Saint, Bishop of Hippo.   2. Jesus Christ—Person and
offices—History of doctrines—Early church, ca. 30–600.   3. God-
-History of doctrines—Early church, ca. 30–600.   I. Title.
BR65.A9S7513   1997
231'.092—dc21
                              96-29594
                                CIP

The Grace of Christ and the Grace of God
in Augustine of Hippo

Contents

Preface

"Books too have their history." This rather trite saying applies to the present study of *The Grace of Christ and the Grace of God in Augustine of Hippo*. Eight years ago, I was invited by the editors of the *Augustinus-Lexikon* to collaborate on the articles "Christ" and "God." It was finally agreed that I alone should write the first of these two articles and be the principal writer of the second. With a view to the discharge of this by no means easy task, I devoted a major part of my scholarly work to Augustine's Christology and his teaching about God. For reasons that I need not go into here, but to my own regret, the two contributions, which were substantially finished by the fall of 1990, could not appear in the *Lexikon*.

I mention all this because it largely explains, and perhaps excuses, the special character of the present work. To begin with, it renders intelligible what at first sight appear to be unconventional limits placed on the study of the two themes. The study of Christ, which forms the first part of the present book, is concerned chiefly, although not exclusively, with passages in which the word "Christ" occurs. The second study, which provides the substance of the second part of the book, does not deal with the whole of Augustine's teaching about God but is limited to the concept of "God." In particular, Augustine's teaching on the Trinity is taken up only to the extent that it deals with "God the Father" and "one God."

In addition, traces naturally remain of my original purpose, which was to write two articles for a lexicon. I have, however, translated the lengthier passages of Augustine and have allowed only shorter, more stereotyped citations to be given in Latin. Furthermore, I took the two themes as the subjects of my lectures in the first semester of the academic years 1990–1991 and 1991–1992 at the Augustinian Patristic Institute in Rome. My presentation may therefore smack somewhat of the classroom.

But the concrete circumstances that led to the present book in its final form have had their advantage as well. Despite the limitations set on them, the two studies combined here bring to light a tension that dominates the entire

1

theological thinking of Augustine. The title I have chosen for the book makes the problem clear, namely, the relationship between the orders of creation and redemption. In addition, the subtitle specifies the question: Is Augustine's theology to be viewed as Christocentric or theocentric? In this connection, I introduce some secondary themes that in my opinion deserve to be looked at more closely. Finally, the fact that I was able to present my interpretation of Augustine first to my students was of no little profit to the present book.

Be all that as it may, it has been a source of great joy to me to be able to devote myself for several years to the Church Father who is dearer to me than all the others. For this very reason, I feel obliged to express my sincere thanks to those who have made it possible for me to bring this work to a happy conclusion. First and foremost, I thank the editors of the Studia Ephemeridis "Augustinianum": Father Vittorino Grossi, the generous director, and Father José M. Guirau, the tireless secretary, who declared their willingness to make my book on Augustine a part of their series. I also thank Mrs. Uta Krewel (Bottrop), Dr. Hildegard König (Tübingen), and my young colleague, Robert Dodaro, all of whom contributed with commendable devotion to the improvement of the book's language and to the clearer presentation of my thought.

In grateful remembrance of the past twenty years, during which my teaching and scholarly research have been devoted for the most part to the Augustinian Patristic Institute, I wish to dedicate this study of a subject that was certainly a favorite of Augustine himself to the professors and students of the Institute. I include in my grateful remembrance all those—men and women, near and far—whose sympathy and interest helped me to find meaning in the part I have played in research into a long past age and at the same time not to forget the people of today.

Basil Studer
San Anselmo, Rome, November 1992

General Introduction

Is it Christ or God who is at the center of St. Augustine's theological thought? The question cannot be evaded if we bear in mind, first, how attached the Bishop of Hippo was to the formula "through Christ as human being to Christ as God" *(per Christum hominem ad Christum Deum)* and, second, how often, especially in his later years, he repeated the words of the Apostle Paul: "The grace of God through Jesus Christ our Lord" (Rom 7:25).[1]

The question of whether we should speak of Christocentrism or of theocentrism in connection with Augustine is in any case a very complex one. This can be easily shown from a discussion that went on in the recent past. About ten years ago, Barbara Aland published a very worthwhile article on *"Cogitare Deum* in den *Confessiones* Augustins."[2] As she explains in her introduction, two things stimulated her interest in what at first glance seems to be a quite narrow subject.[3] On the one hand, she could not allow E. Jüngel to go unchallenged when, in his book *Gott als Geheimnis der Welt,* he appeals to Augustine as supposedly the classical representative of the tradition of a completely incomprehensible God. On the other, she felt obliged to challenge R. Lorenz's claim that Augustine had not succeeded in overcoming a "certain ambivalence in the matter of grace and knowledge" and "therewith, the danger of confusing nature and grace."

She herself thinks that the positions of these two writers are mutually coherent, to the extent that the "monistic metaphysics," to which Lorenz attributes the ambiguity in Augustine's teaching about grace and knowledge, and the tradition of "the utterly transcendent God," which Jüngel claims to find in Augustine, are very similar. At bottom, both positions assume, each in its own way, that there is but a single order of knowledge. As Aland points out further on, behind the problem just indicated lurks the question of how "createdness for God" is related to the grace which is given to us through the incarnation of the Son.[4] In other words, according to Aland, we may ask whether there is a difference in principle or only a gradation between the creative action of God and God's action in grace or between nature and grace.[5]

On the basis of the *Confessions,* to which she deliberately limits her study, Aland attempts to answer the question in the following way.[6] There is a difference between the knowledge of God that reason can attain and the knowledge of God that is obtained with the help of grace. In the former kind of knowledge, it is possible for human beings, at least for a brief, though blessed, moment, to touch, at the apex of their souls, the God who transcends them. Believers, for their part, achieve the same experience of God in their prayer; but while they, like the philosophers, fall back again into the hard reality of the present life, they remain subject to God through their attitude of faith. Moreover, they hope for the everlasting vision of God, with the confidence given to them by their faith in the truth taught them by the "weakness of Christ," which has become the way for them.[7]

Thus, with her eye on the views concerning grace and knowledge that Lorenz proposes, Aland rejects a knowledge of God that is limited in a one-sided way to the possibilities of the human mind; in addition, she traces Lorenz's way of understanding the knowledge of God in Augustine to a failure to distinguish between nature and grace. If she had taken other passages into consideration, especially from the *Expositions of the Psalms,* she could have found even stronger support for her interpretation (she did not appeal to these other passages because she wanted to limit her study).[8]

In the final analysis, Lorenz stands in the line of those modern scholars who have taken their cue from a famous essay of A. von Harnack and have seen Augustine as primarily a Neoplatonic philosopher.[9] It should be remembered, however, that the dean of historians of dogma later nuanced somewhat his judgment on Augustine's theological thought. In doing so, he continued to see a tension in this thought between a more religio-philosophical doctrine on the "grace of God" and a more ecclesiastical teaching on the "grace of Christ."[10] Something of this dialectic can be seen in Pascal, who, as a reminder of a memorable night in his life, sewed into his clothing a paper that contained the following words among others, "'God of Abraham, God of Isaac, God of Jacob,' not of philosophers and scholars."[11] He thus distinguished between the God of faith and the God of the philosophers.

Augustine of Hippo was not in a position as yet to make such a distinction, although he does distinguish between two names in the revelation given to Moses: the "name [of God] in God's eternity" *(nomen aeternitatis),* that is, "the One who is," and the "name given in an act of mercy" *(nomen misericordiae),* that is, "God of the fathers."[12] But even if we see in Augustine the beginnings of a distinction between philosophy and theology in the Scholastic and modern sense of these two terms, he himself always means by "the truest philosophy" a deeper understanding of the Christian faith, in other words, a kind of theology in the later sense of the term.[13] In any case, he also ascribes to reason *(ratio)* possibilities of a knowledge that is not identical in its object with what believing Christians accept on the basis of biblical revelation and seek to understand with their reasoning powers. Thus in his *The Trinity,* he presupposes a concept of God that can be attained with the help of reason and that one must have in mind when one seeks to reflect on the thoroughly theological question of the unity in the Trinity.[14]

At the level of the rational understanding of the faith, Augustine distinguishes both materially and formally between two orders, which however are closely interconnected. He assumes as objective or ontological realities an order of creation and an order of redemption. By this I mean that in various contexts he speaks of God who created us and God who (even more wonderfully) redeemed us. More than anything else, it was the controversy with Pelagius, Julian of Eclanum, and others, in which his teaching on grace was challenged, that compelled him to differentiate between "the gift that is nature itself" *(gratia naturae)* and "the grace by which we are made believers" *(gratia fidelium).*[15]

This tension between "the gift of creation" *(gratia creationis)* and "the gift/grace of redemption" *(gratia redemptionis)* brings with it the problem of theocentrism and Christocentrism in Augustinian thought. As I mentioned earlier, the Doctor of grace undoubtedly cites again and again these words from the Letter to the Romans, "The grace of God through Jesus Christ our Lord" (Rom 7:25). In this context, Christ is consistently seen as mediator between God and humanity. But Augustine can also be content with the other formula mentioned earlier, "Through Christ as human being to Christ as God." Or he will speak of "Christ the way" and "Christ the homeland." The importance of these Christocentric-sounding formulas is clear from the fact that G. Madec has been able to write a book on Christ in Augustine with the title: *La patrie et la voie (The Homeland and the Way).*[16] Although the contexts in which such formulas as these are used make it clear that God is the beginning and the end, they also show how concerned Augustine is to make Christ the center of the activity of salvation.

Similar tensions are also to be seen in the order of knowledge. At the logical level, Augustine likes to appeal to the formula taken from the Latin translation of Isaiah, *Nisi credideritis, non intelligetis* ("Unless you believe, you will not understand," Isa 7:9). Thus, faith in Jesus Christ is in his view the unconditionally necessary basis of religious knowledge, but it is not to be forgotten that from another point of view, he gives priority to reason. Believers not only use their minds to discern how far they may in good conscience rely on faith; to some extent they also use them to control the statements of the Bible. In addition, rational knowledge based on faith is superior to simple faith. On the other hand, Augustine links the "advantage of believing" so closely with the purificatory function of faith that the question arises whether in his view a submission of faith to the divine authority serves only to cleanse the human heart for a truly spiritual knowledge of the truth, or whether, on the contrary, human beings, due to their faith in revelation, experience something to which even their purified hearts cannot give them access.[17] Thus, in an incidental way, the question of Christocentrism or theocentrism arises here once again.

In Augustine's view, faith depends in fact primarily on "the authority of Christ." But to what extent is this authority grounded in the authority of God? At the same time, human beings owe the certainty of their judgment to the presence of the interior teacher. But is not the eternal truth that enlightens the mind identical with the Word that God has spoken?

It is to this very complex set of problems that these two studies of Christ and God are intended to give an answer, or at least elements of an answer. The two studies are to a large extent independent of each other. Each of them takes as its starting point a state of the question that is based on a short review of the literature. In each, this is followed by a survey of the most important of Augustine's writings in chronological order. Each ends with a more systematic overview. This procedure makes it possible to approach the problem in question from two viewpoints and, using mutually complementary results, to reach a more complete general picture. In addition, the material framework is relatively restricted in both studies. The investigation of Augustine's Christology is largely limited to passages in which the word "Christ" occurs. The study of his theology is restricted to passages in which he uses the term "God" in either a specifically Christian sense or in a broad and non-specific sense. Yet even within this limited setting, it is possible to say something important about the question I have raised.

In both investigations, the Trinity is never lost sight of. For when I ask what Augustine means by "God" when the term is used in a broad sense, the Trinity is involved even here. On the other hand, in the discussion of "Christ," we are always talking about the only Son of the Father, who as the Human One *(filius hominis)* communicates divine life in the Holy Spirit. I have chosen to tackle the Christological question first, for this will make it clearer that for Augustine, both in his personal journey and in his theological thought, Christ was the way to God, the Lord and Father.

PART I

The Grace of Christ

Introduction

1. Augustine's Picture of Christ: An Unrecognized Problem

At first glance, the classical histories of dogma by Harnack, Loofs, and Seeberg seem to neglect Augustine's Christology.[1] And in fact, these authors say little or nothing about the constitution of the person of Christ. However, they are very much interested in redemption through Christ. This is especially true of Harnack, who presents Augustine as "reformer of Christian piety" and as a thinker for whom the "humility of Christ" is central.[2] If these three scholars regard Augustine's Christology, in the strict sense of this term, as unimportant for the history of dogma (as they understand this discipline),[3] the reason is first and foremost their focus on "Christ for us," a focus that goes back to A. Ritschl.[4] But their reserve is also explained by the judgment passed by O. Scheel, who in his comprehensive work on *Die Anschauung Augustins über Christi Person und Werk* (1901) had described Augustine's Christology as possessing very little originality.[5] In any case, the negative assessment made at that time of Augustine's contribution to the Church's teaching on the one Christ, true God and true human being, has continued to exert an influence down to very recent times. Even Mühlenberg in his notable essay on Augustine has only a few passing references to the latter's conception of Christ.[6]

And even the leading Catholic histories of dogma do not have very much to say about Augustine's Christology in the narrow sense of the term.[7] But when they limit themselves to this and do not expand their vision to encompass the saint's entire picture of Christ, other reasons are at work than in the case of the Protestant scholars. The approach of Catholic scholars is due chiefly to the overly sharp distinction between the person and the work of Christ that had developed in the Catholic tradition.

It was impossible, however, for Catholics to continue overlooking the extent to which Christology and soteriology go together in Augustine; W. Geerlings, in particular, made this point in his *Christus Exemplum,*[8] as I myself did in my patristic *Soteriologie.*[9] Other prejudices have likewise been overcome in modern research. Scholars no longer accept the one-sided and, in particular, the overly negative view of the Hellenization of Christianity that is to be seen in the classical histories of dogma.[10] They have also recognized that they must not limit themselves to the principal works of Augustine but must take his other writings into account, especially the sermons. The importance of this shift can be seen clearly in the most recent comprehensive presentation of Augustine's Christology by G. Madec.[11] But in order to better understand the change that has taken place between the beginning of the century and today, it will be helpful to look more closely at the factors operating in this development.[12]

2. A Hundred Years of Study of Augustine's Picture of Christ

a) The Influence of Harnack's Views on Hellenization

In 1901, O. Scheel published a comprehensive presentation of Augustinian Christology that is still useful today because of the wealth of material it provides.[13] In his work, he follows the line taken by contemporary historians of dogma, especially Loofs, as he expressly says,[14] but he emphasizes more than the latter does Augustine's dependence on the philosophy of late antiquity. In Scheel's view, the Christology which the young Augustine had worked out prior to 391 formed the nucleus of all that came later.[15]

According to Scheel, since Augustine had, in the course of his conversion, adopted the Platonic tradition and since, on the other hand, he had only vague ideas about Christianity, he simply identified the biblical "Son of God" with the Neoplatonic *nous* ("mind").[16] The divinity of Christ, defined in cosmological and metaphysical terms, was at the center of his thinking; at the same time, while he verbally accepted the humanity of Christ as understood by the Bible, it played no decisive role in his thinking. Seen in this context, the salvation of the human person could consist only in a communion of life with the Logos.[17] "Blessedness" flowed from the vision of "truth," that is, of the divine ideas contained in the Logos. In this approach, Christ is seen simply as a teacher and a model. Through his "instruction," he liberates reason for its union with the truth that is the Word.[18] Consequently, Christ's death and resurrection take second place to the incarnation of the Word. After 391 (Scheel says), this entire doctrine of redemption, which is focused on the self-revealing Logos, is indeed supplemented at certain points (for example, in connection with humility and Christ's mediatorial role), chiefly from Paul, but is not essentially changed.[19]

A Christology interpreted in such radically Hellenistic terms could not go unchallenged. Harnack criticized it severely.[20] To it he opposed a Christology in which the central place belongs to the mediatorship of Christ, which is based on the receptivity of the human soul to the "action of God."[21] Through his own fidelity to God, the human being Jesus leads his brothers and sisters to the gracious Father of them all. In this interpretation, the "humility of Christ" recovers its unique meaning.[22] At the same time, the suffering of Christ is emphasized.[23] As a result, other soteriological themes—the forgiveness of sin, reconciliation with God, victory over the devil—recover their importance.[24]

Seeberg, who attached much more importance than Harnack and Loofs did to the tradition of the Church, put himself on Scheel's side to the extent that he agreed with him on the significance of the Logos for salvation and expressly disagreed with Harnack on the role which the latter assigned to the soul of Jesus in the salvation of humanity.[25] At the same time, however, he asserted that "the religious interest of the great Father of the Church is not one-sidedly in the divinity of Jesus, but rather in this no less than in the humanity."[26] In addition, Seeberg placed a very heavy emphasis on the Western, voluntaristic element in Augustine's teaching on redemption.[27]

In the subsequent period, Scheel's approach was influential for a long time; it can be seen, for example, in O. Du Roy's investigation into the beginnings of Augustine's teaching on the Trinity.[28]

b) The Reaction to the One-sidedly Hellenistic Understanding
   of Augustine's Christology

After 1945, the study of the history of dogma was increasingly carried on in the light of ecclesial dogma and its connection with sacred Scripture. There was also a shift away from an overly pessimistic view of the Hellenization of Christianity (the beginning of which was, in addition, dated much earlier). In particular, the Neoplatonism of Milanese circles and of Augustine himself was seen in a much more positive light.[29]

It was in this new setting that T. van Bavel produced his ground-breaking study of Augustine's Christology.[30] Although his perspective was still that of Neoscholastic dogmatics, his considerable powers of historical criticism enabled him to do more justice to Augustine's contribution to Christology in the narrow sense of the term. He was able especially to show that Augustine's teaching on the communication of idioms had to a great extent anticipated the *Ekthesis,* or credal statement, of Chalcedon.[31] Above all, van Bavel's study of the emotional life[32] and human knowledge of Christ[33] showed that the humanity of Jesus was of much greater importance to Augustine than earlier scholars were prepared to allow.[34]

The interest in ecclesiology that had been growing since 1920 likewise led to a broader understanding of Christology. To some extent before the Second World War, but especially after it, studies and collections of texts were published that shed a bright light on the doctrine of the "whole Christ,"[35] which had been neglected in the classical histories of dogma.[36] Previously, scholars had been interested, at most, in the Christ of *The City of God*.[37]

Finally, an especially powerful impulse in Christology came from scholarly work on the liturgy. In particular, the studies of J. A. Jungmann[38] turned attention to the picture of Christ seen in the prayer of the community.[39] This in turn raised the question of the role of Christ in Augustinian piety and, more specifically, the question of whether this piety is Christocentric or theocentric.[40]

c) The Rounded Approach of More Recent Scholarship

Patristic studies, which had been pursued much more extensively since the fifties, especially in France and Italy, led, especially after 1975, to a more rounded approach to the investigation of Augustinian Christology. This is true first and foremost of the biblical area.[41] Older studies[42] were supplemented (partly in connection with modern editions of individual writings of Augustine) by a whole series of in-depth studies of the Christ of the Psalms, the Christ of John, and the Christ of Paul. The Christ of Augustine's *Expositions of the Psalms* roused particular interest.[43] The introductions of M. F. Berrouard to the *Homilies on the Gospel of John* are especially good.[44] Finally, the word "ground-breaking" must be applied to A. Verwilghen's comprehensive study of Augustine and the hymn in the Letter to the Philippians.[45]

To this context of connection with the Bible, belong to a large extent the studies, old and new, of the titles which Augustine uses for Christ—physician,[46] milk and whey,[47] redeemer,[48] merchant (or trader),[49] jurist,[50] and especially the fundamental title of mediator[51]—as well as studies of the theme "Christ—justice."[52] In relation to this, we should not overlook the fact that the philological interest at work in these word studies was awakened by research into Christian Latin.[53]

Catholic scholars, too, increasingly took into account the soteriological orientation of Christology that has always been stressed, sometimes to an exaggerated degree, in Evangelical scholarship.[54] As I have already noted, the traditional distinction between Christology and soteriology was transcended.[55] The resulting more rounded approach has left its mark especially on a number of studies devoted to the incarnation.[56] But it is to be seen also in investigations of the fundamental theme of the grace of Christ.[57]

For obvious reasons, Christian piety is inseparable from soteriology in Augustine, as is clear from, for example, the study of Schaffner on Christian humility[58] or that of Brabant on Christ as the center of Christian morality.[59] In this context, the various moods, as it were, of Augustinian piety need to be carefully considered, especially the Manichean[60] and Neoplatonic.[61]

Finally, it has become increasingly clear in recent years that in dealing with Augustine's Christology, it is not enough to consider only his philosophical background. It is also, and perhaps even more, necessary to keep in mind his literary education and the Ciceronian ideal of the "wise speaker" *(orator sapiens)*. Not only his sermons but his explanations of the Bible and even his treatises are profoundly permeated by this ideal.[62] How relevant this is even for his Christology has been shown by, for example, the studies of Lütcke on authority,[63] Mayer on sign,[64] P. de Luis on exegesis of the New Testament,[65] and Drobner on person,[66] as well as my own essays on "sacrament and model" and on the formula "to give pleasure and be of profit" *(delectare et prodesse)*.[67]

3. Consequences for Methodology

This historical and critical survey of the study of Augustinian Christology during the past hundred years also provides guidelines for the first part of the investigation I am undertaking here into the relationship between the grace of Christ and the grace of God. The investigation deals with everything that Augustine preached and taught about Christ, which includes the Christ with whom he lived his life. My aim is to bring out as clearly as possible how, under the influence of his personal experiences and encounters, he gave a new philosophical and biblical depth to the picture of Christ he had received from his mother. It is in the light of this development that we shall answer the question that is our ultimate concern here, namely, to what extent Augustine is Christocentric or theocentric and whether we should speak, in connection with him, of the grace of Christ or rather of the grace of God. Behind this question, as I pointed out at the beginning, lies the antithesis between the God of the philosophers and the God of the Bible.[68]

In this first part of the book, I restrict myself to texts in which the word "Christ" appears. The limitation will prove to be hardly a disadvantage. The reason: such texts are so numerous that the entire Augustinian picture of Christ emerges from them. At the same time, this linguistic delimitation makes it possible to discover aspects of Augustinian Christology that would otherwise remain hidden, for example, the association of Christ-formulas and Christological texts of the Bible, an association that varies according to context. Above all, this procedure allows the love of the greatest of Latin theologians for his Lord and Savior to emerge fully.

The procedure I am following also yields the division of the presentation of the grace of Christ into two sections. In the first, more analytic section, I shall study the occurrence and meaning of "Christ" in the various writings in their chronological order. The second section will be more systematic and deal with Christ who as true God and true human being is both way and goal for individual believers and for the entire human race and who is consequently the greatest blessing that God has bestowed on God's creatures.

CHAPTER 1

The Word "Christ": Its Meaning and Use

1. The Numerical Occurrence of the Word "Christ"

"Christ" occurs in the writings of Augustine as an unmodified noun. It also occurs frequently in combination with "Lord" as "Christ the Lord" or "the Lord Christ." A conspicuous formula is the one Augustine likes to use at the beginning of sermons: "Our Lord and Savior."[1] A special favorite is the expression "Jesus Christ our Lord," which evidently reflects Romans 7:25. Unmodified or in these several combinations, the word "Christ" occurs over 20,000 times, whereas the name "Jesus" occurs "only" 4650 times.[2] Since these are "sacred names," the soundness of the text is not always assured. In addition, Augustine also refers to the ancient Christian symbolism of the Greek word *ichthys*, "fish," an acrostic made up of the initial letters of the Greek words for "Jesus Christ, God's Son, Savior."[3]

2. Meaning of the Word "Christ"

In connection with Psalm 103:15, "that he may make his face cheerful with oil," Augustine explains the meaning of the name "Christ" by reference to the grace that has appeared in Christ.[4] In addition, he explains the name itself as follows:

> He is loved by all, he is preached by all; because he was anointed beyond all others, therefore he is Christ. For "Christ" means "anointed"; the name Christ is derived from chrism or ointment. Messiah in Hebrew, Christus in Greek, Anointed in Latin. But his whole body was anointed. Therefore all who come receive grace so that their faces may be made cheerful with oil.[5]

In this explanation, "Christ" is translated as "anointed"; at the same time, the Greek word *christos* is derived from *chrisma,* but is also linked to the Latin *oleum,* "oil."[6] In addition, Augustine notes the Hebrew background, the connection between Christ and Messiah.[7] In this same context, the point is also made that in the incarnation, the Son of God became the "Christ," and this for the salvation of the human race. To this end, as *The Trinity* says more clearly, Jesus received the Holy Spirit at the incarnation; at the beginning of his human existence, he was filled with grace without having any merits as yet. On the other hand, he was not really anointed by the Holy Spirit at his baptism in the Jordan; the anointing at his baptism by John was rather a prefiguration of the reception of the Spirit by the baptized.[8] Furthermore, the title "Christ" is connected with the idea of sending: "God was anointed for us and sent to us; God was a human being in order to be anointed, but God was a human being in such a way as to be God."[9]

All this becomes even clearer when we compare the definition of "Christ" with that of "Jesus." In many passages Augustine interprets the name "Jesus" as meaning "Savior" (see Matt 1:21).

> *Christ Jesus,* he [Paul] says, that is, Christ Savior, *Salvator.* That, you see, is what Jesus means in Latin. Nor should the grammarians ask how good it is as Latin, and Christians should just ask how true it is. *Salus,* you see, is a Latin noun. But as for *salvare* and *salvator,* these weren't Latin words before the Savior came. When he came to Latin people, he coined these Latin words.[10]

In this passage, Augustine regards "Jesus" as a proper name *(nomen proprium),* like the names Moses and Elijah, whereas he understands the word "Christ," like the words "priest" and "prophet," as a title, a symbolic name *(nomen sacramenti).*[11] When used metaphorically,[12] the title "Christ," like the name "Jesus" when this is paraphrased as "Savior," expresses a function in the order of salvation. "Christ Jesus" therefore also means "King and Savior."[13]

Augustine is thus able to locate Jesus in the line of the priests and kings of Israel[14] because by reason of their anointing, the latter proclaimed Christ in advance.[15] Even though they were far from perfect, they too were anointed ones, christs. In like manner, Christians may by reason of their anointing in baptism be called christs; for it was not only Christ as head who was anointed, but his body as well: the anointing belongs to them, too.[16] They are, however, anointed not in an unqualified sense but only by participation.[17]

3. "Christ" as a Proper Name

In most passages, however, Augustine uses "Christ" as a proper name, as a description of the subject about whom his statements are made.[18] It is with this usage in mind that he asks who or what Christ is, and he gives the answer: "The Word to whom the human being belongs."[19] He may make his question more concrete: "Who is the physician with whom we are dealing?" His first answer is "Our Lord Jesus Christ." To the further question, "Who is the Lord Jesus Christ?" he answers with a wide-ranging description of the identity of Christ:

> He is the one who was seen by those who crucified him. He is the one who was arrested, beaten, scourged, smeared with spittle, crowned with thorns, hung on a cross, wounded with a spear, taken down from the cross, laid in a tomb. He is our very Lord, Jesus Christ; he himself is clearly this, and he is the complete physician for our wounds. . . . Is not he himself all this? Yes indeed, but he is not simply what the Jews saw; that is not the whole of Christ. What more is there, then? In the beginning was the Word. In what beginning? And the Word was with God. What Word? And the Word was God.[20]

In such passages the reference to the economy of salvation is always more or less explicitly included.[21]

This way of speaking is evidently inspired by the creed, in which Jesus Christ is the subject of the second article. The sermons in which Augustine explains the baptismal profession of faith[22] or refers to the faith professed in baptism[23] leave no doubt on this point. It is against this background that he often speaks of "Christ born of the Virgin,"[24] or will say briefly and tersely, "Christ was born as God from the Father, as a human being from the mother."[25]

Two distinctions are at work in such passages. First, the statements about Jesus Christ may be either static or dynamic. In the former, Augustine will say that Jesus Christ is God and human being.[26] To this category belong also the statements about the unity of God and the human in Christ,[27] as well as those passages which speak of "believing in Christ," a phrase that in the final analysis means "believing that Christ is God and human being."[28] Dynamic statements, on the other hand, are concerned with the constitution of the subject named Jesus Christ: "The number of the persons is not increased when a human being is joined to the Word, so that one Christ results."[29] Or, more concretely: "In the Word, the [Human One] was sanctified from the beginning of his creation, when the Word became flesh, for the Word and the human being became one person. At that time, therefore, [the Word] sanctified itself in itself, that is, [the Word] sanctified itself as a human in itself as the Word, for Word and flesh are one Christ who sanctified the human being in the Word."[30]

Secondly, we must not overlook the fact that utterances about Christ are on different levels.[31] The name "Christ" may refer to the Word or to the Word made flesh or to the Church as the "whole Christ."[32] Accordingly, Christ exists "before us, for us, in us."[33] Christ is the Christ who speaks through the prophets, the Christ who lived on earth, and the Christ who is head of the

Church.[34] Finally, he is the historical, the mystical, and the eucharistic Christ.[35] In the proper or narrow sense, however, Christ is "the Word made flesh."[36]

4. Writings in Which the Name of Christ Is Lacking
Completely or to Some Extent

Although "Christ" in the sense of Messiah and, far more often, as a proper name occurs with great frequency, it is noteworthy that in a series of works and in lengthy sections of others, the word is missing completely or appears almost exclusively in citations from Scripture.

Now it is certainly not surprising that no mention is made of Christ in the early writings, which are mostly philosophical and rhetorical.[37] Augustine remarks that Alypius did not want Christ mentioned in these works.[38] On the other hand, according to Nebridius, those discussions were about Christ, Plato, and Plotinus.[39] As a matter of fact, the word "Christ" occurs at a crucial point in *Answer to Skeptics:* "I am certain that I shall never depart from the authority of Christ, for I find none that is superior."[40] The same holds for *The Teacher,* where the interior teacher is not only identified with eternal Wisdom but, in reliance on Ephesians 3:16f., is given the name Christ.[41]

But even after 391, there are works in which the name of Christ occurs only infrequently. Thus in *On Teaching Christianity,* Augustine mentions Christ only when he is analyzing biblical or patristic texts in which the name occurs.[42] He does not mention Christ at all in his explanation of the incarnation[43] and only rarely in his explanation of redemption and the mysteries of Jesus.[44]

It is especially striking that in his reflections on the Trinity, Augustine uses the word "Christ" only when discussing the economy of salvation and, in particular, the relevant objections of the Arians.[45] This is true even of *The Trinity:* the word "Christ" does not appear at all in Books 9 and 10 and occurs rather rarely in Books 1 to 7, even though the author discusses the incarnation there. Instead of "Christ," he speaks of "the Word" and "the Son" as well as of "Wisdom." It is likewise characteristic of the *Answer to Maximinus the Arian* that of the twenty points in the first book, only ten speak of Christ, while we look in vain for that name in many chapters of the second book.[46]

No less noteworthy is the fact that the name "Christ" is lacking in long stretches of the polemical works, even though the person of Christ plays an important role in them. Only toward the end of *The Christian Struggle* does the word "Christ" appear a good many times,[47] whereas it occurs only rarely in the earlier expositions of the incarnation and redemption. Even in the *Answer to Faustus,* where it appears more than a thousand times, it is used only once or twice in many books.[48] Likewise, "Christ" is hardly to be found at all in the historical expositions of the anti-Donatist works.[49] A series of anti-Pelagian writings contains the word "Christ" almost exclusively in repeated citations from Paul.[50] Even the *Answer to Julian* has whole sections without a mention of Christ.[51]

It is even more surprising that in many sermons, even in one Christmas sermon and certain Easter sermons, "Christ" occurs either rarely or not at all.[52] Among the *Expositions of the Psalms,* which are concerned basically with the "prophecy of Christ,"[53] there are some in which the word "Christ" is hardly used.[54] In many cases, it is used only in passing, as, for example, in the explanation of the title[55] or of certain words, such as "salvation"[56] or "hand of God."[57] On the other hand, a verse of a psalm or even a single word can give rise to an excursus on Christ or on grace; then the name of Christ suddenly becomes frequent.[58]

The name does, of course, occur often when Augustine is explaining a psalm according to his Christo-ecclesiological method, with the help of which he distinguishes between the head, the body, and the whole Christ.[59] But by no means does he use this method in all the *Expositions.* He leaves it aside throughout the explanations of Psalms 110-117. In these, "Christ" occurs only in citations from the New Testament and especially from Paul and in some formulas. In addition, Augustine may announce this method in the introduction of an *Exposition* but then not follow it throughout.[60] For the most part, he uses it, and with it the word "Christ," in explaining psalms in which the psalmist complains about the distresses and difficulties of human beings and asks God for help.[61] In these cases, the use of "Christ" is also occasioned by an anti-Donatist setting or the liturgical setting of Lent.[62] As is to be expected, "Christ" occurs especially often in exegesis of the strictly messianic psalms.[63] We must also not overlook the fact that Augustine regards certain psalms or psalm verses as addressed to Christ himself and not to God.[64]

In the *Homilies on the Gospel of John,* a last set of sermons, while Augustine uses the word "Christ" more frequently than John himself does, and uses it not only in the sense of Messiah, as John does exclusively, but also as a proper name, he does not use it at all in three of the homilies.[65]

Finally, we should observe that in the *Miscellany of 83 Questions,* the name "Christ" appears in a number of questions either not at all or only in the title,[66] that some books of *The City of God* introduce the name very infrequently[67] or not at all,[68] and that numerous letters do not speak of Christ except perhaps in the address.[69]

It is not easy to explain why Augustine uses the word "Christ" frequently in some works and infrequently or not at all in others. The biblical background certainly plays a decisive role. The context, too, must be taken into account, a point that becomes clearer in what will be said further on. It is even more difficult to determine the extent to which the greater or lesser frequency reflects a development. Be that as it may, there is a striking difference between *Faith and the Creed* (391) and the *Handbook for Lawrence* (421–423). In the former, the word "Christ" appears relatively seldom while in the latter, it is made clear from the outset that Christ is the foundation of the Catholic faith.[70] In any case, the varying frequency of the word "Christ" must warn the reader not to be too quick to speak of a Christocentrism in Augustine.

5. "Christ" in the *Confessions*

It is evident that the varying frequency of the word "Christ" in the different works depends on the biblical background of each. At the same time, we may think that it is also connected with the thrust of a work and even with its literary genre. We must also take into consideration how often, in Augustine no less than in other Church Fathers, one word leads to another. The relevance of this remark may already be seen in the *Confessions*.

When Augustine fell seriously ill as a child, he fervently begged his mother for the baptism of "Christ your God" (*Conf.* 1.11.17). As he expressly says, he, like his mother, already believed in Christ.[71] Because of this belief, which he had acquired with his mother's milk, he regretted later on that he had not found the name of Christ, his redeemer, in the *Hortensius* of Cicero (*Conf.* 3.4.8). On the other hand, the Manichees, whom he came upon next, had the name of God, of the Lord Jesus Christ, and of the Comforter, the Holy Spirit, constantly on their lips (*Conf.* 3.6.10). He shuddered as he thought back to the period of his illness in Rome, because at that time Christ had not yet freed him from original sin and his own sins and he would therefore have gone to hell if he had died (*Conf.* 5.9.16).

At that time, he had advanced to the point of breaking with the Manichees. However, he did not find the saving name of Christ among the philosophers to whom he now turned; thus, he decided to remain, at least for the time being, a catechumen in the Catholic Church (*Conf.* 5.14.25). His mother, who had followed him to Rome, was overjoyed at this decision and, with her trust in Christ, hoped to see her son a "Catholic believer" before she died (*Conf.* 6.1.1). Augustine himself found satisfaction in the fact that the Church, the Body of the only Son of God, the Church in which the name of Christ had been put upon him as an infant, did not teach any silly doctrines about the presence of God (*Conf.* 6.4.5). Despite all his intellectual difficulties concerning evil and God's presence, he felt that he already adhered firmly to the faith of the Catholic Church in Christ the Lord and Redeemer.[72]

In fact, he had already gotten further than that: he believed that in Christ, God's Son and our Lord, and in the Scriptures of the Catholic Church, God had provided a way of salvation leading to life after death (*Conf.* 7.7.11). Augustine was still looking for that way, but he did not find it until he acknowledged the mediator between God and the human race.[73] At that time in fact, he saw in Christ, his Lord, only a human being of surpassing wisdom, a complete human being indeed, but not a human being who excelled all others because he was Truth in person (*Conf.* 7.19.25). His friend Alypius, on the other hand, was of the opinion that in Christ there was God and flesh but not a human soul (*Conf.* 7.19.25).

Having read the books of the Platonists but not yet seeking the way to God in Christ, our Savior, Augustine had become not an initiate but a man condemned to death; he had not yet understood the love that builds on the foundation of humility, on Christ (*Conf.* 7.20.26). He did however come to see, thanks to his reading of the Bible and especially of the Apostle, that everything depends solely on the grace of God, which alone can set us free, through Jesus Christ, from the body of this mortal life (see Rom 7:24f.) (*Conf.* 7.21.27). When he met Simplicius in Milan, the latter tried to encourage him to practice the humility of Christ and to this end referred him to the example of Marius Victorinus, who had unhesitatingly become a servant of Christ and had come to fear remaining outside the Church of Christ and being denied by Christ in the presence of the angels (*Conf.* 8.2.3f.). So too had the Apostle humbled the pride of Sergius Paulus under the yoke of Christ (Acts 13:7-12) (*Conf.* 8.4.9).

In his struggle with himself, Augustine now realized that he could respond to God only if God would enlighten him through Christ (Eph 5:14) and rescue him through Jesus Christ from this body of death (Rom 7:24f.) (*Conf.* 8.5.12). This became fully clear to him when the words of the singing child, "Take, read," drove him to open the Bible and he read Paul's exhortation to renounce earthly joys and ambitions and to put on Christ (Rom 13:13f.) (*Conf.* 8.2.29). Made happy by the conversion that had come at last, he turned in prayer to Christ Jesus, his helper and redeemer, who had laid his light yoke upon him (*Conf.* 9.1.1). During the weeks he spent at Cassiciacum after giving up his teaching post, he experienced a great joy: God also caused his friend Alypius to submit to the name of the Son, our Lord and Savior Jesus Christ, although previously Alypius had not tolerated that name in Augustine's books (*Conf.* 9.4.7).

In his look back at the life and death of his mother, he tells of how God had trained her in the fear of God by the rod of Christ (*Conf.* 9.8.17). He also asks his readers to pray for him to God, the Father of all the brothers and sisters of Christ (*Conf.* 9.12.33). At the same time, he does not dare to say that his mother, who was indeed living in Christ, had never spoken a word contrary to the law of God (*Conf.* 9.13.34).

In his reflections on the presence of God, he refers again at the end of the tenth book to the example of humility and the redemptive activity of Christ, the only true Mediator (1 Tim 2:5); this Christ alone, who died for all (2 Cor 5:15), had kept him from despair (*Conf.* 10.43.68). In the remaining books, in which Augustine reflects on the beginnings of God's mercy, he mentions

Christ only in two formulas of prayer from Paul (*Conf.* 11.2.4; 11.22.28) and in allusions to texts of Paul (*Conf.* 13.7.8; 13.18.23; 13.21.31).

This survey of the *Confessions* undoubtedly sheds light on Augustine's own experiences of Christ. He reveals how he advanced from the still vague belief in Christ that had pervaded him from his earliest childhood to a faith that could answer the claims of reason and enable him to live a chaste life. It becomes clear, in particular, at what an early date Augustine reached the point of seeing in Christ both the Word and a true human being. His account of and reflections on the first thirty years of his life also indicate the exegetical, liturgical, and apologetic, and most other areas in which he was accustomed to use the word "Christ." They show—and this is the most important thing here—why and with what associations he uses it in each context.[74]

6. The Use of Biblical and Exegetical Language

a) Under the Spell of the Pauline Writings

It is the *Confessions* that first make clear the importance of the Pauline writings for Augustine's use of the name "Christ." In this work, a series of the most important Pauline texts, ones Augustine also cites elsewhere, already make their appearance: Romans 5:5; 1 Corinthians 3:1; 11:1; Ephesians 3:14, 19; and above all, 1 Timothy 2:5 and Romans 7:24f. In the last three books of the *Confessions* is also to be seen a phenomenon that will recur repeatedly: the word "Christ," if found at all, occurs only in citations from Paul (or John). This holds first of all for the commentaries on the Letters to the Romans and to the Galatians as well as for the explanations of other Pauline passages, where, of course, the frequent occurrence of "Christ" is to be expected.[75] But the same is true of many sermons,[76] and especially of certain *Expositions of the Psalms*[77] as well as, and above all, of many theological treatises.[78]

Even the anti-Pelagian writings, which deal essentially with the interpretation of Paul's teaching on grace, that is, the "grace of God through Jesus Christ our Lord" (Rom 7:25), are no exception.[79] Thus, in *The Perfection of Human Righteousness,* where the author is discussing the definitions (*definitiones*) of Caelestius, he uses "Christ," with two exceptions, only in citations from Paul, especially in reference to Romans 7:25. The same is true of *The Deeds of Pelagius,* where this passage of Paul is again frequently cited.[80] In like manner, the use of "Christ" is largely restricted in *The Merits and Forgiveness of Sins* to the biblical passages explained there.[81] In *The Spirit and the Letter,* texts that include the word "Christ" come from John as well as from Paul.[82] Augustine does not, of course, make all of Paul's ideas his own in the same degree, but his own usage is determined by the language of the Apostle. If the latter had, in the relevant passages, spoken only of "Jesus" or "Savior" or "Lord," then in Augustine, too, these titles would probably have occurred more frequently than "Christ."

The importance of the dependence on the Pauline writings in the use of the word "Christ" will become even clearer when we discuss the areas of theological controversy. But let me anticipate and note with regard to the interaction of theological questions and Pauline texts that in defending the divinity of Christ Augustine endorses the traditional preference for the hymn about Christ in Philippians 2:5-11. However he refers relatively infrequently to verses 5 and 11, which speak respectively of Christ Jesus and the Lord Jesus Christ.[83] Furthermore, the reader will not be surprised that in *The Trinity* and the *Handbook* Augustine cites the Apostle primarily in his explanations of soteriology.[84] Again, in *The City of God,* citations from Paul mount up in explanations of the end time.[85] Finally, it is also not surprising that in the theology of Easter which he develops in his letter to Januarius, Augustine relies on Paul and therefore speaks of "Christ."[86]

b) The Influence of the Other Biblical Writings

In the Christological exegesis of Genesis 1:1 and the Christological application of the psalms that we find in the *Confessions,*[87] an exegetical field in the broader sense is to be seen. To it belong, first and foremost, the explanations of the gospel stories. In these explanations, we meet the title "Christ" far more frequently than in the gospels themselves.[88] The same holds for the various "Questions" in which Augustine discusses difficult passages of the New Testament.[89] Especially noteworthy are the explanations of the Gospel of John, for in these "Christ" occurs continually.[90] Finally, in the various treatises, the proof from Scripture cites not only Pauline but also other New Testament passages in which the title "Christ" occurs, especially John 17:3.

The exegesis of the Old Testament is focused on Christ in a different way. As for the entire Christian tradition, so for Augustine the books of Israel speak constantly of Christ.[91] He is "the prophesied Christ," as the *Answer to Faustus* puts it and as is to be seen elsewhere as well.[92] Correspondingly, the word "Christ" occurs frequently in sermons on Old Testament passages.[93] The same is true of Books 15 to 18 of *The City of God,* in which Augustine describes the development of the two "cities" on the basis of texts from the Bible. Especially impressive is the Christological interpretation of the relevant psalms.[94] This special love of the Psalter leads us to expect that the Christological interpretation of Jewish prophecy will find its most important application in Augustine's most extensive work, the *Expositions of the Psalms.*[95]

In this work, "Christ" occurs with great frequency in the explanations of the titles: *In finem* ("To the end"), *Psalmus David* ("Psalm of David"), and so on.[96] Also worth mentioning are the methodological introductions in which the author explains how the verses of a psalm are to be distributed among the various voices: Christ the Head, Christ the body, or the whole Christ; as a result, the title "Christ" occurs frequently.[97] It is to be noted, furthermore, how certain key words immediately trigger the mention of Christ: salvation,[98] way,[99] testimony,[100] foundation,[101] rock.[102] Finally, Augustine relates a number of psalms in their entirety, especially prayers and complaints, to Christ and his Church, and therefore speaks continually of Christ.[103] This is also the case, as we would expect, with properly messianic psalms.[104]

The reason Augustine speaks constantly of Christ in this area of exegesis is that in his view, the Bible is nothing but the "the mystery of God that is Christ."[105] This is true, to begin with, of the Old Testament. Referring to the books of the Old Testament, Augustine tells Faustus that Christ speaks from all of the Scriptures.[106] (Here and elsewhere, "Christ" always means "the whole Christ.") "Practically every page tells of nothing but Christ, and the Church spread throughout the whole world."[107] Along the same line, Augustine also says that because the Law is ordered to love, love, that is, Christ, speaks from every psalm.[108] Everyone who has been educated in the school of Christ through the writings of the biblical authors knows that Christ is to be seen and understood in the psalms, the prophets, and the Law, all of which were composed before the coming of Christ.[109] The same is true, meanwhile, of the New Testament writings. While the books of the Old Testament proclaim Christ in advance, those of the New Testament narrate his deeds and thereby exhort to love.[110]

If, then, all of the sacred Scriptures tell of Christ, the ultimate reason for this, according to Augustine, is that Christ himself, the eternal Word of God, speaks in them. It is the Manichees, first and foremost, whom he reminds of this basic truth: "The Christ—that is, the Word of God, which he is—who says in the gospel that he has come to send fire into this world also speaks in the Old Testament when he says, 'I am a devouring fire.'"[111] For this reason, Augustine repeatedly insists that Christ speaks in the prophets or the psalmist.[112] Being the incarnate Word, Christ, unlike a prophet, spoke to humanity not only in words but in deeds: "Let us ask the miracles themselves what they have to say about Christ because they have tongues if they are understood. For since Christ is the Word of God, a deed of the Word is a word for us."[113] In keeping with this, Augustine goes far beyond the practice of the gospels when he so often introduces the sayings of Jesus with such formulas as "Christ says" or "Jesus Christ said."[114]

It is a fact, of course, that the prophetic language of Jesus is often obscure and ambiguous; it contains "mysteries" and "sacred signs" *(sacramenta)*.[115] Augustine seeks not only to call attention to this parabolic language[116] but to defend it with his views, as a rhetorician, on the usefulness of allegories and metaphors.[117] If, then, we do not want to stop at the "history" but also desire to understand the "prophecy,"[118] we must go to the Christ of the New Testament, for only so will the veil be taken from before our eyes. That is why

Augustine, using the words of the Apostle (2 Cor 3:14-16), constantly mentions this necessity.[119]

7. Traditional Language Referring to Christ

Since Augustine composed his *Confessions* a few years after his ordination as a priest, we find in them a language that derives from an already lengthy tradition and, to some extent, from the Bible itself. We find such expressions as "the baptism of Christ," "to believe in[to] Christ," "the name of Christ placed upon me," "Church of Christ," "yoke of Christ," "servant of Christ," "brothers of Christ." All these are traditional usages that belong to three linguistic domains.

a) Liturgical and Catechetical Language

In Augustine's sermons, and especially in those which he delivered in the period before and after Easter, in his own catecheses, and in some of his treatises, he repeatedly uses a whole series of stereotyped expressions current in the preaching of the time. Some examples are "commandment of Christ," "disciple of Christ," "coheirs with Christ," "sacrament of the body of Christ," "spouse of Christ."[120]

The series includes, in particular, formulas having to do with Christian initiation: "to attach oneself to the name of Christ," "to come to Christ" or "to faith in Christ," "to be baptized in Christ";[121] "to believe in[to] Christ";[122] "exorcisms in the name of Christ";[123] "sign of the cross of Christ";[124] "Christ [is] invoked over you";[125] "to receive the sacrament of the body and blood of Christ . . . to have the name of Christ . . . to be called a Christian";[126] "receive and eat the body of Christ, yes, you that have become members of Christ in the body of Christ; receive and drink the blood of Christ. . . . you turn into the body of Christ";[127] "in the memory of Christ's passion and resurrection";[128] "therefore just as, in a certain way, the sacrament of the body of Christ is the body of Christ and the sacrament of the blood of Christ is the blood of Christ, so the sacrament of faith is faith."[129]

Finally, the frequently used "Christ" formulas that are inspired by the baptismal profession of faith also belong here:[130] "Christ born of the Virgin Mary (of a woman)," "Christ who suffered," "Christ crucified," and others of this kind.[131] It is obvious that what Augustine is expressing in these formulas from the tradition is the connection of believing Christians with their Lord and Savior, and the oneness of the Church with its head.

b) Everyday Ecclesiastical Language

Likewise, of no little interest are the "Christ" formulas which Augustine uses in his dealings with his colleagues, with clerics, the ordinary faithful, friends, and officials. Such formulas occur quite frequently in the salutations of letters. For example, "Augustine sends greetings in the Lord to the beloved brothers, clergy, elders, and entire people of the Church of Hippo, whom I serve in the love of Christ";[132] or, "Augustine sends greetings in the Lord to the beloved Lord Jerome, his holy brother and fellow presbyter, who is to be honored in the love of Christ";[133] or again, "Augustine, bishop, sends greetings in the Lord to Lord Cecilian, an outstanding man, truly and deservedly to be honored and received as a son in the love of Christ."[134]

Augustine also uses "Christ" formulas when his aim is to implore a favor of his addressees or to admonish them. "I implore you by the gentleness of Christ";[135] or, "In the name of Jesus Christ we beg you not to do that";[136] or quite solemnly, "For I am sure that Christ dwells in your heart, and in his name I ask you to take counsel of him who presides over your mind that is subject to him";[137] or similar expressions.[138]

Finally, he invokes Christ in greetings and blessings, for example, "Lord, my son, may the mercy of God our Lord keep you happy in Christ."[139]

The extent to which he has made this language of the Church his own emerges with special clarity in a late letter in which he raises the question of when a bishop or the clergy are permitted to flee and abandon the community.[140] In this letter, he uses the following expressions for service of the Church and for the Christian community: "the bonds by which the love of Christ has bound us together" (1); "servants of Christ, ministers of word and sacrament" (2); 1 John 3:13 (3); "ministry of Christ . . . he does not deny Christ" (4); "ministers of Christ and people of Christ, a brother for whom Christ died" (6); "sheep of Christ" and "members of the body of Christ" (7); "Christian peoples" and "presence of the ministers of Christ," with reference to Philippians 2:21 (9); "salvation which is in Christ" (13); "flock of Christ" (14).

The letters of Paulinus and Jerome and others, which contain similar formulas, allow us to speak here of an everyday ecclesiastical language.[141]

How seriously Augustine himself took these references to Christ and was not simply making use of formulaic phrases is shown by Letter 232.6, in which he forbids his pagan addressees to call upon the name of Christ. It is also shown by the way in which he speaks of Christian friendship, of "friends in Christ," and of Christian love.[142] Behind a language that has been molded by the tradition, there is a faith in "Christ present in the Church"[143] and a profound conviction that he is serving Christ in his Church.[144]

c) The Language of Asceticism and Hagiography

"Christ" formulas are very frequent in Augustine's writings on virginity. The following may be mentioned from his principal work on the subject, *Holy Virginity:* "virgins of Christ" (1.1); "may Christ, son of a virgin and spouse of virgins, give aid" (2.2); "members of Christ . . . and themselves virgins and mothers of Christ" (7.7); "a teacher, therefore, of the humility of Christ" (31.31; see 32.32f.); "to suffer for Christ" (47.47). Similar expressions occur in *The Advantage of Virginity*.[145] The same language is typical of other ascetical writings. The final sections of *The Work of Monks* provide good examples: "the poor of Christ," "Christian warfare," "to serve Christ," "soldiers," "servants in Christ."[146]

A typically Christocentric language also occurs in sermons on the feasts of martyrs and in other hagiographical texts: "athlete of Christ";[147] "the feast of a holy virgin who publicly testified about Christ and earned a testimonial from Christ";[148] "to deny" or "confess Christ";[149] "tribute to the victorious Christ."[150] Appropriately, the writings on the saints show the extent to which, in Augustine's view, the perfect Christian life is grounded in Christ. This life consists of naught else but love for Christ and, consequently, witness to the love of Christ in the "city of God."[151]

8. The Word "Christ" in Works of Theological Controversy

Although the *Confessions* is an entirely personal work in which Augustine speaks with his God about himself, at the same time, the major questions that occupied him in his episcopal activity are also touched on. As a result, this account of himself also shows us the way in which he spoke of Christ in theological polemics.

a) "Christ" in the Anti-Manichean Controversy

The reference in the *Confessions* to the Manichees, who always had the name of Christ on their lips,[152] turns the reader's attention to the whole anti-Manichean controversy. In a letter to Bishop Deuterius, Augustine sums up the Manichean heresy in three points: denial of the reality of Christ's incarnation; erroneous understanding of the patriarchs, the prophets, and the Law; descent of the godlike soul into this world and the necessity of setting it free.[153] In the *Revisions*, he mentions only the first two errors, but in addition accuses Faustus of an adulteration of the New Testament writings.[154] He thus mentions all four of the themes that he develops in his anti-Manichean writings and in which he speaks especially of Christ.

Augustine first comes out against the Docetist tendencies of the Manichees.[155] Against these, he emphasizes Christ "born of the Virgin (of a woman)"[156] and Christ who suffered and died.[157] In addition, he takes pains to explain, in the light of Paul, the true meaning of the "flesh of Christ" and of his members.[158] In order to combat the illusory Christ of the Manichees, he emphatically exhorts his Christians, in connection with 1 John 4:1-3: "So meanwhile, dearly beloved, turn your ears away from every debater, preacher, writer, whisperer who denies that Jesus Christ has come in the flesh. So turn the Manichees away from your houses, your ears, your hearts. The Manichees, you see, deny quite openly that Christ has come in the flesh. So their spirits are not from God."[159]

In the same sermon, Augustine refutes the Manichean doctrine of the good and wicked natures. In doing so, he reminds his hearers that everything has been created through Christ and that the real incarnation of Christ as the means of salvation restores and lifts up not a nature that is wicked in itself but a nature that has become wicked.[160] In order to refute the Manichean thesis on the divinity of the soul, he then shows them that the wickedness of the soul consists in error and weakness *(infirmitas)* or, in other words, has its ground within the soul itself; finally, he refers again to the real incarnation as the source of salvation.[161]

In defending the Old Testament against the Manichees, Augustine develops the basic theme of the "prophecy of Christ," which had already been taken up by Christian theology at an early date. In his polemic with the Manichees, this theme acquired new relevance.[162] His most extensive explanation of the theology of prophecy is found in the *Answer to Faustus,* Books 12 and 13.[163] Here he responds to Faustus' claim that the prophets did not in any way proclaim Christ in advance. He offers two arguments. First, he goes back to the words of the Apostle and the words of Jesus himself.[164] Then he gives proof to the contrary in the form of a wide-ranging typological explanation of the history of Israel,[165] the "prophetic nation."[166] He also takes as his basic principle that the entire Bible, even if not always with equal clarity, proclaims Christ.[167] For this reason, he speaks continually of Christ: of the prefigurations of Christ and the prefigurations, too, of those who reject Christ[168] and those who believe in Christ.[169]

In these passages, Augustine is dealing with the proclamation in advance of Christ and the Church.[170] He justifies this Christological and ecclesiological interpretation not only by the authority of the Apostle[171] but also by the language of allegory[172] and by references to allegory in Philo[173] and the pagans.[174] In the thirteenth book, Augustine again tries to prove the usefulness of prophecies for belief in the divinity of Christ. His aim here is to counter the objection of Faustus that the prophecies would not help a pagan to believe the prophets and, through the prophets, Christ.[175] In response, he shows how prophecies written, as the Jews attest, long before the coming of Christ[176] have been fulfilled in the history of the Church: in persecutions of the Church, in the spread of the Church, and in the Church's internal difficulties.[177] In the process, he also points out emphatically that it is only through Israel and its prophets that the pagans have been instructed about the one true God[178] and about Christ, God's messenger.[179]

In the discussion of the Christian meaning of the Old Testament, Augustine was ultimately forced to take up the question of the "authority of the faith." In doing so, he developed the insights into the relation of faith to reason that he had acquired during his own conversion. Against Faustus, he emphasizes first of all the need of witnesses and signs for faith in Christ,[180] as well as the purifying power of simple faith.[181] The "authority of the faith" itself is derived primarily from the Bible[182] or, more accurately, from the agreement between the apostolic and the prophetic writings,[183] whereas it has no support from the authority of pagan[184] or even Manichean writings.[185] For its part, the authority of the Bible acquires its full force from the authority of the Church.[186] For this reason, at the end of the entire work, Augustine once again emphatically warns his readers to hold fast to the authority of the Scriptures because this has been preserved intact through apostolic succession since the time of Christ.[187]

In the thirteenth book, meanwhile, he places less emphasis on tracing this Church-supported authority back to the authority of Christ himself.[188] Perhaps Faustus' stress on the "reputation of Christ" *(fama Christi)* deterred Augustine from referring specifically to Christ.[189] Elsewhere, he is perfectly clear on the point. Not only does he insist that Christ, the Word, spoke in the prophets[190] and that one must go to Christ in order to understand the Old Testament.[191] In *The Advantage of Belief,* he also criticizes heretics who are unwilling to believe unless they have achieved rational insight; in his view, they are not Christians at all.[192] At the same time, he insists that within the Church, the reason for believing is that Christ has given the Church such great authority.[193] But this emphasis on authority in the controversy with the Manichees did not keep Augustine from also subjecting their objections to a historical critique, especially their objections to the Gospel of Matthew.[194]

Also to be noted is his view that even the just of the Old Testament were justified by faith.[195] In the final analysis, their faith was the same as the faith of Christians. The only difference was that they lived in a different order of signs: they believed in the future coming of Christ, whereas Christians believe that he has already come.[196]

The fact that in all his discussions with the Manichees, Augustine constantly speaks of Christ[197] will cease to surprise if one bears in mind the importance Christ had for them.[198] They even regarded Mani as an apostle of Christ.[199] They also spoke of Christ in their explanations of "the savior who saves and must be saved."[200] A typical example is Fortunatus, who in his debate with Augustine speaks of "Christ the Savior" and in addition appeals to the relevant passages in Paul.[201] Above all, they cultivated a real Christ-centered piety. In both East and West, Christ had a place in Manichean teaching: he brought light and salvation.[202] Proof of this is the way in which the Manichees confessed Christ. Thus, in Faustus' confession of faith as cited by Augustine we read:

> Therefore, we worship the one deity under the threefold name of the
> Father, God almighty, of Christ [the Father's] Son, and of the Holy

Spirit. . . . The Son, however, dwells in this second and visible light; because [the Son] is twofold, according to the Apostle who says that [the Son] is the wisdom and power of God, we believe that his power resides in the sun and his wisdom in the moon.[203]

In the anti-Manichean controversy, Augustine thus links the concept of Christ with statements about the true humanity of the Redeemer, with the idea of prophecy and fulfillment, and with the norm of authority: Christ is the truly incarnate Son of God, in whom the prophecies of the biblical authors have been fulfilled and on whom the authority of the Scriptures but also of the Church is based.

b) Apologetics

Augustine was helped on his way to the whole Christ by the philosophers. To his disappointment, however, they themselves did not speak of Christ; they did not know the incarnate Word.[204] With this statement in the *Confessions,* we touch on the realm of apologetics; here, too, Christ has an important place.

We meet the theme in the sermons in which Augustine comes to grips with the remnants of contemporary paganism—with its customs and its criticisms of Christianity.[205] The sense of Christianity's superiority that finds expression in these sermons is especially characteristic of his addresses on the feasts of the martyrs.[206] The sermons recently discovered in Mainz can also be regarded as belonging among the sermons of this kind. In these, Augustine invites pagans, who evidently have entered the basilica of Boseth, to convert to the Christian faith.[207] In so doing, he speaks of the "Church of Christ" (no. 4), of "believing in Christ" (no. 19), of the "name of Christ" in whom all earthly events take place (no. 20), of "the cross of Christ on the foreheads of kings" (no. 24). In a special way, however, he urges on them the "humility of Christ, the medicine that cures pride" and, in keeping with this, concludes his invitation to conversion with these words: "Let the proud, then, drink the cup of the humility of the humiliated Christ. Let them deign to be humble; let them now recognize the medicine meant for them; let them come and believe" (no. 26).

The language of apologetics likewise characterizes the letters which Augustine exchanged with pagans, especially with pagan intellectuals. In his letter to Volusian, in which the issue is the incarnation of Christ, he speaks continually, of course, of Christ.[208] In his letter to Dioscorus, a young Greek who has asked him all kinds of questions, he is no less explicit. He speaks there of "the Christian faith,"[209] of "the Christian era" and the subjection of Platonic philosophers to Christ the King,[210] of the salutary humility which Jesus Christ came into the world to teach,[211] and of the growing reputation both of the name of Christ and of those who have acknowledged Christ to be Wisdom itself and have entered into his service *(militia).*[212] Also of interest is the correspondence with another pagan, Longinianus. Here Augustine asked

Longinianus what he thought of Christ, but he was understanding when the man gave him an evasive answer.[213] The name "Christ" also occurs with remarkable frequency in a letter in which Augustine answered the questions of pagans, especially questions about the resurrection, the delayed coming of Christ, and the prophet Jonah.[214] Typical, finally, is the way in which, in a letter to the pagan residents of Madaura, the Bishop of Hippo denies them the right to greet him with the name of Christ.[215]

The language of apologetics undoubtedly finds its most impressive use in *The City of God*. Thus, the name of Christ already appears in the introduction, in which the author chastises pagans for their ingratitude in defaming "the Christian era" and in blaming the sufferings of Rome on Christ.[216] In keeping with this apologetic tone, "Christ" occurs rather frequently in the first three books.[217] In Books 4 to 10, however, it is less frequent and is entirely missing from Book 6. Since in the second half of the work (Books 11–22) Augustine is making use of a great deal of the results of his exegetico-theological work, there is room to distinguish to some extent between the apologetic,[218] the anti-Manichean,[219] and the liturgical[220] ways of speaking of Christ. Especially striking in these books is the kind of exegesis in which "Christ" is accompanied by applied biblical testimonies, more specifically, the typological explanations of the histories of the patriarchs and the monarchy,[221] the prophecies of Christ and the Church,[222] the eschatological texts of the New Testament,[223] and the Pauline texts on the resurrection.[224]

In this apologetic usage, the first thing that strikes the reader is the fact that Augustine often speaks at the same time of Christ, Christians, and pagans,[225] as well as of the "Christian religion" and the name of Christ.[226] In this setting, the Church, "the family of Christ," is presented, not only in the biblical and apocalyptic sense but also in the political sense, as "the city of Christ, the unconquered king."[227]

Far more impressive, however, is the way in which Augustine repeatedly contrasts the pride of the pagans and the philosophers, which at bottom is the pride of the demons, with "Christ's way of humility." At the climax of Augustine's debate with the Platonic philosophers, we read: "What reason is there for your refusal to become Christians on account of opinions which are your own, though you yourselves attack them? It can only be that Christ came in humility, and you are proud."[228] So, too, he emphatically proclaims Christ as crucified, as foolishness to the pagans.[229]

But the theme that is of the most far-reaching importance for the Christology of Augustine is that of the "universal way," which those false mediators, the demons, cannot open up. This way was opened by Jesus Christ, the one true mediator between God and humanity, through his sacrifice on the cross.[230]

Noteworthy, finally, is the conception of Christian history. On the one hand, Augustine repeatedly refers to "the Christian era," which began with the "coming of Christ"[231] and which has been wholly victorious since even the Roman emperors submitted to the name of Christ.[232] On the other hand, knowledge of "sacred history" and, above all, of the central event that is the incarnation of Christ is not based on fables and myths but on a reliable written history.[233] In the final analysis, this last deserves to be trusted because of the promises made by the prophets and Christ himself which have been fulfilled in the Church.[234] It is precisely along this line that in the second half of his *The City of God,* Augustine tries to show against Porphyry[235] that Christians can achieve knowledge of the "universal way."[236] Thus, he uses history in his effort to penetrate the mystery of God that has been revealed in the one mediator, Jesus Christ.

We should observe that Augustine earlier uses the apologetic language of *The City of God* in another less well-known but nonetheless remarkable work, *The Consent of the Evangelists.* Before giving, in Books 2 to 4, exegetical proof of the essential agreement among the four gospels, he takes up, in Book 1, the pagan objection that Christ left no writings behind him.[237] In doing so, Augustine uses almost exclusively the title "Christ."[238] At the same time, he opposes Christianity to paganism, speaking of "the enemies of the name of Christ,"[239] of "those who praise Christ [but] are malicious detractors of the Christian religion,"[240] as well as of "the Christian faith"[241] and even of "the King of the Christians."[242]

Here again, the expression "the Christian era," which occurs several times, deserves special attention.[243] By it Augustine means the period in which idolatry has been vanquished, as the prophets had promised. Pagans may claim to "praise Christ" but they resist becoming Christians. They see Christ as indeed a wise person but they refuse to recognize him as the one in whom the God of Israel, the only true God, has announced the end of idolatry.[244] Finally, in this work Augustine already sets forth his doctrine of the one mediator between God and humanity and thereby responds to the pagan objection which he had mentioned at the beginning: Christ, having become head of his Church, led the evangelists by the hand and thus excluded any contradiction from their writings.[245]

c) "Christ" in the Realm of Dogma

Since in the *Confessions* Augustine describes—from his later vantage point—the development of his initially still vague faith in Christ,[246] we must also take current dogma into account, as this had developed in the orthodox Churches as a result of the Trinitarian and Christological controversies of the fourth century. His references to "my God, the humble Jesus" and "the whole human being" that was "in Christ"[247] echo both the Arian and the Apollinarist controversies with which, especially the former, he dealt in detail and in the process spoke repeatedly of Christ. He did so whenever the scripture reading in the liturgy or elsewhere gave him the opportunity. The opportunity arose especially in his ongoing commentary on the Fourth Gospel,[248] but also in many expositions of the Psalms[249] and in other exegetical sermons.[250] These controversies, which by now had become traditional, were reflected even more strongly in his explanations of the orthodox faith.[251] But they also became a matter of present relevance when he directly opposed contemporary Arians.[252] In addition, there was the affair of Leporius.[253] Finally, in his various descriptions of heresies, Augustine comments on the two errors of which we are speaking here.[254]

Two points may be mentioned that will help us understand this dogmatic context. First, the word "Christ" occurs here only when Augustine is speaking of the "economy of salvation," that is, when he is speaking of Christ who is both God and human being.[255] Second, it is to be emphasized that "Christ" is always conceived as the subject of both divine and human predicates.[256]

In the entire area of dogma that is inspired by the tradition of the fourth century, it is the two-part formulas that stand out the most. In this context, those statements may be regarded as fundamental in which Christ is represented as God and human being or simply as the God-human: "True human being, true God: God and human being, the whole Christ. This is the Catholic faith."[257]

Following the anti-Arian tradition, in which the primary issue was a clear description of the sonship or generation of Christ, these basic statements are made more precise by means of antitheses in which the twofold origin of Christ is expressed. Following the confession of faith, Augustine speaks first and foremost of "Christ," the "Son of God" and the "Human One" *(filius hominis)*: "According to the true Catholic faith our Lord and Savior Jesus Christ is Son of God according to his divinity and son of David according to the flesh."[258] Accordingly, Christ is "born of God and, by the power of the Holy Spirit, of the Virgin Mary."[259] Both births are described as wonderful.[260]

Using a more biblical language, Augustine distinguished, as the tradition did, between Christ as only-begotten *(unigenitus)* and first-born *(primogenitus).*[261] This expresses more strongly than other antitheses the fact that Christ is the natural and not the adopted Son of the Father.[262] Accordingly, Augustine repeatedly says, in strongly anti-Arian language, that as God, Christ is equal to the Father *(Patri aequalis),* while as human being he is less than the Father *(minor Patre).*[263]

Just as often, he uses more technical terms and speaks of the two substances or two natures of Christ.[264] The same idea, but without direct reference to the two births, is also expressed in the two biblical themes that had long since become part of the Christian tradition: "the Word was made flesh" of the Johannine Prologue and "in the form of God, in the form of a slave" of the Letter to the Philippians. Augustine uses both passages separately[265] but often together as well.[266] In doing so, he gives his personal explanation of "Word" as meaning God's speaking[267] and paraphrases "flesh" as "the likeness of sinful flesh" (Rom 8:3).[268] He lays great stress on the "canonical rule" that governs the use of two-member formulas in accordance with the traditional rules for the communication of idioms; in other words, he distinguishes between the (biblical) assertions made about Christ as God and those made about Christ as human being.[269]

At the same time, it is of interest for the doctrine of the Trinity that in his anti-Arian writings from a later period (after 419), he applies the "less than the Father" not only to the incarnation but also to the eternal origin of the Word from the Father.[270]

Somewhat less numerous than the two-member formulas are those with three members. These originate in the anti-Apollinarist tradition;[271] in them, the human element is described as consisting of "(rational) soul" and "flesh": "Nor, as some have said, was there simply flesh and Word; there was flesh and soul and Word."[272] In using these formulas, Augustine is not simply endeavoring to prove the existence of the human soul of Christ from the relevant passages of Scripture, especially Matthew 26:38 and parallels.[273] Rather, he is also explaining the character of this soul, inasmuch as he ascribes to it all human (non-sinful) weaknesses, which it has freely accepted.[274] The Docetist tendencies of the Manichees and Priscillianists are opposed in the formula "Word and human spirit and human flesh," with texts of Scripture being supplied for each element.[275]

After 360, writers had begun to balance the Christological antitheses used against the Arians with formulas emphasizing unity, these being taken partially from earlier traditions. We find these in Ambrose, Damasus, and Jerome among the Latin writers.[276] Augustine himself did not hesitate to follow this tradition. We find such formulas, therefore, in sermons from around 400 or earlier.[277] Thus, we read in an explanation of the multiplication of the loaves:

> [Christ] must be feared, but he must be loved even more. He is human being and God; the one Christ is human being and God, just as one human being is body and soul; not, however, God and human being as two persons. In Christ there are indeed two substances, God and human being, but one person, so that the threefold Trinity might remain and not become fourfold with the addition of a human person.[278]

The analogy with the unity of the human being, to which allusion is made here, is developed elsewhere,[279] especially in the letter to Volusian,[280] with the aid of Neoplatonic anthropology.[281] Augustine's intention in using this already traditional comparison is to safeguard the immutability of God. The same is true of the idea of God and flesh being united by means of the soul.[282] In addition, Augustine developed a noteworthy teaching on the communication of idioms.[283]

For the rest, Augustine's conception of the oneness of Christ is shown, although with more or less clarity, in the various, likewise traditional ways of describing the incarnation[284]: as an event *(fieri),*[285] a taking on *(susceptio)*[286] or assumption *(assumptio),*[287] a drawing close *(accedere),*[288] or even a mingling without confusion *(mixtio sine confusione).*[289] Although in using these terms Augustine is clearly starting from the teaching of the faith according to which only the Son became a human being,[290] he does not yet arrive at the technical formulation of the dogma. That is, he does not use the expression "the one person of Christ" in order to describe the starting point of the incarnation. In his thinking, "the one person of Christ" is rather the result of the ineffable union between the godhead and the humanity in Jesus Christ.[291]

d) "Christ" in the Anti-Donatist Writings

It is perhaps permissible to see the references in the *Confessions* to "your one Church, the body of your only Son,"[292] and "the faith, within the Catholic Church, in your Christ"[293] as allusions to the Donatist controversy. In any case, the anti-Donatist writings can be seen as a special setting for Christology. "Christ" has an important place in these writings, apart from the sometimes lengthy historical disquisitions in which the word occurs hardly at all.[294] The same is true of a series of letters,[295] numerous and sometimes famous sermons,[296] many of the *Expositions of the Psalms,*[297] and especially the early homilies on the Gospel of John.[298]

In these writings, Augustine obviously keeps in mind the fundamental outlook of his adversaries.[299] In his view, the Donatists have a correct teaching about Christ but not about the Church of Christ. They acknowledge that the Church has a head and a body, but they do not know where the true Church of Christ is.[300] In their ignorance, they call into question three points in particular: the universality of the Church, that is, "the Church spread throughout the entire world"; the holiness of the sacraments administered in the Catholic Church and thus the true meaning of "the communion of the holy" *(communio sanctorum);*[301] and the coexistence in the Church of the just and sinners, the "mixed body," or the nature of the "society of the holy" *(societas sanctorum).*[302]

To these three questions, Augustine gives answers that are completely Christological. In doing so, he takes as his starting point the principle that the same sacred Scriptures that proclaim Christ also contain the real truth about the Church of Christ. "In the Scriptures we learn Christ, in the Scriptures we learn the Church. . . . See the Scriptures we have in common, see where we know Christ, see where we know the Church. If you hold fast to Christ, why do you not hold fast to the Church?"[303] It is in the words of Christ, then, not in the words of human beings, that we find the answer to the question of where the Church is.[304]

In answer to the first and decisive question, he maintains that Christ is not here or there but everywhere and that therefore the Church, too, must be universal: "If you attend to Christ, he is everywhere. You say, 'Christ is here'; but I say, 'He is everywhere.' . . . See what Church I point out to you. See what Christ bought, see what he redeemed, see for what he shed his blood."[305] In addition, Augustine continually harks back to more or less biblically inspired themes, all of which underscore the point that Christ is the Lord of the "one Catholic Church," the one, all-embracing Church.[306]

Thus, he very often refers to what the Apostle says about the seed that is Christ (Gal 3:16).[307] No less frequent are his admonitory references to the "inheritance of Christ" that includes all nations (allusion to Ps 2:2).[308] Along this same line are the exhortations in which Augustine calls to mind the "oneness of Christ,"[309] "the peace of Christ,"[310] or "the love of Christ."[311] More vividly but no less biblically, he depicts the Church as the one bride of Christ,[312] as the chaste virgin who clings to Christ alone (see 2 Cor 11:2f.).[313] In doing so, he is obviously taking notice of the exegesis of the Song of Songs, which the Donatists had cited.[314]

More concretely, he speaks of the "altar of Christ," beside which no other altar may be built.[315] By this, he also conveys that the one Church of Christ is founded on the Eucharist: on the "table of Christ,"[316] the sacrifice of Christ,[317] and the reception of the body and blood of Christ.[318] Finally, it is especially in this context of the Eucharist, and often with anti-Donatist echoes, that he develops his doctrine of the "whole Christ," the head and members that make up the one Christ.[319] Here he is clearly influenced by Tyconius, a Donatist,[320] yet the prosopic exegesis he uses, which distinguishes "the person of the head" and the "person of the body" as subjects of various statements *(voces),* has roots that go far deeper.[321]

The other two questions are also answered by reference to Christ. On the one hand, Augustine sees the holiness of the sacraments as originating in Christ. He presupposes that Christ is the "originator of the sacrament," the sole teacher of true baptism,[322] and the only true priest.[323] Accordingly, the decisive factor is not the integrity of the human minister but the sacramental presence of Christ. It is Christ and not the holder of office who is the "origin," "root," and "head"; it is not the "conscience of the minister" that is decisive for the faith of the baptized, for it is Christ who gives faith.[324]

By means of this Christological grounding, Augustine ensures the holiness of baptism even in those cases in which one does not know whether the baptizer is interiorly a member of the Church.[325] For this reason, he does not weary of repeating to his faithful that Christ himself baptizes.[326] Likewise, he repeatedly speaks of the "baptism of Christ," partly in opposition to the baptism of John.[327] Nor does he fail to say more precisely in this context that Christ baptizes "by the invisible action of majesty": "Christ baptizes not by a visible ministry . . . but by hidden grace, by hidden power in the Holy

Spirit."[328] This means that when baptism is administered in the name of Christ and with his words,[329] it makes the baptized person a member of the Church of Christ, even though it may not bestow the "justice of Christ," since the "sacraments of Christ" have their salutary effect only in the Catholic Church that is connected in oneness of life with Christ its head.[330]

Augustine sees the valid celebration of the Eucharist as depending, like baptism, on the name of Christ and on Christ's consecratory blessing.[331] At the same time, he also resolves the third and most thorny difficulty by reference to Christ. During the time of this world, the "body of Christ" is "mixed":[332] both good and bad Christians belong to the Church.[333] In other words, "even the wicked are gathered together in the sharing of Christ's sacraments."[334] Only Christ, the Lord of the Church, knows who belongs to him interiorly as well. At the end of time, as judge of the living and the dead, Christ will separate true and false Christians and thus make known to all who his members are.

e) The Anti-Pelagian Semantic Field

In the *Confessions,* finally, Augustine also anticipates his teaching on grace against the Pelagians.[335] According to what he says, Pelagius himself interpreted the work in this way.[336] In one sense, this anti-Pelagian semantic field is doubtless identical with the general exegetical and especially with the Pauline semantic fields, which we saw earlier. But here the Pauline and other biblical texts are brought to bear in an original way.

In his work on *Heresies,* in which Augustine outlines his teaching on grace in a positive way and at the same time defines the errors of his Pelagian adversaries,[337] it is remarkable that he does not put the emphasis on Christ. In fact, however, as he insists elsewhere, the Pelagian views on grace call the redemptive work of Christ into question. Thus, they empty the cross of its meaning.[338] If their view is accepted, Christ died in vain (Gal 2:21).[339] For this reason, Augustine repeatedly describes them as enemies of the grace of Christ.[340] In other words, the Doctor of grace does not weary of following the Apostle (Rom 7:24f.) and presenting his own theology of grace as a doctrine of "the grace of God through Jesus Christ our Lord."[341] He does not, therefore, simply observe that the entire Bible is about this divine grace of Christ,[342] but he also entitles one of his writings *The Grace of Christ.*[343]

It cannot come as a surprise, therefore, that in his anti-Pelagian treatises, sermons,[344] and letters,[345] Augustine constantly speaks of Christ. This is of course true, first of all, of expositions in which he cites the Pauline testimonia.[346] But in this regard, the reader is immediately struck by the fact that Augustine appeals to a relatively few passages which recur more or less frequently. Among these, as the subject requires, citations from the Letter to the Romans take first place since the divergent interpretations of this Letter form the most hotly controverted point in the dispute between Augustine and

Pelagius. These passages include Romans 5:1-12, especially 5:5 and 5:12,[347] Romans 7:24f.,[348] Romans 8:3,[349] and Romans 8:28ff.[350] Also frequently cited are Galatians 2:21,[351] Galatians 3:26,[352] Galatians 6:2,[353] 1 Corinthians 1:17,[354] 1 Corinthians 15:21f.,[355] Philippians 2:21,[356] and 1 Timothy 2:5.[357]

At the same time, Augustine also uses the word "Christ" in expressions of his own, although these are often derived from Paul or other biblical writers.

He speaks of Christ, to begin with, in many passages in which he is dealing with baptism. He often uses such phrases as "regeneration in Christ," "to be reborn in Christ," or similar formulas,[358] as well as "the baptism of Christ."[359] He repeatedly recalls that Christ is "Jesus" and "Savior" even for little children.[360] So too, he speaks of Christ when the subject is the origin of human sinfulness or the need which the entire human race has of redemption. In this context, it is the many forms of the Pauline Adam-Christ antithesis that stand out.[361] Thus, the origin of all human beings from Adam is seen as the counterpart *(forma e contrario)* of rebirth from Christ.[362] Here the "flesh of Christ" himself is exempted from any sin; it is only a "likeness of sinful flesh" (Rom 8:3).[363]

On the other hand, Augustine fundamentally agrees with Julian that Christ is "the supreme form of justice,"[364] although he has reservations about the imitation of Adam and the mere imitation of Christ.[365] Furthermore, "Christ" is frequently found in connection with the theme of the just persons of the Old Testament. Augustine's view is that they, too, attained their salvation only through faith in the incarnation of the Son of God, through "faith in Christ foretold."[366]

Finally, "Christ" also appears in texts in which the interplay of divine grace and human freedom is discussed.[367] Christian freedom is possible only on the basis of the love that is poured out into hearts by the Holy Spirit (see Rom 5:5), but this Spirit is the one whom Christ promises and gives[368] and whose outpouring therefore presupposes "faith in Christ."[369] The joy that uprightness gives *(delectatio iustitiae)* also comes from Christ.[370] At the same time, the Father draws human beings to Christ: "Therefore to be drawn to Christ by the Father and to hear and learn from the Father that one should come to Christ: this is naught else than to receive the gift of faith by which one believes in Christ."[371] For the rest, passages are not lacking in which we find the themes mentioned here brought together. A good example is the letter in which Alypius and Augustine inform Paulinus of Nola about the Pelagian heresy.[372]

9. The Originality of Augustine's Use of the Word "Christ"

External influences undoubtedly played their part in Augustine's varied use of the word "Christ." These different uses followed the tradition of the

Church in large measure.[373] In particular, his way of speaking of Christ in the great controversies was determined by external factors inasmuch as in these controversies he continually paid heed to his adversaries, who in their own way appealed to Christ: to the Christ-centered piety of the Manichees, to the radical following of Christ of the Donatists, to the Paulinism of the Pelagians, and to pagan opposition to Christians and their Christ. Nor is there any denying that Augustine's use of "Christ" often sounds quite stereotyped. That is the impression given by the salutations of letters, standard phrases of the Church's everyday language, stock explanations (that "rock" means "Christ," for instance), and countless echoes of Paul. But we may not underestimate the underlying lively faith in Christ present in the Church. Moreover, the not infrequent passages in which Augustine speaks directly to Christ attest to his deep love for his Lord and Redeemer.[374]

We may go further. It seems justified, in light of all that has been said, to speak of a theology that is stamped with the name of Christ. In particular, questions asked of Augustine by others were the occasion for giving to some extent a systematic form to his reflections on the central importance that Christ had for him. This is true not only of the Letter to Volusian, on which there is general agreement.[375] In addition, the rather special questions which Dardanus put to him regarding Luke 23:43 and 1:42ff. led him to distinguish between Christ as God and Christ as human being as well as between Christ's various modes of presence—everywhere; in individual souls; in the Church— and thus to present his correspondent with a complete Christology.[376] In a less technical but no less comprehensive way, Augustine presents his teaching on Christ in his explanation of the messianic Psalm 109. In addition, we may see Christological syntheses in some of his overviews of heresies.[377] Here again, Augustine is doubtless dependent on the tradition. It is worth noting, however, that even in these instances, he thinks in terms of Christology and traces all errors in the faith to mistaken understandings of Christ.[378]

Finally, it is not eccentric to see in the *Confessions* the beginning of a Christological synthesis. By this I mean that insofar as he contrasts here the Word of God which, according to him, the Platonists had discovered, with the incarnate Word of John as understood in the ecclesial tradition, he already gives the main lines of his antithetical Christology. The sense, however, in which it is permissible to describe his piety and theological thinking as Christocentric must still be shown in detail.

CHAPTER 2

The Christocentrism of Augustine

1. Christ Is All

"Christ delights in the truth, delights in blessedness, delights in righteousness, delights in everlasting life, all of which are Christ."[1] Thus Augustine to his faithful in Hippo. But he spoke even more vividly to women consecrated to God: "The joy of Christ's virgins is from Christ, in Christ, with Christ, after Christ, through Christ, on account of Christ. The special joys of virgins of Christ are not the same as those of persons not virgins, even though the latter also belong to Christ."[2] For him, Christ was the goal of all longing: "Let all sighs be sighs for Christ; desire him alone, who is the most beautiful of all and who loves the ugly in order to make them beautiful; run to him alone, sigh for him alone."[3] For this reason, his prayer to God could only be prayer with and to Christ: "As priest he prays for us, as head he prays in us; we pray to him as to our God."[4]

It was in such language as this that Augustine daily gave eloquent expression to his "Christ is all," both in his pastoral and theological activity and in the whole of his own life.[5] His conversion, as he describes it in the *Confessions,* was in fact nothing but a turning to the whole Christ: to the "wisdom and power of God,"[6] to the Word with God and the Word with us.[7] On the other hand, Christ represented the solution to his major problems. Christ was his starting point for tackling the difficulties of the Manichees with the Old Testament and with religious knowledge: the "Christ who was prophesied" and "Christ as authority." His solution in the Donatist crisis was "Christ in the Catholic Church," which is "the inheritance of Christ," "the one Christ, head and body." "The grace of God which through Jesus Christ our Lord frees us from the body of death" was the central motif in his disputes with the Pelagians. "The one mediator between God and humanity, the human being Jesus Christ" was the password in controversy with the pagans, since "the humble Christ" alone opened the "way of universal salvation."

It is not surprising, then, that when he sums up his theological thinking in his *Handbook,* he should base it on "the foundation that is Christ."[8] In a theology that is thus grounded entirely in the Bible, the only task could be to show how in the Bible Christ is "narrated."[9] The extent to which Christ was at the center of the life and work of the Bishop of Hippo will become even clearer when we try to give a summary overview of his Christological thought on the basis of the most important texts, especially those in which the word "Christ" occurs frequently.

2. One Christ, God and Human Being

a) God and Human Being

In countless passages, Augustine uses verses one to three and fourteen of John's Prologue to express the mystery of Christ. The Word is God and is with God, and the Word was made flesh: these statement are for him the answer to the question of who or what Christ is. "You know who Christ is (I am speaking to Catholics because you have believed correctly): he is not the Word alone nor the flesh alone, but the Word who became flesh in order to dwell among us."[10] Implicit here is that the one Christ is both God and human being, the Son of God and the Human One: as God, equal to the Father; as a human being, our brother, who is Life in himself and the beginning of our resurrection. Thus he says in an explanation of John's Gospel:

> Because the Catholic faith holds the truth of both [humanity and divinity] and proclaims what it believes, it acknowledges Christ to be both God and human being. For both are written and both are true. If you describe Christ solely as God, you deny the instrument of salvation by which you have become healthy; if, on the other hand, you describe Christ as a mere human being, you deny the power by which you have been created. Hold, therefore, believing soul and Catholic heart, to both; hold fast to both, believe both, in your belief confess both. Christ is both God and human being. As God, Christ is equal to the Father, one with the Father. What is Christ as a human being? As a human being he was born of the Virgin and derives from a human being mortality but not any wickedness.[11]

In another homily we read the following: "This Christ is the Son of God and the son of a human being. In the beginning was the Word, and the Word was with God, and the Word was God; it was in the beginning with God. See how [the Word] gave him life in [the Word's very self]. But because the Word was made flesh and dwelt among us, a human came into being of the Virgin Mary."[12]

Using John's language, Augustine also expresses the union of the divine and the human in dynamic terms: "The Human One *(filius hominis)* was sanctified in the Word at the beginning of his creation, when the Word became flesh, for the Word and the flesh became one person. At that point, then, the Word sanctified itself in itself, that is, itself as a human being in itself as the Word. For the one Christ is Word and human being, sanctifying the human being in the Word."[13]

Augustine repeatedly linked this Johannine language, which he preferred, to the "form of God" and "form of a slave" of the hymn in the Letter to the Philippians.[14] Thus, he can exhort his listeners as follows in his explanations of the Fourth Gospel:

> Learn this same truth from the words of the Apostle. *Have this mind in you,* he says, *that was in Christ Jesus who, though he was in the form of God, did not think equality with God a booty to be clung to.* What does [John] mean if not that as far as the Word is concerned, Christ Jesus is God with God? But see what follows: *but he emptied himself, taking the form of a slave, being made in the likeness of human beings and found in human form.* And of whom is [John] speaking if not of the same Christ Jesus? But everything is already here: the Word in the form of God, which assumed the form of a slave; and the soul and the flesh in the form of the slave that was assumed by the form of God.[15]

Following the Latin tradition, Augustine was able to express the same truth with the aid of the antitheses seen in the history of salvation: "creator—re-creator"[16] or "[God] created—[God] re-created"[17]; "maker—redeemer" or "former—re-former"[18]; "creator—savior."[19] He spoke similarly of "majesty" and "humility."[20] In more concrete terms, he said emphatically: "Could anything be more certain than our good fortune, when the one who prays for us is the very one who gives us what he prays for? Christ, you see, is [human being] and God; he prays as a [human being], he gives what he prays for as God."[21]

In all these statements, which are inspired more or less directly by the Bible and especially by John and Paul, a strong tendency to make distinctions emerges. Augustine liked to talk about Christ in the language of antithesis. In doing so, he was undoubtedly following the anti-Arian tradition.[22] Not without reason does he appeal to the "canonical rule" according to which a distinction must be made between the divine and the human in Christ.[23] But we must not overlook the fact that the contrast between Christ-as-God and Christ-as-human being is influenced by the rhetorical taste for antithesis that was widespread at that time. Also to be explained by both traditions, but primarily by the second, is the tendency in many passages to assign the same value to the opposed elements.

In contrast, there are other, no less important passages especially in the early writings, in which Augustine clearly gives priority to the divine over the human. This is true of his explanations of Wisdom as being the only Son, who is consubstantial and coeternal with the Father and who assumed the whole human being,[24] or his explanations of the Word, who assumed soul and flesh into union with [the Word's] person.[25] But it is true also of the statements that the human being Jesus participates in the divine wisdom.[26]

Finally, this Christological dualism became a given in the struggle for a rational understanding of the Christian faith, for while the young Augustine found it easy to see in Christ the eternal Word, only gradually was he able to realize that the incarnation of the Word provided the only practicable way to [Christ's] divinity.[27]

b) The One Christ

Despite all the emphasis on the distinction of the divine and human in Christ, Augustine never forgets to underscore the unity of Christ. Following a tradition already in process of consolidation, he resolves the tension that arises from the contrast between God and human being or, more accurately, between Son of God and Human One, by saying of Christ that he sees [Christ] as the subject, the "one person," in "the one Christ."[28] Like his predecessors, he excludes any division of the one Christ.[29] Even his comparison with the oneness of the human being is not new. Augustine's original contribution consists in the way in which, with the aid of prosopic exegesis as well as of Neoplatonic anthropology, he develops the thesis of the "one person" or "the oneness of the person of Christ"[30] and, consequently, of the human being as "one person."[31] Especially to be noted in this context is that he connects the oneness of the person of Christ with his reflections on the presence of God: "But this human being is in God in a way different from how this God is in the human being; for God is there in a way peculiar to [God]. For the one person is God and human being, and the one Christ Jesus is both. Christ is everywhere inasmuch as he is God, but in heaven inasmuch as he is a human being."[32]

There is another explanation that can be regarded rather as independent, the one in which Augustine, with the Apollinarists in mind, defines the oneness of Christ by reference to the soul and the body or to the state in which Jesus was between his death and his resurrection. Thus, the one Christ suffered and was sad;[33] so too, the one Christ was buried, even though the flesh alone lay in the tomb.[34]

But Augustine was not satisfied to emphasize the one Christ, the only Son of God, the oneness of the person, the coming together of Word and flesh in the oneness of the person. He also concerned himself more than his predecessors had with the logical consequences. He built upon the theory of the communication of idioms, which the Nicene theologians had developed, by explaining more fully why human qualities may be attributed to the Son of God and divine to the Human One on the basis of the oneness of the person.[35]

He first does so in detail, it is true, in controversy with the Arians, even though he had spoken long before of "God born," "God crucified," and "the flesh of God."[36] In this explanation, "the oneness of the person of Christ Jesus our Lord" consists in the fact that the divine and human natures reciprocally communicate the names proper to each, in such a way that the Son of God is called a human being and the Human One is called God, while the one Christ is called both.[37]

Even though Augustine does not carry this reasoning further by an analysis of the concept of person, he does indicate, in his reflections on the oneness of Christ, that in his view, this oneness has its basis in the eternal sonship of Christ. In other words, he does not yet know the formula "one of the Trinity," but at the same time, his manner of ascribing the incarnation to the Son alone is no longer far removed from that formula.[38]

3. Through Christ as Human Being to Christ as God

The answer to the question of who Christ is always includes, more or less explicitly, his role in salvation. The one Christ, God and human being, is always seen also as Savior. To put it in John's words: the Word not only became flesh but also dwelt among us. Thus, Augustine says, for example:

> [The one] who was God became a human being; by assuming what [God] was not, while not losing what [God] was, God became a human being. In this fact you find something for your weakness and something for your fulfillment. May Christ raise you up through [Christ's] humanity; may [Christ] lead you through [Christ's] divinity and allow you to reach what [Christ] is as God. The whole of preaching and the whole of salvation consists in this . . . that both souls and bodies arise.[39]

a) The One Mediator between God and Humanity

Following the Apostle, Augustine likes especially to express the "for us" in terms of mediation.[40] In fact, the relevant text on the subject: "There is one God; there is also one mediator between God and humanity, the human being Christ Jesus" (1 Tim 2:5), is one of the biblical texts that Augustine cites most often. Moreover, it is frequently cited along with various other favorite texts: John 10:30; 17:20-23; Romans 5:13; 1 Corinthians 15:21f.; Ephesians 1:22f. For this reason alone, we will not be surprised to find that the idea of mediation lies behind all the fundamental themes of Augustinian theology. Christ shows himself to be not only authority but present in the Church, not only sacrament and example or model but the universal way of salvation; Christ is all of these as the Son of God who became a human being in order to be mediator between God and humanity.[41]

It is quite obvious that the idea of Christ as mediator takes a number of forms in Augustine. However, I may say, with some simplification, that he uses it in two perspectives. Looking at it from a more philosophical viewpoint, he understands Christ the mediator to be "between" *(medius)* God and human-kind, and thus as one who belongs both to the creator and to creatures and who possesses both immortality and mortality and therefore can lead human beings out of the present state of transitoriness to permanent blessedness.[42] In this context, the problem of the one and the many is more or less clearly discernible.[43]

But mindfulness of his Neoplatonic partners in dialogue also determined, to some extent, the other and doubtless stronger trend, according to which Augustine regards Christ the human being as mediator.[44] This means that as human being Christ makes possible the revelation of eternal Wisdom, that is, the Word, in whom all the thoughts of God are contained. With this in mind, Augustine confesses:

> I sought a way to obtain strength enough to enjoy you; but I did not find it until I embraced "the mediator between God and [humanity], the [human being] Christ Jesus" (1 Tim 2:5), "who is above all things, God blessed for ever" (Rom 9:5). He called and said "I am the way and the truth and the life" (John 14:6). The food which I was too weak to accept [you] mingled with flesh, in that "The Word was made flesh" (John 1:14), so that our infant condition might come to suck milk from your wisdom by which you created all things.[45]

First Timothy 2:5, however, played a decisive part in this second perspective, inasmuch as that passage speaks of redemption.[46] Accordingly, as mediator, Christ is first and foremost the one who has offered the sacrifice of reconciliation;[47] he became sin, that is, the sacrifice by which human beings are reconciled with God (see 2 Cor 5:21).[48] The death which Christ freely took upon himself became the victory over death itself. The mediator who gives life thus conquered the demons[49] and the devil, the originator and mediator of death.[50] The self-surrender to this reconciling and victorious sacrificial death also involved the perfect righteousness of Christ: as mediator, Christ was the immortal righteous one, the human being who was "righteous with God" and who, therefore, because of the righteousness that united him to God, was able to justify sinners who had fallen under the power of death and to bring them life and peace.[51]

b) Christ the Way—Christ the Homeland

Insofar as the basic theology of the mediation of Christ puts the emphasis on the human being Jesus,[52] it is admittedly less consonant with the antithesis-centered Christology that constantly dominates the theological thought of Augustine and his proclamation of the faith. In the context of this theology of mediation, it is rather another theme that pushes to the fore: the theme of "through Christ as human being to Christ as God" or, as the case may be, the variations of it that are seen in the antitheses "Christ the way—Christ the homeland" or "the way by which we go—the goal to which we go."[53]

The importance of this theme is already obvious from the simple fact that Augustine repeatedly cites the words of Jesus, "I am the way, the truth, and the life" (John 14:6), perhaps, even as often as the words from the first Letter to Timothy.[54] As a matter of fact, both texts are often combined in the same passages.[55] In addition, Augustine expressly connects the idea of mediatorship with that of the way:

> For this is "the mediator between God and [humanity], the [human being] Christ Jesus." As [human being] he is our Mediator; as [human being] he is our way. For there is hope to attain a journey's end when there is a path which stretches between the traveller and [the traveller's] goal. But if there is no path, or if a [person does] not know which way to go, there is little use in knowing the destination.[56]

Augustine developed this theme in one of his most famous passages: in the seventh book of the *Confessions,* as he looked back on his reading of the Platonists, he did not hesitate to acknowledge that contemporary philosophers knew the homeland, the "Word with God"; but at the same time he reproached them for not knowing the way, the Word incarnate.[57] The same manner of approaching a subject lies behind the basic theme of the "universal way" in Book 10 of *The City of God.* Here again, Augustine sees Christ the way as including both the incarnation of the Son and the "grace of God through Jesus Christ our Lord." At the same time, he identifies the "homeland" more clearly with what we believe and to some extent know: the Father, the Son, and the Spirit.[58] In the final analysis, this can also be seen as the context for those passages in *The Trinity* in which the author, without engaging in polemics, connects Christ with knowledge and wisdom, with belief in the temporal and understanding of the eternal.[59]

Furthermore, behind this antithesis of knowledge and wisdom lies the antithesis of authority and reason that plays a decisive role in Augustine's first works: "We follow a twofold way: either reason or, in any case, authority."[60] Christ certainly does not come into the field of vision here. Nevertheless, as Augustine emphasizes even in other early writings, the authority of the faith ultimately rests on the authority of the incarnate Christ.[61] On the other hand, human reason, too, ultimately turns to Christ as the interior teacher who is word and wisdom.[62] According to Augustine, then, all of religious knowledge is founded on Christ, true God and true human being. In faith, human beings acknowledge the "external Christ," while in rational knowledge they gaze upon the "interior Christ"; for in their souls they are enlightened by the divine

Word as the true Teacher, while the incarnate Word summons them from externals to the interior. "The one true teacher, the unchangeable Truth, the only interior teacher, teaches us, but he has become an external teacher in order to call us back from things external to what is within."[63]

Augustine says the same at the end of the first book of *The Consent of the Evangelists,* where he contrasts Christian teaching about the true mediator, Christ, who as the Wisdom of God assumed the human being into the unity of [Christ's] person, with the pagan conception of Christ as simply a wise man; he expressly cites words from Plato's *Timaeus* and says, "[Christ], who is Truth in matters eternal, is our faith in created things."[64] Christ thus grounds faith in history and thereby opens the way to eternal truth.

Against the same philosophical background, but not without polemical overtones, Augustine also spoke to his faithful on the theme of Christ as way and Christ as homeland. Thus, the beginning of the Prologue of John provided an occasion for attacking the "wisdom of the proud"[65] and urging his community to the Christian life:

> Cling to Christ according to what he became for us, so that you may reach him according to what he is and according to what he was. He came in order to become for us [var.: what he was not]. He became for us that by which the weak are carried and may cross the sea of this world and reach the homeland, where there will no longer be need of any ship because there is no sea to cross.[66]

Frequently, however, the philosophical controversy is hardly perceptible any longer, as, for example, when we read in an explanation of the Prologue of John:

> If you seek the truth, hold to the way, for the truth itself is the way. One and the same is that to which you go and that by which you go; you do not go through one thing to another nor do you come to Christ by anything other than Christ: you come through Christ to Christ. How do you come through Christ to Christ? Through Christ as human being to Christ as God; through the Word made flesh to the Word that was in the beginning, God with God; from that which human beings ate to that which the angels daily eat.[67]

In any case, it is remarkable that Augustine should develop this theme in speaking to the ordinary faithful. Two points are noteworthy. First, he manages to find quite simple formulas, such as "by whom we go—to whom we go" *(qua imus—quo imus)* and "we are going to him, we are going by him, we are not going off the rails" *(ad illum imus, per illum imus, non perimus).*[68] Second, probably under the influence of the Nicene tradition, he reduces the theme to the Christocentric antithesis, "through Christ as human being to Christ as God." A good example is an explanation of John 14:6:

> Now, because Christ . . . is, with the Father, truth and life, the Word of God, of which it is said *The life was the light of [humankind]* (Jn 1:4); thus, because [Christ] is, with the Father, life and truth and we had no way of getting to the truth, the Son of God, who is always in the Father truth and life, became the way by taking [on human nature]. Walk along the [human being] and you come to God. You go by [Christ], you come to [Christ].[69]

Or, in language even more Nicene: "You believe in Christ who was born in the flesh, and you will arrive at Christ who is born of God, God with God."[70] A similar statement occurs at the end of a survey of heresies: "To confess that Christ is God, equal to the Father, and true [human being] . . . to confess both is to be a Catholic. As such, you have a home country, you have a way to it. . . . [Christ] is the home country we are going to, [Christ] is the way we are going by. Let us go to [Christ] by [Christ], and not get on the wrong track."[71]

Because this reduction comes closest to the fundamental Christological theme "one Christ, God and human being," it is certainly legitimate to organize the varied themes of Augustinian Christology with it in mind—this despite the fact that a richer range of metaphors is used in developing the "way—homeland" theme than the theme of mediation. Nor is it out of place in the process to distinguish a more individual and a more social point of view. Augustine himself provides a basis for doing so when he explains in a sermon: "When you believe in Christ, by your believing in Christ, Christ comes into you, and you are somehow or other united to [Christ] and made into a member of [Christ's] body. And this cannot happen unless both hope and charity come along too."[72] Through genuine Christian faith, a person attains to Christ; but in union with Christ, the person also belongs to Christ's body, which will be completed in the resurrection.

4. The Way Is Faith in Christ

Augustine is not satisfied with the general statement about salvation, namely, that "Christ is the way and the homeland." Rather, with his eye on the consummation, he plumbs it more fully by developing the Pauline theme of justification through faith. In the process, he emphasizes three points of view in particular: Christ as teacher of faith, as example of humility, and as source of grace. At bottom, he is always dealing with the way, which consists of faith in Christ. In this sense, the *Handbook* speaks of the way "by which we go to God; this way is faith in Christ, a faith that works through love."[73]

a) Christ, the One Teacher

To reach Christ as God through Christ as human being means, more specifically, to travel the way of faith. For when the Bishop of Hippo repeatedly describes the Christ life with the verbs "go, walk, sail, travel, pass time, cross," what he is referring to is simply believing in Christ.[74] According to the basic demand made of every Christian, anyone who does not believe in Christ on the cross will not reach the everlasting vision of Christ: "Christ is never going to be seen on the cross again; but unless we believe that he was once so to be seen, in a manner in which there would be no expectation of seeing him again, we shall not come to see Christ as he is to be seen forever."[75] In the exposition of Psalm 123 Augustine is even more explicit:

> What does being pilgrims mean? We walk by faith, [the psalmist] says, not by vision. Pilgrims therefore walk by faith, they are not yet in the homeland but still on the way; those however who do not believe are neither in the homeland nor on the way. Let us, therefore, so walk that we remain on the way; for the King of the homeland has become the way. The King of our homeland, the Lord Jesus Christ, is there the truth but here the way. Whither are we going? To the truth. By what way are we going? By faith. Whither are we going? To Christ. By what way are we going? Through Christ.[76]

This fundamental faith in Christ embraces the entire economy of salvation that is decreed by the Trinity and summed up in the profession of faith.[77] More particularly, as Augustine emphasizes with his eye on the Pelagian heresy, Christians must believe in the one Mediator, the human being Christ Jesus, and in his resurrection, and therefore in his incarnation and death.[78] It is worth noting, however, how Augustine can focus belief in Christ on his resurrection. Even Jews and pagans, he thinks, believe that Christ lived and died, but only Christians believe that he rose from the dead.[79] In the context of anti-Pelagianism, on the other hand, he can focus rather on the idea of justification:

> Faith in Christ consists in believing in him who justifies the wicked; it means believing in the mediator without whose mediation we are not reconciled with God; it means believing in the Savior who has come to seek and rescue what was lost; it means believing in him who said "Without me you can do nothing." Therefore those who do not know the justice by which God justifies the wicked and seek to establish their own justice by which the proud are proven guilty, these cannot believe in him.[80]

This faith in Christ, moreover, has its origin in Christ himself. For when persons walk in faith toward the truth, it is the divine truth itself, in its real incarnation, that grounds their faith, so that it is through the human being, Christ, that the way to God becomes possible for them. "In order to give a [person's] mind greater confidence in its journey towards the truth along the way of faith, God the Son of God, who is . . . Truth [itself], took [on human

nature] without abandoning . . . godhead, and thus established and founded
this faith, so that [humanity] might have a path to [humanity's] God through
the [human being] who was God."[81] This idea of faith as grounded in the incarnation is not limited to learned treatises but is also the content of Augustine' sermons. We read, for example, in one of the sermons, "It is good for us
to believe in Christ, especially because he himself openly said what you have
heard, that he came into the world to be light that those who believe in him
will not walk in darkness but will have the light of life."[82]

In summary, then, it may be said that the way of faith consists in unre-
servedly following Christ who came into time in order to lead humanity to
eternity. To believe in Christ means, consequently, to take the economy of salvation seriously. This is to say, in more technical language, that Christ is the
"authority behind faith." If human beings want to come to faith, they must
submit to the various forms of this authority: the Scriptures, the preaching of
the Church, and Christ.[83]

Meanwhile, since the adult Christian's faith in Christ seeks understanding,
the way to the homeland, the way to truth, is always also a way of deeper
knowledge.[84] Faith in Christ is thus open in principle to the understanding of
Christ.[85] Christians are therefore not satisfied with milk, the food of the weak;
rather, they eat solid food and savor the bread of the angels. Through faith in
the incarnation, they attain to knowledge of the Word. They go beyond Christ
as human being to Christ as God.[86] But Augustine is not satisfied with faith in
the incarnation and with the further knowledge of the Word. He also contemplates the various mysteries of the life of Jesus in order to account for the
mercy of God.[87] He even goes into the weaknesses of Christ, his tears and anguish,[88] in order to finally lead by this means his faithful into the mystery of
"being commended to the love of God."[89]

But Augustine does not understand the way of faith to be simply a progressive enlightenment of the heart. By a growing faith, Christians also attached themselves more interiorly to Christ. Those who believe in Christ are
freed from sin and through their faith in Christ attain to the grace of divine
adoption: "The medicine for all the wounds of the soul, and the one way of
atoning for all human delinquency, is to believe in Christ. . . . By believing
in [Christ], they become children of God, because they are born of God adop-
tively by the grace which consists of faith in Jesus Christ our Lord."[90] More
concretely, those who believe in Christ keep themselves free from the sin of
unchastity; they do not forget that they belong to the body of Christ; they do
not scorn the Christ within them; they take seriously the warning, "Spare a
thought for Christ in yourself, recognize Christ in yourself."[91]

Faith in Christ, understood in this more comprehensive way, likewise has
its origin in Christ. He is head of the "school of Christ."[92] Not without reason
does Augustine repeatedly remind his hearers at the beginning of his sermons
that Christ is the real teacher, who proclaims the faith through him (Augustine)

and opens up its deeper meaning,[93] nor does he ever weary of reminding them of Jesus' own words about the "one teacher" (Matt 23:8ff.).[94]

Behind this Christian conviction, there is undoubtedly the philosophical idea of the interior teacher who causes eternal truth to reveal itself in the mind of the human being and the idea of the divine wisdom in which all human knowledge is a participation. But there are four points that must not be overlooked. According to Augustine, it was also by his human words and actions that Christ introduced people to the meaning of Christian life.[95] Christ is also the one from whom real understanding of the Bible comes; for this reason, human beings owe their knowledge ultimately to the divine wisdom. In the course of the years, moreover—and this is the third point—this early insight of Augustine found expression in a way that takes greater account of the responsibility of the Christian conscience.[96] Finally, as interior teacher, the Lord teaches through the Spirit, whom he promised, and through the love which the Spirit gives.[97] To the extent that Christ is in this full sense both the authority that grounds faith and the interior teacher, and combines in himself both the knowledge through which human beings have access to temporal realities and the wisdom that discloses eternal realities to them, he guarantees the process of maturation in which Christians move beyond faith to knowledge.

b) Example of Humility

The way to the homeland proves to be a way of faith. But walking by faith in Christ, who leads to certain knowledge and ultimately to the full vision of the Word, requires a whole series of human attitudes. Among these, humility takes first place. Only those who are ready to admit their own powerlessness and to entrust themselves without reserve to a superior authority can believe in Christ and therefore travel the way that ends in the vision of God and thus in everlasting blessedness.

It was chiefly through his debate with contemporary philosophy that Augustine came to insist on the way of humility.[98] In particular, he criticized the Platonists because in their pride they did not recognize the incarnation of Christ and therefore, despite all their grasp of the end of the human person, they missed the way to it.[99] Behind this criticism, there no doubt lies the idea that pride is the greatest human sin. In any case, it is for this reason that Augustine urgently exhorts Dioscorus, a Greek, to humility:

> My dear Dioscorus, my desire is that you submit yourself to [Christ] with all devotion and that you provide yourself with no other way to grasping and retaining the truth than the one provided by [the one] who as God saw how weak our human steps are. That way is, first, humility; second, humility; third, humility. And as often as you might ask, I would say the same. It is not that there are not other precepts, but unless humil-

ity precedes and accompanies and follows upon all our good actions . . . pride will snatch everything from our hand as we congratulate ourselves over some good deed. The other vices are certainly to be feared in the form of sins, but pride is to be feared even in our good deeds, lest our praiseworthy actions be lost through the immoderate desire of praise.[100]

Behind this earnest exhortation to humility there also lies, of course, the experience of Augustine himself, who suffered so greatly from his inability to submit to God in all things.[101]

But there were other reasons as well why the Bishop of Hippo was so bent on presenting humility as a basic Christian attitude. In language that was at times quite eloquent, he repeatedly urged it upon his faithful. Thus, he says in a sermon on Matthew 11:25:

So [God] hid . . . from the proud, [the one] who through . . . creation had given those diligently seeking the creator hints of [God's self] alone. So it was well said by the Lord, *You have hidden these things from the wise and the knowing;* whether from those who with their complex calculations and skillful researches made such thorough investigations into created nature, but failed totally to recognize the creator, or from those who recognized God but did not glorify [God] as God or give thanks, and were unable to see things straight and as they are, because they were proud. So, *You have hidden these things from the wise and the knowing, and have revealed them to the little ones.* What little ones? The humble.[102]

This humble faith has its origin in the incarnation of God. Christ abased himself in order to break the arrogance of human beings and thus also to conquer pride as the origin of sin: "That high priest, you see, who dwells in this house, our Lord Jesus Christ, was pleased to offer himself as an example of humility, to ensure the return of humankind which had gone out from paradise through pride."[103] The example of Christ's humility, which led him to his self-abasement in the incarnation, his acceptance of death, his triple temptation by the devil, his mocking by the Judeans, and his mistreatment by the soldiers, became "the remedy for pride" for all.[104] Augustine never tired of reminding his faithful of this example of humility. Thus, he says in his exposition of Psalm 31:6 (he is also referring to the pride of the philosophers):

Everywhere are to found excellent precepts concerning morals and discipline, but this humility is not to be found. This way of humility comes from another source: it comes from Christ. What else did he teach by humbling himself and becoming obedient unto death, even death on a cross? What else did he teach by paying a debt which he did not owe, so that he might free us from our debt? What else did he teach by being baptized, though he had committed no sin, and being crucified, though he was not guilty in any way? What else did he teach but this humility? Not

without good reason does he say: *I am the way and the truth and the life.*
By this humility human beings draw close to God, for the Lord is close
to those of contrite heart.[105]

Or, again, in an explanation of John 14:6:

> Christ the way is the humble Christ; Christ the truth and the life is
> Christ exalted and God. If you walk along the humble Christ, you will ar-
> rive at the exalted Christ; if in your sickly health and debility you do not
> spurn the humble one, you will abide in perfect health and strength with
> the exalted one. What else, after all, was the reason for Christ's humility,
> but your debility? You were, you see, completely and irremediably in the
> grip of your debility; and this was the fact that made so great a doctor
> come to you. . . . Because you were not able to go to him, he came to
> you. Why? Let us see. It was because pride would not allow us to return
> to life.[106]

Christ's role as exemplar is not limited, however, to humility. He also provided human beings with the example of a life of faith. His entire earthly
existence was nothing but a manifestation of the standard and rule of discipline.[107] In his life but especially in his death, Christ preceded us in the righteousness in which the commandment of love is summed up.[108] In doing so, he
showed how even in the direst distress human beings can hold fast to their
love of righteousness, that is, to the will of God.[109] In particular, Christ gave
the example of a virginity consecrated to God. For in Christ we see the most
excellent teacher and exemplar of virginal integrity.[110] But, more than any
other, this typically Christian way of life is not possible without humility; for
that reason, virgins must also learn from Christ to be meek and humble.[111]
Consequently, Christ's role as exemplar was most clearly shown in his humility.

c) Exemplar of Grace

In addition to humility, other human attitudes are required if one is to journey to the eternal homeland through faith in Christ. Above all, the way of faith
is inconceivable apart from hope and love. Belief in Christ always means hope
and love as well. "You believe in Christ, you see, when you both hope in
Christ and love Christ. Because if you have faith without hope and without
love, you believe that he is the Christ, but you don't believe in Christ."[112]
For this reason, Augustine constantly stresses the point that genuine Christian faith must find fulfillment in active love. "Faith cannot work well, except
through love. Such, you see, is the faith of the faithful; it mustn't be the same
as the faith of demons, because the demons too believe, and tremble. So the
faith to be admired, the true faith of grace, is the sort that works through
love."[113] As here, so in many other passages, Augustine refers or alludes to
James 2:19;[114] even more frequently he cites Galatians 5:6.[115]

In the difficulties and afflictions of the present life, however, it is not possible for believing Christians to persevere in docility to God and love of all their fellow human beings unless they arm themselves with the patience that allows them to hope unwaveringly in God. In other words, they must constantly be aware that they are redeemed only in hope and not yet in reality. They must have not only a firm faith but also a solid hope. Our hope, too, must be unchanging and strongly anchored in God. Just as God, on whom it relies, remains immovable, so hope must be steady. Only in the present time is it possible to speak of hope. The time will come when there will be hope no longer, but only the reality sought. In this world there are in fact numerous ills, interior and exterior; troubles do not cease but even increase. All who are on the way to God must experience them. But the entire Bible tells them that they should endure the present, hope in the future, and love God whom they do not yet see so that they will be able to embrace God when they see God at last.[116] Not only the inner self but also the outer person will rise to life. Consequently, only when Christians place their hope entirely in Christ can they love in the full sense and thus live out their faith in Christ. Most especially must they believe in the resurrection of Christ and hope for their own resurrection.[117]

Precisely then, because faith in Christ cannot exist without hope and love, the way of faith necessarily proves to be the gift of God, "the grace of God through our Lord Jesus Christ."[118] Faith itself, too, certainly originates in the prevenient kindness of God.[119] Even its first beginning is given to human beings by God, as Augustine insists especially to the monks of Gaul.[120] But in his view, experience makes even more evident that grace is the source of hope and love.[121] He does not tire of citing the Apostle's words about the love that is poured out in our hearts by the Holy Spirit.[122] Only with the help of grace can Christians hasten joyfully along the way of the commandments[123] and love uprightness even in the extreme afflictions of life.[124] Only by the power of grace can they place their trust entirely on God and persevere in this hope to the very end. Augustine even devotes a special work, *The Gift of Perseverance*, to this basic concern in his teaching on grace.[125]

In light of all this, it is understandable that Augustine should speak of Christ as "exemplar of grace." In fact, not only does he join the ancient tradition taken over by Christians and especially by Lactantius in emphasizing that Christ taught by word and example and had to reinforce his teaching by his example.[126] He also adds the idea of help to teaching and example. Thus, he writes at the beginning of 412, "At the time that Christ knew to be most opportune and had ordained from eternity, [Christ's] teaching came to humanity and [Christ's] help in grasping eternal salvation."[127] He had already explained: "Let us observe our Lord, our true example and help. Can we prove he's our help? *Without me you can do nothing* (Jn 15:5). Can we prove he's our example? *Christ suffered for us*, Peter says, *leaving us an example, to follow in his steps* (1 Pt 2:21)."[128]

Especially impressive in this context is his discourse on sacrament and ex-ample or model in the fourth book of *The Trinity.*[129] There he explains that the death and resurrection of Christ are the sacrament of the inner self and the model for the outer self.[130] By his death and resurrection, Christ conquered sin and laid the foundation for justification; at the same time, Christ showed that human beings need not be afraid in the face of death and began the series of resurrections.[131]

But it was undoubtedly the controversy over the Pelagian conception of Christ's example that led Augustine to lay even more emphasis on the heal-ing, illuminating, and strengthening grace of Christ.[132] Because human nature was corrupted by the sin of Adam, it needed to be restored in its innermost depths; and because this is not yet accomplished by baptism alone, it also needed the helping grace of the redeemer throughout later life for every step toward eternal salvation. For this reason, Augustine gives the following sum-mary in *Nature and Grace,* when speaking of growth in love and growth in righteousness:

> The beginning of love is the beginning of righteousness. Progress in love is progress in righteousness. Great love is great righteousness. . . . I wonder whether love may not be able to keep growing when it has de-parted from this mortal life. In any case, let it be so full everywhere and always that nothing can be added to it. But it is not poured out in your hearts from our inner resources of nature or will, but by the Holy Spirit who is given to us and who aids our weakness and works for our health. For it is the grace of God through our Lord Jesus Christ.[133]

Consequently, a simple imitation of Christ is not enough. The danger of the Pelagian heresy consisted precisely in this, that it saw the grace of Christ as consisting in imitation of him and not in the giving of the Spirit whereby this imitation first becomes possible. In other words, if justification comes simply from imitation, then Christ died in vain.[134] In the incarnation, there-fore, Christ became both an example of living and an example of grace.[135]

Augustine succeeds in giving an especially profound expression to grace as the source of the life of faith, in the full and comprehensive sense of the phrase, by taking over a Pauline theme, that of "Christ dwelling in your hearts through faith" (Eph 3:17). He repeatedly harks back to it both in his theologi-cal writings and in his sermons.[136] Christians may not allow their faith to sleep. If it does, it must be awakened, as the disciples awakened Christ in the boat.

> If faith is within, then Christ is there, sighing; if faith is within us, Christ is within us. . . . Rouse Christ as he sleeps there. The reason why you are tossed by the waves and are ready to return evil for evil is that Christ is asleep in the boat. He sleeps in your heart when you forget your faith. If you rouse Christ, that is, renew your faith, what does Christ, now

awake in your heart, say to you? I heard the words: "You have a demon!"
(John 7:20) and "I have prayed for them." The Lord hears and is patient;
the servant hears and takes offense![137]

Because of faith, Christ is present in the life of Christians. Christ in hearts
is faith in Christ; Christ is awake in those whose faith does not sleep.[138] Here
Christ guides the entire lives of believing Christians: Christ enlightens them,
gives them patience, enables them not to feel superior in time of prosperity
and to praise God even in adversity.[139] As interior teacher he grants them certain knowledge but also directs their consciences.[140] Because Christians keep
Christ present through faith, Christ himself sighs and hopes in them.[141] With
Christ in their hearts, they can resist everyday temptations.[142] If they awaken
Christ in their hearts, they remain at peace even in the storms of the homeland.[143]

This Christ whom Christians must always awaken in themselves can evidently only be the grace of God through our Lord Jesus Christ: "Grace is
poured forth, faith starts working through love, Christ who was already
dwelling in [Zacchaeus'] heart is welcomed into his house."[144] The truth of
this can be seen especially in the fact that, like the Apostle, Augustine links
the presence of Christ in the hearts of believers with the indwelling of the
Holy Spirit. Thus, he bids his faithful ask God to "give you through [God's]
Spirit to be strengthened with power, and to have Christ dwelling in your inner
selves through faith."[145]

5. The Way of Universal Salvation

> The Apostle says, "In your inner selves Christ dwells in your hearts
> through faith." This is the life of hearts that makes us live for ever and
> ever, from the beginning of faith to the goal which is vision. He says,
> "May you be rooted and grounded in love and be able to comprehend
> with all the saints." This is the communion that will exist in an inde-
> scribable divine and heavenly state; there the poor will have their fill,
> those who do not seek what is their own but what is Jesus Christ's, that
> is, who do not seek their private advantage but take thought for the com-
> mon good, where the salvation of all is found. For because of the bread
> that gives such persons their fill, we, the many, are one bread, one body,
> as the Apostle says somewhere.[146]

Accordingly, the way of faith is not simply a way which the individual
travels with Christ. It is rather a way of universal salvation, on which Christ
leads all together to the homeland. The boat in which Christians are to rouse
their faith is the ship of the Church.[147] In it, individuals also profess the faith
that they carry in their hearts.[148] It is together with others that individual Christians are one human being with the Christ who is present in the Church; they

form the whole Christ which from Abel to the end of time is maturing to full stature; they belong to the city of which Christ is the king.

a) Christ, the Shepherd of the Church

Christ lives in the Church. From 391 on, at the latest, this conviction permeates all of Augustine's writings, especially his anti-Donatist works, his expositions of the Psalms, and his apologetic work, *The City of God.* The presence of Christ appears, first of all, in those who have responsibility in the Church. He, the supreme Shepherd, leads his flock through the shepherds of the Church.[149] He does so through word and sacrament, that is, through the activity of those by whose agency the communion in the sacraments is established and maintained.[150]

As Shepherd, Christ is, first, the teacher of the faith.[151] Nowhere does Augustine say this as clearly as in his sermon *On Learning Christianity.* After referring to Sirach 51:31, 36, he explains: "The word *disciplina* ['instruction'] comes from *discere* ['learn']. The house of instruction is the Church of Christ. What, then, is learned here or why does learning take place here? Who are the learners and from whom do they learn? They learn to live rightly. They learn to live rightly in order that they may live forever. Christians do the learning, Christ does the teaching."[152] Augustine develops this thought chiefly through the image of the school. In order to initiate his followers into the faith, Christ runs a school: "Christ is the one who teaches; his chair is in heaven, as I said a moment ago. His school is on earth, and his school is his body."[153]

In this school, Christ is the real teacher and addresses Christians, who are his students. The bishop, on the other hand, who runs the school in Christ's name, is a fellow-student of the students.[154] Augustine brings up this last point more than once, as, for example, in the wholly ecclesiological exposition of Psalm 216: "We protect you because of our office of stewardship, but we desire to be protected along with you. To you we are shepherds, but together with you we are sheep under that Shepherd. To you we are teachers from the place where I stand, but in this school we are fellow learners with you under that one Teacher."[155]

In the school of Christ, the circle of disciples that Christ gathered around himself during his earthly life lives on.[156] The work done in the school is chiefly the reading and explanation of the sacred Scriptures, all of which are concerned with Christ.[157] Thus, Christ speaks both in the Scriptures and in the expositor. Just as formerly he was not silent either in the prophets or during his days on earth, so he is not silent now.[158] At the same time, Christ proclaims himself: "Christ preaches Christ."[159] Augustine does not forget, however, that Christ does this work with the help of human beings.[160] He takes for granted, above all, that Christ runs his school in the worship of the Church.[161] There Christ breaks not only his bread but also his word.

This brings us to the second aspect of Christ's work as Shepherd: he also administers the sacraments. He himself performs these simple New Testament signs through which the continuation of his presence and thus the holiness of his Church are ensured.[162] For this reason, Augustine, like Ambrose, calls Christ the author of the sacraments.[163] It is Christ who primarily baptizes.[164] In the Eucharist, which is celebrated in his name,[165] the sacrifice is present in which he, as true Priest, unites the whole human race with God.

> It follows that the whole redeemed community, that is to say, the congregation and fellowship of the saints, is offered to God as a universal sacrifice, through the great Priest who offered himself in his suffering for us—so that we might be the body of so great a head—under the "form of a servant." . . . This is the sacrifice of Christians, who are "many, making up one body in Christ." This is the sacrifice which the Church continually celebrates in the sacrament of the altar, a sacrament well-known to the faithful, where it is shown to the Church that [it itself] is offered in the offering which [it] presents to God.[166]

In the celebration of the Eucharist, the body is also fed. It lies with Christ himself on the altar. Therefore, the faithful receive their own mystery, and to this, too, they say Amen.[167]

b) One Human Being

Because Christ is present in the Church through word and sacrament, the Church forms one human being with Christ: "Because Christ's possessions reach to the ends of the earth, and [Christ's] possessions are all the saints, and all the saints form one human being in Christ (since in Christ there is a holy unity), this one human being says: 'From the ends of the earth I have cried to you, when my heart was in anguish.'"[168] Whereas Adam through the sin of disobedience gave rise to the generation of sinners, the "condemned mass," a new people is born through rebirth in Christ.[169]

In this community of the reborn, Christ proclaims himself as the good news. "Christ proclaims himself as the good news; he also proclaims himself in his already existing members so that he may bring others and so that those who were not members may come and be joined to his members through whom his good news is preached. Thus, there will be one body under one head, possessing one spirit, living one life."[170] Together with his faithful, Christ prays to the Father, intercedes for his followers at the Father's right hand, even prays to himself.[171] Thanks to his presence, Christ celebrates Christ in the liturgy. For not only Easter but every celebration of the Eucharist is a memorial of the death and resurrection of Christ, and it is Christ who celebrates this memorial of himself.[172]

So, too, Christ is hungry in the community of those who believe in him, while in their poor, Christ himself receives the gifts of compassion. With this in mind, Augustine reminds his faithful: "Look, Christ is not commanding you anyway; Christ is asking you, Christ is in need. *I was hungry,* says Christ, *and you did not give me to eat* (Mt 25:42). It's for your sake he was willing to be in need, so that you would have somewhere to sow the earthly things he has given you, and from them reap eternal life."[173] Because Christians can receive Christ in the poor, they are not deprived of the presence of Christ.[174] In the final analysis therefore, Christ lives in the love of Christians for their neighbors: "And there will be one Christ loving himself, for when the members love one another, the body loves itself."[175] In the members, Christ fulfills his own commandment.

But in this one human being, the suffering of Christ also continues to the end of the world. Thus, Augustine says in commenting on the words "you all kill" of Psalm 61:4:

> Can there be so much room in one human being that this one can be killed by all? But by this 'one human being' we must understand our own person, the person of our Church, the person of the body of Christ. For the one human being with its head and body is Jesus Christ . . . two in one body, speaking with one voice, enduring the same suffering, and when evil is past, enjoying one rest. Christ's suffering is therefore not in Christ alone, yet the sufferings of Christ are only in Christ.[176]

Consequently, in one human being, Christ is tempted and Christ overcomes the tempter.[177] In a very special way Christ suffers in his martyrs.[178]

Finally, in the glory of the resurrection, Christ ascends to heaven and thereby begins the ascension of his whole body, which in hope already dwells with him at the Father's side.[179] Augustine does not say anything more about how he understands the presence of Christ in heaven and in us, although he does offer some points of departure for such an understanding.[180]

c) Founder and King of the City

The "passing over of Christians" *(transitus christianorum),* which has its exemplar in "the passing over of Christ" *(transitus Christi),*[181] does not how-ever take place all at once. Rather, it is accomplished in a historical process that began with Abel and will be complete only in the resurrection of all the just. Augustine often returns to the theme of "the Church beginning with Abel."[182] He also leaves no doubt about the fact that only in the future will the one human being reach the perfection of the full Christ. The images of a jour-ney, a sea voyage, and a "walking with spiritual steps," as well as the frequent antithesis of hope and reality, are very clear in this regard.

The lengthy historical development of the whole Christ is often presented by Augustine as a struggle between Christ and the devil.[183] The gradual formation of the whole Christ thus proves to be a continual victory of the Just One and his followers over the one who has been the adversary from the beginning. This basic concept in Augustinian theology is found above all in *The City of God,* as well as in many sermons and expositions of the psalms that reflect the same apologetic situation. In these writings, Augustine develops the antithesis between the two loves, the love of Christ and the love of the world or of the devil.[184] He expresses the same idea in the politically oriented images of the city of God and the city of the devil or, in terms that are even more biblical, in the contrast between Jerusalem and Babylon.[185] He regards Christ himself as king of the citizenry of God.[186] We must not, however, overlook the fact that in *The City of God,* Augustine not only describes Christ as the true king,[187] but also speaks of God as "founder and king of the glorious city of God."[188]

The first source of his historical conception of the opposition between Christ and the devil was the Bible, in which the Christ event was foretold by the prophets and then reported in the story of Christ and the first community.[189] But an impulse also came from Porphyry, according to whom, a "universal way" cannot be historically demonstrated either in the "truest philosophy" or in the teachings of Indian sages or in the experience of the Chaldeans.[190] In answer to this entirely negative view, Augustine sought to show from the history of the city of God—from its origin, its continued existence, and its end—that in Christ, the one true mediator, God wills to lead all, even ordinary human beings, to eternal salvation.[191] To this end, he refers especially to the "Christian ages,"[192] the time between the first and second comings of Christ, in which the prophetic promises have been fulfilled, as can be shown to anyone from the very writings preserved by the Jews. This is true especially of the age of Theodosius, which most clearly manifests the fulfillment of the promise of a universal Church.[193]

d) The Whole Christ

In the final analysis, the history of the city of God that is gradually establishing itself on earth is nothing other than the incarnation of God in the most comprehensive sense. Foretold by the prophets, established in principle by Jesus' birth from Mary and his death and resurrection, the formation of the whole Christ takes place in the Church, where the unparalleled presence of God in Christ takes its full form. Augustine refers to this basic reality not only by speaking, as he does from early on, of the head and members that make up the whole Christ. He also coins a technical terminology to deal with this reality, for he speaks not only of the one person of Christ but also of "the one person of the Church."[194]

Augustine presents this doctrine of the whole Christ, of the comprehensive incarnation of God, in an entirely realistic setting. In a theology that is marked by Christian hope, he reminds his hearers and readers in a great variety of expressions and with great intensity that the whole Christ lives in hope and advances through faith, not through vision.[195] Christ must be born ever anew in the hearts of the faithful.[196] In his Church the city of God is still always on pilgrimage, even though it is already awaited by the heavenly Church.[197]

6. The Supreme Grace of God

Jesus Christ, the one mediator between God and humanity, is also the way that leads to the homeland; he is this for individuals and for the entire human race. He is the foundation of Christian and ecclesial life. But this entirely Christocentric understanding of human existence emerges into full clarity only when we bear in mind that for Augustine everything is God's grace and that the incarnation in particular is the greatest of all graces. On the other hand, it is precisely due to this that Augustinian Christocentrism becomes relativized. The "way to Christ through Christ" is, in the final analysis, "a way to God through Christ in the Spirit."

a) The Form of Righteousness

A life lived in faith is entirely a gift of God. Augustine therefore constantly cites the text: "What do you have that you have not received? And if you received it, why do you boast as if you did not receive it" (1 Cor 4:7).[198] This is already true of creation, which came into being through the eternal Word; but it is even more true of the greater grace thanks to which human beings have become believers through the incarnate Word.[199] This grace of God, however, has its effect through Jesus Christ our Lord.[200] It originates in his saving work on earth, as becomes clear especially in the theme of the reconciliation by which God's enemies become God's friends.[201] So, too, all justification goes back to Christ: he baptizes in the Church; his sacrifice is celebrated in his name; he suffers and conquers in his members; he constantly intercedes for them at the right hand of the Father.[202] Those who acknowledge all this are on the way of Christ.[203]

But Christ is not simply the source and origin of grace.[204] His human life is also the exemplar of all grace. Through the grace by which the human being Jesus became the Son of God and therefore a completely righteous person, they, too, are justified who believe in him; as Christ was born of the Spirit, so believers are reborn of the same Spirit.

> In our head, therefore, let the fountain of grace show itself to us;
> from there it is poured out on all his members according to the measure
> of each. The same grace by which that human being from his very begin-

ning became the Christ, makes others Christians from the beginning of their faith. From the Spirit from which he was born, these are reborn. The same Spirit who made him sinless effects the forgiveness of sins in us.[205]

There is a hint here that the righteousness, in which Christ persevered to the end and in which he died as a righteous person for the wicked, is ultimately rooted in his eternal Sonship,[206] and that in this respect he is the model for the righteousness of Christians, who have in their own way become God's children through the grace of baptism.[207] Above all, Christ is the exemplar of all grace because in his incarnation it became clear that grace is a completely free gift of God's love. "You will not dare to claim that because of previous merits the human being Jesus Christ became son of God from the very outset, that is, in the womb of the Virgin. Therefore, it was by the same grace by which his members become good after being wicked, that that human being was good from the beginning."[208]

Augustine can hardly find satisfactory words for praising this freely bestowed beginning of all grace, which goes back ultimately to the predestination of Christ. Thus, he says, for example, in *The Predestination of the Saints:* "This, then, is the predestination of the saints, which shone out most clearly in the Saint of saints and which no one who has correctly understood the words of truth may deny. For we have learned that even the Lord of glory himself was predestined insofar as the human being became the Son of God."[209] Moreover, "the one who made for us the Christ in whom we believe is the one who also made us believe in Christ; the one who made the human being Jesus 'the pioneer and perfecter' of our faith also gave human beings the origin and completion of faith in Jesus."[210] It also goes without saying that the Christ who without any merits on his part was anointed the Son of God in the incarnation and filled with the grace of God, is also the exemplar of all predestination.[211]

Implicit in all these assertions is that Augustine regards the incarnation of Christ as a unique grace. He also says as much explicitly: "As regards that [human being] taken up by the Word, it's all grace, it's unique grace, it's perfect grace."[212] It is the supreme example of the graciousness of grace. At a decisive point in his attack on Roman paganism he writes:

> If only you [Porphyry] had recognized the grace of God through our Lord Jesus Christ! If only you had been able to see [Christ's] incarnation, in which [Christ] took a human soul and body, as the supreme instance of grace! . . . The grace of God could not be commended in a way more likely to evoke a grateful response, than the way by which the only Son of God, while remaining unchangeably in [the Son's] own proper being, clothed [the Son's self] in humanity and gave to [humankind] the spirit of [the Son's] love by the mediation of a [human being], so that by this love [human beings] might come to [the Son] who formerly was so far

> away from them, far from mortals in [the Son's] immortality, from the
> changeable in [the Son's] changelessness, from the wicked in [the Son's]
> righteousness, from the wretched in [the Son's] blessedness.[213]

In this view, it is also perfectly clear that no human being, either before or
after the incarnation of Christ, can be justified without this grace. Even in the
Old Testament, the grace of Christ was needed for justification.[214] It was
through the grace of Christ that the righteous of that time believed in the
promises, while later on it was by the same grace-given faith that Christians
believed in the one who had come.

> Saving faith in the mediator between God and humankind rescued
> the righteous who prior to [Christ's] incarnation believed that [the Son]
> would come in the flesh. Our faith and theirs is one and the same because
> what we believe has occurred, they believed was to come. . . . The
> sacraments could differ according to different times and yet take their
> place most harmoniously in the unity of the same faith.[215]

Even in that former time, justifying faith was possible because Christ had appeared to the ancestors and had spoken through the prophets.[216] In the Old
Testament, there were even martyrs who accepted death in the name of
Christ.[217] Even then, there was an economy of salvation, that of "the Church
that began with Abel."[218]

It is in light, then, of the "grace of the Head," the graciousness of the incarnation of Christ, that the magnificence of Augustine's Christocentric vision
of history becomes fully clear. Because at the same time he anchors the mystery of Christ in Christ's eternal Sonship and this in the life of the triune God,
he makes it clear, in addition, that the economy of salvation is likewise a reflection of the everlasting love that unites Father and Son from all eternity. But
this is something that must be discussed in greater detail.

b) Through Christ, in the Holy Spirit, to God the Father[219]

"Through Christ as human being to Christ as God." This faith in Christ undoubtedly permeates the entire theological thinking and feeling of Augustine.
His "Christ is all" must not, therefore (as I have already suggested), be turned
into an absolute. He himself leaves no doubt on this point, for in one of his
final works he speaks of the school of the Trinity:

> This school is far removed from the fleshly senses. There the Father
> is heard and teaches in order that human beings may thereby come to the
> Son. There, too, is the Son . . ., for [the Son] is the Word through whom
> [the Father] thus teaches, but [the Son] accomplishes this not through the
> ear of the flesh but the ear of the heart. At the same time, the Spirit of the
> Father and the Son is also there. It too teaches, but not separately [from

the Father and the Son], for we have learned that the actions of the Trinity are indivisible.[220]

This last statement certainly bears the stamp of the anti-Arian tradition of the fourth century, a stamp that becomes more noticeable in the later works of Augustine. But the same trinitarian orientation also marks the more personal *Confessions.* In these, Augustine constantly addresses himself to God who through the Son and Spirit has bestowed God's mercy on Augustine,[221] or else he speaks of "the Christ of God."[222] God's mercy had from the beginning placed in his heart the name of Christ, which he did not find in the philosophers, the name of his Savior, the Son of God.[223]

In fact, we will correctly interpret Augustine's "Christ is all" only if we keep in mind that Christ's gift of grace begins where all life has its source.[224] Even the watchword of Augustine's teaching on grace—the grace of God which sets us free through Jesus Christ (Rom 7:24f.)—already forbids a Christological reduction.[225] Such a reduction is even more clearly excluded by the basic concept of sending, apart from which the name "Christ" loses its deeper meaning.[226] Even though, by reason of Christ's sending in the incarnation, Christ does not cease to be equal to the Father, the Father is nonetheless the one who sends Christ.[227] The very anointing by which the human being is anointed as the Christ is understood by Augustine in trinitarian terms: "The Son was anointed by God the Father when [the Son] became a human being, while yet remaining God; [the Son] was filled with this anointing, that is, with the Holy Spirit."[228]

The same is true of the revelation given by Christ, for in the final analysis this is attributed to the Father. Augustine indeed says, "Christ is shown to Christ through Christ," but we must not overlook the context in which this is said: "When, then, the Father shows [Christ] to the members of Christ, [the Father] shows [Christ] to Christ. This is a great but real marvel: Christ is shown what Christ already knew, and [Christ] is shown to Christ through Christ."[229]

Finally, the extent to which the faith in Christ, by which believing Christians journey to the everlasting homeland, has its origin in the Father is shown by passages in which Augustine, referring to John 6:44, explains that the Father draws us to Christ. For example, he says, "To be drawn by the Father to Christ and to hear and learn from the Father that we should come to Christ is nothing else but to receive from the Father the gift of faith in Christ."[230] Along the same line, he comments on Psalm 85:11 that God always extends God's hand to those who journey on the way: "For in giving [God's] Christ, God extends [the divine] hand; extending [the divine] hand, [God] gives [God's] Christ. [God] leads to the way by leading to your Christ; [God] leads along the way by leading in [God's] Christ; Christ, however, is the truth."[231] Elsewhere, he says more precisely that the Father leads us to Christ by revealing Christ to be God.[232] Lastly, the love that is poured out in hearts through the Holy Spirit, and without which full faith in Christ is not possible, has its origin in the Father.[233]

The way of faith not only begins in the Father; it also ends in the Father. It is true that Christ is not only the way but also the truth and the life.[234] In Christ, all who believed in him amid the darkness of this world will have eternal life in the light of the vision.[235] So, too, Christ is wisdom for all souls,[236] and in Christ these souls become themselves the throne of wisdom.[237] As Word, Christ is the bread of the angels and the saints.[238] Some day, moreover, he will be the whole Christ along with the angels and all human beings who have believed in him.[239] In this sense, then, Christ himself is also the homeland,[240] both for the individual soul and for the pilgrim Church—now in hope, some day in reality.

But in its fullest sense, the formula "through Christ as human being to Christ as God" says that Christ the human being leads to the wisdom and truth of God, that is, to the one who in the final analysis reveals the Father. "Through Christ as human being to Christ as God; through the Word made flesh to the Word that was in the beginning, God with God."[241] Accordingly, Augustine regards God as the homeland: "There we shall always have one living Father, we shall have our homeland."[242] In the same line of thought, he speaks of the vision of God[243] and describes this vision as never ending happiness *(fruitio)*[244] as well as eternal salvation and an everlasting song of praise.[245]

Nor is the basic theme of mediatorship opposed to this orientation that is theocentric in the New Testament sense of *theos*. It is true that in keeping with the Nicene tradition, Augustine understands the "God" with whom the human being Christ Jesus unites humanity to include Christ as God. He gives even the "God" of 1 Timothy 2:5 a trinitarian meaning.[246] Nevertheless, Christ always remains for him the "door to the Father": "If Christ preaches himself and by preaching enters into you, it is through himself that he enters. He is also the door to the Father, for there is no way of reaching the Father except through him. For there is one God and one mediator between God and humanity, the human being Christ Jesus."[247] It is also to be noted that the mediation of Christ not only awakens a purifying faith that causes human beings to turn in upon themselves and find the truth of God in their hearts. It also reveals the depths of the wholly other God: God's humility and the proof of God's generous love, the love, that is, that has its origin in the Father.[248]

All this is confirmed by Augustine's conception of prayer. Not only does he stress, with the tradition, that the Eucharistic Prayer is addressed to the Father;[249] he also sees the psalms as first and foremost a prayer to the Father. Even though he is familiar with prayer to Christ as God,[250] he gives far greater preference to "praying with Christ, in the Spirit, to the Father."[251]

This orientation of the economy of salvation to its first source and ultimate end will emerge more clearly in the second part of this book, which will be devoted to Augustine's concept of God. But it must be noted here that no matter how much we acknowledge the theocentrism of Augustine, it would be incorrect to interpret the formula "through Christ as human being to Christ as God" as meaning that the incarnation of the Word loses its meaning after the last judgment. Even though it might be possible thus to interpret certain statements in which Augustine distinguishes between the order of faith and the order of vision,[252] we must take into account that he evidently did not deal with the question of the salvific meaning that the glorified humanity of Jesus has for eternal life after the last judgment.[253] In any case, he expressly rejected, although without further discussion, the theory of a transformation of the human nature of Christ into the Word.[254]

Above all, relying on the New Testament, he understood eternal life to include a "reigning with Christ."[255] At the end of *The City of God,* he describes life in heaven as also including "singing the Lord's mercies for ever." "Nothing will give more joy to that City than this song to the glory of the grace of Christ by whose blood we have been set free. There, that precept will find fulfillment: 'Be still, and know that I am God.'"[256] Astonished at the mystery of Christ, the saints will dwell in the vision of God, the author of all grace.[257] If God is then all in all, they will know that it is God who fills them: "Restored by [Christ] and perfected by [Christ's] greater grace we shall be still and at leisure for eternity, seeing that [Christ] is God, and being filled by [Christ] when [Christ] will be all in all."[258]

PART II

The Grace of God

Introduction

1. The God Question in Augustine and Its Relevance Today

Although Augustine of Hippo does not go down equally well with all theologians today, it is nonetheless very noticeable how many of them have been fascinated by him and still are.[1] To cite only the German-speaking world, notable examples can be given: Adolf von Harnack, Reinhold Seeberg, Romano Guardini, Berthold Altaner, Erich Przywara, Hans Urs von Balthasar, and Ladislaus Boros. No less noteworthy is the fact that these and other friends of Augustine have interested themselves in his conception of God.[2] This fact need not surprise anyone who reflects that the Bishop of Hippo had to deal with those intellectual and religious currents of thought that focused their attention chiefly on the question of God: Gnostic dualism that lived on in Manicheism, and the Stoic and Platonic traditions with their inclination to monism.

The importance of Augustine's properly theological thought becomes even clearer when we realize that in his *The City of God,* the most important apologia from Christian antiquity, Augustine used the so-called "tripartite theology" as his point of departure in his critique of Roman religion.[3] More clearly than all the other Church fathers, and even more unambiguously than Lactantius and Eusebius of Caesarea, he gives in this critique the reasons why Christians found the theology of the myths meaningless, shows how carefully they distinguished what was useful and what useless in the theology of the philosophers, and demonstrates the dangers they had to take into account in making political theology their own.[4]

The importance that has been attributed in our time to Augustine's teaching on God becomes even more explicable from the fact that the question of God dominated Augustine's own religious experience. The often repeated motto, "I am determined to know God and the soul,"[5] shows that after self-knowledge there was in his early years only one other object worthy of a scientific and theological quest: God. And when, later on, he devoted his best energies to bringing home the Church's teaching on the grace of Christ to the bishops and faithful of his time, he did so because he was convinced that anyone who "makes pointless the cross of Christ" is thereby attacking the very dignity of God. His entire religious thought stood under the sign of the tension between faith in the one mediator, Jesus Christ, the source of truth and grace, and the deep insight that God is the beginning and the end.

Those, therefore, who take up the question of God in Augustine are not simply tackling a question that has acquired a central place in modern scholarship on Augustine. Even more, they are striking to the heart of Augustine's own religious thinking and feeling. They have in mind Augustine's perhaps most frequently cited words, "You stir humanity to take pleasure in pleasing you, because you have made us for yourself, and our heart is restless until it rests in you."[6]

2. A Century of Scholarship

Here again, a survey of modern scholarship would be helpful in getting a clearer grasp of the state of the question. Such a survey, however, would be a difficult, almost impossible undertaking. Moreover, there is no point in attempting a complete review of the immense literature on the subject. We must be satisfied from the outset with a somewhat arbitrary selection of representative studies. At the same time, it is only with difficulty that the numerous studies of the God question in Augustine can be grouped according to their main types. An introduction to this literature must therefore always remain provisional.[7]

a) Philosophically Oriented Studies

Augustine has always been a subject of great interest even in philosophical circles. It may, in fact, be asserted that the philosophical aspects of his concept of God are the ones that have been discussed the most. This is already evident from the many studies of the proofs for God's existence in Augustine.[8]

Discussions of Augustine and the "God of the philosophers" have to a great extent been connected with the broader problem of the Hellenization of Christianity. In the case of Augustine, this has meant in particular the question of his Neoplatonism as well as the more specialized question of the historicity of his *Confessions*. The year 1950 may be taken as marking a turning point in the investigation of this set of questions.[9] It seems reasonable, therefore, to deal first with the literature published before that date, then with works published after it, and only then to glance at presentations of Augustine's teaching on God.

aa) *Scholarship before 1950*

In 1887, in a work which I cited earlier, A. von Harnack, still a young man, suggested a distinction between the Augustine who wrote his *Confessions* when already a Christian bishop and the Augustine who at the time of his conversion wrote dialogues that continued to be entirely shaped by Neoplatonism.[10] Following von Harnack, F. Loofs in his manual on the history of dogma and W. Thimme in a monograph on the intellectual development of Augustine during the years 386 to 391 emphasized the predominance of Neoplatonic thought over the ecclesial thought of the convert of Cassiciacum.[11] This approach to the biography of Augustine found its keenest expression in P. Alfaric's *L'évolution intellectuelle de Saint Augustin,* published in 1918. According to Alfaric, Augustine was converted first to Neoplatonism and only later on, thanks to the philosophical "conversion," did he become "Catholic." For this reason (Alfaric argues), the account of his conversion in the *Confessions* is to be regarded as tendentious; in other words, it reflects Augustine's later situation in the Church.

The sharp response from C. Boyer, who in his study *Christianisme et néoplatonisme dans la formation de saint Augustin* (1920) emphasized the influence of Monica and Ambrose, did little to change the critical approach to the historical value of the *Confessions.* All the same, some writers, such as K. Holl (1922) and J. Norregard (1923), did tone down the importance of Neoplatonism in the conversion of Augustine, giving greater attention once again to his Christian parentage and his ideas on authority.

bb) *The New Approach of P. Courcelle*

In 1950, P. Courcelle published his *Recherches sur les Confessions de saint Augustin.*[12] In this book, he took the results of previous study and developed them further. He was able to show that during the period of Augustine's conversion, there was a group of Neoplatonic philosophers in Milan, among whom Ambrose may be numbered. Although not all the details of Courcelle's thesis won agreement, its substance was accepted. According to this, it is meaningless to distinguish between a Neoplatonic and a properly Christian phase in the life of Augustine. We may assume rather a meeting and even a partial identification of Neoplatonic and Christian ideas.

Positions similar to those of Courcelle were subsequently adopted by J. J. O'Meara in various studies,[13] by R. Holte in his valuable book *Béatitude et Sagesse,*[14] and by other authors. On the other hand, there are still differences of opinion on the extent to which the Neoplatonic philosophy of Plotinus reached Augustine through Porphyry.[15] In recent years, however, there has been still another shift. Scholars are again taking much more seriously the influence of the faith which Monica and his Christian environment passed on to the young Augustine; this is true especially of G. Madec in his various studies of the *Confessions* and Augustine's early writings.[16]

cc) *The Study of Augustine's Teaching on God*

The divergent judgments of the Neoplatonic influences on the intellectual development of the young Augustine are reflected in studies of his teaching on God and in presentations of it in histories of dogma. As early as 1873, A. Dorner strongly emphasized these philosophical influences. Von Harnack and Loofs followed the same line, as I mentioned earlier. Seeberg, however, showed himself much more reserved on this point. It was chiefly R. Jolivet and E. König who reacted against the exaggerated estimates of Neoplatonic influence.

In addition, during the last forty years, this opposite view has been strongly supported by the investigations of P. Hadot, J. Pépin, G. Madec, and others into the sources of the philosophical thought of Augustine and other Christian writers of his time.[17] It is not surprising therefore that in more recent studies of Augustine's teaching on God, its Neoplatonic background should be taken into account in a calm and impartial way and be critically evaluated.[18] This does not mean that the question of the Hellenization of Christian theology and in particular of the theological thought of Augustine is thereby excluded. We are far from having reached complete clarity on the extent to which the biblical message concerning the one Lord and God, the God of Israel and the Father of Jesus Christ, was rethought in the light of Greek philosophy.[19]

K. Flasch, in his quite recent *Logik des Schreckens,* has taken a unique position of his own. According to his exposition of this in his penetrating introduction to the second of the *Quaestiones ad Simplicianum,* in 396–397 Augustine relinquished his Neoplatonic approach to the doctrine of God and developed a new picture of God by reference to the absolute gratuity of grace, which he had discovered at that time.[20]

b) The Study of Manichean Influences on the Theology of Augustine

In his well-known book on the intellectual development of Augustine, Alfaric took up—as the subtitle of the work promised—not only Augustine's Neoplatonism but also the question of his Manicheism.[21] According to A. Schindler, Alfaric's observations on this second subject are still worth considering.[22] In a short note, G. Quispel goes even further: in his view, we are now sufficiently familiar with the Neoplatonic background of Augustine's thought; it is all the more urgent, therefore, to shed more light on his relations with Manicheism.[23] Others are more reserved on this point, but they do speak of a basic Manichean mood, of some common tendencies, that influenced especially the composition of *The City of God* and Augustine's teaching on grace.[24]

In any case, it is remarkable that Augustine was for nine years a member of the Manichean sect in Africa;[25] that during the first years of his pastoral activity he had to engage in disputation with the Manichees; and finally, that his Pelagian adversaries represented him as being a Manichee. We may therefore expect that his properly theological thinking will take on sharper contours for us when we take Manichean influences into account, even if these were only such as are felt in any response to a different intellectual movement. This will be made clearer below, in the chapter on the question of God in Augustine's anti-Manichean writings. For the moment let me simply point out that there is quite a considerable body of literature on this question, including some that is very recent.[26]

Also worthy of note is the way in which E. Przywara in his incomparable book on Augustine, *Die Gestalt als Gefüge,* compares the Neoplatonic and Manichean approaches in Augustine's teaching on God. In his Neoplatonic vision of things (Przywara says), Augustine conceived of God as "the Light of the universe." When adopting the Manichean and, even more, the anti-Pelagian perspective, he experienced God as impenetrable darkness. Yet precisely for this reason he came to realize that it is only in the extreme abasement of the Son that God finally reveals the divine self as love.[27]

c) Monographs of a Neoscholastic Kind

The majority of books that deal with Augustine's teaching on God, either exclusively or in combination with other themes, delve into the philosophical aspect and are therefore obliged to deal also with the influence of the philosophical traditions of antiquity, especially the Platonic. Not all of these studies, however, are affected by the debate over the Hellenization of Christianity. On the contrary, they have in common that they proceed systematically rather than historically. They care little, therefore, about the chronology of Augustine's works or his interior development. Rather, they present Augustine's teaching on God in the setting of modes of thought taken over from medieval Scholasticism. Consequently, they speak to such questions as the possibility of knowing God and proving God's existence; the divine nature; the most important attributes of God and their interconnection; as well as the relationship of God to the world and to human beings, that is, divine providence and predestination.[28] This kind of approach is to be found especially in the articles in the *Dictionnaire de théologie catholique,*[29] to some extent even in E. Gilson's classical introduction to Augustine's thought,[30] but also in more recent monographs.[31]

d) Studies of Augustine's Exegesis and Preaching

In addition to historical and systematic studies of Augustine's teaching on God, there are noteworthy investigations of his interpretations of the Bible and his activity as a preacher. The former touch on our subject inasmuch as they deal with the exegesis of the relevant texts; especially important here are works on Augustine's exegesis of Genesis[32] and on the use and interpretation of the psalms in the *Confessions* and in the expositions of the psalms.[33] Also of interest in this context are the introductions to Augustine's great apologetic work, *The City of God,* since here Augustine uses many of his own explanations of the biblical books from Genesis to the Apocalypse of John.[34] As for the sermons, a special interest attaches to those dealing with the creed.[35]

3. Thoughts on the Appropriate Method

a) The Principal Difficulties in a Presentation
   of Augustine's Teaching on God

Despite its brevity, the preceding survey of Augustinian scholarship during the last hundred years makes it quite clear how difficult it is to properly evaluate Augustine's teaching on God and to present its main lines. As the reader will have seen, one must come to grips especially with four difficulties.

First of all, in all the works of his that have survived, Augustine evidently acts as a "theologian" and speaks constantly of God. He likes to speak of "the truest philosophy," but by this he means theology in the present-day sense of the word. All he has in mind are the efforts of Christians to gain a deeper understanding of their faith, to think out the reasons for the mystery, and thus to show themselves not only lovers of wisdom but also lovers of God. With this in mind, A. Schindler comes to the conclusion, at the end of his excellent thirty-page survey of Augustine's interior development and theology, "This means that the doctrine of God and the essential features of Christology form a background for everything else I have presented."[36] This statement certainly applies more to the teaching on God than to the Christology. Even though the Christological passages in Augustine's writings are very numerous, God is everywhere seen as the beginning and the end, as the "subject" (to use the language of Scholastic theology). Anyone wanting to speak of Augustine's picture of God must therefore go into all of his writings, which is an impossible undertaking.

Next, a reading of Augustine's writings makes it immediately clear that the Latin word *Deus* ("God") is an equivocal one. When Augustine uses it spontaneously, without further theological reflection, and especially when he uses it as the subject of a sentence, *Deus* means the God of Israel, the God of the prophets, and the God of Jesus Christ, or, in short, the Father whom Christians confess in the first article of the baptismal creed. But Augustine also uses the word to express the fact that the Father, the Son, and the Holy Spirit are a single God and equal in nature. Likewise, he also calls Jesus Christ or the Holy Spirit "God." Particularly worth noting is the Christological use of the word, as, for example, in the frequently occurring formula "through Christ as human being to Christ as God." We must therefore always take the ambivalence of the word into account.

More complex than the two difficulties named is a third: the fact that readers of Augustine's works are faced with a Greco-Roman reinterpretation of the Bible. Augustine undoubtedly believes in the God announced in the prophetic and apostolic writings. Nor can anyone fail to see that he sticks to the wording of the biblical books, especially when dealing with the Book of Psalms. At the same time, however, neither is it possible to overlook the fact that he hears the language of the Bible as a Latin speaker of the imperial age. Above all, he relies on the Latin translation of the Bible that in turn goes back to the Septuagint. In doing so, he constantly follows the earlier Latin tradition, which likewise is largely dependent on the Greek tradition. In other words, whenever he preaches and teaches about God, his words, especially in his citations and paraphrases of the Bible, have Latin and Greek overtones. For example, when, together with the biblical writers, he calls God "Lord" and "Father," he awakens in his hearers images current in Latin North Africa around the year 400. He speaks to them of God as the father of a household, thereby reflecting the way in which the Romans of the time thought of the *pater familias.* But how is one adequately to bring all these nuances into play?

Last, one must keep in mind the intellectual development which Augustine undoubtedly experienced in the forty years of his theological labors. True enough, the intuitions that played a decisive role in his full return to the Catholic faith remained characteristic of his thinking until the end of his life. But it is no less certain that his pastoral experiences, the continual battle against errors, the critical responses to the objections of both pagans and Christians to divine providence, and the daily obligation of exhorting and encouraging his faithful, all led him to rethink his initial insights. There are even scholars who think that over the years Augustine became more pessimistic precisely in his teaching about God. He moved (they say) from the God of light to the God of darkness who arbitrarily determines everything in advance.[37] This assessment of his teaching on God is in fact one-sided, but this is not disagreeing with the underlying idea that Augustine did undergo an intellectual development. It is, however, not easy to represent this development in a handy way and without all too many repetitions.

b) Methodological Consequences

If we are to effectively meet these difficulties facing a survey of Augustine's teaching on God, we must undertake a selection of texts. To come to grips with all the writings in the same measure would be a completely impossible undertaking. The study that follows will therefore be restricted to the most important works or groups of works and within these, at least in part, to those writings in particular that seem most representative of the main questions Augustine took up in his theological thinking.[38]

The writings selected are to be discussed in chronological order. This principle is applied, however, with flexibility. In the discussion of a basic text, earlier or later but in any case more secondary passages will also be introduced. Thus in the section on *The Literal Meaning of Genesis,* passages from other writings on God as creator will also be taken into account. In particular, the chronological order will be set aside at the beginning and the end of the entire discussion, which will begin with the *Confessions,* fundamental on the question of God, and end with the preaching to the faithful, constant throughout Augustine's entire priestly ministry.

Furthermore, it will be my concern in this study to bring out, above all else, the biblical background of Augustine's picture of God. This will not, however, prevent attention to the shades of meaning that come from his cultural environment and the concerns at work in his pastoral ministry. The point is to take adequately into account the fact that his teaching on God, as well as his entire theological thought, has its basis in the Bible, but in the Bible as read and explained in the imperial Church of the fourth and fifth centuries.[39]

Finally, for all these reasons, there can be no question of presenting the entire teaching of Augustine on God. Attention will be directed rather to the meaning of "God" *(Deus)* as Augustine uses it. This implies two things. First, we shall be looking to see with what meaning and in what contexts Augustine uses the word "God." Second, we shall keep in mind that when Augustine speaks of "God," he means in the first place the Father, to whom the (Latin) Bible is primarily referring when it speaks of "God."[40] This does not mean, however, ignoring the fact that Augustine also speaks of the Son and the Holy Spirit or the entire Trinity as "God" and that, of course, he acknowledges the equality of the three persons as understood by Nicea and accepts the principle that all the external divine works are common to the three persons.

c) Division of the Study

In light of the previous considerations, this second part of the work will have four chapters. The first, "God in the Writings of Augustine the Seeker," will, in addition to the *Confessions,* deal also with the philosophical dialogues and the anti-Manichean writings from the first period of Augustine's literary production (386-400). The second chapter will be on "God in the Major Theological Works"; here the principal works of Augustine—*The Trinity, The Literal Meaning of Genesis,* and *The City of God*—will be discussed. The third chapter, "God in the Christian Program of Life," will first discuss two letters (147 and 187) in which Augustine takes up questions having to do with the vision of God and with the presence of God; it will then turn to the anti-Pelagian writings, the *Expositions of the Psalms,* and the baptismal catecheses. In the fourth chapter, a concluding overview, the principal traits of Augustine's picture of God will once again be emphasized.

CHAPTER 1

God in the Writings of Augustine the Seeker

1. "Lord my God": God in the *Confessions*

In the *Confessions,* which is surely his best known work, Augustine undoubtedly gives a unique expression to his picture of God. Already a bishop with some experience behind him, but still seeking inner peace, he turns with all his heart to his God and Lord.[1] This masterwork of late antiquity undoubtedly also raises numerous historical, literary, and theological questions, but it is not possible to enter here into such a complex set of problems.[2] This much, however, may be maintained: modern scholarship sees the *Confessions* as containing, on the one hand, a largely reliable historical account and, on the other, further reflection that mirrors the religious experiences which the author had had by the time the work was composed. A. Trapè expresses the generally held view by distinguishing between "the Augustine presented in the narration" *(Agostino narrato)* and "Augustine [who] narrates" *(Agostino narrante).*[3]

These remarks suggest three steps in describing the intellectual and spiritual journey of Augustine. The first is to describe the events and experiences of his life that led him to the point of recognizing and accepting God, not only academically but existentially, as "Being itself" *(ipsum esse).* He tells of these events and experiences in order to show others the way to God. A second step will turn to the God of dialogue. Any description of Augustine the narrator will include a formal aspect and an aspect concerned more with content. In the former, we are dealing with the basic literary character of the *Confessions.* As is generally recognized, the *Confessions* are shaped by the Book of Psalms. In his conversation with God, Augustine expresses himself in the manner of the psalmist. When this fact is noticed, it becomes clearer how much the God of the *Confessions* is a God of dialogue. Augustine is in fact not seeking simply to deepen his knowledge; rather, he is involved with his God, invokes that God, tells God of his own wretchedness, and praises the divine mercy. In short, he speaks with the Lord his God.[4]

Finally, in his conversation with God, Augustine is telling himself and his readers who the God is with whom he is speaking: the God who is before and above all things and at the same time closer to us than we are to ourselves. But this all-transcendent and at the same time all-present God is viewed not only ontologically but also historically. God manifests the divine self in the history of sin and of justification. This implies that human beings know God not only because God enlightens them *(illuminatio Dei)* but also and above all because God is constantly mindful of them *(memoria Dei).*

a) Augustine's Spiritual Journey

Anyone dealing with the *Confessions* will usually think immediately of the conversion which the young African professor of literature underwent near Milan in 386. And yet it is obvious that the so-called conversion of Augustine cannot be tied down to the scene in the garden when he heard a child singing "Take, read; take, read," opened the Letter to the Romans, and read the liberating words of the Apostle.[5] His conversion took place rather in the course of an intellectual, ascetical, and religious process. Indeed—and this is not always given adequate attention—his was not in the final analysis a conversion in the usual sense of the word, or at least not a conversion from paganism to Christianity. In the course of a long and difficult ascent, Augustine reached the conviction that the faith of his childhood fully satisfied his academic and ethical expectations.[6] Numerous scholars have described this journey to full acceptance of the Catholic faith. They have, however, also given varying assessments of the account in the *Confessions,* together with the allusions in the early writings.[7]

Augustine was never a pagan. On the contrary, he was born into a Christian family. He did, of course, have pagan acquaintances; and in any case, he was familiar with the pagan life of the time, as his criticisms of contemporary paganism show.[8] But he himself emphasizes the Christian influence which he experienced from his earliest childhood. He remarks in connection with his reading of Cicero's *Hortensius,* "This name of my Saviour your Son, my infant heart had piously drunk in with my mother's milk, and at a deep level I retained the memory" (*Conf.* 3.4.8; Chadwick, 40). He had seen how people prayed and had learned from them to turn to God in his childish distresses (*Conf.* 1.9.14). As a child, he had also heard of the promises of eternal life, for the entire household professed the Christian faith, except for his father, who did not, however, stand in the way of his mother's devotion (*Conf.* 1.11.17).

In his youth, then, Augustine never questioned the existence of God. His difficulty was rather in picturing God to himself and understanding God's relationship to the world.[9] After his disappointing reading of Cicero and his still greater disillusionment with the Bible, he was introduced to the Manichean community of Carthage, which promised him the resolution of his problems without recourse to any authority.[10] At that time, his Christian beliefs were inundated by "splendid hallucinations" (*Conf.* 3.6.10; Chadwick, 41). He saw himself therefore incapable of imagining an immaterial reality, and this was the principal reason for his aberrations (*Conf.* 4.16.29; 5.10.19f.; 5.14.25; 6.3.4). Even after he turned away from Manicheism, he was still unable to rid himself of his material images of God (see *Conf.* 7.5.7). He imagined a God spread out over endless space (*Conf.* 7.14.20).

When, however, he came upon the writings of the Platonists, he found a spiritual God. As he looked back, he thought: "I was astonished to find that I already loved you, not a phantom surrogate for you. But I was not stable in the enjoyment of my God" (*Conf.* 7.17.23; Chadwick, 127). Yet shortly before this revolutionary experience, he was still utterly confused, without any light, his eyes fixed on things instead of on God (*Conf.* 7.7.11). If at this decisive point we recall the words at the beginning and the end the *Confessions*—"You have made us for yourself, and our heart is restless until it rests in you" (1.1.1; Chadwick, 3) and "In your gift we find our rest. There are you our joy. Our rest is our peace" (13.9.10; Chadwick, 278)—it becomes clear that here is the heart of the work: the soul, created in the image of God, that seeks its center of gravity in God and not in itself also rediscovers its place in the structure of things.

Augustine did not acquire this right attitude to reality all at once. He had to struggle for it. Above all, he had to gain clarity on the problem of evil. In this regard, the books of the Platonists served only as an admonition, a shock. Augustine therefore had to confront in all honesty the truth that as creator, God transcends all things. He had to find his God—eternal truth, true love, and beloved eternity—within his own heart (*Conf.* 7.10.16).[11] In the final analysis, the discovery that he made, with the help of Plotinus as read through the eyes of Porphyry, was of God as "Being itself" *(ipsum esse)*. For him, however, the God thus discovered was identical with the "God who is" who was revealed to Moses. For this reason, he would never cease preaching to his faithful both "God who is," which is the name of God in eternity, and God the Father, which is the name expressing God's mercy.[12]

The lengthy process of Augustine's conversion was climaxed by his decision to receive baptism. It also included, therefore, the renunciation of his professional career and the choice of a philosopher's life ("retirement to philosophize," *otium philosophandi*). Augustine speaks very little of his baptism, but we should not on this account play down its importance. His account of the conversion of Marius Victorinus makes clear how he esteemed Christian baptism (*Conf.* 8.2.3-5).

Even though the discovery of "God as being itself" forms the center of his story, we must nonetheless understand this in the context of the spiritual transformation by which Augustine moved from a still rather vague faith to a considered and freely accepted faith.[13]

b) The God of Dialogue

In modern scholarship on the *Confessions,* a great deal of importance has been given to the determination of its literary genre.[14] In particular, various writers have endeavored to define more precisely the meaning of the words "confession" *(confessio)* and "confess" *(confiteri).*[15] In light of this, it might have been expected that more attention would be paid to the influence of the psalms on the *Confessions.*[16] In any case, we do have a study of this precise question from the year 1955.[17] Apart from the influence of Christian hymnody and ancient poetry, it is the extensive use of the language of the psalms that explains one of the most important literary characteristics of the *Confessions:* the interior dialogue that gives it its form.

The fact that in the *Confessions,* Augustine is in fact speaking to his God is repeatedly emphasized.[18] Indeed, it does appear at first sight that he is engaged in a monologue. In his words, expositions, narratives, and questions he answers himself, as he does in the preceding early dialogues, of which he himself says, "Augustine [talks] with Augustine."[19] But if we listen more attentively, we become aware of the invisible partner in dialogue who supports Augustine in his search for the truth, approves or rejects his solutions, and finally leads the process to its conclusion. This partner is the truth, God.[20] In other words, in the *Confessions,* Augustine lets God teach him. God reveals the meaning of life to him, and all with a view to those who will read his account. Augustine thus ceaselessly turns to the Lord, his God. He constantly speaks the divine name and invokes God (*Conf.* 1.1.1); he even beseeches God (*Conf.* 10.37.62). In the last books, he is still speaking with his God.[21]

Augustine owes this way of conversing with God to the sacred Scriptures and especially to the Book of Psalms. Readers can gain certainty on this point simply by looking at some invocations of God and their contexts in the first book of the *Confessions.* In addition to the well-known beginning (*Conf.* 1.1.1-2.4), the following examples may be given: "Who then are you, my God? What, I ask, but God who is Lord? For 'who is the Lord but the Lord?,' or 'who is God but our God?' (Ps 17:32)" (*Conf.* 1.4.4; Chadwick, 4); "In your mercies, Lord God, tell me what you are to me. 'Say to my soul, I am your salvation' (Ps 34:3)" (*Conf.* 1.5.5; Chadwick, 5); "You are being in a supreme degree and are immutable. In you the present day has no ending, and yet in you it has its end. . . . They would have no way of passing away unless you set a limit to them. Because 'your years do not fail' (Ps 101:28), your years are one Today" (*Conf.* 1.6.10; Chadwick, 8).[22]

Two points may be noted. First, although he speaks of God more often as "Lord God" than as "Father," he means by "Lord our God" the God of the ancestors, the God of Israel, the God of Jesus, that is, the one whom Christians confess in the first article of their baptismal creed.[23] But we should not forget the second point, namely, that some invocations reflect the religious language of Latin pagans. This will likely be true at least of the following instances: "Most high, utterly good . . . perfection of both beauty and strength" (*Conf.* 1.4.4; Chadwick, 4-5); "gentle Father" (*Conf.* 1.18.28; Chadwick, 20) and "Father of piety" (*Conf.* 13.24.36; Chadwick, 295)[24]; "Yet, Lord, I must give thanks to you, the most excellent and supremely good Creator and Governor of the universe, my God, even though by your will I was merely a child" (*Conf.* 1.20.31; Chadwick, 22). Whereas such titles and expressions from the Greco-Roman tradition may presuppose a personal God,[25] it must be admitted that the biblical climate of the entire work greatly augments this personal character.

The pronounced dialogue form of the *Confessions* thus makes it utterly clear that despite all the philosophical speculations they contain, they bear witness to an entirely personal God, a God to whom human beings turn with reverence and wonder, a God to whom they say "thou" as they do when speaking to another beloved human being, and in whom they find one who understands them and is so good to them.[26]

c) The All-Transcending and Utterly Close God

In his *Confessions,* then, Augustine is speaking with his God. Inasmuch as he addresses God repeatedly as "Lord" but also describes God as a kind Father, he constantly recognizes both the transcendence and the closeness of this God. He does so with the optimism with which he ascends from the beauty of created things to the beauty of their Creator. But he also contrasts human wretchedness and God's mercy in the manner which he developed from 396 on, at the latest. In order that we may better understand these two approaches to God, we must also describe in more detail the way in which God helps human beings to a deeper vision of the divine beauty and mercy by enlightening them and remembering them.

aa) *God, the Creator within Us*

At the beginning of the *Confessions,* Augustine asks God, "Who then are you, my God?" He himself knows no better answer than, "What . . . but God who is Lord?" (*Conf.* 1.4.4; Chadwick, 4).[27]

He then develops this answer with a flood of titles for God that are borrowed from the language of both the Bible and paganism. Here are the opening words of the series: "Most high, utterly good, utterly powerful, most omnipotent, most merciful and most just, deeply hidden yet most intimately present, perfection of both beauty and strength, stable and incomprehensible, immutable and yet changing all things, never new, never old, making everything new . . ." (*Conf.* 1.4.4; Chadwick, 4–5).

In his literary analysis of this unique passage, G. Buisson brings out its stanzaic structure, its antitheses, its harmony, and its biblical background.[28] In our present context, the most important point is what he says about the use of antithesis: "In this passage, antithesis has countless brilliant facets. It is sometimes quiet ('most beautiful—most strong'; 'stable—incomprehensible'), sometimes animated ('always active—always in repose'); here it is gathered up into two words ('loquacious—mute'), there it spreads out and is intensified (str. 3.3-4; 7.3-4)."

This use of antithesis marks not just the beginning of the first book of the *Confessions,* but the entire work.[29] Not only does it show the author's rhetorical skill; it also reflects the dialectic at work in his theological thinking.[30] The following examples may serve to back up this last point: "deeply hidden and yet most intimately present" (*Conf.* 1.4.4; Chadwick, 4-5); "if only they [the Manichees] could see the eternal to be inward" (9.4.10; Chadwick, 162); "you were more inward than my inmost part and higher than the highest element within me" (3.6.11; Chadwick, 43); "you . . . are most high and most near, most secret and most present" (6.3.4; Chadwick, 93-94).[31]

This last passage explains why God is at the same time far and near. God is distant, over us, because God is our Creator.[32] With the aid of Cicero and especially of the Platonic tradition, Augustine had discovered that God is truth *(veritas)* and changeless being *(ipsum esse).* But, following the Judeo-Christian tradition, he also reached the point of distinguishing between God as Creator and all good but mutable things.[33] At the same time, he also came to realize that as our Creator, God is also near to us, carries us in the divine hands, guides our life, and brings to life everything good in us: "When people see these things with the help of your Spirit, it is you who are seeing in them" (*Conf.* 13.31.46; Chadwick, 300).[34]

bb) *The Just and Merciful God*

In the *Confessions,* Augustine tells how he sought God. It was not, however, only the weakness accompanying creaturehood that stood in the way, but also the wretchedness of the sinner. This ethical orientation of his spiritual journey is a solid historical fact. At that time, Augustine was in fact under the spell of the question of evil (see *Conf.* 7.7.11; 7.13.19). He had preferred to make an evil principle responsible for his moral difficulties (*Conf.* 5.10.18). Because he was sick, he could not imagine God.[35] In other words, because he was offended by reality, he thought that he had no alternative but to accept the existence of two principles.[36] For this reason, he also felt liberated when he found the moral strength to abandon himself to God or, better, when God healed him (*Conf.*

8.12.29f.; 7.8.12). This entire outlook corresponded in large measure to the mind of antiquity, according to which philosophical reflection was always accompanied by moral effort. But Augustine went even further. He also reflected on his return to God in light of the discovery which he made in about 396–397 of the necessity of grace, while he was studying the Letter to the Romans.[37]

Because of his religious experiences, Augustine came to see the distance and nearness of God in connection with sin, which separated sinful human beings from their holy God.[38] Consequently, God's distance signified God's anger and demand for everlasting righteousness. God's nearness, on the other hand, signified the divine mercy and the completely free condescension of the eternal God (see *Conf.* 4.4.7).

Consequently, when Augustine speaks of the mystery of God at the beginning of the *Confessions,* he invokes God as "most merciful and most just" and refers to God's anger and jealousy while at the same time calling God "my holy sweetness" (*Conf.* 1.4.4). In like manner, he praises the divine mercy that has called him from "the region of dissimilarity" to a closeness in which the human being knows God and realizes that he or she has been created in the image of God.[39] When Augustine thus places himself in this historical and existential perspective, he recalls, before all else, the eternal love of God, which he himself has come so late to love: "Late have I loved you, beauty so old and so new; late have I loved you. And see, you were within and I was in the external world and sought you there. . . . You touched me and I am on fire to attain the peace which is yours."[40]

cc) *God Who Enlightens and Remembers*

In the seventh book of the *Confessions,* there is a famous passage in which Augustine describes his ascent to the always existing God.[41] Even though he had never doubted the existence of God, he felt the need of a rational justification of the faith in God that he had inherited from his family. The effort to do this was stimulated by his reading of Cicero's *Hortensius.*[42] The great Roman orator had taught him that human beings must seek their happiness in wisdom, in God who is Truth.[43] Therefore, his journey to God consisted to a large extent in an ever new reaching out for truth. And, in fact, he never ceased to invoke the truth, to speak of it, to reflect on it.[44]

In order to understand better this seeking after the truth, we must take two things into consideration. First, we must not overlook the fact that Augustine frequently attends to truth of a mathematical, scientific kind. It is in view of this kind of truth that he comes to certainty about the existence of God.[45] Second, and this is even more important, he shows himself convinced that human beings have God alone to thank for the truth.[46] As he repeats over and over, God is our light.[47] Thus, human beings cannot know the truth unless they are enlightened by God.

It is not easy, however, to define more closely the enlightenment or illumination to which Augustine keeps coming back in various contexts. Perhaps we may briefly describe his conception of it as follows. The enlightenment does not affect sense knowledge nor does it extend to the entire range of intellectual knowledge. Rather, it makes judgment possible in accord with rules derived from the highest truths of an ethical, esthetic, and logical kind. When human beings turn to these truths—the good, the beautiful, and the true—they experience the nearness of God. This explanation by E. Gilson was also adopted by R. Holte, although the latter extended it to the "natural" human being, who glimpses the eternal ideas in a mediated way.[48]

Augustine's teaching on enlightenment thus points to the bridge that to some extent enables human beings to cross the abyss dividing their creatureliness from the divine Creator. But the *Confessions* also speak of a more radical self-transcendence. Sinful human beings also return to their Father. That is, Augustine confesses not only the sublimity and closeness of God; he tells also and above all of the mercy in which, while safeguarding the divine justice, God reaches out to human wretchedness.

This basic theme of the *Confessions* finds its most profound expression in what Augustine has to say about the "memory" of God and human beings.[49] In his interpretation of the first verses of Genesis in the last three books of the *Confessions* (11–13), he stresses that God has been mindful of humanity. Thanks to this mindfulness of God, if nothing else, human beings can remember their own past and place themselves before God in the present; they can remember God and thus exist in the image of God.[50]

This teaching on memory obviously brings human beings close to God. It allows them to be seen as beings who share in the spiritual life of God. They, like God, are spirits.[51] Moreover, this conception of memory, with the aid of allusions to the Bible, heightens the necessity of God's healing human beings. It is possible for wretched humanity to confess and be delivered from their wretchedness because God has not forgotten them. They owe their very salvation to the immutable will of God who shows mercy on those to whom God shows mercy and is compassionate toward those to whom God is compassionate (see Rom 9:15). I must show, later on, why and when Augustine came to deepen further this intuition of 396–397 which already fully controls his *Confessions*.[52]

If we review what Augustine says in the *Confessions* about his Lord and God, we find that his spiritual journey led him, by way of the truth, to the unchangeable and solely good God. But this God is also the God of personal dialogue, the God who helps human beings and intervenes in their history, the God whom one may address as "Thou." It was precisely in this continual exchange with God that Augustine experienced the transcendence and closeness of his God, but of a God who also enlightens God's sinful creatures and cannot forget them because God has always been mindful of them.

2. The God of Wisdom and Beauty

The foregoing look at the God of Augustine's *Confessions* took as its start-ing point the now commonly accepted view that in this autobiographical work, a distinction must be made between the story *(narratio)* and reflection on it *(meditatio)*. As the Bishop of Hippo confessed his own wretchedness and the divine mercy, he recalled what he had thought about God as a young man. It is obvious, meanwhile, that his earlier writings, composed between 386 and 388, more immediately reflect his theological thought during those years.[53]

These works of the catechumen and neophyte have greatly interested scholars down to our day. This is not surprising when we keep in mind how many questions they raise concerning their precise chronology, their histori-cal context, their biographical reliability, their literary character and sources, as well as, in particular, the rather difficult questions they pose on the rela-tionship between Christian faith and ancient philosophy.[54] In what follows, I shall concern myself only with this last set of questions. Even here there can be no question of discussing all aspects of the matter, but I must address my-self at least to those that make possible a clearer grasp of the sense in which Augustine speaks of God in these writings which are clearly philosophical in orientation.

I have no intention, however, of distinguishing in principle between these so-called philosophical works of Augustine and his theological works. Although the later distinction between philosophy and theology is already announced in a fashion, such a division is not appropriate.[55] The first writings, which were com-posed or at least begun before 389, deserve to be called philosophical only be-cause in them the contrast between Christianity and the philosophical culture of antiquity seems to be more clearly defined. In reality, even in these writings, the author is always engaged in theology, in a reflection that even in questions of anthropology and the theory of knowledge is based on the faith.[56]

Now, it is evident that the teaching on God, which we are discussing here, is at the center of these early writings. Augustine himself emphasizes this at the beginning of the *Soliloquies:* "I wanted to know God and the soul."[57] This basic theological orientation is undoubtedly connected with the fact that Augustine's conversion consisted first and foremost in the effort to bring his inherited faith in God into harmony with his scientific concerns.[58] But this existential search, which is so characteristic of these writings, does not allow us to be satisfied with the distinction made by those scholars who would see three aspects in the idea of God in these works: God as Being beyond all becoming, God as the fullness of all perfections, and God as truth.[59] Rather, we must attempt to grasp the spiritual and intellectual circumstances within which Augustine was at this time reflect-ing on the mystery of God. Furthermore, it has rightly been said that his concept of God arose out of the crisis that was occupying all his thoughts and affections, and that consequently he experienced his God primarily as redeemer.[60] In what follows, then, I shall describe the various ways in which Augustine and his friends drew nearer to God in their conversations and meditations.

a) God, the Source of Happiness

Answer to the Skeptics[61]

The first work of Augustine that has come down to us is the three books of the *Answer to the Skeptics (Contra Academicos* or *De Academicis)*. It was composed at Cassiciacum in the fall of 386.[62] This work, the fruit of a joint reading of Cicero,[63] does not say much about God.[64] It reflects rather Augustine's intention of engaging his friends, especially Licentius and Trygetius, in an *exercitatio* or exercise in dialectical argument.[65] The point was to demonstrate that a wise person is capable of reaching a more certain knowledge of truth. But at bottom, Augustine intended to give a rational justification for having himself abandoned skepticism at his conversion.[66] In any case, when he endeavored to find an answer to the question of whether the happy life presupposed knowledge of the truth or only a search for the truth, he was laying the foundation for the later, more detailed discussion of the certainty of truth, without which no one can live happily.

As early, moreover, as the third book of the *Answer to the Skeptics,* the theme of the divine authority required for religious knowledge is announced. Augustine also speaks explicitly here of the Most High God who in the divine goodness sent the authority of the divine intellect into a human body in order to awaken and instruct souls through the words and deeds of the incarnate mind of God and thereby to enable them to enter into themselves and remember their heavenly homeland, without having to engage in philosophical discussion.[67] Authority, which is the basis of Christian faith, also grounds the certainty that there is an absolute truth.[68]

The Happy Life[69]

On November 13, 386, in celebration of Augustine's birthday, he and his friends broke off their discussion of the Academics for three days and, as it says in *The Happy Life,* held a spiritual banquet in the form of conversations on human happiness and the conditions for it.[70] Later on in the *Revisions,* when referring to those friendly conversations, Augustine observes that the answer to that basic question was simply that "the happy life consists in the perfect knowledge of God."[71]

The discussions themselves, however, were less simple. As we learn from the book on *The Happy Life,* during the first two days, the subject of discussion was the complexity of the striving for happiness in which all human beings are engaged. In these first steps, the participants reached the conclusion that human beings can only strive for an abiding good, that is, God. But at this point, the question arose of whether they can already possess God in the seeking of God or only in the knowledge of God.

On the third day, in a hardly interrupted lecture, Augustine tried to answer this question. In connection with the reading of Cicero, he proved that the lack *(egestas)* of wisdom is reason for the failure to attain to a lasting happiness and that, on the other hand, a good measure of wisdom can guarantee true happiness.[72] If, then, the soul becomes absorbed in eternal wisdom, it need not fear either the lack of a sufficient measure or any deprivation.[73] In confirmation of this view regarding not-too-little and not-too-much, Augustine appealed to texts of the Bible in which the Son of God is described as the Wisdom and the Truth of God. In this way, he came to the conclusion that God alone is the measure *(modus)* of the wisdom of the wise soul and that therefore the wise, moderate soul possesses God and so is happy.[74]

This conclusion proves to be, at bottom, a solution provided by faith. Augustine does, however, expound it with the tools provided by Stoic philosophy, according to which, happiness is to be found in reason and consists in measure.[75] Following Plotinus, he also expresses his views on union with God through the Word. In his concluding reflections, however, he also recalls the already mentioned passages of Paul (1 Cor 1:24) and John (14:6).[76] He himself will later on judge this attempt at an understanding of the faith to have been hardly successful.[77]

In any case, at that time he, together with his mother and his friends, had already achieved important results. They not only understood that true happiness consists in a possession,[78] but they also realized that the everlasting good must be God and consequently that the wisdom required for happiness cannot be merely moral but must be a wisdom that unites with God as the principle of unity.[79] By interpreting Cicero in the light of Plotinus, they even found a certain correspondence between the three principles that ground happiness, according to Plotinus, and the Christian Trinity. They speak of the Holy Spirit as the ray of truth that bids human beings enter into themselves in order to find with the help of truth the Father, who is the supreme measure.[80] God the Father is thus seen—and this is the decisive point here—as the goal of human longing. All salvation originates in God, the only and true God, the Father, the Lord, the liberator of souls.[81]

b) Human Beings, Created as Images of God[82]

Soliloquies[83]

While Augustine was staying at Cassiciacum with Monica and his friends, he also took time for solitude and meditation. In such periods of quiet, he liked to converse with himself,[84] once again taking up, but now for his personal profit, the problems he had been discussing with his friends. The work entitled *Soliloquies* brings together these very personal reflections. Augustine was aware of having created a new literary genre.[85] He was convinced, however, that there was no better tool for seeking the truth than to proceed by questions and answers, including those one puts to oneself.

During the discussions on the possibility of gaining a certain knowledge of the truth and thus attaining to the happy life, Augustine had forced himself to face the question of the nature of the soul. Therefore, on this point, too, he wanted to test the data of faith with the aid of reason. Consequently, he asks God at the beginning of the *Soliloquies* that he be able to know nothing but God and the soul.[86] However, he is undoubtedly interested primarily in the soul, that is, in its immortality.[87] As he shows, especially in the second book, the soul must be immortal because immortal truth is present in it and because the soul itself cannot live without truth.[88]

In his reflection on the soul, he also clarifies his ideas of God. The eternity of truth proves not only that the soul is everlasting but that God, too, is eternal.[89] The way in which he contemplates God and the soul at the same time is already clear in the lengthy prayer that begins the *Soliloquies*.[90] In this prayer, which Du Roy calls a first summary of Augustine's understanding of the faith,[91] a wealth of invocations of God, in part philosophical, in part natively biblical, comes gushing forth.[92]

According to Solignac and in particular Du Roy, this prayer also has a trinitarian structure.[93] At the beginning (they say), Augustine addresses God the Father, Creator of the universe.[94] He then invokes God the Truth, that is, the Son.[95] This is followed by an invocation of the Spirit, the God through whom we overcome the enemy.[96] In the fourth part of the prayer, Augustine addresses the entire Trinity, the one God.[97] Finally, after a reference to the quest for God, he once again addresses the Father, the supreme Good, the most kind Lord and Father, the wisest and best Father.[98]

But this trinitarian structure is by no means obvious.[99] Augustine constantly prays to God, whom he occasionally calls Father, but he addresses himself neither to the Son nor to the Holy Spirit. At most, it might be said that he has the divinity in mind, the divine substance, in which "begetter and begotten is one"[100] or "are one."[101] In addition, even though always addressed to God the Father, his prayer obviously describes many activities of God so that it is possible to ascribe the various events of salvation to the Father or to the Son or to the Holy Spirit. But this is surely not an adequate reason for speaking of the prayer as trinitarian in character. But even if one nonetheless prefers to accept this trinitarian orientation,[102] prayer to the Father predominates in this lengthy outpouring of invocations. The exhortation at the end of the first book is a good confirmation of this. There Augustine encourages himself to entrust himself wholly to "the most merciful and beneficent Lord."[103] Thus, he does not pray here any differently than in the *Confessions,* where most of his prayers are addressed to the Lord our God, who creates and acts through the Word and the Spirit.

The Immortality of the Soul[104]

A draft of the third book of the *Soliloquies* has come down to us under the title of *The Immortality of the Soul.* Augustine outlined it before his baptism, and it was published without his consent. No one will be surprised, therefore, at its insipid argument. Nonetheless, since in this work Augustine continues his thoughts on the nature of the soul that are set down in the other two books of the *Soliloquies,* he has some interesting observations on God. God is regarded as the Creator to whom the soul owes its life.[105] The author also emphasizes that God alone is superior to the rational soul and that in God's constant care God will never force the soul to change into a body.[106] God is thus seen as at once transcendent and immanent.

The Magnitude of the Soul[107]

After his baptism (387–388), Augustine composed the treatise *The Magnitude of the Soul,* the main thesis of which is that the soul is not great in a spatial sense but is nonetheless great because it is ordered to virtue and contemplation. In this context, Augustine endeavors to lead his partner in dialogue to a rational quest for what is true.[108] In doing so, he takes up some Plotinian and Porphyrian themes but relies even more on the Bible, especially Paul, and on the teaching of Mother Church.[109]

Following the Christian tradition with its Platonic bent, he therefore teaches that the soul is immortal because it is created in the image of God[110] and that it is to be formed anew in the likeness of the Son, who is the image of the Father.[111] In like manner, he describes the true life as a gradual ascent in which, thanks to the intellect and truth, the soul finally reaches the ultimate ground, the supreme Creator and source of the universe.[112] In the hymn-like final section, he maintains in a summary that the soul, though entirely immaterial and closest to God, is not what God is; therefore, in accordance with the teaching of the Catholic Church, it may under no circumstances worship any creature but only the Creator of all things: changeless Source, changeless Wisdom, changeless Love, the one perfect, eternal, and changeless God.[113] In addition, this concluding passage already anticipates the correlation which Augustine establishes in *The City of God* between the divine Trinity and the three parts of philosophy: physics, logic, and ethics.[114]

c) Enlightenment

The Teacher

In the Thagastan community in which Augustine lived after his return to Africa, he also had a conversation, in 398, with his son Adeodatus, for whom he had a high regard.[115] This exchange of thoughts between father and son has come down to us in the dialogue on *The Teacher*.[116] The partners in dialogue took as their starting point the question of the significance of speech and whether it can be used both to teach and to learn or rather only to teach.[117]

In the detailed discussion[118] in which they defined teaching as a communication[119] that uses signs, they reached a paradoxical conclusion: on the one hand, communication *(docere)* is impossible without signs;[120] on the other, nothing is understood through signs[121] but only brought to mind.[122] After this lengthy joint exercise, Augustine had the final say. He was able henceforth to maintain his thesis that Christ is the sole teacher of truth. That is, when Jesus spoke to us from outside us, he was simply telling us that he dwells in us in order to be our teacher in the true sense. If, then, people want to understand what they hear or have heard, they must consult their interior teacher.[123] At bottom, Augustine is already claiming here that as the incarnate Word, Christ speaks externally through human beings while as eternal Word, Christ speaks within.[124] The idea of interior enlightenment thus expressed is not proposed here for the first time,[125] but it appears more clearly here than elsewhere.[126]

As for Augustine's picture of God, which is our question here, it is worth noting that in *The Teacher,* he speaks of God as Truth or, more specifically, of Christ the Truth and, more specifically still, of the truth of God.[127] There is thus a close connection between "God the author of nature" and "God the teacher of truth." The presence of God as enlightener is, as Augustine was to say more clearly in *The City of God,*[128] nothing else than a form of God's presence as creator.[129] Precisely in thus seeing God as his creator, he moves beyond the Neoplatonic theory of illumination and adheres to the Christian tradition.[130] In the same context, he reflects on memory,[131] of which he will later say that Christ has deposited therein the eternal unchanging truth. This teaching on memory then becomes the basis for his conception of God as spirit[132] and especially for what he has to say about the Trinity as memory, intellect, and will.[133]

d) The Question of Evil

Order[134]

In November 386, after the interruption represented by the dialogue on *The Happy Life,* the murmur of water during the night and the scurrying of a mouse gave the friends at Cassiciacum another occasion for interrupting the dialogue on the Academics.[135] For these phenomena of nature led them to discuss the causality and order in the world.[136] As we know from the *Confessions,* questions about evil and the disorder in creation had been occupying Augustine for quite some time.

In any case, according to the notes that were revised to form the two books entitled *Order,* Augustine and his friends spent those days talking about providence, which is seemingly called into question by disorders and evil. They also discussed unity, which is the key to the entire set of problems.[137] In their exchange of ideas on these difficulties, they reached the point of condemning the objections against providence as rebellion *(impietas)* against the good and wise God[138] and as a lack of a comprehensive grasp of the various causes at work.[139] But in this vision that was wholly dependent on Plotinus, they did not take moral evil, or sin, into consideration.[140] They did, at any rate, stress the fact that God always loves the good but cannot love evil, even though God always integrates it into the order of things,[141] and this in accordance with the divine justice.[142] Above all, they reached a definition of the order according to which God governs the whole of creation.[143]

These discussions filled the first book. But because the entire set of problems seemed to overtax his partners in dialogue, Augustine, being both paternal friend and leader of the discussions, shifted to the question of whether wise persons should follow an order in their study of the liberal arts.[144] In answering this question, they came to the conclusion that the goal of any such order should be a participation in the oneness of God and at the same time a contribution to the unity and beauty of the world.[145] But they did not pay any further attention to the moral viewpoints involved in this quest of unity. As in the first book, so in the second, Augustine emphasizes the kindness and gentleness of God.[146] As for their final point, the two ways of knowledge, namely, authority and reason, I shall speak of these further on.[147] It is worth noting in passing how in setting the scene for the nocturnal dialogue with his friends, Augustine mentions some details such as the irregular murmur of the water and Licentius' expulsion of a mouse; by means of these references, he illustrates the rational discussion and explains by concrete examples what is to be thought about the order which providence has established in the world.[148]

Music, Book 6

According to the second book of *Order,* which was composed in 386, the liberal arts make possible an ascent to God. Convinced of this opinion, Augustine undertook the composition of a work that would deal with all seven arts. However, he completed—and this not until later on—only the six books on music. In the sixth book,[149] he returns to the theme of the harmony of creation, but he looks at it now chiefly from the viewpoint of numbers and rhythms. Following this Pythagorean and Neoplatonic line of thought, he offers a very optimistic vision of creation. Thus toward the end, he speaks of the ideal, spiritual rhythm that originates in God and is communicated to the soul; and in this connection, he praises God's creation and providence, but without going any further into the problem of evil.[150]

It is significant, however, that in this context he already defines sin as a perversion of the turning to God in love and as a reversal of the order that should exist between enjoyment and use. In a correct order, all functions of the soul show themselves to be beautiful in their rhythms, to the extent that they are ordered to a good end: care for the body's well-being, zeal for a good relationship with other people, everything. Therefore, no rhythm of any kind is to be excluded from the realm of divine providence, not even the rhythms that spring from the deadly ruin caused by sin, for even these have their beauty. But human beings neither love these nor try to find happiness through use of them. Their experience of them is like that of one being carried down a river on a plank to which one clings for life: one cannot simply let go of it as an encumbrance, but neither can one cling to it as a permanent support; one can only make good use of it.[151]

In the so-called philosophical writings, then, God is seen first of all as the source of happiness for the human soul. Possession of God makes the soul happy. But this possession of God that produces happiness presupposes wisdom and certainty regarding truth. Two things make it possible for the soul to attain to wisdom. First, it èxperiences the truth thanks to its likeness to God, since it is immortal and therefore spiritual as God is.[152] Second, the truth of God's very self illumines it and thus enables it to judge about things. Thanks to the admonition given it by the Holy Spirit and to its enlightenment by the Son, who is the power and wisdom of God, the soul that is on its way to God the Father, the supreme good, also understands the order created by the wise and good God; indeed, it even understands evil, which God does not will but which nonetheless has a place in the rational order that is always supported by the providence of a just God.

In this vision of the eternal and blessed God, two points are especially important. First, under the influence of the philosophy of his day, Augustine sees God first and foremost in God's relationship to the soul, which seeks its happiness in knowledge of the truth.[153] God is therefore seen as the Light that illumines the interior of the human person and as the Orderer who guarantees the rational structure of the world. Second, the ever deepening Christian experience that Augustine acquires through the reading of the Bible and the study of the Church's teaching leads him to become increasingly aware that evil consists not simply in ignorance but in an arrogant turning away from God and that the soul therefore needs not only a true God but a forbearing one who frees it from the burden of sin.[154]

It is not easy to determine the extent to which Augustine gives a new interpretation of the Christian faith with the help of ancient philosophy or, to put it differently, the extent to which he has made the elements of this philosophy his own in relation to the Christian tradition, which becomes increasingly important to him. In any case, it is certain that when the young Augustine reflected on God and the soul, he was not satisfied with the data of faith but strove for a deeper grasp of these with the help of the scientific methods at his disposal.[155]

3. God in the Anti-Manichean Writings

The writings which Augustine composed between 388 and 400 bear the mark, for the most part, of an anti-Manichean tendency. F. Decret has made an exhaustive analysis of these writings in his study of Manichean Africa.[156] According to Decret, initially, and especially in *The Catholic Way of Life and the Manichean Way of Life*—a work begun in Rome and completed in Thagaste—Augustine adopted a rather defensive attitude; he contrasted the pure life of Catholics with the immoral attitude of the Manichees and denounced the corruption seen in the leading circles of the Manichees.[157] The work *True Religion* can also be regarded as typical of this approach of Augustine.[158] Although this book shows a clear anti-Porphyrian emphasis in its introduction and conclusion,[159] it is nonetheless primarily an attack on the Manichees.[160] In it, he endeavors to show rationally how, thanks to the incarnation of Christ, even sinners can turn back to God; how even evil has a place in the order willed by God; and how the return to God follows the path of faith and reason.

The writing of *The Two Souls* in 391–392 represents a turning point. Augustine, now a priest, undertook a scholarly critique of Manichean teachings.[161] In his *Answer to Adimantus,* written between 392 and 395, he went a step further; in it he tackled directly such writings of the Manichees as he had come to know.[162] This method can be seen above all in the extensive work *Answer to Faustus* and to some extent in the record of the discussions with Felix and Fortunatus.[163]

For all their polemical character, these writings reflect a great familiarity with the sect, to which Augustine himself had belonged for nine years.[164] In these works, Augustine takes up three sets of questions: the problem of evil and of the origin of sin, the problem of a knowledge based on authority, and the problem of biblical interpretation.[165] In the passages in which Augustine summarizes Manichean views as he sees them,[166] the main lines of his anti-Manichean polemics show in a perhaps somewhat different light.[167] Nonetheless, they are easily reducible to the sets of questions just identified.

In any case, the question of God, too, is always on the agenda in all the questions raised.[168] Readers will not be surprised at this if they bear in mind that the decisive issue in Augustine's "conversion" to Manicheism and then in his entrance into this Gnostic-Christian sect was the rational justification of his faith in God.[169] In his view, the nature of evil can be understood only in light of knowledge of the good and, indeed, only in light of the knowledge of God, the supreme Good. So too, the authority on which the faith that leads to knowledge is based is ultimately the authority of God alone. Finally, one can resolve the hermeneutical question only if one believes that God is the author of the writings of both the Old and the New Testaments and that these writings therefore contain nothing unworthy of God.

An assessment of Manichean influences on the question of God in Augustine himself would certainly be desirable.[170] Obviously, he, too, speaks of the God of light. Even more important may seem the connection between "May I desire to know God and the soul" in *Soliloquies* (1.2.7) and Manichean theology and anthropology.[171] Finally, the Manichees, too, even if in their own way, allowed for a progression from faith to knowledge.[172] A good many scholars, A. Adam for example, emphasize these similarities;[173] others, W. Geerlings for one, suppose at least a similar spiritual climate.[174] In any case, like all controversialists, Augustine was influenced in the way in which he posed and discussed questions by the adversaries whom he so passionately attacked.[175] But by no means did he deny them all sympathy and mutual understanding.[176]

a) God Is Not the Originator of Sin[177]

For many years, Augustine had already been preoccupied with the question of evil, the question of all the disorder in the world.[178] After his baptism and during the first period of his pastoral activity, he had inveighed against the Manichees, who were quite influential in Roman Africa. Now he felt obliged to take up this very difficult question once again.[179] His intention, as he explicitly says at the beginning of *True Religion,* was to substantiate by rational means the traditional faith in this matter.[180] But his renewed treatment of these problems led him beyond the point he had previously reached. Whereas previously he had followed Plotinus in addressing the general question of disorder, he now opened up tortuous trains of thought on sin as a flouting of the law and an expression of pride and on the origin of sin. In doing so, he continually followed the lead of the ontology that he had taken over from the Platonic tradition and that he regarded as compatible with the Catholic faith.[181]

This further conceptual development can be seen in *Free Will.*[182] The first book of this explicitly anti-Manichean work reports a conversation which Augustine had with his intellectually very open-minded friend Evodius during the winter of 387–388 in Rome. The other two books, however, were added later in Africa and completed around 395.[183] The Roman dialogue focuses on the nature of evil. Starting with the question of whether God is the author of evil (1.1.1), the two partners in dialogue try to reach an answer, following two trains of thought. First, they explain the concepts of evil deeds, of passions, and of law (1.3.6–6.15). In speaking of law, they distinguish between temporal and eternal law, the latter being innate in the human heart.[184] They therefore see sin as consisting in the fact that reason does not subject the passions to itself and the will does allow itself to be guided by eternal law.[185] Both of these viewpoints lead them to the conclusion that sin cannot be caused by God but originates in free will (1.7.16–16.35).

The point of the second book is to show, by means of an ascending dialectic, why human beings may believe in the existence of God. To this end, the first step is the ascent from being through life to knowledge. A second step leads through the external and internal senses to reason. In a third step, the partners in dialogue move beyond reason, with its eternal laws of numbers and its eternal norms of wisdom, to God, who is Truth and Wisdom itself.[186] Thus, it is seen, from a new vantage point, that God can be the source only of good things, including the very will that has become sinful.[187]

The third book, finally, turns into a hymn to divine providence. This last includes the foreknowledge by which God foresees every action without in any way doing violence to human freedom (3.2.4-11). Even sin is not a challenge to providence, since by means of an appropriate punishment sin is again integrated into the providential order of things (3.5.12–16.46). Not even the premature death of children, the suffering of animals, or the very sin of Adam with all its consequences justifies doubts about the beauty of divine providence.

In thus solving the entire problem of evil by reference to the goodness of God, who wills only the good, *Free Will* is marked by an impressive unity.[188] Later, in the anti-Pelagian controversy, instead of insisting on human freedom, Augustine will emphasize the grace of God, but without thereby sacrificing his ideas on the order established by the wisdom and goodness of God.[189] He will, however, impose on himself a greater reserve in face of the ineffable mystery of God.

The points which Augustine made perhaps most clearly, and certainly most extensively, in *Free Will* he confirmed in his other anti-Manichean writings:[190] all things have been created by God and have not emanated from God;[191] sin, however, cannot come from the changeless and good God, but originates in the free human will;[192] nevertheless, sin can never interfere with the order that is willed by the good and just God, an order in which good things serve to console human beings while evil things serve to educate or punish them.[193] This last summarizing theme, which had been announced as early as 388 in *The Magnitude of the Soul*, at the end of which Augustine presents a first sketch of *Free Will*,[194] found its fullest expression in *True Religion*, where he says:

> Neither the sins of the soul nor the punishments it endures can in the slightest disfigure the universe. For if a rational being is free of sin and subject to God, then everything else is subject to [God's] rule. A sinful being, on the other hand, is expelled to the place to which it belongs by its nature, so that the beauty of the universe, whose creator and ruler God is, is not spoiled. There are thus three things which show the beauty of the universe to be irreproachable: the damnation of sinners, the testing of the righteous, and the perfection of the blessed.[195]

I do not raise the question here of the extent to which Augustine the con-troversialist has presented an accurate picture of the dualism of the Manichean tradition.[196] The point to be emphasized is that according to Augustine, God cannot be the author of evil but constantly preserves the beauty of the universe by punishing sinners in God's incorruptible justice (a point which the Manichees, too, were ready to concede).[197] God is always the God of what is good and is more powerful than any evil. It is worth noting, meanwhile, how in this context of the justice with which the Most High God, planner of every-thing, punished humanity at the beginning, Augustine contrasts this justice with the mercy by which God liberates humanity in subsequent history.[198]

A further point in these reflections: the god of darkness cannot be the equal of the God of light nor as eternal as God is. The god of darkness, as the Manichees portray this god (in Augustine's interpretation of them), is no real god at all.[199] The God of light is the only true God.[200] There is no denying, however, that in a number of respects Augustine made the theological position of the Manichees more inflexible than it really was. In his view, the logic of the Manichees themselves forced them to hold an absolute dualism and to ac-cept the coeternality and complete equality of the principle of good and the principle of evil. In reality, the Manichees in their religious practice prayed only to the God of light and were therefore, at bottom, monotheists.[201]

b) Knowledge Based on Divine Authority[202]

During the years of suffering that led to his conversion, Augustine saw himself constantly faced with the problem of human religious knowledge.[203] Amid his expectations of a knowledge of truth that would finally bring happi-ness, he found himself confronting the difficult fact that he had to seek the eternal in the things of time, that is, he had to overcome the uncertainty and weakness that hinder sinful nature from achieving knowledge of God. How-ever, he realized at last that the passage from time to eternity can be accom-plished only by those who rely in faith on that authority which, according to the testimony of the Catholic Church, has manifested itself in divine revela-tion. At the same time, he also understood that such a revelation requires legit-imation by clear pieces of circumstantial evidence and that it be plausible to all. That is, he realized the need of a historical revelation that can be tested in a scholarly way, but also a revelation that calls for a love which is open to past and future and at the same time purifies faith.

This problem of knowledge and authority makes its appearance even be-fore the anti-Manichean controversy.[204] Augustine had touched on it when he reflected on the conditions of knowledge in general, as the discussions at Cas-siciacum, set down in the philosophical writings, attest. Thus, a famous pas-sage in *Order* says that human beings reach knowledge by two paths, the path of authority and the path of reason. The first path must come first: without faith, which relies on an authority, there can be no rational knowledge.[205] The connection between authority and reason will occupy Augustine again in the Manichean controversy. The reader will be familiar with the Letter to Consentius, in which Augustine urges Consentius to love knowledge.[206] No less noteworthy is the warning against an explanation of the Bible that contradicts reason.[207]

His debates with Manichean positions, from 388 to 400 and even thereafter, forced Augustine to clarify further these decisive questions, with a tendency, of course, to emphasize authority and faith.[208] This tendency is perfectly understandable when we reflect that Augustine had joined the Manichean sect in order to find a rational answer to the questions haunting him and that this very sect, which had promised him knowledge, had fobbed him off with faith.[209] The extent to which the search for the correct solution of this problem affected him finds expression in the often cited passage from *Answer to the Letter of Mani Known as "The Foundation"*: "I would not believe the gospel were I not moved by the authority of the Catholic Church."[210]

Augustine's effort to determine the meaning of authority and reason may be seen very clearly in the fourth part of *True Religion,* where he explains that human beings attain to true salvation through authority and reason.[211]

But it was chiefly *The Advantage of Believing* that was devoted to these questions.[212] As the title already suggests, this work expresses more clearly than others of the same kind the conviction that human beings must first believe in order then to be able to know. It was with this understanding that Augustine had cited in an earlier work the words from the Book of Isaiah, "Unless you believe, you will not understand."[213] Although he makes faith an unconditional requirement for human knowledge, he admits that a certain kind of knowledge must precede faith. Before people believe, they must be certain that they can trust the authority that instructs them.[214] Consequently, in the third part of *The Advantage of Believing,* Augustine develops an entire theory about the ascertainment of authority: the authority of Jesus (which the Manichees, too, acknowledge),[215] miracles, the conversion of so many people to faith in the true God, and the virtues.[216]

Finally, he felt obliged, in *Answer to Faustus,* to go into the question more deeply, especially in reference to interpretation of the Bible. While Secundinus had warned his adversaries against trying to prove everything at any cost,[217] Faustus had shown himself far less credulous. That is to say, he had called for a faith accompanied by reason and discernment (16.8; 33.3) and had sharply criticized the New Testament stories (18.3; 33.2). For this reason, Augustine had to set greater store on the scientific justification of authority.[218]

This further step is not surprising if we reflect that in the interval, he had engaged more intensely in exegetical work and in his *On Teaching Christianity,* had even developed a theory about taking history into account in exegesis.[219] In the concluding summary of this comprehensive work *(Answer to*

Faustus), he emphasizes not only historical criteria but philosophical ones as well. That is, he reminds the Manichees here that people have good grounds for following the authority of the sacred Scriptures. In fact, ever since the time of Christ, this authority has been protected, recommended, and clarified by the apostles and their successors, the bishops. It is therefore not accepted credulously but is acknowledged on the basis of a reasonable certainty or at least by the same sound human reason with which people are convinced of the absolute immutability of God.[220] This virtually programmatic passage is further confirmation that in the Manichean controversy the question of God was much more important than the problems of biblical interpretation.[221]

In his reflection on human knowledge, Augustine presupposes the distinction between divine authority and human authority.[222] The authority that goes back to God is therefore authentic and the highest form of authority, but it does not impinge directly on human beings.[223] Rather, it is present in the authority of Christ, in the authority of the sacred Scriptures, or in the authority of the Church.[224] When God thus exercises the supreme divine authority in these various forms of authority, God shows the divine self primarily as truth, as remedy for ignorance, and as enlightenment of the human heart. This conviction, which had already been characteristic of Augustine's philosophical writings, also permeates his writings against the Manichees.

But the anti-Manichean controversy led Augustine to develop three further aspects of God-as-Truth. First, he emphasizes more strongly than in the past the distinction between God who makes possible human knowledge of the eternal laws and the divine norms, and God the creator of all that is good and true.[225] Second, he expressly develops the picture of God who directs history and through the temporal dispensation makes knowledge of eternal truth accessible. Finally, and above all, Augustine here presents a God who must be loved. The faith that is the basis of knowledge is impossible without love for God. Only when believers love God do they trust themselves to God's authority; only when they obey God's first commandment is their faith purified and strengthened. In short, their love of God allows them to pass from time to eternity.[226]

c) The Problem of Biblical Interpretation

With his answer to the question of what evil is and whence it comes, Augustine cleared away a troublesome obstacle on the path to the beatifying knowledge of eternal truth. At the same time, by showing the connection between authority and reason, he outlined in a positive way the passage from this changeable world to the immutability of God. These two main questions in the Manichean controversy run together with a third: the question of biblical interpretation. This is true especially of the connection between knowledge and authority. That is, the question of how eternal truth becomes accessible to human beings through sensible signs is concretized in the question of how the biblical narrative ("the historical narrative") and indeed the entire revelatory event ("history itself"[227]) are part of the temporal dispensation of the eternal God.[228] In any case, when it came to exegesis, the dispute in which Augustine was engaged had to do with two questions: the question of the unity of the two Testaments and the question of how to explain biblical statements about God that are unworthy of God.

The problems of interpretation occupied Augustine first in his polemic against Adimantus, a disciple of Mani and a propagator of Manicheism in Africa.[229] As this work shows, Augustine had to debate three series of topics *(capitula)* with this resolute adversary of the Old Testament: the evil God of the Pentateuch and the prophets; the curse on anyone hanged on a cross (Deut 21:23); and the carnal prescriptions of Deuteronomy, along with the morality and gross rituals of the Law.[230]

In response to the views of his adversary, Augustine insists, especially at the beginning of his work, on the unity of the two Testaments; he gives numerous examples of the harmony between them.[231] In particular, he explains the error of the Manichees, and of all who see such an opposition between the Old and New Testaments, by the fact that they are unable to distinguish between times[232] and between shadow and reality.[233] Above all, they have failed to understand that by God's will the entire temporal dispensation is ordered to the truth, to Christ.[234] For proof, Augustine goes back, as he already had in *The Literal Meaning of Genesis,* to the spiritual exegesis of Old Testament texts[235] and in addition explains the metaphorical and anthropomorphic expressions of the Bible by the same method.[236] He also combats other theories of the Manichees, such as reincarnation[237] and the myth of Jesus as passible *(Jesus patibilis).*[238]

The critique of the Manichean interpretation of the Bible takes on even more distinctive traits in the much more extensive work, *Answer to Faustus.*[239] In response to Faustus' less penetrating criticisms, Augustine goes more deeply into what the two Testaments have in common and what distinguishes them. Along this line, he develops more fully than before the distinction of times.[240] Here again, he sheds light on the harmony between the two Testaments by means of images, such as shadow and reality,[241] and in doing so relies on traditional teaching about prophecies and prefigurations.[242] He also sets great store by the distinction between various Old Testament prescriptions in order to refute objections against the allegedly immoral and gross regulations of the Law.[243]

Finally, he gives very clear expression to the Christological orientation of the entire Bible, as can be seen especially in this passage, "Christ meets me openly or secretly and refreshes me everywhere in those books, everywhere in those Scriptures, as I scour them and yearn in that sweat of human damnation."[244]

Two new traits are, however, peculiar to the *Answer to Faustus.* First, as we would expect in so extensive a work, Augustine explains in much greater detail his ideas on the agreement of the two Testaments, on the value of the laws and prophecies, and on other matters.[245] Second, he can now rely on clearer conceptions of language and signs.[246] This second fact is not surprising since while composing the *Answer to Faustus,* he had already finished the first two books of *On Teaching Christianity* with their theory of things and signs.[247]

Following the exegetical principles that earlier Christian writers had already applied against the Gnostics and, to a certain extent, against the Jews as well, Augustine naturally joins his predecessors in stressing the uniqueness of God. The God of the Jews is no other than the God of the Christians. God shows the divine self in the Old Testament as good and in the New as jealous, and conversely. God is the Lord of creation and the Father of all human beings. Accordingly, God reveals the divine self not only as the author of both Testaments but also as the director of the temporal dispensation that has led to Christ, the mediator between God and all of humanity. Augustine's anti-Manichean exegesis, in which he excludes all passion from God and shows himself fully aware of the difficulty of speaking about God in an appropriate way, is for him a further confirmation that God is immutable and at the same time ineffable.[248]

Excursus: A New Turning Point in Augustine's Theological Thought?

We may consider as part of the controversy with the Manichees the work in which, in 397, Augustine answered eight questions put to him by Simplician of Milan.[249] The answer to the second question, which takes the form of a commentary on Romans 9:9-29, is the longest and by far the most important.[250] K. Flasch regards it as marking a turning point in the teaching of the Bishop of Hippo on grace and on God.[251] He is able to appeal to Augustine himself, who toward the end of his life represented his explanation of the Apostle in 397 as having been something new.[252] However, we must not overlook the fact that this exegesis of the difficult chapter of the Letter to the Romans had been in preparation for some years.[253] In addition, Augustine was not only under the influence of the Paulinism current at the end of the fourth century but he also read the letters of the Apostle chiefly with an eye on his own positive and negative experiences of the attitude which the Manichees adopted toward Pauline theology.[254] Precisely this circumstance shows that we are quite justified in placing the *Miscellany of Questions in Answer to Simplician* among the anti-Manichean writings of Augustine.[255]

According to Flasch, the answer to Simplician's second question focuses essentially on the following ideas:[256] Even in 397, Augustine holds fast to his philosophical insights, namely, that God is good and that everything God has made, especially the human person, soul and body, is also good. "Nothing in all this is evil, God hates nothing in all this. How, then, can [God] hate Esau?" Augustine's answer to this question, which was a burning one for Christians who like Simplician had received a Neoplatonic formation, is this: God does not hate Esau the person, God hates Esau the sinner; God does not hate God's creature as such, but the one who has deliberately become a sinner. But that is not the entire answer, since Jacob, too, was a sinner and Esau was not a sinner in God's eyes because of some sin committed before birth or because of deeds which God foresaw he would do. What God hated was the sin in Esau, while in Jacob God loved the divine grace bestowed on him with the forgiveness of guilt. "God always hates sin, but in one person [God] punishes it with damnation, in another [God] forgives it through grace."

With regard to Augustine's teaching on God—and here we are largely in agreement with Flasch[257]—three conclusions emerge from this theory on the relationship between God and human beings, a theory certainly suggested by Paul. First, in it Augustine is evidently still holding fast to his Neoplatonically tinged concept of God. He does not deviate from the divine transcendence which he has discovered with the help of the Platonic works.[258] God remains the only, the great God.[259] But God is no longer the "ungrudging" God who pours out all God's goodness.[260]

Second, Augustine develops here his conception of the justice of God. He has earlier spoken of the divine justice. Now, however, he does not strive simply to reconcile this justice with the part played by evil and sin in the order of the world; rather, he also seeks to come to grips with the fact that there is such a thing as damnation.[261] He supposes the fact of damnation because of his pastoral experience that there are human beings who refuse to be converted. In order, then, to preserve the divine justice itself, he modifies the Pauline concept of righteousness, without therefore excluding that there are at least traces of righteousness in human life.[262] Most importantly, however, he constructs his concept of original sin, which allows him to assume that Esau and Jacob and all human beings, including little children, have in justice deserved to be damned. But God would, without consideration of merits and purely out of grace, preserve at least some from everlasting punishment.[263]

By taking this position, Augustine undoubtedly limits the saving will of God,[264] but he does so in order to protect the justice of the one, good, and just God, even in view of the damnation of human beings, which he regards as certain.[265] If he thus changes his conception of justice—in Flasch's view, he "empties it"[266]—he makes it clear how much the justice of God matters to him, above all because he wants to be true to the Bible.[267]

Third, and last, the theological voluntarism of Augustine emerges much more clearly than in the past. In order to remove every reason for human beings to plume themselves,[268] Augustine now excludes any interaction between

God and human beings.[269] God alone acts; human activity does not enter the picture. Augustine certainly intends to maintain human freedom,[270] but his view now is that human beings can no longer freely choose the good; they can only sin freely. Grace liberates them to do what is good; it instills in them a joy in what is good and thereby moves their wills.[271] Instead of expressly saying that God works together with human beings in such a way that their freedom is not abolished but perfected, he excludes human autonomy even for the beginning of faith.[272] Thus, the divine will is seen as absolutely sovereign while human freedom is seriously called in question.[273]

Nonetheless, although Augustine did not achieve a true synthesis of grace and freedom, as Flasch rightly emphasizes,[274] we may not deny him the right, amid this dialectic forced on him by an extremely difficult problem, to take the side of what seemed obvious in light of his knowledge of the Bible and his pastoral experience.[275] Even among the ancient philosophers, there were some who gave the divine decree of fate priority over human dignity. And in this case, the middle way would of course be preferable. But who always and consistently follows the middle way? Is it not typical that in the defense (which often has a "rhetorical" ring to it) of his own concern in his presentation of the lordship of God, Flasch allows the fatherhood of God to be shortchanged?[276] He dwells on the "terrors" (of the Lord) but says nothing about the "consolations" (of the faithful and lenient Father).[277] Finally, one might also ask Flasch why he does not go into the humility of God as revealed on the cross of Christ. It must certainly be admitted that this question does not arise. But should it not be mentioned when one intends, as Flasch does, to tackle the questions of the Milanese priest along with their entire literary context, including the early *Expositions of the Psalms?*[278]

Above all, one can ask whether Flasch takes seriously enough the Creator God whom Augustine, following the Bible and the Nicene tradition, presupposes even in his answer to Simplician.[279] This concept is not only the basis of what Augustine says against the Manichees regarding the origin of all good and the just rule of God in history. It also lies behind what Flasch regards as the novelty of 397: the definition of God as eternal, immutable will.[280] Augustine certainly did not succeed in bringing the divine unity and human unity into full harmony. He did, however, clearly bring out the absolute transcendence of the omnipotent God of the Bible, in line with western voluntarism (with Ambrose, for example) and its distinction between nature and grace.[281] This is to say that the year 397 saw new elements enter Augustine's picture of God but is not to be regarded as a new turning point.

CHAPTER 2

God in the Major Theological Works

1. God the Father—One God

a) The Problem of *The Trinity*[1]

Because the Father, the Son, and the Holy Spirit are one God, the question of God is always present in Augustine's trinitarian statements and reflections in numerous sermons[2] and letters.[3] This is true, above all, of *The Trinity,* a major work composed between 399 and 421. According to the general introduction to the work, the unity of the Trinity is the problem: "We are seeking the unity of the three."[4] The subject of the study is how the Father, the Son, and the Holy Spirit, whom Christians confess in the baptismal creed, are one God. In more technical language, the question is how Father, Son, and Spirit, who exist together from eternity and also work together outside the divinity since the beginning of creation, are one in the divinity,[5] and how their equality manifests their unity.[6] In this connection, Augustine also reflects on why the Son alone became a human being, even though the external divine activity is common to all three persons.[7]

This entire broad set of problems that are discussed in *The Trinity* obviously includes the problem of God in the narrower sense. This is clear from passages in which Augustine explains the biblical terms, wisdom, charity, gift, and spirit, in a trinitarian perspective.[8] That is he explains in this connection how these biblical titles befit the individual persons as well as all the persons together; in doing so, he applies the distinction between "properly ("peculiarly") and "in common" ("universally"). Thus, he establishes, in particular, that "spirit" is used of all three persons in common, but properly or peculiarly of the Holy Spirit.[9]

We are, however, in no way forcing the theological approach that makes its appearance here if we extend the same distinction to the term "God." In this sense, the Father is to be called God in the proper sense, but the Son and the Spirit, or the entire Trinity as the case may be, can be called God in common. Still, the common concept of God is not distinguished in its content from the concept as used in the proper or peculiar sense. The Father is indeed said to be "properly God," but this simply makes the point that what is being asserted when "God" is said of all three persons together, is ascribed to the Father as the origin within the godhead (*principaliter*, "as source"). As Augustine expressly insists, the Father is "God who is from no one."[10]

In this perspective, the main question in *The Trinity* is how the concept of "God in common" or "God universally" is used of the Father, the Son, and the Spirit, that is, of the entire Trinity. Only in the second place does the question arise of how the Father is called "God in the proper sense." But in both cases, the meaning of "God" is, at bottom, simply presupposed.

Augustine himself was clear in his own mind about this foundational presupposition. This is clear from the beginning of *The Trinity,* where before starting his reflections on the Trinity, he excludes the three possible errors that can be found in the doctrine of God (in the narrower sense).[11] Those who intend to think about the unity of the Trinity must not think of God as a bodily being or as if God were the same in being as the soul or as if God begot God's own self.[12] How important this strictly theological point is to him is shown by the confirmation of it at the beginning of the decisive eighth book, where he also gives a positive description of the picture of God with which one must start if one wants to reflect on the Trinity which Christians confess in the baptismal creed.[13] According to what is said there, it is already of great importance that one know what God is not. It is better, however, to bear in mind that God contains all good in the divine self (God is "the good of every good"), that is, God is the immutable, supreme Good.

The importance of these preliminary considerations on God for the understanding of this major theological work can hardly be exaggerated. When Augustine investigates the question of the unity of the Trinity and in the process takes a stand ultimately on the very concrete question of the relationship between the New Testament *theos* and the Latin word *deus,* which the Nicene tradition applies in the same way to the Father, the Son, and the Spirit, he obviously presupposes at every point a rather clearly defined idea of God. For this reason, it is also legitimate to investigate the question of God in the strict sense without going into the questions of trinitarian theology in detail.

b) The Biblical Foundation of Faith in the Trinity

In the first four books of *The Trinity,* it is chiefly in light of the theophanies narrated in the Bible that Augustine discusses the question—which is his chief interest—of the relation between equality and unity in the Trinity.[14] Insofar as the tradition of the fourth century is in the background of these reflections, they cannot be described simply as a "proof from Scripture."[15] They should rather be called a dogmatic description of what is believed about the Trinity as this emerges from the traditional understanding of the biblical passages in question. In any case, it is the Nicene faith in the identical essence of Father, Son, and Spirit[16] and in their common action that Augustine makes his starting point.[17]

He comes to the following conclusion:[18] all three persons are equally invisible;[19] the context in the Bible must therefore show which of the three persons has appeared or whether possibly all three have manifested themselves.[20] It also emerges that the completely invisible divine substance itself was not to be seen with the eyes in any theophany;[21] rather, all appearances were mediated by angels[22] or by a temporarily assumed form created by the entire Trinity[23] or, in the supreme instance, the incarnation, by a humanity assumed into personal unity but nonetheless created.[24] In grounding this thesis, Augustine also discusses, although rather incidentally, the universal causality of God, which is at work in all changes in creatures, even in the human soul,[25] and which directs everything,[26] including even the sacrament of the Eucharist[27] and miracles[28] as well as all second causes.[29]

Finally, in Augustine's remarks on perfect equality, he also stresses the point that while all external divine activity is common to the Father, Son, and Spirit,[30] the Son alone became a human being and the Holy Spirit alone appeared in the form of a dove or of fire.[31] Nor does he fail to emphasize that according to the Bible, the Father has never been sent.[32] He thus suggests that the one divine activity and the one divine being have their origin in the Father.[33]

c) The Dogmatic Formulation of Trinitarian Belief

In Books 5–7, in which Augustine discusses, with cautious reserve,[34] the theological terminology that had developed in the tradition, he concerns himself primarily with the question of how we are to speak of the one God as a single substance and of the Father, Son, and Spirit as three persons.

According to the tradition, the Scriptures justify calling God a substance or, better, an essence.[35] This means that everything accidental, and therefore all change, is excluded from God.[36] More exactly, not everything said of God is said in terms of substance; relational statements are also made of God. But neither intratrinitarian relational statements (such as "unbegotten") nor extratrinitarian relational statements (such as "origin") are to be understood as accidental; therefore, they do not signify any change in God.[37] When, later on, biblical words referring to all three persons (the terms appropriated to the individual persons, including "spirit,"[38] "love," "eternity," "form") seem to introduce a plurality of names into God, we must not forget that everything meant by them is identical with the one being of God.[39] Since being and wisdom in particular are identical in God, it can be said of all three persons that they are the eternal wisdom.[40] In this connection, Augustine developed the fundamental distinction between "properly" (or "peculiarly") and "in common" (or "universally"), which was to help him distinguish the various ways in which the Scriptures and the tradition speak of the wisdom, the love, and the spirit of God.

As for the application of "person" to the Trinity, Augustine would prefer to avoid it.[41] He does of course acknowledge this usage in the Latin tradition, although it is not to be found in the Bible itself.[42] Insofar as "person" serves to make a clear distinction between Father, Son, and Holy Spirit, we may undoubtedly speak of "persons."[43] But since "person" befits Father, Son, and Spirit, it is a general name and one that is also applied to human beings.[44] Above all, it is a term that has an absolute and not a relative meaning. Therefore, "person," like "essence," ought to said of the one God.[45] Being the one God then, Father, Son, and Spirit are the one, simple, and immutable essence. This means, on the negative side, that neither the categories nor the predicables of the Aristotelian tradition are applicable to God.[46] On the positive side, it means that apart from the relational distinctions between Father, Son, and Spirit, everything ascribed to the one God in the sacred Scriptures and the Christian tradition is identical with God's one, immutable being.

d) Theological Investigation of Belief in the Trinity

After these explanations of a dogmatico-exegetical and dogmatico-logical kind in the first seven books, Augustine passes in the eighth book to the second part of *The Trinity,* in which he takes a more speculative approach[47] to the equality of persons and the unity of essence.[48] Here, after some remarks on God as supreme Truth and supreme Good,[49] he shows that there is no "form of triuneness" on the basis of which we can love the Trinity as such, in the way, for example, we love justice on the basis of the "form of justice" and are filled with loving wonder at it in Paul.[50] If we want to love God not only as the one God[51] but as the Trinity, there is only one possibility: to acquire, with the help of images from the created world, some rough understanding of how Father, Son, and Spirit are one God, and in this way to deepen our love of the Trinity.[52] Since, however, the inner self, the mind, is created in the image of God,[53] the search for this knowledge and love based on images leads through the interior life of the human being.[54] In lengthy discussions of the various images and vestiges, Augustine finally reaches the "image of wisdom": the human person is most the image of the triune God when he or she remembers God *(memoria Dei),* knows God *(intellegentia Dei),* and loves God *(amor in Deum).*[55]

e) Results for the Doctrine of God in the Narrower Sense

In this entire intellectual effort to draw closer to God as Trinity, Augustine makes a whole series of fruitful statements about God as such. For one thing, by his distinction between "properly" and "in common" ("universally"), Augustine here conveys a much clearer idea of what he understands by God the Father as well as by "the one God," which is what the Trinity is for him. What all three persons, or the Trinity as the case may be, have in common and what is ascribed to the Father properly and as origin is the divine essence. In other words, when we call the Son and the Spirit "God" and speak of "the Trinity, which is one God," but then also describe the Father as, in a radical sense, "properly God," we mean in every case the immutable and eternal Being.[56] The divine essence itself is thus described as supreme Truth and supreme Good. In addition, Augustine explains that everything said in the Bible about the three persons and the one God is identical with God's being; and this includes eternity, wisdom, and blessedness.[57]

Because in his intellectual effort to find a perfect image for the Trinity, Augustine turns first and foremost to the mental life of the human person, he also projects an image of the inner world of God. Consequently, in this comparison between God and the soul, more than in other settings, the one God is seen not simply as an incorporeal and immutable being but also as the God who knows and loves.[58] In other words, God is not simply acknowledged by human beings as the all-transcendent Being, but is reverenced as supreme Wisdom by those who strive for wisdom[59]; moreover, as Love, God is the goal of all human desire.[60]

While everything that the Bible (as understood in the Christian tradition) says about Father, Son, and Spirit or, as the case may be, "the Trinity that is one God," is said about the divine essence, the same is not true of statements that apply to the three persons individually, that is, that have to do with their relations with one another. Only the Father is unbegotten, only the Son is begotten, only the Holy Spirit proceeds from both. It is in terms of these differences that the external divine activity, in particular, is to be explained. Father, Son, and Spirit always work together in creation and history. It is "the Trinity that is one God" which reveals itself in the external divine activity. Nonetheless, only the Son and the Holy Spirit were (or are) sent into the world. Their manifestations are effected by the one God; at the same time however, only the Son or the Spirit can be said to be sent. Since in the Bible the Father is represented only as the one who sends and never as one sent, it becomes clear that the Father must be regarded as "God who is from no one," as the source of all divine life, as the origin of the divine essence, and therefore as God "in the proper sense."[61]

When seen from the human side, all these statements about the one God mean that the Christian is in the presence of a unique mystery. This is certainly true first and foremost of the Trinity: believers cannot derive a "form," or likeness, for it from anything in their experience.[62] But in the final analysis, even the "one God" as such, the divine being that is predicated of all three persons "in common," is also wrapped in an impenetrable mystery. Human beings can indeed rise from creation to the godhead, but on this earth, full knowledge of God is fleeting at best and always remains only a rough groping for God.[63] Perhaps what really dawns on one in this drawing near to God is simply the incomprehensibility of God.[64] But this insight has the advantage of spurring Christians on to seek God ever more and to find their fulfillment in this tireless seeking.[65]

Therefore, because Christians stand here before a mystery, they are thrown back wholly on faith. Only in faith do they know the Trinity. But faith also sustains them in their seeking after the one God. In this effort to know the one God, human beings grow in love, and it is precisely this love for the one God who is accessible through creation that makes it possible for them to love also the Trinity, which can be known only by faith. For those who love God love Love, and in this love, they love the fact that the Trinity is the one God.[66]

Finally, in his reflections on the procession of the Holy Spirit from the Father and the Son, Augustine presupposes that the inner life of the Trinity is knowable only on the basis of the Easter mystery. The economic Trinity alone reveals the immanent Trinity.[67] The point is thereby made more clearly than elsewhere that the act of faith does not simply purify the eyes of the spirit for a perfect knowledge of the one God. Faith in Jesus Christ, who on the cross and in the resurrection proved himself to be the Son and therefore also the one who communicates the Holy Spirit, also opens to believers new horizons in the knowledge of God. Christians know through faith that the Father is the one God, not alone but together with the Son and the Holy Spirit.

2. God the Creator[68]

a) The Importance of *The Literal Meaning of Genesis*

It was not long after beginning *The Trinity* that Augustine also began his extensive explanation of the first two chapters of Genesis. The time he required for the work known as *The Literal Meaning of Genesis (De Genesi ad litteram)* was less than for *The Trinity,* but it nonetheless took several years (404–414). He had already set himself to explain the beginning of the Bible,[69] and he would come back to it again later on.[70] So, too, there is no doubt that he developed his thoughts on the subject in light of both a long tradition and his own experience.[71] But his most thorough and at the same time most original presentation of the matter is contained in *The Literal Meaning of Genesis.* The truth of this claim can already be seen in the method applied here.[72] Namely, he avoids a Christological interpretation of the text[73] while consciously bearing in mind the ineffable mystery of the divine activity that began history and gave things their meaning.[74] With reverence in face of the unfathomable mystery of the all-transcendent God, he offered the most profound reflections on the history of the origin of heaven and earth as told in the Bible (see Gen 2:4a). More clearly than elsewhere, except perhaps in the *Confessions,* he expressed his ideas on God and God's relation to creation. Thus, *The Literal Meaning of Genesis* contains the end result of what he had learned in his discussions with Manicheism and Neoplatonism, but also in the study of the Bible that he undertook as a result of his contact with Ambrose.[75]

It is noteworthy that by "God" he usually means the Father,[76] who created the world through the Word and in the Holy Spirit.[77] This can be seen even where he speaks of the Trinity as creator:

> It is the Blessed Trinity that is represented as creating. For, when Scripture says, *In the beginning God created heaven and earth,* by the name of "God" we understand the Father, and by the name of "Beginning," the Son, who is the Beginning, not for the Father, but first and foremost for the spiritual beings [God] has created and then also for all creatures; and when Scripture says, *And the Spirit of God was stirring above the water,* we recognize a complete enumeration of the Trinity.[78]

There can, however, be a tension between God the Father and the one God: "We say, then, that the sovereign, true, one, and only God, Father, Son, and Holy Spirit, that is, God and [God's] Word and the Spirit of both, the Trinity without confusion and without separation. . . ."[79] Nonetheless, completely in line with the Bible, "God" is used first and foremost for the Father.

b) Augustine's Theology of Creation

The best way to start a presentation of Augustine's theology of creation[80] as developed chiefly in *The Literal Meaning of Genesis* is with the distinction between "founding" or "establishing" *(conditio)* and "governing" or "administering" *(administratio),* which controls his explanation of the story of creation.[81] The formulation of the distinction certainly goes back to the classical period of Latin. It is found in Cicero, who is probably following Poseidonios and says in his *The Nature of the Gods,* "I say, then, that the world and all its parts were established in the beginning by the providence of the gods and are governed for all time by the same providence."[82] Prior to Augustine, Tertullian had already distinguished between "found" *(condere)* or "establish" *(instituere)* and "govern" or "administer" *(administrare).*[83] Another distinction of the same kind, seen in the formula "founder and ruler" *(conditor et rector),* was also used by both pagan and Christian writers.[84]

The way, however, in which Augustine himself uses the distinction between creation and government, both in *The Literal Meaning of Genesis* and elsewhere,[85] is also connected to some extent with the double story of creation in the Bible. In his discussion of it, he also draws upon the following three texts of the Bible.[86] According to Sirach 18:1, God created all things together.

Therefore, when Genesis 2:2 speaks of God resting, we must understand that everything had been done. On the other hand, according to John 5:17, God does not cease working;[87] rather, God continually governs what God established at the beginning. Accordingly, Augustine does not, like Philo, Origen, and Gregory of Nyssa, use the two accounts to contrast a purely spiritual creation with a spiritual-corporeal creation.[88] Instead, he distinguishes two phases in the one creation: "There are two moments of creation: one in the original creation when God made all creatures before resting from all [God's] works on the seventh day, and the other in the administration of creatures by which [God] works even now. In the first instance, God made everything together without any moments of time intervening, but now [God] works within the course of time."[89] At that time, then, God created, now God continues to govern.

In the first moment of creation (the *conditio* or founding), Augustine distinguishes two aspects. He does this first in connection with his considerations on the knowledge of the angels.[90] In his view, the angels have a threefold knowledge. They see things in the Word, they see them in their created reality, and they relate this vision to God. Consequently, the "reasons" *(rationes)* of things exist first in the Word, then they are made real in elements and seeds, and this along with time.[91] In the fifth book, Augustine develops similar thoughts, but without relating them to the knowledge of the angels.[92] Thus, he reaches the point of making a general distinction between "reasons in the Word (before time)" *(rationes in Verbo [ante saecula])* and "causal reasons" in the elements (from the beginning of time) *(rationes causales [a saeculo])*. This distinction is presupposed in the following formulation: "[God's very self] exists before time. But when we speak about the beginning of time, we think of creatures such as the world, with which time began. Creatures which are born in the world are said to be in time."[93] Here, too, the important distinction between "now" *(nunc)* and "then" *(tunc)* finds expression in the distinction between "from the beginning of time" *(a saeculo)* and "in time" *(in saeculo)*.

Two qualifications may be added. First, although creation did not take place in "temporal days," it does have to do with time, for at the creation, time also began.[94] Second, as already indicated, in this foundation of the movement of creation, the "causal reasons" were also included, as was the "connection of causes,"[95] that is, the order which this movement was to follow.[96] From this, two conclusions follow. While the first moment, that of creation, was primarily ideal but also real insofar as it already included time ("from the beginning of time"), the second moment is completely real, for in it, creatures exist in the reality of time *(in saeculo)*. But in this movement, no "new kinds" *(nova genera)* arise.[97] What happens in this movement is rather a development of the "causal reasons" that have been installed from the beginning.[98] "God, then, creates no new creatures, but [God] directs and rules by [God's] governance of the world all the things [God] made together, and thus [God] works without ceasing, resting and working at the same time."[99]

c) Statements about God Contained in the Theology of Creation

In connection with the doctrine of the twofold creation, Augustine makes a whole series of fundamental statements about God. To begin with, he describes God as the wise and generous creator. God does not create blindly; God knows what God is doing. God knows creatures in the "eternal reasons" *(rationes aeternae)* that are contained in God's Word.[100] Precisely on this account, creatures bear the mark of God's rationality. In addition, as the Scripture says, God has created all things with measure, number, and weight (Wis 11:21); as a result, all things participate in the wisdom which God is in the divine self.[101] But this also means that human beings can know God through creation.[102] They do not know creatures, however, in the way in which God knows them in God's eternal and changeless knowledge before God even created them. Therefore God is ultimately closer to human beings than things are.[103]

At the same time, moreover, Augustine stresses the fact that the divine goodness underlies creation. God does not create simply because God wants to but out of God's overflowing goodness; that is, God does not need creatures but wants to give them a share in God's everlasting blessedness.[104] In doing so, God proves the divine love in two ways: "There are, it should be noted, two purposes in God's love of [God's] creation: first, that it may exist, and secondly, that it may abide."[105] This twofold love, which begins and preserves and which corresponds once again to creation and government, has a different effect on heavenly and on earthly beings: "Some abide in the most exalted holiness next to God, transcending all the changes of time; but others abide according to the determinations of their time, while the beauty of the ages is unfolded by the coming and passing of things."[106]

What has been said contains a second statement: God sustains the creation and in the divine providence leads it to its fulfillment.[107] In other words, God does not leave the world to the play of chance.[108] Rather God continues to be the cause of the ongoing existence of all things; were God to withdraw, the world would fall back into nothingness.[109] Augustine describes this ongoing divine causality with the term "government," a term that includes both the motion given to things and providence.[110] When he speaks of "movement," he means that God continually moves the world, keeps it in motion.[111]

Two things are included in this last statement. First, there is a movement that embraces everything, even the smallest and least important element;[112] yet in this movement of all things, God remains unmoved.[113] As Augustine explains in detail, especially in answering the question of how God spoke to Adam, God works in time and space without God's eternity, truth, and love being affected in any way.[114]

In this connection, Augustine distinguishes between God's activity in nature and God's activity in wills.[115] God moves natures so that they exist. Wills, on the other hand, God directs so that good wills are fruitful, while evil wills do not go unpunished and in this way are, despite everything, integrated into the order which God has established.[116] The freedom that God thus gives to human beings is, however, grounded in the nature which God has established. (In the course of the Pelagian controversy, Augustine would understand this conception of freedom more narrowly but would not abandon it in principle.)[117] At the same time, the divine activity is further specified from another point of view. While God acts directly in natures to call them into existence and while God also enlightens the angels without any mediation so that they may participate in God's truth and blessedness, God acts on human wills mediately with the aid of spiritual or corporeal creatures. This cooperation of second causes itself takes place within an order in which lower creatures remain subordinate to higher and God stands over the entire order.[118]

In this detailed description of the movement given by God, the second element in governance, namely, providence, is also included. In God's providential movement, God follows the order which God has established.[119] Consequently, divine providence is simply the development of the "causal reasons" which God introduced into the elements of the world when God first founded it and which were already contained in the divine Word. If in this description of providentially caused movement as an unfolding, Augustine gives the impression of a predetermination,[120] he corrects the impression in another image, a comparison of the development of the world with the growth of a tree.[121] In this context, however, he does not go into the question of the inequality of human beings in happiness and misery; but in another passage, he does point to the cross, from which alone the depths of this mystery can be glimpsed.[122] Elsewhere, he has, in addition, allowed more independence to temporal events, speaking of "the beauty of the ages [that] is unfolded by the coming and passing of things."[123]

Finally, the theme of the twofold creation gives expression to the tension that exists between the eternity of the changeless God and God's activity in time, which God has created along with changeable creatures, whether spiritual or corporeal, which are always in movement.[124] In this conception, creatures somehow exist outside God in their own natures. They are, however, connected with eternity. Their movement originates in One who remains immovable; it occurs in accordance with the possibilities contained in the causal reasons;[125] it also leads back to God, who is after all things.[126] At the same time, Augustine is fully aware that the movement of changeable creatures by the changeless God remains impossible to grasp. He does not speak in a purely negative way, but says rather that God moves the divine self and creatures outside of time and space.[127] He also compares God and the soul: as the soul moves the body without itself thereby moving in space, so God moves things without the divine self entering into the movement of time.[128] But this comparison leads him only to place a still greater emphasis on the mystery of the divine activity in space and time: "For if [inquiring human beings] cannot yet grasp what takes place in [themselves], how much less will [they] comprehend what is above [them]!"[129]

For a complete understanding of this theology of creation, we must add that it undoubtedly contains philosophical considerations similar to those of the Stoicism which Cicero had accepted and, above all, to those of contemporary Neoplatonism.[130] It is to be noted, however, how in his thoughts on creation and providence, Augustine takes biblical texts as his starting point and repeatedly makes these his guide. An important stimulus came from Genesis 2:2f., "On the seventh day God rested."[131] Now, God certainly did not rest like a human being wearied by labor but as God alone can rest. Yet when the Scripture expressed itself in this manner, which was suited to human understanding, it did not do so in vain or in a way unworthy of God. Apart from explanations of a rather moral type, Augustine understands by the "rest of God" the completion of the "first foundation" and the absolute lack of neediness on God's part. The supreme being is blessed in itself, even while allowing others to participate in its blessedness.

Also of interest to Augustine was the question of how old Adam was when created.[132] In this context, he explains the manner in which possible and real beings, the natural course of things, and miracles are contained in the "causal reasons."[133] According to this explanation, God in his omnipotence and wise providence establishes the laws governing things, but without binding the divine self to these laws.[134] On this same basis, that is, once again on the basis of the Bible, when explaining the formation of the woman, Augustine also distinguishes the mystery of grace from that of creation. The grace by which sinners are rescued belongs among the motives hidden in God, which come into play not in creation but only in providence.[135] Therefore, according to the Apostle, the mystery of grace is not hidden in the world, where the causal reasons of all things that have a natural origin are hidden, but in God, who has created everything.[136]

Finally, the question of how God spoke with Adam spurred Augustine to a profound discussion of providence, which I dealt with above.[137] At the same time, this question provided him with an opportunity of distinguishing the direct knowledge of God that the angels have, from the indirect knowledge of God that human beings have.[138] These more philosophical reflections are, however, based once again on the Bible. In light of John 5:17, 20f. and 1 Corinthians 15:36ff., Augustine excludes any limitation of God's activity.[139] It is also understandable in light of the Bible that he likes to use political expressions and images for God's action in the world: rule, govern, administer, and so on.[140]

Even in the area of the doctrine of creation, the focus is always on the understanding of the faith. Following the Bible, Augustine endeavored to gain a more exact understanding of the sense in which God is to be viewed as creator. To this end, however, he also took ideas from the Stoic and Neoplatonic traditions, in which the description of divine providence played an important role. The extent to which the faith allowed him to go beyond the philosophical thought of his time is clear especially from his reception of the Christian conviction that God "creates from nothing." No less distinctive, moreover, is his idea, inspired precisely by the biblical story of creation, of a God who speaks to human beings and loves them, without being dependent on them. In light of all this, one will be still less inclined to speak of a revolution in the doctrine of God that took place around 397. Even though Augustine composed *The Literal Meaning of Genesis* after 400, the work shows how fundamental the biblical teaching on God the creator had been for him a good while before he wrote his answers to Simplician.[141]

3. The God of Sacred History

a) The Theological Significance of *The City of God* in General

When the lamentations of Christians and the objections of pagans against divine providence continued unabated after the fall of Rome in 410, Augustine felt compelled to defend the Christian religion in a large-scale apologia which he himself entitled *Books on the City of God*.[142] But the debate with Roman paganism which this defense involved had long before become a consuming preoccupation of his. In this context, he had also already appealed to history, in which the two cities symbolized by Jerusalem and Babylon are in opposition from its beginning to its end.[143] This theme was now to be fully developed in *The City of God*.

It is to be expected that precisely in this context, Augustine would further develop his idea of God. The accuracy of this prognostication is already clear from a preliminary answer to the two difficulties that the title of this section, "The God of Sacred History," may suggest.

First, there is the possible question of whether, in *The City of God*, God is in question at all. Despite the title of the work, this query is not groundless. For while in his great catechetical instruction, Augustine had presented Christ as king of the city of God,[144] it is not so clear what "king" means in the present work. To be sure, Christ is a number of times described as "king and founder of the city";[145] but in a no less uncompromising way, it is said that God is the founder of the city,[146] and there is no doubt that "God" means the Father.[147] This acceptance does not of itself contradict the fact that in his apologia, Augustine is attacking in particular the philosophy held by the

Roman pagans, for in his view Porphyry, whom he has first and foremost in mind, acknowledged the God of the Jews and at the same time also spoke of "God the Father."[148]

The second objection is more important: Is it justified, when referring to *The City of God,* to speak of "the God of sacred history"?[149] It must certainly be admitted that this expression does not occur, but it is a fact that in the fifteenth book, in which Augustine begins his presentation of the development *(excursus)* of the two cities,[150] he speaks several times of "sacred history." He uses the expression especially in passages in which he is defending the credibility of the biblical account of history.[151] As I will have to show in greater detail, the emphasis in the second part of *The City of God* is precisely on this historical account, on the "knowledge of history" *(cognitio historialis).* In this second part, Augustine seeks to confirm the refutation of Porphyry, which he had undertaken in the first part, by showing from the biblical history that there is indeed a universal way of salvation.[152] The sacred or divine history undoubtedly tells us that human beings either turn to God in love or deny God their love. But the historical account of God's activity in the world is also concerned, in the final analysis, with God's guidance and judgments or, better, with the God of whom the Bible tells. In view of this "story of the deeds of God," it is quite legitimate to describe the idea of God that finds expression in the most powerful apologia from Christian antiquity as "the God of sacred history."

b) The Basic Idea of the First Ten Books of *The City of God*

Although the main theme of *The City of God* (around 410) was not new, the external events of that year did cause Augustine to concern himself in a more thorough way with the action of God in history. In any case, in the first book, where he refers in detail to the conquest of Rome, he describes God as an educator who is testing Christians by misfortune and in patient mercy desires to lead pagans also to conversion[153] and who has the power to bring good even out of evil.[154] Therefore, Christians had no need to hesitate in answering the question "Where is your God?" As the family of the supreme and true God and as believers in the perhaps hidden but always active presence of God, they possessed a consolation that is not deceptive but is based on a firm hope.[155]

Moreover, the pagan objection that the abolition of the traditional form of worship was responsible for everything led Augustine to prove from history[156] that the pagan gods were unable to ensure the earthly prosperity of the Romans. In doing so, he was, at bottom, refuting the political theology of Varro.[157] If the Romans achieved glory in their history, it was not due to the worship of their gods, who had no concern for the morality of the citizens, but on the contrary encouraged them to immorality,[158] and had not protected them from disasters even before the rise of Christianity.[159] The Romans owed their fame rather to their moral strength[160] and, above all, to the true, almighty, and just God,[161] who takes care of both the good and the wicked.[162]

In fact, in the pre-Christian history of Rome, it became clear that God alone, the author and giver of all good, gave earthly kingdoms to the good and the evil, and this in accordance with an order that is unfathomable to us but completely clear to God; that the divine self is not above this order but is its master and governor; and that if in the process God allowed human beings to enjoy earthly happiness, God did so in order to bring them, as God did the people of Israel, to a desire for true blessedness.[163] Without undermining human freedom, God has foreseen and preordained everything; for as "the cause which is cause only, and not effect," God knows and determines all other causes in advance.[164] It is precisely because God does what God wills and does not suffer what God does not will, that we call God "all-powerful."[165]

In saying all this, Augustine does not, however, exclude the basic principle of the Roman political theology, according to which, worship is the basis of the salvation of the people; but it must be the worship of the true God,[166] for God alone is the master and governor of all present things.[167] On the other hand, the principle is breached insofar as by giving earthly blessings, God intends to awaken the desire of eternal blessings and, when all is said and done, desires to be worshipped in view of these. God does govern the destinies of nations, but is even more the creator who intends to bring human beings to everlasting happiness through a history of prosperity and disasters.[168]

Consequently, the second part of the attack on the pagans must show that the gods can guarantee human beings a supraterrestrial happiness even less than they can an earthly one.[169] That is why the issue is the refutation of Varro's political theology.[170] And yet, in these five books (6–10), Augustine's criticism is not aimed primarily at these Stoic conceptions; for while these identify God too closely with the world, it is not worthwhile, in his opinion, to continue debating with them.[171] He turns instead to the contemporary Platonic tradition as represented especially by Porphyry.[172] The reason is that this tradition accepts the existence of God and of God's concern for humanity, as well as worship of God for the sake of everlasting life, even though, illogically, it puts up with polytheism.[173] He views it, in particular, in light of its division of the philosophy of God into three parts: God as origin of things, as light of minds, and as end of good action.[174] For this reason Augustine also prefers the Platonic tradition to all others.[175]

On the basis of these considerations and after a survey of Varro's teaching on demons,[176] Augustine presents Platonic teaching on everlasting life[177] and on the mediation of demons.[178] He thereby prepares the way for his own positive thesis, according to which Christ alone, the true mediator between God and humanity, opens the way to salvation for all by enabling them to enter through love into his sacrifice and thus become the city of God.[179]

In thus linking mediation and true worship so closely, Augustine certainly has in mind the teaching of Apuleius and Porphyry on demons.[180] He takes over from these writers the idea of a spiritual worship that is to lead to a life of happiness in God. At the same time, passages of Scripture, which clearly become more frequent in the tenth book, compel him to return to his main thesis about the two cities. Thus, while the God of history moves into the background in the debate with the Platonists,[181] this God appears once again as soon as the emphasis falls more on the Bible.[182]

The thesis on the true mediatorship, which is directed chiefly against Porphyry, seems to have little relation to history. In fact, however, it includes a consideration of history and a historical picture of God, and this in two ways. On the one hand, the sacrifice offered by Love proves to be a historical reality, something that is gradually brought to completion. The way was prepared for it in the Old Testament by miracles, theophanies, and sacrificial actions, and at the present time it finds expression in the sensible manifestations of mercy.[183] It reaches completion also on the social and therefore, necessarily, the historical level.[184] Furthermore, and above all, this sacrifice would not have been possible without the incarnation and the cross.[185] In these, it has its historical foundation, and it remains effective in history insofar as the memorial of it is daily celebrated in the liturgy of the Church.[186] The anti-Porphyrian teaching on the mediatorship of Christ supposes, then, a God who never ceases to act in history.

On the other hand, the refutation of Porphyry leads Augustine to demonstrate the existence of the universal way of salvation from the knowledge of history.[187] He is thereby able to answer at the same time the question of why Christianity appeared so late on the scene. The knowledge of history is based chiefly on the fulfillment of the Old Testament prophecies. In Augustine's view, there is no more compelling proof than this, as even the Platonists allow.[188] Concretely, this knowledge of history consists in reflection on the origin, development, and end of the two cities and thus in a meditation on history that necessarily presupposes a God who acts in history.[189] How accurate this statement is can also be seen in the themes which Augustine takes up in passing when dealing with the tripartite history of the two cities.

c) The Two Cities according to the Historiography of the Bible

If the increased appeal to the Bible in the tenth book of *The City of God,* the positive part of the apologia, led to a greater attention to history, this is all the more true of Books 11–22.[190] By this I mean that in his efforts to confirm, on the level of the knowledge of history, his thesis on the universal way peculiar to the Christian religion, Augustine relies extensively on the biblical writings, beginning with Genesis and ending with the Apocalypse of John.[191] To this end, he makes use of the rhetorical pattern of beginning, continuation, and end,[192] as applied in fourth-century historical writing with its panegyrical tendency.[193] Moreover, Augustine had already called for the use of this kind of historical approach in catechesis,[194] and he had also practiced it, in at least an inchoative way, in his own sermons on the baptismal creed.[195] In such a "narration of events," God inevitably appeared primarily as a God of history: as the one on whom the narrative focused and thus as the God who acts in history.

This statement applies first of all to Books 11–14, in which Augustine treats of the creation of the angels and of the fall and its consequences for human life in the flesh. To begin with, in connection with the creation of the angels, he makes a series of statements about God, their creator: about the knowledge of God that is gained from the created order, from knowledge of truth by the soul, and from faith in Christ;[196] about God's transcendence of time and space;[197] about God's simplicity and immutability,[198] which, however, exclude neither the trinity of persons[199] nor the "multiplicity" of God's wisdom;[200] about God's power to integrate even evil into the beauty of the world order;[201] about God's knowledge, in which all things are present to God;[202] about God's goodness, because of which God has created everything.[203] In the process, Augustine does not neglect to point out the trinitarian aspects of the divine creative activity,[204] but this must be dealt with elsewhere.

Further questions about the origin of the two communities, of the angels and good human beings, and of the demons and sinners[205] give Augustine an opportunity to make it clear that everything originates in God;[206] that God is "the supreme existence and the author of all existence whatsoever"[207] and therefore the efficient cause of all good but not of evil, which arises from a defective cause;[208] and that God and God's providence are in no way open to challenge.[209] The reflections on the creation of the human being that make up a good part of the twelfth book also lead Augustine to go more deeply into the question of time and eternity. In doing so, he does not shrink from saying that the fact that God has created the human being in time without a new act of the will is an impenetrable mystery,[210] but he categorically rejects the idea of a plurality of worlds.[211] At the same time, he agrees that God's knowledge also embraces the infinite.[212] Finally, he again reminds his readers that every being outside of God has its origin in God, while God is not subject to any passivity.[213]

The exposition of the fall and its consequences in Book 13 contains no significant references to the being and activity of God. The same can be said in large measure of Book 14, which deals with human lusts. At the end of this book, however, Augustine does stress the point that God has foreseen human frailty and integrated it into God's providential design and that God can bring good even out of evil.[214] With these concluding reflections, he completes the more static teaching—but a teaching nonetheless necessary for an understanding of God's action in history—on the relationship between the eternal, immutable God and creatures that are changeable and also caught up in time.

He turns now to the more dynamic perspective of a history of salvation and damnation, wherein God asserts the divine justice toward sinners and reveals the unmerited mercy with which God fills up the number of the elect.[215] If God allows the sin of the angels and human beings a place in the divine providence, God does so only in order to teach through historical experience what a difference there is between the individual's arrogance and divine aid[216] and, in the final analysis, in order to make it clear, through the contrast between selfless love of God and self-love with its contempt of God, that God is all in all.[217]

In Books 15–18, the subject is the development of the two cities.[218] Whereas the first three books, which dealt with the period from Abel and Cain to the Babylonian captivity, had been concerned almost exclusively with the development of the city of God, in the eighteenth book, which takes us down to Augustine's time, it is the juxtaposition of the worldly city and the city of God that is discussed.[219] In all four of these books (15–18), however, historical thinking comes even more to the fore. This is already made inevitable inasmuch as here Augustine is basing his thought to a great extent on the historical and prophetic books of the Old Testament.[220] But this historical emphasis is heightened by the fact that at the same time, with the help especially of Eusebius, he endeavors to correlate the events narrated in the Bible with those of general world history.[221]

In this meditation on history, which he distinguishes from philosophical reflection,[222] he has little to say about the role of God. He does, however, end this second section of Part 2, on the historical coexistence of the two cities, with the following lapidary statement, "Nevertheless, both cities alike enjoy the good things, or are afflicted with the adversities of this temporal state, but with a different faith, a different expectation, a different love, until they are separated by the final judgment, and each receives [its] own end, of which there is no end."[223]

In these books, to speak more specifically, he harks back to three themes that illustrate the historical action of God. First, he reminds his readers more than once of the providence that has controlled both the rise and the fall of the various empires.[224] Providence also ordained that even outside Israel, the people of God, there should be human beings who lived lives pleasing to God.[225] This is the context also for the strong emphasis on the unmerited election of the citizens of the city of God.[226]

Another theme which Augustine had to take up, especially in connection with the history of Abraham and the other patriarchs, was that of promise and prophecy.[227] In light of these, the events reported by the inspired writers always referred also to Christ and his Church.[228] Augustine does not, however, fail to point out that depending on God's intentions, some of the promises were fulfilled in the fleshly Israel, others in the Church, and still others in both.[229] Above all, he stresses those promises that have been fulfilled in the victorious spread of the Christian religion, despite the obstacles, both internal and external, which the Church faced.[230] In the background here is the idea that God repeatedly consoles the Church but at the same time seeks to keep it free of all arrogance by means of the trials God sends.[231]

Finally, a decisive factor in Augustine's meditation on history is that it is based on the historiography of the Bible, which is guaranteed by the authority of God's very self. Unlike the philosophers, who are at odds with one another, the biblical writers, who agree with one another, bring out the true meaning of the history they narrate.[232] It may be noted in passing that on occasion, Augustine also turns his attention to the anthropomorphic language of the Bible as he explains the wrath of God[233] or God's "descent"[234] or God's speaking with the angels.[235]

In the final four books of his apologia, which were not composed until around 426, Augustine treats of the end of the two cities. He begins with a rather philosophical discussion of happiness, in which he has Varro, Cicero, and Porphyry chiefly in view.[236] Here he takes as his guiding idea that the perfect happiness of the Christian people cannot be found in the present life nor consist either in the virtue of the individual or in the coexistence of many, but solely in everlasting peace.[237] For this everlasting peace and the preliminary peace that leads to it, his favorite name is "the tranquillity of order."[238] But this kind of peace comes from God alone, the God who "created all things in supreme wisdom and ordered them in perfect justice," for God gives human beings what they need for their earthly lives in order to guide them to obedience and then to everlasting peace in the resurrection.[239]

Thus, a submission in faith to the eternal law is required of mortal human beings.[240] This attitude of faith must, in turn, be translated into action in the life of society.[241] This kind of faith-based life for God and neighbor can, however, come only from God: God must cause it to arise and grow through the divine teaching and grace.[242] On the other hand, a life of faith can lead only to God, so that God may be all in all.[243] In this context, Augustine also holds the view that while it is still on its pilgrimage, the heavenly city adapts itself to the community of the earthly city as long as the worship due to the one God is not put at risk and earthly peace remains always directed to God.[244] God, for God's part, must therefore act in history so that a perfect tranquillity of order may come into being.

The accuracy of this claim is confirmed by the way in which Augustine distinguishes between the city of God and the pagan city, namely, by the fact that the former, unlike the latter, is built on justice.[245] This justice, in turn, includes a subordination to God and above all, excludes all worship but that of the true God, the God of the prophets and of the promises now being fulfilled, the God therefore of sacred history, but also the God whom Varro calls the "supreme God" and Porphyry, the "great God."[246]

The historicity of this God of peace is also confirmed by the way in which, in his attack on Roman paganism, Augustine uses the testimony of Porphyry, who despite his hostility to Christians, recognized the God of the Jews as the supreme God.[247] This representative of the best of all philosophies even spoke of "God the Father"[248] but illogically did not accept the Jewish principle, which must have been known to him, that God alone is to be worshipped.[249] On the other hand, as Augustine acknowledges, he agrees with Porphyry that justice must be based on devotion, which includes love of God, neighbor, and self.[250] But in his own case, this basic conception is more open to a God of history, not only inasmuch as he, unlike Porphyry, gives love a social dimension and thereby makes it a factor in human history but also, and above all, inasmuch as he sees the return to God made possible by the sacrifice of Christ on the cross, thanks to which the city of God becomes a single sacrifice.[251] The reference to the passion of Christ is not explicit, but he does speak of the one sacrifice of Christians and of the eucharistic celebration of this mystery. In doing so, he specifically refers the reader to his earlier development of the same theme.[252]

In Book 20, Augustine takes up the last judgment, the final act of history. Here again, God is thought of as a God of history. This is already made clear in the introduction where, following the Bible, Augustine explains that God is, before all else, a judge of humanity.[253] At the same time, he emphasizes here the inscrutability and justice of the divine judgments, in accordance with which the good must endure evils while the wicked experience good things.[254] But as the final act, the judgment itself is part of history. Augustine therefore sets it in the context of historical events, the course of which he derives from the final chapters of John's apocalypse[255] and from other eschatological passages of the New and Old Testaments.[256] Finally, the historicity of God is also confirmed by the basic thesis of the *Homilies on the Gospel of John,*[257] namely, that God will entrust the final judgment to the incarnate Son[258] and will bring it to pass through the coming of the Human One.[259]

In the last two books of *The City of God,* Augustine first takes up the end of the city of this world and then the end of the city of God.[260] In dealing with the former, he discusses chiefly the question of the eternity of hell fire,[261] while in dealing with the latter, he focuses mainly on the resurrection of the body. But in answering both questions, he develops a theology of miracles.[262] In it, miracles are seen as a revelation of God. Above all, the omnipotence of God plays a central role.[263] Just as God constantly works miracles—first and foremost the miracle of creation[264] and the miracle of the ever more widespread belief in the resurrection of Christ[265]—and permits miracles to be worked by the angels and even by demons, so too can God, in God's wise omnipotence, allow the damned to burn in a fire that does not consume them[266] and can transform the bodies of the just for life in heaven.[267]

In the background of this teaching on God's omnipotence is the idea that the always immutable God can intervene to alter the course of nature that was set at the creation.[268] Hereby, the author addresses once again an important theme of the theology of history. At the same time, it is God's omnipotence that allows God to permit the fall of some of the angels; for God knew that the divine power was great enough to bring good out of this evil and to replace the fallen angels with human beings.[269] Since the presence of the Pelagian controversy can be clearly sensed in the last books of *The City of God,* it cannot surprise us to find that in these books God is also seen in light of the history of unfaithfulness on the one hand and gracious justification on the other. But this aspect of the matter needs to be discussed in greater detail elsewhere.[270] So too, the question of the vision of God, which Augustine goes into in detail in the last book, must be taken up later on.[271]

At the same time, mention must be made here of the lengthy debate with the "compassionate Christians" on the limitation of the punishments in hell.[272] Augustine refutes these Christians, who in his view are overly generous, by referring to the revelation of damnation, which he regards as explicit,[273] and to the *lex orandi,* that is, to the prayer to be spared the pains of hell;[274] in addition, he corrects their arguments from the Bible.[275] In this discussion, he is guided, in the final analysis, by the thesis he has already defended, that the providence of God includes justice and that, as the Christian tradition had long claimed, God is simultaneously just and kind.[276] In addition, he maintains here, as elsewhere, that God's foreknowing and preordaining always coincide.[277]

Finally, the historicity of God is once more brought out fully in the concluding chapter of the entire work. Here, Augustine describes the plenitude of bliss as the sabbath that follows upon the six ages of the world. On that last day, human beings will do naught but give completely free and endless praise to the God who now fills all and to God's unmerited mercy;[278] therein, they will have reached the goal of their love.[279]

In light of the foregoing exposition, the picture of God that is given in *The City of God,* which is surely the most important apologia from Christian antiquity, may be outlined as follows. First of all, we are struck by the numerous but not surprising philosophical statements that occur in a refutation of contemporary Platonism. God is described as founder and governor, as creator and administrator, as author of all essences and cause of all things, as origin of things in accordance with foreknowledge and will. It is also presupposed that God can be known not only by the wise but also, though in a different way, by simple folk as well.

Nor is it surprising to find that in a discussion focused in large measure on the political theology of the Roman imperial age, metaphors and ideas with a political origin are applied to God. Thus, God is seen as king and emperor, as lord and ruler. True peace is God's gift, and only in the order which God establishes is justice to be found.

Closely associated with these political categories are metaphors from private life as understood in contemporary views of society. Thus, God is also represented as the father of the household and as educator.

A further distinctive element is the importance which this apologia gives to the fulfillment of Old Testament prophecies and to miracles. These presuppose a God who stands above the natural order which the divine self has established and who can intervene in history in accordance with "reasons" which God has, as it were, reserved to the divine self.

Finally, and above all, a look back at the sections dealing with history in the first ten books and at the presentation of sacred history in the other books can only make clear how much God is, for Augustine, a God who in immutable freedom and wise love guides the destinies of humanity and leads it to that goal where happiness takes the form of unending praise of God's mercy which has operated in time.

If, in addition, we reflect that Augustine the apologete has measured the Christian usefulness of philosophical expressions and sociopolitical metaphors by the standard of the biblical historical narrative and that at the same time he distinguishes the orders of grace and nature, we can no longer doubt that for Augustine God is, in the final analysis, the God of the prophets and apostles and the God of Jesus Christ.

CHAPTER 3

God in the Christian Program of Life

1. The Vision of the Omnipresent God

a) Introductory Remarks on Letters 147 and 187

During the early years of the writing of *The City of God*, Augustine also had occasion to hold forth on a subject dear to his heart: the perfect union of the human being with God. First, the question was put to him of whether human beings can see God with their eyes or, more specifically, of how the passages of Scripture that exclude a vision of God are to be harmonized with those that assert such a vision.[1] Somewhat later he was obliged to answer two further questions: How is the text, "Today you will be with me in Paradise" (Luke 23:43), to be understood, and then how are we to understand the knowledge which a child in its mother's womb has of God (Luke 1:41-44)?

The two responses, Letter 147, written in 413–414, and Letter 187, written in 417, are closely connected with each other in method and in content. Both deal with questions of an exegetical kind.[2] It is also true, of course, that Augustine always starts with philosophical presuppositions. But we are immediately struck by how closely he tries to stick to the relevant biblical texts. In the first of the two letters, he also relies on the exegesis of Ambrose.[3] As a result, his expositions are in large measure circumscribed by the two exegetical questions.

At the same time, the two questions, on the vision of God and on the presence of God, also belong together from the viewpoint of their content. Only what is present can be seen, and only what is present in a new way can be seen in a new way: this is something Augustine presupposes throughout the two documents.[4]

b) The Treatise on the Vision of God (Letter 147)

At the beginning of the first of the two letters, which he addresses to Paulina, a nun, and which he himself describes as a treatise on the vision of

God,[5] Augustine explains his views on religious knowledge.[6] His first reason for beginning with these methodological reflections on prayer and knowledge, seeing and knowing, knowledge and belief, and on divine and human faith, is to ground the approach he takes to the Bible.[7] But already in these reflections, he is also announcing the connection between presence and vision, which he regards as fundamental.[8] In addition, with the help of his analysis of religious knowledge, he is able to exclude a vision of God by the bodily senses.[9]

The content of his answer to Paulina can be summed up as follows, with the help of the recapitulation which occurs in the middle of the letter.[10] According to the explicit testimony of Scripture and especially of Matthew 5:8, "Blessed are the pure of heart, for they shall see God," there *is* a vision of God.[11] God is by the divine nature invisible, but God can be seen if God wills to be and as God wills to be.[12] This is true not only of God the Father but of the entire Trinity.[13] In the present world, however, God allows the divine self to be seen or perceived solely through a created form *(species)*.[14] Only in ever-lasting life will God be seen as God is, as Augustine repeatedly says, especially in view of Exodus 33:13, "Show me yourself" *(ostende mihi temetipsum),* and 1 John 3:2, "When [God] appears, we will be like him and will see him as he is."[15]

The vision of God may not, however, be understood as being the same as the vision we have of visible things.[16] It occurs, rather, inasmuch as the only-begotten Son of God reveals the substance of the deity to those who are worthy of it. Following Ambrose's explanation of John 1:18, Augustine describes this revelatory activity of the Son as a "narrating" *(narratio),*[17] in which the Son, as the Word, does not sound in our ears but, in keeping with the text, "Whoever sees me, sees the Father" (John 14:9), shines in the mind as the radiant image of the Father.[18] This narration is already at work in faith. It is with this in mind that Augustine cites the following words of Ambrose, that "outstanding desirer of the vision":

> Those who grasp the omnipresence of God with a mind that rises above itself see God, even though God seems to be absent. Those, on the other hand, who are not capable of this should pray and act so as to attain to it. But let them not turn to a human expositor in order with [that one's] help to read what they cannot read. Let them turn rather to the divine Redeemer in order to become capable of that of which they are incapable.[19]

On the basis of faith, human beings can in any case, even in this life, have a knowledge of God.[20]

Furthermore, the extensive exegesis of Ephesians 3:18, which Augustine undertakes following Ambrose, leads him to a more concrete conception of the vision of God. For the knowledge of "the love of Christ that surpasses knowledge," which is included in the vision of the Son and the Father, extends not only to the substance of the deity but to God's hidden counsel of grace and thereby ensures the peace that transcends all understanding.[21]

Behind these explanations of the varying degrees of the vision of God lies the conviction that God is by God's very nature invisible.[22] Augustine himself derives this basic view chiefly from biblical texts. In doing so, he certainly presupposes the philosophical principle that the unchangeable is also invisible.[23] He supports this principle with biblical texts[24] and without any further philosophical discussion of it. But he evidently joins the preceding tradition in accepting that the simplicity of God—what God has, that God is—excludes any and every translation into a form required for visibility.[25]

In his reflections on the vision of God, Augustine also presupposes that the vision is a grace. The invisible God allows the divine self to be seen when and where God will. Here Augustine explicitly follows Ambrose, according to whom the suddenness of God's self-manifestations especially is proof of the freedom of the self-revealing God.[26] Even though the Bishop of Milan continued a long-lived current of tradition in his thesis on the created form God uses in the divine manifestations *(forma electa),* we must regard as original with him the heavy emphasis on the divine will, which finds expression especially in the antithesis between nature and grace and which Augustine makes his own.[27]

These theological considerations are confirmed by certain anthropological presuppositions. Human beings are capable of seeing God if God decides to communicate the divine self to them. They long for this vision of God that will complete their being.[28] But they want to see God's very self and not just enjoy a manifestation of God.[29] To this end, they must be not only morally worthy but also ontologically disposed: they must have pure hearts[30] and even, so far as this is possible, be filled with God *(plenus Deo).*[31] They must therefore cling to God and prepare a spiritual dwelling for God within themselves "in order to hear [God's] silent story and see [God's] invisible form."[32] The devil, the demons, and sinners are therefore excluded from the vision.[33] Conversely, God can show the divine self to the just, and this in a spiritual, not a corporeal way, only if they belong wholly to Christ and if they, like Christ, undergo a transformation to a glorified life.[34]

In any case, Augustine seems to assume that Paul and Moses—but not Peter[35]—were deemed worthy of seeing God even in the present life. Paul experienced a kind of ecstasy and was transported to heaven.[36] Moses' deepest wish—to see God—was fulfilled: he not only saw him "in a riddling way" but beheld the divine glory "face to face."[37]

c) The Treatise on the Presence of God (Letter 187)

The Letter to Dardanus is concerned, as I said, with two exegetical problems. In both questions, but especially in the first, the issue is the presence of

God, and it is not without reason that Augustine himself describes this letter as a treatise on the presence of God.[38] But this basically philosophical problem is complicated by the fact that Augustine also brings in secondary questions, such as the meaning of "paradise,"[39] and in addition has to take into account that Christ is both God and human being.[40]

Once again, the best way to gain an overview of the answer to both questions is to start from the summary with which Augustine himself ends his letter.[41] Here he speaks, to begin with, of the presence of God in general. In addition, he distinguishes between "presence" and "indwelling," as he has several times earlier in the letter.[42] Accordingly, God is everywhere wholly present *(ubique totus praesens)*. God is present not just in one part of reality but everywhere; and God is not just partially present in a part but is wholly present in every part.[43] Indeed, God is not enclosed as in a vessel, as though God could not exist apart from the things in which God is present; rather, God is in the divine self.[44]

This completely nonspatial omnipresence becomes intelligible only when we rid our minds of all material representations, and this is difficult, if not simply impossible.[45] At least, however, the presence of God may be compared with that of light or sound.[46] Above all, human beings must think of it as they do of wisdom and immortality or health.[47] In any case, they must exclude from God both quantity and quality.[48] In positive terms, the omnipresence of God consists in this, that God is the creator of all things, governs them all without effort, and carries them like feathers in the divine hands.[49] It is to be noted that Augustine ascribes this creative omnipresence not only to God the Father but also to the Son and to the Spirit, and thus to the entire Trinity, which is one God.[50]

The indwelling of God is something different. For although God is everywhere present through the presence of God's divinity, God is not everywhere present through the grace of the indwelling.[51] The indwelling takes place in the individual justified human being and in the Church as the body of Christ: in "the most blessed temple" and in "the most blessed temples."[52] But it does not take place with the same degree of intensity in all. It is "stronger" in those human beings who are holier than others and who are therefore more like God and closer to God.[53] In other words, whether a person is more or less filled by God and in particular by the Holy Spirit depends on the capacity of the individual and also on the grace given to the individual.[54]

The indwelling of God is to be understood as in reality a dynamic occurrence. It already takes place in the unbaptized, depending on their predestination; in them, God prepares a dwelling for the divine self.[55] But it is also a gift that is given in baptism to little children, who are as yet unable to know God.[56] God dwells even more in those who are called but do not yet know God to the degree possible on earth, although they are striving for a greater knowledge.[57] God is nearer still to those who are advancing and who persevere in this advance.[58] Finally, the indwelling reaches its full form in eternal life.[59] Augustine sums up his thinking on the indwelling as follows, "When you think of God's indwelling, you think of the unity and communion of the saints, first in heaven, where [God] is said especially to dwell because there [God's] will is done perfectly by those in whom obedience dwells, and then on earth, where [God] builds and dwells in a house that will be consecrated to [God] at the end of time."[60]

Although Augustine closely connects this progressive event with the capacity and knowledge of human beings, it is clear that in his view, it is even more an effect of God's grace and love.[61] God acts: God builds a dwelling for the divine self.[62] The grace-character of the indwelling is most clear in its highest form: the "assumption of the human being into Christ," in whom the divine plenitude dwells bodily.[63]

It is inevitable that after his reflections on the presence of God in general and on the indwelling, which is to be distinguished from it, Augustine should take up the presence of the God-human being in particular and thereby arrive at his real question. Here he makes a threefold distinction. Inasmuch as Christ is God, everything said about the presence and indwelling of God holds for Christ. As God, Christ is everywhere wholly present. So too, as God, Christ dwells in the individual and in the Church as in a temple. As human being, however, and because of his real corporeality, Christ has a place in heaven. Between Christ's death and resurrection, however, in his soul he was in the underworld, in his body he was in the tomb.[64] As human being, then, Christ is not everywhere; rather, he is there whence he will some day come.[65]

d) Concluding Assessment

Although Augustine does not in this context use the distinction between nature and grace, he does quite explicitly distinguish in Letter 187 between the order of creation and the order of salvation. In the former, God is everywhere wholly present and as the creative substance rules over all things. In the order of salvation, on the other hand, God dwells more fully in those who more fully acknowledge God with the help of the divine grace. Thus, the treatise on the presence of God is in substantial agreement with the treatise on the vision of God. The self-communication of God—whether described in the cited scripture texts as "appearance" or "dwelling"—is completely dependent, as is creation as well, on the divine will. God thus shows the divine self to be the gracious God.

At the same time, God comes to human beings to the extent that they purify their hearts and strive with devout faith to attain to a greater knowledge of God and a more faithful fulfillment of the divine will. God thereby shows the divine self to be a demanding God, the Holy One for the holy (the frequent contrast between God the just and God the merciful does not apply here).

Furthermore, although Augustine connects the grace-character of the indwelling with the unique grace of Christ's mediatorship only in passing,[66] he does explicitly insist that the inaccessible God can be known only through the divine Word; God is to be seen only because God's only-begotten Son tells of God.[67]

In accordance with the Christian tradition, which is deeply rooted in the Bible but also in the Greek religious spirit, Augustine thus considers the vision of the invisible God and therewith the union with the wholly other God to be the supreme goal of human striving. Yet more than any other spiritual writer, or in any case more than the Neoplatonic philosophers, he makes the attainment of this profoundly human ideal depend solely on the will of the gracious God. At the same time, as he had done in an inchoative way in the writings at Cassiciacum,[68] he connects the divine condescension with the incarnation of the Son of God, who is the supreme proof of the graciousness of the gracious God.

2. God Merciful and Just

Around the year 412, Augustine entered upon a series of debates that were to be in all probability the supreme challenge to his intellectual powers and that later found their place in history as the "Pelagian controversy." We would expect that precisely in this dogged struggle over the deepest meaning of Christian life, he would have to clarify his original theological thinking. We will appreciate better the extent to which this was in fact the case if we distinguish two periods in the history of these quarrels about grace: the period before 418 and the period after.

a) The Idea of God in the Anti-Pelagian Writings before 418

As the final work of this period, *The Grace of Christ and Original Sin,* and the Canons of the Synod of Carthage in 418[69] make clear, the issues in this first period (412–418) were universal original sin and the absolute necessity of interior grace for salutary action. Celestius and Pelagius, each in his own way, had denied the inherited sinfulness of all human beings and had defended the possibility of perfect righteousness in this world.[70] Their main concern was the dignity of the free human being. Augustine, on the other hand, took into account the need all human beings have of redemption, and he maintained the necessity of an interior helping grace that God gives with utter freedom on God's part. His concern was "the grace of God through Jesus Christ our Lord" and therefore the dignity of God. In fact, his anti-Pelagian position includes a whole series of statements about God. In large part, these had long been dear to him,[71] but they appeared now in a new light.

The first point to be noted is the theological consequences of the fact that in the debate about the Pelagian concept of nature, Augustine recognizes the goodness of creation but at the same time stresses the need human beings have of redemption.[72] This means, more precisely, that he distinguishes between the gracious character of creation, which is called into being by divine love, and the gracing of sinful humanity, which springs from the prevenient love of God.[73] This is to say unambiguously that God is both creator and savior. Thus, he reproaches Pelagius:

> When he believes that in defending nature he is taking up the cause of God, he fails to see that in claiming human nature to be sound, he is rejecting the compassion of the physician. For the creator of this nature is also its savior. We ought not, therefore, praise nature so highly that we are forced, and are even convinced, to say that a savior is unnecessary. Let us then honor human nature with the praise it deserves and refer this praise to the glory of the creator. But let our gratitude to [the creator] for creating us be such that we are not ungrateful to [the creator] for healing us.[74]

Later on, when his adversaries accuse him of Manicheism, Augustine will emphasize this antithesis even more.[75]

Furthermore, in this context, Augustine also takes up one of his basic theses, according to which, the human person or, more particularly, reason must be subject to God; in this sense, God the creator is first and foremost a master *(dominus).*[76] On the other hand, in connection with divine redemption, he repeatedly makes the point that the "righteousness" of God is not God's own righteousness but the righteousness by which human beings are justified.[77]

It goes without saying, of course, that Augustine connects the saving work of God with our Lord and Redeemer, Jesus Christ.[78] But the point he repeatedly emphasizes against the Pelagians is that it is the grace of God that is given to us through Christ.[79] It is indeed Christ who justifies us,[80] but in justifying us, Christ reconciles us with God.[81] Even though the sinful human being must turn to Christ, the invitation to do so comes from the Father.[82] At the same time, salvation consists not only in association with Christ the Savior but also in membership in the kingdom of God.[83] In this context, we must not fail to realize that throughout this controversy, which is always carried on in the arena of the Bible, Augustine means by *Deus* the Father, as does the New Testament itself.[84]

The disputes over the dignity of the free human being also led Augustine to investigate more fully how the grace of God works in the human heart. In this connection, he developed the thesis that in what is most their own, their wills, human beings are dependent on the help of God.[85] But he goes even further and describes this helping grace as an action of the divine Spirit,[86] as an inspiration to active love.[87] Thus, it is not simply by the action of free will, which human beings have by their creation, and with the support of the law of God that they are led to a life of righteousness; in addition, they receive the Holy Spirit, through whom they acquire a delight in the supreme good that is God's very self.[88] But this is not by any means to say that violence is done to them. Rather, God draws them to the divine self by means of God's over- whelming light and the sweetness of God's love.[89] On the other hand, this in- terior action of God does not completely restore the interior balance of the person, even if a miracle of divine omnipotence were to free that person com- pletely from the law of sin.[90] For this reason, Christians must constantly pray for the grace of God.[91] God will then give them joy in what is good[92] and per- severance to the very end.[93]

This emphasis on the helping grace of God that acts entirely from within already led to an unavoidable tension. On the one hand, the Christian life thus made possible by divine grace seems to be an easy thing.[94] On the other, Au- gustine sees this action of God in enlightening and drawing as something completely unmerited. It is also given only to those chosen by God and thus has its origin in the utterly free decree of God.[95] This tension was, however, not something new. It went back to the years 396–397, when in answering questions on this subject from Simplician of Milan, Augustine had developed the idea of the complete gratuitousness of divine grace. In his *Revisions,* he himself speaks of the explanation of Romans 9:9-29 that he gave at that time as having marked a turning point in his teaching on grace.[96]

b) The Idea of God in the Later Anti-Pelagian Writings

In the second period of the controversies concerning grace (418–430), three issues called for even more detailed discussion. Julian, the most astute of Augustine's adversaries, forced the latter to greater precision regarding the concept of corrupted nature and, more specifically, the concept of concupis- cence. Furthermore, monastic circles in North Africa and Gaul forced him to distinguish more precisely between the action of grace and the action of the free will. Finally, at the beginning of these twelve years, but especially toward the end of them, Augustine had to take an unambiguous position on the ques- tion of predestination. As a result of all these discussions, there was a further clarification of the picture of God.

When Julian and others accused Augustine of Manichean errors[97] and, at the same time, shifted the discussion primarily to the New Testament area, they gave him the opportunity to state more precisely the teaching on God that he had defended against the Manichees, and this in two respects.

On the one hand, he had to make it clearer that God is the author of na- tures without thereby being the author of disorders.[98] Accordingly, there is no substance that is not from God.[99] Even in wicked human beings God is the creator of good.[100] In particular, marriage, unlike concupiscence, is from the true and good creator.[101] In this process of clarification, the goodness of God is defined more closely: "It follows that the only creator of natures is the creator of good things and that [the creator] is therefore good; but [the creator] is greatly different from [the creator's] creatures and superior to them by reason of [the creator's] supreme goodness, for [the creator] cannot be in any way corrupted, and this due not to a reception of grace but to a property of [the creator's] nature."[102] But if God is by nature immutable and can therefore only be good, this does not mean that God is not free.[103]

On the other hand, the biblically based objections of Julian led Augustine to make his concept of God more concrete and more biblical. He speaks of God as loving [God's] creation but also loving to judge humanity: "God loves human beings so much that even when they are evil [God] loves them as human beings, although [God] hates them as evil. Thus the wicked whom God hates are human beings, since God loves what [God] has made, and are wretched, since God loves judgment."[104] More accurately: God loves all souls but prefers some, not because of their merits but thanks to God's own generosity.[105]

The discussions on grace and freedom, especially as we see them in *Grace and Free Will* (425–427), compelled Augustine to reflect more deeply on the action of God in the hearts of human beings. On the one hand, he maintains consistently that God may not be made responsible for sin. God acts in wicked human beings without on that account being the author of their sin.[106] If God hardened the heart of Pharaoh, God did it for a legitimate reason without thereby removing Pharaoh's freedom.[107] God could with all the more reason allow evil in human beings since in the divine goodness and omnipotence, God can bring good out of evil.[108] "God is so good that [God] can make good use even of what is evil; as omnipotent, [God] would not allow this evil to be unless [God] were able to make good use of it by [God's] supreme goodness. If [God] did not do so, [God] would seem to be rather impotent and less good, as being unable to make good use even of evil."[109]

On the other hand, in this context, Augustine presents God as the ultimate and true source of salvation. Everlasting life consists precisely in this, that in crowning human merits, God is crowning God's own gifts.[110] This is an instance of "grace upon grace."[111] Everlasting life brings to fulfillment a human love that has always and at every point been forestalled by God's love.[112] God's grace, which illumines human thought and sustains human love, shows itself to be an irresistible power.[113] It virtually creates the action of the human will: "All who are saved and come to the knowledge of the truth are saved by [God's] will and come to that knowledge by [God's] will. Even those who, like children, do not yet have the use of free will are reborn by the will of [the one] by whose creative action they are born. Those who already have the use of free will cannot will except by the will and help of [the one] who prepares the will."[114] The human heart, then, is entirely in God's power.[115] That in saying this Augustine had to reckon with the dilemma of freedom or grace had not escaped him earlier. But in the past, he had abstained from trying to solve this riddle.[116]

Finally, in the writings in which he had to give a complete answer to questions regarding foreknowledge, predestination, and perseverance, Augustine could not avoid giving clearer expression to his conception of the all-transcending will of God. He was clear from the outset, however, that he was dealing here with an impenetrable mystery. The choice of the children who are to receive the grace of baptism before their premature death[117] as well as the gift of perseverance granted to the redeemed[118] are based on the unfathomable but just decision of God.[119] And yet, even though the depths of the wisdom and love of God cannot be plumbed, we may not be silent about the mystery of divine predestination; otherwise, we run the danger of denying the gratuitousness of divine grace.[120] We must, of course, speak of this mystery in a correct way. Thus, the faithful should pray in fear for perseverance and at the same time set their entire hope on the mercy of God.[121] In any case, Christians may not question the decisions of God.[122] Rather, they must acknowledge that God is not unjust toward those whom God does not deliver from the "condemned mass" and that God acts out of pure kindness toward the others whom he does deliver.[123]

In this connection, Augustine also introduces the distinction between predestination and God's foreknowledge. According to this distinction, God knows and wills in advance the salvation of the rescued with the same infallibility with which God knows and wills those who are lost.[124] God does not, however, determine that anyone shall sin, an action that presupposes the free act of the creature; God determines only their just punishment.[125] This doctrine, which may have been occasioned by certain passages of the Bible[126] but which no one prior to Augustine maintained in this form,[127] is by any account still harsh enough. In practice, it calls into question the universality of salvation.[128] Consequently, it shows God as a master who arbitrarily intervenes in the destinies of human beings.[129] It is probable that Augustine himself could tolerate such a harsh teaching only because he was convinced that the omnipotent God will somehow, despite everything, carry out the plan of eternal wisdom. Thus, he says in *Correction and Grace:*

> Therefore, we confess, to our salvation, what we rightly believe: that the God and Lord of all things—who created everything as very good and foreknew that evil would arise out of good and who knew it to be more in keeping with [God's] omnipotent goodness to bring good out of evil than not to allow evil at all—so ordained the life of angels and human beings that [God] might show in it, first, what their free will can do, and then, what the blessing of [the divine] grace and . . . just judgment can do.[130]

In this hope, which doubtless was supported by his concept of order, Augustine was all the more justified inasmuch as, according to him, God had in complete freedom predestined the Son to be the Head of all the elect.[131]

In light of this background, it is doubtless legitimate to ask whether the picture of God that Augustine projects in the anti-Pelagian and related writings can really become the basis for a program of Christian life. The first point to be made in response is that in this body of writings, Augustine is not presenting an utterly new teaching. To a great extent, he only sets new emphases. The most original of his contributions is perhaps the antithesis between creator and savior, which was imposed on him by the twofold attack on the Manichees and the Pelagians. Rather new, also, is the way in which he insists on interior grace that is irresistible. More than in the past, he now stresses the point that delight in the good *(delectatio boni)* and even in God can come only from God's self. The love of God has to be poured into the human heart by the Holy Spirit (see Romans 5:5). The least novel characteristic of the Augustinian teaching on grace is probably the third, its pronounced voluntarism: God acts as God wills. This axiom does not appear first at the supposed turning point of 397; it is also in Ambrose, and is already to be seen in Irenaeus at the latest.[132] In any case, Augustine does speak more clearly now of predestination to good and predestination to punishment. Connected with this is the henceforth urgent admonition to work out our salvation in fear and trembling (see Phil 2:12).

As early as the fifth century, this particular aspect of the Augustinian teaching on grace was felt to be scandalous and inhuman,[133] and many Christians are no less offended by it today than at that time; quite the contrary, in fact. The offensive harshness of a thinking that climaxes in this twofold predestination cannot be denied. At the same time, however, we must bear in mind—and this may be said as at least a rough answer to the question of why this position was accepted—that Augustine could never escape the thought of the unparalleled greatness of God. He felt constantly compelled to stress the radical difference between the creator and the creator's creatures. It is in this intention of allowing nothing to detract from the dignity of God that we may see the real heart of a logic which he carried to its extreme.[134]

Now, this acknowledgment of the Lord and Father in Augustine's conception of God is also unconditionally a part of the program of Christian life. Christians must realize clearly that they owe everything to their creator and redeemer. "[God] made us, and not we ourselves" (Ps 99:3): this is a conviction that must never vanish from the heart of a Christian believer.[135] But is not this basic insight at one with the picture of God given in the Bible and does it not reflect, in the final analysis, the attitude of Jesus, for whom the Father was everything?

3. The God of All the Faithful

As the *Confessions* bear witness on almost every page, Augustine found the way to his God primarily through the psalms.[136] He led his faithful and especially those consecrated to God along the same way. He explained to them the psalms, which were sung in the liturgy and were read in private.[137] The God whom Augustine proclaimed in his explanations was the God of everyday life, of human cares and afflictions, of the heart's experiences, of yearning love. It is of all the greater interest to consider this locus of encounter with God inasmuch as Augustine's "most wide-ranging work," the *Expositions of the Psalms,* reflects the major part of the pastoral activity of the Bishop of Hippo and is therefore representative of the concerns he had in the rest of his preaching.[138] Certainly, it will also be worth our while to at least look more closely at the sermons on the Creed and on the Eucharistic prayer.

a) The Unfathomable Mystery of God

Following the lead of the psalmists, Augustine never wearies of speaking of the greatness of the divine creator who has made everything in heaven and on earth.[139] The traces of this omnipotent God are consequently to be found everywhere.[140] God's unfathomable wisdom fills the entire creation.[141] By this mighty will, God has made all creatures, in utter freedom and unmoved by any necessity, but simply as it pleased the divine self: God's will is the cause of all things.[142]

Like the psalmists, however, Augustine also realizes that this immense, wise, and almighty God is a stone of stumbling for many individuals.[143] Even though Christians do not question God the way pagans do,[144] they nonetheless often murmur against God.[145] Perhaps not openly, but they do it in their hearts.[146] In their foolishness they do not understand that God may let sinners prosper while overwhelming the righteous with suffering.[147] They do not realize that God means to educate human beings.[148] They do not see God as the physician who wants to heal wounds and who even has the power to give the blind a light that comes from the divine self.[149]

At the same time, those who truly believe do not dispute with God.[150] They do not think of accusing God of evil.[151] They do not bend God's will to suit themselves.[152] Instead of murmuring, they align their judgment and entire behavior with the will of God.[153] God's will is for them the yardstick for their lives.[154] If despite all their efforts, Christians cannot understand God, they entrust themselves wholly to the divine wisdom and place their entire hope in the divine goodness.[155] Neither in happiness nor in misfortune do they cease to yearn for God.[156] In prayer, they reach out to God with even deeper interior desire.[157] In this context, Augustine appeals to many of the psalms as he reminds his hearers that God is both just and merciful. As truthful and just, God punishes sinners; as merciful, however, God raises them up and consoles them.[158]

b) Praise of the Transcendent God

In face of the unfathomable mystery of God, Augustine can think of nothing better than to urge his faithful to praise God.[159] In his view, the praise of God is the chief task of believers.[160] In doing this, however, human beings do not do God any service since God has no need of their praise.[161] Rather, by praising God, they profit themselves; they are enriched and thereby give their life its true meaning.[162]

How preoccupied Augustine was with this most important of human tasks emerges in an especially fine way in the many passages in which, following the psalmist, he seeks in ever new turns of phrase to bring out the two meanings of "confess to God" *(confiteri Deo)*.[163] For example: "The words do not always refer to the confession of sins; this devout 'confession' may also mean the praise of God. In the former confession persons lament; in the latter they display their joy; in the former they show their wounds to the physician; in the latter they thank [the physician] for their healing."[164] In their distress *(miseria)*, they should confess their sins to God, while with their gaze on God, who is both just and merciful, they should sing of the divine acts of mercy *(miserationes)* and praise the kindly judgments of God.[165] Because Augustine felt it his duty, in line with the Psalter, to encourage his faithful to the praise of God, he loved also to explain the Easter Alleluia. This word, or rather two words, means: "Praise the Lord."[166]

But Augustine is not content with these general explanations of the meaning of praise of God. On the contrary, he can become quite concrete. Praise of God must pervade the entire day; in this way, the day will become a practice for everlasting life: "You praise when you are engaged in business; you praise when you take food and drink; you praise when you rest on your bed. When do you not praise? Our praise of God will become perfect when we reach that city, when we become the equals of the angels of God. . . . Let us practice for this perfect praise by the praise we now offer through good works."[167]

To praise God for all eternity is thus the goal of all of human life.[168] Consequently, the sacrifice of praise does not take place only in the liturgy and in prayer. Rather, it must permeate the entire day of Christians through the keeping of the commandments, through good works and humble submission to God, and through the surrender of oneself.[169] This obligation applies to both good and bad days.[170] Like Job, Christians must recognize that God gives them everything they have and that God can take it away again and yet can only be praised.[171] It is precisely thus that they prove that they have the right attitude.[172] In all this praise, the faithful are already joining in the song of praise that is the occupation of the angels;[173] at the same time, they give expression in their praise to the truth that the entire creation proclaims the praise of God.[174]

The motive for this adoration and praise is ultimately the greatness of God who created the world and has still more wonderfully redeemed it.[175] God is to be praised first of all because God alone is good in the true sense[176] and because God is above all things.[177] Especially to be praised is God's eternity: God's years have no end and there is no change in God.[178] God does not, however, remain inactive; rather, God works in repose.[179] God, the fullness of all joy and the embodiment of all riches, is precisely the divine self.[180] Since God is "Being itself" *(ipsum esse),* God cannot change.[181] It is for this reason that our salvation is to be found in God alone; God alone is our final refuge.[182] It was God who initiated the history of salvation,[183] and God has stood by and now stands by all the divine promises with unshakable fidelity.[184] God's everlastingness is therefore also the reason why human beings can hope to reach their reward in God and to possess God as their sole inheritance.[185] Their praise of God will in fact never end,[186] for the divine beauty will unceasingly delight them anew.[187]

c) The Indescribable Greatness of God

In responding to their call to perpetual praise of the one and only God, human beings come up against their own limitations. What creature can praise the creator as the creator deserves?[188] Even though the greatness of the infinite God becomes clear to human beings in creation and in history, they cannot comprehend their God; much less can they put their admiration into words. Their thoughts and language always fall short of the reality.[189] Creatures do indeed provide them with images and modes of expression, but no comparison is worthy of God.[190]

And yet even the desire to praise God is already a form of praise.[191] More importantly, human beings always have available wordless song, jubilation without words.[192] To the extent that they ceaselessly praise God, even without words, they ceaselessly reach out to their God; in their mute praise they experience their God.[193] God is in fact nearer to them than they are to themselves[194] and acts on them in a wholly interior manner.[195] They become increasingly aware that they owe everything to God.[196] They realize, above all, that they can only praise God, since God praises the divine self in the divine self.[197] As their love grows, human beings come closer to their God. Their love for God becomes so pure that they no longer ask for any other reward save God alone.[198] For this very reason, their hope is also strengthened and their desire intensifies for that life in which they will never cease to sing God's praises in love.[199]

Thus, Augustine endeavors to bring his people closer, in the truest sense, to the ineffable God. He does this, as the ineffable mystery of God itself requires, through the images provided by the psalms. He calls God a refuge,[200] our portion,[201] the reward of the just,[202] an inheritance,[203] light and fountain,[204]

king and ruler,[205] dwelling and house,[206] and a possession in which human beings possess God and are possessed by God.[207] In doing so, Augustine does
not neglect to explain in detail the anthropomorphic manner of speaking that
is common in the psalms.[208] Above all, he opens the eyes of the faithful to God
in the light of experiences in which he has shared the psalmist's own experiences of nearness and distance from God.[209] Nor does he forget the social dimension. He speaks of his experience of God in the context of the struggle
between Jerusalem and Babylon and consequently sees God as founder and
king of the "glorious city."[210]

What he says about God cannot, of course, be separated from the perspective that controls his entire exposition of the psalms, namely, the perspective
of the whole Christ.[211] If we want to understand fully what Augustine is saying about God in his exegesis of the psalms, we must not forget, in particular,
the tension that exists, even here, between statements about "God in the
proper sense" and statements about "God in the general sense."

In fact, there are many *Expositions* in which the text of the psalm or its traditional interpretation leads Augustine to understand "God" and, even more,
"Lord" as referring to Christ. A typical example is the explanation of Psalm
46, which in the Christian tradition is connected with the ascension of Christ
and in which, consequently, the words "God has ascended with jubilation" are
understood of Christ.[212] Interesting as well is the exegesis of Psalm 85. Here
Augustine not only makes the point that the Word through whom God created
everything is one God with the Father, but he also specifies that "we pray to
[Christ] as our God."[213] In addition, he extends the knowledge of the one God,
of which St. John speaks (17:3), to include Christ: "You are to understand that
[Christ] too is the one true God because Father and Son are one true God. The
meaning, then, is 'that they may know the one true God, that is, you and the
one you sent, Jesus Christ.'"[214]

As we would expect, in some explanations, there are also expressions that
match more or less closely the well-known formula "Trinity, which is God."
Thus, Augustine regards as legitimate the question of whether in Psalm 81:1,
the words "God has stood in the congregation of the gods" refer to Father,
Son, and Holy Spirit, that is, the entire Trinity; for when all is said and done,
"each is God, and the Trinity is one God."[215]

At the same time, there are *Expositions* in which "God" is understood exclusively, or at least in the majority of instances, as the almighty creator, the
God of the ancestors, and the Father of Jesus Christ. This is clear when "God"
is distinguished from "the only Son" or when the text speaks of God who
shows the way of salvation through God's Word and Spirit.[216] Thus, in those
Expositions of the Psalms in which he exhorts and consoles his faithful and,
above all, asks them to praise and thank God, or in which he speaks of God
who created the world and is active in the history of humanity and is near to
all who place their hope in God—in these expositions, under the influence

especially of the biblical writers, he is thinking first and foremost of the Father. At the same time, however, he feels obliged to make it clear, in accordance with the Nicene tradition, that the Father is always present to us with the Son and the Holy Spirit, with whom the Father is one God.[217]

d) The God of the Baptismal Catecheses

The manner in which Augustine proclaimed God to his faithful emerges in particular from the way in which he made full use of the language of the Bible and the liturgy in introducing them to the faith and prayer of the Church. From the very beginning of his priestly ministry, he had frequent occasion for doing this in the form of baptismal catecheses. What this work meant to him is also clear from a discourse addressed in 391 to an episcopal synod[218] as well as from two writings addressed to a broader readership.[219] On such occasions, he was, of course, obliged to go into the first article of the Western baptismal creed, "I believe in God the Father almighty," and in doing so, to take into account the Milanese and African additions, "creator of all things, king of the ages, immortal and invisible."[220]

Augustine usually begins his explanations with thoughts on the religious meaning of faith and the profession of faith. Here he lays special emphasis of the meaning of the phrase "believe in God" (*credere in Deum*).[221] This phrase signifies faith in the full sense of the word, that is, a trusting surrender of one's whole life, such as a human being ought to make only to God.[222]

In the profession of faith in "God, the Father almighty," "God" means the Lord and God of the Jewish law, the prophets, and the psalms: the creator of heaven and earth, the God of the people of Israel, the God whom Jesus of Nazareth called his Father.[223] "God" is thus to a certain extent the proper name of the Father, whom Christians confess in the first article of their baptismal creed.[224] This meaning of "God" is already suggested by the fact that even in other settings, Augustine often speaks of God who acts through God's Word or the Lord Jesus Christ and through the Holy Spirit.[225] In fact, the explanations of the baptismal creed leave no doubt on the point. "God" and "Father" always go together in these contexts. "Notice how quickly it's said, and how much it's worth. [God is] God, and [God is] Father; God in power, Father in goodness. How lucky we are to have discovered that our God is our Father!"[226]

In addition, God and the Son are clearly different in the explanation of the second article of the Creed,[227] even though the attributes of the Father are afterwards ascribed to the Son, who is with the Father, and even though the same thing happens with the Trinity, which is one God.[228] The same is to be said in particular of the explanation of the phrase "at the right hand of the Father," that is, "God" here means the Father.[229]

All this becomes even clearer if we take into consideration the explanations of the Our Father.[230] These are also part of baptismal instruction, which includes the meaning not only of "believing" but also of "calling upon the name of God."[231] Thus, we read: "Well then, you have both received, and retained, and given back how you are to believe in God; be ready to receive today how you are to call upon God. As you heard when the gospel was read, the Son himself taught this prayer to his disciples and his faithful followers. . . . Its opening words are, *Our Father who art in heaven.*"[232]

In Augustine's view, Christians must first believe in God; only then can they invoke God as Father, as the Son of God taught us. Moreover, according to Augustine, this Christian way of praying was something new. It was not yet provided for in the Old Testament law, although even in that period, the prophets made it clear that if the Israelites had not deviated from the commandments of God, whom they were bound to serve and who is also the God of Christians, God would indeed have been their father, as God in fact became in the New Testament according to the testimony of the apostles.[233] As the explanations of the various petitions also show, especially of "Thy will be done," which has reference to the final judgment (Matt 25:25, 34, 41), the heavenly Father is always equivalent to "God."[234] There is therefore no reason for understanding "God" any differently in the baptismal creed.[235]

"God," then, is the proper name of the Father, whereas "Lord," the divine name Adon-Yhwh of the Hebrew Bible, is usually used by Augustine of Christ, following the lead of the New Testament. But Augustine also likes to call the Father "Lord" when this is suggested by the scripture passages he has just cited or when the Roman idea of paternal authority *(potestas patris)* is in the background.[236] Accordingly, Augustine can remind the faithful of the privilege they have in being permitted to call the Lord their Father.[237] In his earlier answer to Faustus the Manichee, he had already explained how "Father" and "Lord" go together with "God":

> If [God] is not rightly called "Father," then we are wrong in saying "Our Father, who art in heaven" to [the One] of whose substance we have not been born, but by whose grace and merciful will we have been adopted, as we are told by apostolic teaching and utterly reliable truth. Indeed, we have [the One] as God and Lord and Father: God, because we have been created by [the One] through the mediation of human parents; Lord, because we are subject to [God]; Father, because we have been reborn through adoption by [God].[238]

If the name of father belongs to God in a special way, the reason undoubtedly is that Jesus Christ calls God his Father. Augustine himself develops this meaning, but only in the second article of the creed, the one on the "only Son."[239] He does so especially when he is giving a dogmatic description of the profession of faith in Jesus Christ and following the anti-Arian tradition. In this context and in his explanations of the third article of the creed, he also uses "God" for the Son, the Holy Spirit, and the Trinity. In contrast, when dealing with the first article, he calls God "Father" in relation to creation and to the human race.[240] In any case, in catechetical instructions on the creed, he dwells only briefly on the first article, linking goodness with the name "Father," as I pointed out above, and reminding his hearers of the dignity of Christians, who may call God their Father.[241]

On the other hand, in explanations of the Our Father, which continue the explanations of the creed, he goes into greater detail. He emphasizes especially the point that God is the Father of all: of masters and slaves, emperor and soldiers.[242] At the same time, he describes his listeners as his own children and as his brothers and sisters from the same Father.[243] But this Christian dignity brings with it a duty. Christians, who pray to the Father in heaven, must so live that they are worthy to attain to their inheritance; masters must regard their slaves as their brothers and sisters, since the Lord Christ, too, was willing to have them as his brothers and sisters.[244]

In contrast, when preaching on the baptismal creed, Augustine likes to hold forth on the words "God almighty." It is with these that he begins his actual exposition.[245] In his earliest explanation (391), which is strongly anti-Manichean in character, he emphasizes three aspects of God's omnipotence.[246] God is called "almighty" because with complete freedom God creates everything out of nothing and makes it good and beautiful. God is almighty also because no one can challenge the divine will, while God alone can bring good even out of evil. Finally, God is almighty because God cannot deny the divine self (see 2 Timothy 2:13) and can do nothing which God may not will.[247]

In his late work, the *Handbook on Faith, Hope, and Charity,* Augustine deals in great detail with the burning question of how the omnipotence of God is compatible with the existence of evil.[248] He concludes his reflections on this subject, in which the idea of evil as a privation of good is central, as follows:[249] "We may by no means doubt that the cause of the good things belonging to us is solely the goodness of God but that the cause of evils lies in a will that deviates from the changeless good while seeking a changeable good; this was true first of the angels, then of human beings."[250]

In another baptismal catechesis, Augustine connects God's omnipotence with the divine saving action. God is so powerful that even the greatest sinner may hope for the divine mercy: "So let us believe in [God], and promise ourselves everything from [the divine] kindness and mercy, because [God] is almighty. That's why we believe in God the Father almighty."[251] God's omnipotence was also needed for the making of all creatures: for the great and the small, the immortal and the mortal, the spiritual and the corporeal, for everything that God willed to make. But God cannot die or sin, lie or be deceived, for if God could, God would not be omnipotent.[252]

Finally, Augustine takes up, though not in detail, the earlier mentioned additions to the creed that were made to the original text in the African Church, obviously with an antiheretical intention.[253] He explains the sense in which

God was, before all time, the creator of all things; that God is beyond space and time; and that God's eternity transcends all human thought and language.[254]

e) God in the Eucharistic Prayer

For a full understanding of belief in God the Father almighty, as this finds expression chiefly in the instructions for baptism, we must also bear in mind the fact that in addition to the Our Father, the highest form of liturgical prayer, the "prayer of the priest" *(prex sacerdotis)*, is also addressed to the Father. Unfortunately, Augustine gives us only hints of the actual wording of this prayer, the character of which had already been fixed by the tradition.[255] And yet, the way in which Augustine explains the words "Let us give thanks" is very instructive. Christians have God to thank for the fact that they should lift up their hearts to their Lord Jesus Christ.

> That's why the bishop, or the presbyter who's offering, goes on to say, when the people have answered *We have lifted them up to the Lord,* why he goes on to say, *Let us give thanks to the Lord our God,* because we have lifted up our hearts. Let us give thanks, because unless [God] had enabled us to lift them up, we would still have our hearts down here on earth. *It is right and just* to give thanks to the one who caused us to lift up our hearts to our head.[256]

In like manner, other sermons remind us that the "Let us give thanks to God," and thus the entire eucharistic prayer, is addressed to God the Father.[257] This is confirmed by other passages in which Augustine speaks of "God's altar," at which prayers or sacrifices are offered to God.[258] The finest expression of this orientation to the Father occurs in a sermon on Pentecost in which Augustine stresses the point that one cannot receive "the sacrament of unity" if one is not prepared for peace, and then closes with his customary prayer:

> Turning to the Lord, God the Father almighty, with pure hearts let us give [God] sincere and abundant thanks, as much as we can in our littleness; beseeching God in [God's] singular kindness with our whole soul, graciously to hearken to our prayers in [God's] good pleasure; also by [the divine] power to drive out the enemy from our actions and thoughts, to increase our faith, to guide our minds, to grant us spiritual thoughts, and to lead us finally to [God's] bliss; through Jesus Christ his Son. Amen.[259]

Even though Augustine in his prayers often addresses Christ or even the whole Trinity or attests to the fact of such prayer,[260] he nonetheless makes it clear that for him, as for the entire early Christian tradition, the addressee of liturgical prayer is God the Father.

In the sermons on the psalms, then, and even more in instructions on the baptismal creed and on Christian prayer, Augustine makes it clear that he considers "God" to be first and foremost the almighty creator, the God of Israel and the Father of Jesus Christ, but without forgetting that the Son, too, and the Spirit and indeed the entire Trinity are to be confessed as God. It is true, therefore, that in a special way that God the Father is above all things. In even the severest afflictions, Christians should entrust themselves to the Father's wisdom and love. They are to praise and bless the Father even though their words will never be adequate for this and they might better be silent. In the final analysis, no more is being said here than had been said in the writings from Augustine's years of seeking and in the major theological works. Here, however, Augustine's words are more gripping and more in touch with the afflictions and joys of everyday life; they make clearer what it means for Christians to pray and suffer with Christ, and consequently, they no doubt lead believing listeners more deeply into the mystery of the ineffable God.

CHAPTER 4

The Principal Features of Augustine's Picture of God

"God" is the proper name of the Father, in whom Christians profess their faith in the first article of the baptismal creed. It is with this meaning that Augustine speaks of "God" when he spontaneously uses the word in the context of the Bible, especially the psalms, and of the liturgy.[1] But he also gives the name "God" to Christ, the only Son of God, and to the Holy Spirit. In addition, he stresses the fact that the Father, the Son, and the Spirit are one God. He thus speaks frequently of "the Trinity, which is one God."[2] Along this line, he says explicitly, "But all this that I have said, and anything else that in a similarly human way of speaking may be regarded as suitable to say about God, fits both the whole which the one God is and each of the persons in this trinity."[3]

There are even some statements in which, contrary to Augustine's usual manner of speaking,[4] the words "God" or "one God" precede the enumeration "Father, Son, and Holy Spirit."[5] This represents, however, a more reflexive way of speaking that is found chiefly in Trinitarian and Christological passages.[6] But even in such explanations of a dogmatic or polemical kind, the title "God" belongs most properly to the Father. While the Son and the Holy Spirit are called "God" according to the common application of the word, the Father alone is called "God" in a proper sense.[7] The reason for this is that the Father alone is "God from no one,"[8] "God who begot the Son,"[9] "the source of all godhead,"[10] "the fountain of goodness."[11]

These two meanings of "God," which were made clear beyond a doubt in the preceding chapters, must also be kept always in mind in these concluding reflections. Even here, our concern is always first of all with what lies behind the title "God the Father" and only then with what lies behind the "common" title "God"; first, therefore, with what the Father is, and only then with what the Son and Spirit or the "one God" is by derivation.[12]

1. A Double Perspective

Even though Augustine approached the question of God from different angles depending on his theological and pastoral concerns, he almost always adopted a double perspective. On the one hand, he made it clear that for him, God the Father, who with the Son and the Holy Spirit is one God, is in the most profound sense the unchangeable God, Being itself (*ipsum esse*). This basic insight was so important to him that he constantly returned to it even in his sermons to the people.[13] He owed this insight to the lengthy, painful process that is generally known as his "conversion," in which, having once been seized by the love of wisdom, he gradually came to the discovery of what truly is and thus to the conviction that the faith of his childhood could stand up even to the requirements of contemporary science.[14]

The *Confessions,* in which Augustine calls that "conversion" to mind in God's presence, are not, however, the only access to his youthful experience of God. In his early philosophical writings and in his later controversy with the Manichees, he deepened his understanding of what he had experienced down to the period in Milan. The *Confessions* are therefore to be regarded rather as the concluding evidence for the genesis of Augustine's idea of God. At the same time, however, the *Confessions* mark not only an end but also a beginning. As the major theological works in particular attest, the philosophically shaped picture of God acquired in the earlier years remained determinative in the period from 400 to 430. Not just in the time when he was searching, but also in the period of his theological maturity, God was for Augustine the unchangeable being. But later on, when he was beset by many other problems, he would not have held so unwaveringly to this central idea in the philosophical tradition of antiquity if he had not been convinced that God in God's very self had revealed to Moses on Sinai this truth of which the greatest philosophers were persuaded.[15]

It may even be claimed that in later years, as opportunity offered, Augustine further developed his conception of the unchangeably existing God or at least placed it in a new light. Thus, his study of the Church's doctrine of the Trinity led him to explain in great detail the essence of God, the fact that God is, what is proper to God,[16] and therefore God's simplicity as well.[17] At the same time, in these "exercises of the mind," he came to a more accurate grasp of the spirituality of God as compared with the interior life of human beings.[18] Furthermore, the study of the first chapters of Genesis, but also the debates with the Arians, were the occasions for his linking the unchangeableness of God more closely with God's eternity.[19] His explanations of the invisibility and omnipresence of God ran along the same lines. God is by nature invisible and appears only when and as God wills because God is unchangeable.[20] In these areas as elsewhere, Augustine did, however, try to base himself on the Bible; and he liked to cite 1 Timothy 1:17, which speaks of the immortal, invisible, and only God.[21] So too, God's "being everywhere in [God's] entirety" means God's separation from both changeable space and changeable time.[22]

Above all else, it was very important that in opposition to the Pelagians, the Bishop of Hippo should make clear in what sense God remains unchanged by the divine foreknowledge and forewilling. Augustine had himself to a large extent caused the Pelagians' resistance to his teaching on grace by his earlier explanations of the Letter to the Romans. Yet their obdurate reaction led him to reinforce the position he had taken in 397.[23] In the process, the ancient conception of supreme and unchangeable being was definitively raised to a voluntaristic and personal level. God therefore appears more clearly than before as eternal will or, better, as eternally loving.[24] In complete freedom and independence, God has not only called the whole of creation into existence but is able in the divine omnipotence to integrate even evil into the order of the divine justice and goodness. As God has foreseen and forewilled, sinners are justly damned while the just are rescued out of pure grace.[25] Even though it must be admitted that Augustine struggled with this conception more than with his other teachings and that he nevertheless endeavored to be there for all the faithful as their pastor, he did not succeed in bringing this doctrine into harmony with the Christian faith in its entirety.

Finally, we must not overlook his clashes, both the more public and the more private ones, with Roman paganism.[26] In these, Augustine emphasized chiefly the truth that God, as creator and as king of the heavenly city, enters into the historical struggle of the two loves, without thereby being changed.[27] In addition, he links his more philosophical ideas of the immutability, goodness, and omnipotence of the one "who is supremely creator" with the idea of creation from nothing.[28] In particular, in this kind of apologetic setting, he was able to show, in the light of his baptismal faith, the sense in which God, as wisdom and object of true love, must be the subject of the whole of philosophy. Accordingly, physics deals with wisdom as the cause of things; logic is concerned with wisdom as "trust in reasoning" *(fiducia ratiocinandi),* that is, as the trust that is the basis of all knowledge; and ethics shows that wisdom is the final good.[29] Augustine thus provided a further proof that in his view, the Christian faith in God does not contradict authentic ancient philosophy according to his simplified understanding of it.

On the other hand, Augustine never tires of proclaiming God in God's relation to us. In full continuity with the Bible, God is for him Lord and Father. As Lord, God is the creator of heaven and earth, as well as the one who directs all times. All creatures, spiritual and corporeal, but especially all human beings, are subject to God.[30] Like slaves, they belong to the one who as the real Lord has no need of them.[31] So, too, God is Father of all human beings, the God who in the divine goodness cares for every being. But God is also the common Father of all who believe in Christ; God accepts them as God's own children and leads them to their everlasting inheritance.

As the *Confessions* and, in addition, an early baptismal catechesis show, these functional conceptions characterized Augustine's picture of God from the outset. In his reflections on his own life's journey, he very frequently addresses God, as the psalmist does, as Lord and God, but also as a kind Father.[32] And for his catechumens, he coined the formula "God in power, Father in goodness."[33] The defense of the Old Testament against the Manichees likewise led him increasingly to emphasize the fact that God is at once the just Lord and the kindly Father.[34]

At the same time, there is no doubt that after 400, he significantly extended his understanding of the functional aspects of his picture of God. The controversy with the Arians gave him the opportunity, especially after 418, to define more closely the role of the eternal Word in creation and with it the divine activity in general.[35] Above all, it forced him to distinguish more clearly between the eternal sonship of Christ as the Son born of God and the divine filiation of believers as children by adoption through grace.[36] Thus, following the Nicene distinction between "by nature" and "by will," he gave clearer expression to the fact that God's action in creation and history is completely free. The dispute with the Pelagians, for its part, gave Augustine the opportunity of defining more precisely his conception of the Father as giver of all gifts in the orders of creation and salvation and thereby to distinguish more clearly between the grace of creation and the grace of redemption.[37]

Finally, anyone who wants to comprehend the way in which, from the beginning to the end of his seeking and his teaching, Augustine understood God's relationship to creation and history must not overlook the point that his ideas of God's lordship and fatherhood, which in their substance come from the Bible, bore the mark, to a greater or lesser extent, of his Roman environment.[38] By this I mean that the two principal aspects of "God in relation to us" according to Augustine correspond to what the Romans understood by the concept, fundamental in their thinking, of the "father of the household" *(pater familias)*.[39]

For the most part, Augustine simply presupposes the application of this idea to God, although he does at times speak explicitly of God as father of the household,[40] usually in connection with the parables of Jesus.[41] In addition, he uses the term, in a transferred sense, not only of God but also of Christ or of human beings who have a responsibility for the kingdom of God.[42] On the other hand, he does not fail to define what *pater familias* means: "master of the house."[43] This definition shows that Greek has no equivalent term for *pater familias.* Thus, when Augustine joins the Latin translators of the Bible and the Latin ecclesiastical writers in speaking of *pater familias,* he is thinking not only of the head of the household but also of the Roman father of the family, in whose eyes an attitude of dutiful respect was more important than the simple possession of control.[44]

The idea of "father of the household" has in fact two components: The head of the household has authority over the family—over wife, children, freedmen and women, and slaves. In addition, he has the power to issue commands *(imperium)*. His subjects, for their part, owe him obedience and submission. In return, the father of the household has a duty to take care *(diligentia, cura)* of the members of the family. He must look after them *(consulere)*. The members of the family show him a filial and grateful love *(pietas)*. This reciprocal relationship of duties and rights *(officium imperandi et oboediendi)*, which is to ensure harmony among the fellow members *(concordia cohabitantium)*, is present even in a home in which the head has no children; but it is only in a family with sons and daughters that it achieves its full form. In this case, the exercise of paternal authority and paternal attentiveness extends to the education of the children. Through instruction or discipline, the children are to be made capable of preserving the family property and thereby ensuring also the worship of the ancestors.[45] With these connections in mind, Augustine even says that the father of a household will look after only those sons who accept being educated and thus give their father a legitimate hope that the family inheritance will be preserved.[46]

The Romans, however, did not limit the concept of *pater familias* to the household and the preservation of domestic peace. They transferred it also to the common life of the state. Accordingly, a magistrate had paternal authority and was at the same time bound to exercise a paternal attentiveness. Furthermore, at the cosmic level, there was the "parent of all," the supreme godhead, which ruled over human beings and at the same time looked after them with loving care.[47] It is obviously in tune with this tradition that Augustine describes God as "emperor"[48] or "governor of the world."[49] In view of this, we understand better why in the first, introductory book of *The City of God,* he speaks of the family of God in connection with the divine education of the human race.[50] The ruler of the heavenly city is thus seen from the outset as its educator and father. Despite all his reservations when it came to the Roman state, even Augustine could not close his mind to the political categories of his time.

As we read the not very numerous but nonetheless important passages that develop the theme, it strikes us immediately that the concept of father of the household, which Augustine, following Varro, develops especially in his remarks on peace in the nineteenth book of *The City of God,*[51] is not simply applied to God but is also used in reinterpreting theological texts of the sacred Scriptures.[52] Following Proverbs 3:11f. and especially Hebrews 12:1-6, he develops the theme of the Father who chastises the Father's son out of love and thereby educates him for his everlasting inheritance.[53] In the process, he comes to the conclusion that one whom God does not chastise must fear not being loved by God.[54] In Augustine's view, this "law of the father" found its supreme application in the life and death of Jesus. By teaching God's own Son obedience in order to educate him as leader of the faith (see Hebrews 5:10), God showed how, in the final analysis, God meant to be understood as Lord

and Father. However, along with this paternal discipline which God applied to
God's own Son and which people today understand even less that the people
of Hippo and Carthage did, God lets them see that God intends to assert God's
all-transcendent greatness by means of God's still greater love.

2. The Tension between God in the Divine Self
   and God in Relation to Us

God who exists in the supreme degree and unchangeably—God who is
Lord and Father: this antithesis, which Augustine sees as fundamental, undoubtedly contains an immense tension. He does not try to avoid the dialectical challenge. He opens himself to it especially in sermons and writings in
which he explains the account of God's appearance to Moses on Horeb or at
least refers to the divine name that was revealed on that occasion.[55]
His main thoughts on the subject can best be brought together in connection with a sermon that he preached on Exodus 3 in 397 or perhaps as late as
412.[56] After briefly explaining the miracle of the burning bush[57] and then giving a somewhat more detailed answer to the question of who appeared
(Christ? or the Lord through an angel?),[58] the preacher turns to the two names
of God that are revealed to Moses.[59] When the angel or the Lord through an
angel answered Moses' question about God's name by saying, "I am who I
am; this is what you shall say to the children of Israel, 'He who is has sent me
to you,'" God was referring to the being of God, to God's name as the unchangeable one *(nomen incommutabilitatis).*[60] God meant by this answer to
say that God alone, who does not change, possesses true and genuine being.[61]
This implies that God is eternal[62] and therefore is in no sense created.[63] But
God did not give only the name that befits God in God's eternity *(nomen
aeternitatis);* God also deigned to take a name given in an act of mercy
(nomen misericordiae), and therefore God also revealed the divine self to
Moses as the God of Abraham, the God of Isaac, and the God of Jacob.
Augustine further distinguishes these two names as being a name for God
in God's self and a name for God in relation to us. "That name in [the divine
self], this one for us. For if [God] wanted to be only what [God] is for [God's
self], what would we be?"[64] It is a distinction very dear to him, as we can see
from other passages; he returns to it on more than one occasion.[65] At the same
time, however, he knows that it is very difficult to grasp the meaning of the
first name. Moses himself realized that in the words "I am who I am. He who
is has sent me," a very great deal was being said to humanity, but also that they
revealed an immense distance. He felt far removed from God and utterly unlike God. Therefore, the desire arose within him of seeing God as God is (Ex
33:13, 18). But when he surrendered his hope of understanding what God is
in the divine self, God rekindled his hope with the second name.

> When, therefore, [Moses] despaired as one so very unlike that (divine) excellence, (God) raised him from his despair because [God] saw him fearful. It is as though [God] were saying: "Because I said *I am who I am* and *He who is has sent me,* you realized what being means and, at the same time, you despaired of fully understanding it. Be hopeful, for *I am the God of Abraham, Isaac, and Jacob;* I am indeed what I am, I am being itself, I exist as identical with being, but in such a way as not to abandon humanity.[66]

In another passage, Augustine makes his point even more clearly: "Who can grasp that existence? Who can share it? Who will pant after it? Who will long for it? Who dare . . . think [they] can be in its presence? Weak mortals, do not despair! [God] says: *I am the God of Abraham and the God of Isaac and the God of Jacob.* You have heard what I am in myself; hear also what I am for your sake."[67]

He goes on to say in what sense God intends to draw nearer to humankind:

> This eternity, then, has called us, and the Word has burst forth from eternity. Eternity already was, the Word already was, but time was not yet. Why was time not yet? Because time, too, is something that is made. How was time made? *All things were made through him, and apart from him nothing was made.* O Word before time, through whom times were made! O Word born in time, even though [the Word] is eternal life, calling creatures of time and making them eternal![68]

Thus, through the incarnation of the Word, through Christ who was from the lineage of Abraham,[69] God made it possible for human beings to understand what God is. God's Word spoken in time is to become for them a Word for eternity.[70]

3. The Idea of God and Religious Knowledge

The tension between the essential name and the name revealed in mercy, between statements about God in the divine self and statements about God in relation to us, becomes fully intelligible, however, only when we view it in the context of Augustine's teaching on religious knowledge. Augustine himself clearly points us in this direction. On the one hand, he emphasizes on several occasions the difficulty and even the impossibility of understanding the essential name. He speaks of a "despair" in the presence of the wholly other God.[71] He cites Psalm 30:23: "I said in my ecstasy: I have been cast forth from the face of your eyes."[72] He underscores the great difficulty of attaining stability of heart and contemplation.[73] At the same time, he makes the name given in mercy the basis of hope,[74] regarding it as a condescension of God, as an easing of our condition,[75] and as a consolation.

When, in addition, he brings into play the theology of the incarnation that he derived from the Prologue of John, he gives us to understand that here again, as throughout his theology, the issue is understanding of the faith, the knowledge that is built on faith in Christ the incarnate Word; in other words, the issue is a faith that progresses to a deeper knowledge, or to "reason" in the Christian sense of the term. According to this understanding of faith, God in the divine condescension communicates God's own self even to simple believers; for them too, God is the God of the ancestors.[76] All who open themselves to the action of the Spirit succeed, as far as this is possible on earth, in understanding God more fully. Admittedly, they do not grasp God's essence, but they do understand that God is and is above all else. Even if they can only experience this in brief, happy moments, they nonetheless remain subject to God in humility and continue to hope for the full, everlasting vision of God.[77]

Moreover, as is clear especially from the eighth book of *The Trinity,* Augustine distinguishes between the knowledge of God as such and the knowledge of the Trinity. While Christians are able, even in the present world, to rise up, on the basis of their faith, to an at least momentary knowledge of the one God, they are unable in this life to know the "form of the Trinity" and are therefore all the more radically dependent on the hope of someday seeing God as God is.[78]

This conception of faith progressing toward knowledge includes what is meant by the terms "negative" and "positive" theology.[79] In fact, Augustine constantly endeavors to scale the heights of God along a negative path. Convinced that human beings have a clearer understanding of what God is not than of what God is,[80] he seeks to rise up to God by a kind of process of exclusion. Even though this negative theology denies that anything it meets in its ascent through creation is God, it nonetheless leads to the supreme Being. It makes it possible for human beings to find God, to glimpse God's presence, and to be united with God in love.[81] On the other side of the coin, God is also the goal of a positive theology in which God is equated with a clear, unambiguous content: with the "is" of truth, goodness, beauty, with the "Today."[82] Consequently, Augustine also repeatedly undertakes to climb the ladder of the degrees of perfection in creation to the goodness and beauty of the creator.[83]

But the contrast between the name given in mercy and the essential name, a contrast that to some extent corresponds to the advance from faith to knowledge, raises another problem that is not to be taken lightly. For it can hardly be denied that Augustine gives preference to a rational knowledge that is based on faith and to some extent anticipates the vision of the eternal God. He himself takes very seriously the exhortation he gives to young Dioscorus, "Have a great love of understanding."[84] He repeatedly explains that spiritual persons, awakened as it were by faith, know their only God and Lord in their hearts. Readers are therefore inclined to assume that for Augustine himself, the communication of the name given in mercy is simply a way to religious knowledge in the proper sense, a basis for the purifying faith that leads persons to enter into themselves and thus to know the truth. On the basis of their faith in the action of God in history, they would simply enter into themselves and there come to know the eternal being of God, insofar as this is possible on earth.[85]

But if we look more closely, we can see that all the soteriological statements associated with the name given in mercy have to do not only with the act of faith but with its content as well. The action of God in the history of Israel, in the life of Jesus, and in the existence of the Church, which is spreading throughout the world in keeping with the promises, is not limited to awakening in human beings a faith that simply purifies their hearts and thereby enables them to know the truth. God's action also reveals a God whom human beings cannot find simply by entering into their hearts.[86] It opens the eyes of faith to a God who in complete freedom has made everything out of nothing.[87] It shows God to be an inscrutable will that chooses what it wills to choose.[88] But the same action also makes God known as the loving power that overcomes evil not only in the life of the individual but in the history of humanity as a whole.[89] Above all, it "commends" the love of the humble God.[90]

In this way, a synthesis of those opposed tendencies that threaten to tear apart the Augustinian picture of God is also effected.[91] As for the composer of the account of the divine appearance on Horeb, so for Augustine: God was at once a revealed and a hidden God. In his Neoplatonic approach, he had understood God as completely Light, as true and light-filled being. In an anti-Manichean and even more in an anti-Pelagian perspective, he experienced God as inscrutable, fearsome darkness. But precisely in this negative vision, he understood that in the final analysis God revealed God's innermost self only in the humiliation of the cross of Christ[92] and that only in God's humility did God give the final and complete proof that God is love.[93] In Augustine's eyes, the death of Jesus was the most convincing proof that behind the impenetrable mystery of the irreversible divine will there was "God is love."

Summary

"Through Christ as human being to Christ as God." In this terse formula, for which Augustine had an unmistakable predilection, almost his entire teaching on Christ, the Lord and redeemer, is summed up. Even the repetition of the name Christ is already noteworthy since it indicates the great importance this biblical name had in the eyes of the Bishop of Hippo. He also knew, of course, the messianic meaning of "Christ," as used especially in the Gospel of John. But like Paul, he used "Christ" first and foremost as a proper name. It is obviously also due to the Apostle that Augustine speaks so frequently of "Christ" and in such varied contexts.

The formula cited also gives clear expression to the fundamental structure of Augustinian Christology in the strict sense of this word. It brings out the Christological dualism which he regards as fundamental and according to which Christ is God and a human being. This fundamental bipartite statement does not simply reflect the Western tradition, the representatives of which, beginning with Tertullian, never tired of distinguishing God and human being in Christ, a distinction that was even more emphasized under the influence of the Arian controversy.[1] The Christology based on this distinction also characterizes the religious development of Augustine himself as reflected in the *Confessions,* especially in the seventh book. Before his baptism, he had connected Christ with the idea of beatifying truth that he had taken over from Cicero and, consequently, had identified Christ with the *nous* of the Neoplatonic tradition. At the same time, however, he had not forgotten the Christ of his childhood faith and came to realize ever more fully, especially in his disputes with the Manichees, that this Christ truly became a human being. It is in this area that he came, in the course of time, to see the gulf separating Christianity from the philosophy of that age.

Although the formula "Through Christ as human being to Christ as God" shows primarily the basic dualistic tendency of Augustinian Christology, it nonetheless also includes the unity of Christ. For in naming Christ as both God and human being, it makes Christ the sole subject, the one who is at the same time God and human being. In this respect, the formula corresponds to the second article of the creed, which Augustine so often explained to his faithful and which says, "I believe in Jesus Christ, the only Son of God." In his catechetical instructions and on other occasions, he also gave a technical formulation of the unity of subject, speaking first of the unity of person and then also of "one person." In doing so, he followed both the traditional person-exegesis and the philosophical anthropology of his time; out of these presuppositions, however, he not only developed a notable doctrine on the unity of the person of Christ but also drew up the rules to be followed in speaking of the Lord and Savior.

"Through Christ as human being to Christ as God" is, however, not primarily a Christological formula, that is, a summarizing statement about the person of Christ. The main point that finds expression in it is that the salvation of human beings has its basis in Christ. If one adopts this soteriological perspective, one is immediately struck by the "through" and the "to." The two prepositions make it unambiguously clear that Christ is both the gateway and the goal. This is to say, in the language of the Fourth Gospel, that Christ is the way leading to truth and life (see John 14:6). With his Neoplatonic partners in dialogue in mind, Augustine expresses the same thought by speaking of Christ as the way and the homeland. Accordingly, the one Christ is, as human being, the way of universal salvation and as God, the eternal homeland. But Augustine can also place the emphasis on the "through." Then, as he constantly repeats, following 1 Timothy 2:5, Christ as human being becomes the mediator between God and humanity.

It was precisely this predilection for the mediatorship of Christ which urgently required him to move beyond the seemingly Christocentric framework of the formula. In the latter, Christ is undoubtedly seen as the homeland. But, as the contexts in which the formula is used often suggest, Christ is this as the Word that speaks of God and reveals the almighty Father from whom the Word itself has its eternal origin. This is already to say that Christ can be the way only because he is the Son whom God not only begot but sent into this world because in the divine love, God wanted to offer sinful humanity this one way back to God. In other words, in Christ, God is reconciling the world to the divine self, as Augustine, following Paul, repeatedly insists.[2]

All this applies to the individual human being, as Augustine explains especially in his early writings and his studies of the grace of Christ, but also, to some extent, in the *Expositions of the Psalms*. But it likewise applies to the whole of humanity, to the "one human being," a theme that Augustine also develops in the explanations of the psalms, as well as in the anti-Donatist writings and, above all in *The City of God*. At both levels, Christ is both way and homeland. But he is these because God is the beginning and the end.[3] Accordingly, the way of faith, which God opens up by the divine grace, leads both individuals and the Church, in which the heavenly city is already present, to the eternal community where, after the kingdom has been restored to God, God is all in all.

Augustine's teaching on God shows how legitimate it is to understand the seemingly Christocentric formula in a theological and even a theocentric way. Augustine does not speak of God only when there is a question of the divinity of Christ. At least as often, if not oftener, he uses the word "God" in the sense it has in the first article of the creed. In fact, he uses it in two senses: he uses it in a strict sense of the God of Israel and the Father of Jesus Christ, the "almighty Father," while in a "general" sense or with a "common application," he uses the name "God" for "Jesus Christ, the only Son of God" and for the Holy Spirit and the entire Trinity. In view of this, we are justified in saying that everything he associates with the word "God" is attributed first of all to the Father, who is "God from no one," and only in a derived sense to the Son and the Spirit and to the Trinity as such. His first and most spontaneous usage is in accordance with the Bible and especially with the New Testament way of speaking of *theos,* but also with the liturgy, as the eucharistic prayer in particular makes clear. His further and more deliberate way of speaking follows rather the Christian tradition as this developed especially in the fourth century during the Arian turmoil.

It is in this twofold perspective of "God in the proper sense" and "God in a common sense" that everything which Augustine preached to his faithful about God is to be understood and everything which he further developed, in collaboration with his friends and adversaries, in his theological thought. That twofold perspective can be seen first of all in a distinction that runs through all of his writings: the distinction between God in the divine self and God in relation to us. By "God in [the divine self]," he undoubtedly understands the supreme, immutable, and eternal being: pure existence. When he speaks of God in this more philosophical way, there are good grounds for thinking that he very often has in mind God in an anti-Arian sense, that is, the sense in which the Father and the Son and the Holy Spirit are described as one God. But even in that context, there is something that must not be overlooked: when he is following the Old Testament and especially when he has the first article of the creed in mind, the word "God" refers first (directly, *in recto*) to God the almighty Father and Creator of heaven and earth.

When it comes to "God for us," the question is somewhat different. Inasmuch as God created the world and now not only governs it "naturally" but "graciously" changes it by intervening in history, God reveals (according to Augustine) the divine power and fatherhood. Meanwhile, Lord and Father are titles which the Bible uses for the God of Israel and the God of Jesus Christ. In the New Testament, the first of the two titles is certainly reserved for the Son. But when Augustine adopts the language of the Old Testament and especially that of the psalms, he will also speak of "the Lord our God" and mean the one whom Christians confess first in their profession of faith.

At the same time, "Father," both in the sense of Creator and in the sense of Father of believers, is used by Augustine mostly as a title of the first person of the Trinity. In principle, one could also give the name "Father" to the Son and to the Holy Spirit, and even to the entire Trinity, inasmuch as the divine action in relation to what is outside of God, including creation and adoption, is common to all three persons. But in his use of the name "Father," Augustine sticks very close to the New Testament. This is even the perspective that governs his exegesis of Exodus 3:14. By "God of the Fathers," who is identical with "He who is," he means in principle "God, the Father almighty."

Since Augustine's teaching on "God in [the divine self]" and "God for us" is fully intelligible only in light of this conception of the connection between faith and knowledge, we must expect that the distinction between God in the proper sense and God in a common sense will apply even here. Christians believe in God who created the world out of nothing and who reveals the divine self in history, which is entirely oriented to Christ; on the basis of this purifying faith, they rise to a direct, even if momentary, knowledge of God or at least to a firm hope of one day seeing God as God is. But while this Christian faith embraces the Father, the Son, and the Holy Spirit and therefore the Trinity, which is one God, rational understanding of the faith is limited during this earthly life to God as such, that is, to what can be said properly of the Father and commonly also of the Son and the Spirit, and even of the entire Trinity.[4]

In light of these considerations on God and religious knowledge, we understand better the sense in which the seemingly Christocentric formula "through Christ as human being to Christ as God" is to be understood as at bottom theocentric. That is, it is not speaking of an abstract divinity but presupposes that "God is the Father." At least in passages strongly influenced by the language of the Bible, the Father is seen as one who draws to Christ and thereby opens the way of faith, and the homeland is identified with the "God in all" of Paul. As the exegesis of 2 Corinthians 5:19 in particular shows, Augustine is certainly not always consistent. He is often inclined to follow the anti-Arian tradition and understand by "God" the entire Trinity or the godhead, which works in the human Christ.[5] But by and large, he thinks predominantly of the Father, the "God who is from no one," as the beginning and end of "through Christ to God."

This fundamental observation implies that there can be no radical opposition between the grace of God and the grace of Christ, between creation and redemption. God, the almighty Father, who with utter freedom created the world through the Word is also the God who out of completely unmerited kindness has redeemed sinful humanity through the incarnate Word.[6]

This might doubtless be understood as meaning that the grace of Christ is in the service of God's freely bestowed favor and brings its plans to fulfillment against all opposition. The grace of Christ would then prove to be "the grace of God through our Lord Jesus Christ," that is, the gracious action of God, present in Christ and restoring creation.

On the other hand, it is only insofar as the grace of Christ opens up new horizons that the depths of the grace of God reveal themselves fully. It is only the mystery of Christ that makes it known that the omnipotent God has created everything from nothing through the Word and in the power of the Spirit.[7] Above all, it is only the humility of the crucified Lord that reveals (or "commends," as Augustine likes to say) in a unique way that the grace of God has its origin in a love which is God's very self. The extent to which Augustine himself is interested in the elevation of the order of creation by the order of redemption (or we might say, with the Easter *Exultet,* interested in the "happy fault") is made clear in his reflections, taken to some extent from Ambrose, on the relationship between nature and grace, to wit, while God "governs" creation "naturally" through the rational causes that are part of the created order, it is through "causes" hidden in the divine self that God intervenes "graciously" in the human history of salvation and damnation.[8] It was only from sacred history that Augustine could gain this profound insight. His great defense, *The City of God,* and especially its profound reflections on miracles, leave no doubt on this point.[9]

A further point emerges from what has been said. If one is determined to contrast the grace of Christ with the grace of God, one cannot achieve this simply by linking the latter to the God of the philosophers and the former to the God of faith. In response to such a view, it must be said first of all that even in regard to the order of redemption, the insight of faith goes beyond a simple acceptance of the gospel. Above all, the point must be stressed that the grace of God, insofar as this refers to the completely free act of creating, can be fully understood only in the light of faith.[10] This means that the purification of the human heart for knowledge of eternal truth is not the sole function of the faith that works through love. Rather, this faith makes it possible for the human mind to gain a fuller insight: that the one who is called "God" in the proper sense stands at the beginning and end of all things.

I need not emphasize once again that these concluding reflections may not be denied a certain contemporary relevance. On the one hand, it should have become clear that behind Augustinian theocentrism, as it has been presented here, there is a theology of the Trinity which may no longer be contrasted as a Western theology of unity to an Eastern theology of triuneness. Once it is clear that Augustine regards God the almighty Father—whom Christians confess in first place and to whom they address their solemn prayer; the God who, as Augustine understands God, is properly God because "[God] is from no one"—as the beginning and end of creation and history, there is no longer any basis for presenting his theology of the Trinity as one which, unlike that of the Greeks, takes unity rather than triuneness as its point of departure.[11]

In addition to this result, which is significant for the dialogue with the Orthodox Churches, there is another that is perhaps even more important. If we pay closer attention to the expositions in which Augustine, following closely the Bible and the liturgy, speaks of the mystery of love that God has made known to us in the humility of the crucified Lord, we will no longer be satisfied with a piety in which the "Trinity which is one God" remains simply an ineffable mystery of which we can speak, at best, in the traditional forms set down in the feast of the Trinity. Rather, while cultivating a very simple attitude of faith that is nourished by the psalms and Paul and John, we will experience the greatness of the Christian vocation, namely, that we are called to be children of the Lord our God, along with Jesus Christ, the only Son of the Father, in the love that is poured out in our hearts by the Holy Spirit.

Abbreviations

ASE	*Annali di storia dell'esegesi*
Aug	*Augustinianum*
AugLex	C. Mayer (ed.), *Augustinus-Lexikon*. Basel, 1986ff.
AugMag	*Augustinus Magister*. Congrès international Augustinien. Paris 21–24 Sept. 1954. 3 vols. Paris, 1954–55.
BA	Bibliothèque Augustinienne
Bettenson	St. Augustine. *The City of God*. Trans. H. Bettenson. New York: Viking Penguin Inc., 1984. Cited as: Bettenson with page number.
BLE	*Bulletin de littérature ecclésiastique*
CCL	Corpus Christianorum Scriptorum Latinorum
Chadwick	St. Augustine. *Confessions*. Trans. H. Chadwick. New York: Oxford University Press, 1991. Cited as: Chadwick with page number.
CSEL	Corpus Scriptorum Latinorum Ecclesiasticorum
DSp	*Dictionnaire de spiritualité*
DTC	*Dictionnaire de théologie catholique*
EECh	A. Di Berardino (ed.). *Encyclopedia of the Early Church*. 2 vols. New York: Oxford University Press, 1992.
HDG	M. Schmaus, et al. (eds.). *Handbuch der Dogmengeschichte*.
Hill	St. Augustine. *Sermons*. 10 vols. Brooklyn and Hyde Park, NY: New City Press, 1990–95. Cited as: Hill with volume and page number.
Hill	St. Augustine. *The Trinity*. Brooklyn: New City Press, 1991. Cited as: Hill with page number.
NBA	Nuova Biblioteca Agostiniana
NRT	*Nouvelle revue théologique*
OCA	Orientalia Christiana Analecta
RAC	*Reallexikon für Antike und Christentum*
RAE	*Revista agustiniana de espiritualidad*
REAug	*Revue des études augustiniennes*
RechAug	*Recherches augustiniennes*
RELat	*Revue des études latines*
RSR	*Recherches de science religieuse*
RThom	*Revue thomiste*
RTAM	*Recherches de théologie ancienne et médiévale*

RUnivOtt	*Revue de l'Université d'Ottowa*
TLZ	*Theologische Literaturzeitung*
TRE	*Theologische Realenzyklopädie*
TRev	*Theologische Revue*
TTZ	*Trierer theologische Zeitschrift*
ZKG	*Zeitschrift für Kirchengeschichte*
ZKT	*Zeitschrift für katholische Theologie*
ZRG	*Zeitschrift für Religions- und Geistesgeschichte*
WissWeis	*Wissenschaft und Weisheit*

Notes

General Introduction

1. All scriptural translations and references are from the Vulgate, unless otherwise indicated.

2. B. Aland, *"Cogitare Deum* in den *Confessiones* Augustins," *Pietas: Festschrift B. Kötting* (Münster, 1980) 93–104.

3. Ibid., 93f.

4. Ibid., 95.

5. A similar question arises in connection with the problem of the relationship in Augustine between knowledge of the Trinity and knowledge of the incarnation, inasmuch as there are those who presuppose that Augustine derived the triadic structure in God from the Neoplatonism of his time. On this subject, see P. Du Roy, *L'intelligence de la foi en la Trinité selon saint Augustin* (Paris, 1966), and the criticisms of his thesis on the priority of the doctrine of the Trinity, as voiced by G. Madec on several occasions and by J. Verhees, "Augustins Trinitätsverständnis in den Schriften aus Cassiciacum," *RechAug* 10 (1975) 45–75. See also J. Plagnieux, "L'influence de la lutte antipélagienne sur le *De Trinitate* ou le christocentrisme de saint Augustin," *AugMag* (Paris, 1954) 2:817–826, since in this study of the anti-Pelagian (i.e., soteriological) revision of the *De Trinitate*, the question of the relation between Trinity and incarnation is also raised.

6. I report Aland's solution in a simplified form since I cannot go into all its nuances.

7. See especially Aland, *"Cogitare Deum,"* 95–98, with her discussion of *Conf.* 7.10 and 7.17f.

8. In a reprint of his article "Gnade und Erkenntnis bei Augustin," *Zum Augustinus-Gespräch der Gegenwart,* ed. C. Andresen (Darmstadt, 1981) 2:43-125, especially 124, K. Lorenz sticks to his opinion. Even if one accepts his criticisms of Aland's article, the discussion to which her work has given rise makes it possible to clarify the subject of the present book.

9. A. von Harnack, *Augustins "Confessionen"* (Giessen, 1988 [rpt. from *Reden und Aufsätze,* vol. 1, Giessen, 1904]) 51–79.

10. A. von Harnack, *Lehrbuch der Dogmengeschichte,* 4th ed., vol. 3: *Die Entwickelung des kirchlichen Dogmas* (Tübingen, 1910; rpt., Darmstadt, 1964) 4f.: "Augustine as Reformer of Christian Piety and Teacher of the Church."

11. Pascal, *Pensées,* trans. A. J. Krailsheimer (Baltimore: Penguin Classics, 1966) no. 913, p. 309.

12. See especially *Serm.* 7.7. Various dates have been proposed for this sermon; see P.-P. Verbraken, *Etudes critiques sur les sermons authentiques de saint Augustin* (Steenbrugge, 1976) 54.

13. See B. Studer, *La riflessione teologica nella Chiesa imperiale (sec. IV e V)* (Rome, 1989) 117ff.

14. See *Trin.* 1.1–2.4; 8.2.3–3.5.

15. The distinction is explicitly made in *Serm.* 26, which is assigned to 417–419. See especially 26.7: "So apart from that grace by which human nature was established—which is common to Christians and pagans alike—the greater grace is this, not that we were created human beings through the Word, but that through the Word made flesh we were made believers" (Hill 2:96). See also the *Adnotationes in Iob* (ca. 400): "the grace of creation"; *En. Ps.* 135.4 (414–418): out of divine goodness God created us, out of mercy God freed us from our wretched state; *Praed. sanct.* 5.10 (418–419): thanks to the "gift *(gratia)* of nature" all have the ability to believe and love, but it is only by the "grace that makes human beings believers" *(gratia fidelium)* that they can in fact believe and love. On the more undifferentiated concept of grace as it appeared before 397, see K. Flasch, *Die Logik des Schreckens: Augustinus von Hippo, Die Gnadenlehre von 397* (Mainz, 1990) 276f.

16. G. Madec, *La patrie et la voie: Le Christ dans la vie et la pensée de saint Augustin,* Jésus et Jésus-Christ 36 (Paris, 1989).

17. On this question, see B. Studer, *"Credo in Deum Patrem omnipotentem:* Zum Gottesbegriff des heiligen Augustinus," *Dominus Salvator: Studien zur Christologie und Exegese der Kirchenväter,* Studia Anselmiana 107 (Rome, 1992) 401–430, especially 410–418. Originally in *Studia Ephemeridis "Augustinianum"* 24 (1987) 163–188.

Part I, Introduction

1. See A. von Harnack, *Lehrbuch der Dogmengeschichte,* 4th ed., vol. 2: *Die Entwickelung des kirchlichen Dogmas,* pt. 1 (Tübingen, 1909; rpt., Darmstadt, 1964) 179–184; 358–361; F. Loofs, *Leitfaden zum Studium der Dogmengeschichte,* 6th ed. (Tübingen, 1959) 285ff.; R. Seeberg, *Lehrbuch der Dogmengeschichte,* 3rd ed., vol 2: *Die Dogmenbildung in der Alten Kirche* (1923; rpt. Darmstadt, 1953) 424–429, 559ff.

2. Harnack, *Dogmengeschichte,* vol 3: *Die Entwickelung des kirchlichen Dogmas,* pts. 2–3 (Tübingen, 1910; rpt., Darmstadt, 1964) 59–92, 126–134, 233f. On this theme, see W. Geerlings, *Christus Exemplum: Studien zur Christologie und Christusverkündigung Augustins,* Tübinger Theologische Studien 13 (Mainz, 1978) 12–20.

3. See especially Seeberg, *Dogmengeschichte,* 251.

4. On Harnack, see E. P. Meijering, *Theologische Urteile über die Dogmengeschichte: Ritschls Einfluss auf von Harnack.* (Leiden, 1978) 34–50.

5. O. Scheel, *Die Anschauung Augustins über Christi Person und Werk unter besonderer Berücksichtigung ihrer verschiedenen Entwicklungsstufen und ihrer dogmengeschichtlichen Stellung* (Tübingen, 1901) 464.

6. E. Mühlenberg, "Augustin—Die Schöpferische Grundlage der Tradition," *Handbuch der Dogmen- und Theologiegeschichte,* ed. C. Andresen (Göttingen, 1982) 1:406-463.

There is even less in J. Pelikan, *The Christian Tradition: A History of the Development of Doctrine,* vol. 1: *The Emergence of the Catholic Tradition (100–600)* (Chicago, 1971). A more profitable work is J. N. D. Kelly, *Early Christian Doctrines,* 2nd ed. (London, 1960), especially 390–395 (teaching on redemption), 412–417 (mystical body of Christ).

7. See J. Liébaert, *Christologie: Von der Apostolische Zeit bis zum Konzil von Chalkedon (451),* HDG, vol. 3, fasc. 1a (Freiburg, 1965) 97f.; A. Grillmeier, *Jesus Christus im Glauben der Kirche* (Freiburg, 1979) 1:597–604.

8. Geerlings, *Christus Exemplum.*

9. B. Studer, with the collaboration of B. Daley, *Soteriologie: In der Schrift und Patristik,* HDG, vol. 3, fasc. 2 (Freiburg, 1978) 156–174 ("The Revelation of the Love of the Humble God according to Augustine"). See also B. Studer, *Trinity and Incarnation: The Faith of the Early Church,* trans. M. Westerhoff, ed. A. Louth (Collegeville, 1993) 167–185, where the doctrine of the Trinity is related to the theme.

10. On Harnack, see Meijering, *Theologische Urteile,* 76–80.

11. G. Madec, *La patrie et la voie: Le Christ dans la vie et la pensée de saint Augustin,* Jésus et Jésus-Christ 36 (Paris, 1989).

12. On this subject, see Geerlings, "Die Christologie Augustins: Zum Stand der Forschung," *Internationales Symposion über den Stand der Augustinus-Forschung,* ed. C. Mayer and K. H. Chelius (Würzburg, 1989) 219–230, and, earlier, his *Christus Exemplum,* 1–9. For assessment of modern histories of dogma generally, see W. D. Hauschild, "Dogmengeschichtsschreibung," *TRE* 9 (1982) 116–125; and the several contributions, especially those of B. Lohse and L. Scheffczyk in *Dogmengeschichte und katholische Theologie,* ed. W. Löser et al. (Würzburg, 1985).

13. See above, at the beginning of this Introduction, and the detailed analysis of his work in Geerlings, "Die Christologie Augustins," 220–225.

14. Scheel, *Die Anschauung Augustins,* vol. 7.

15. Ibid., 460.

16. Ibid., 76f. On this point, see Loofs, *Dogmengeschichte,* 283ff.

17. Scheel, *Die Anschauung Augustins,* 77f.

18. Ibid., 78.

19. Ibid., 562, with the author's concluding judgment. See Geerlings, "Die Christologie Augustins," 224f., and Loofs, *Dogmengeschichte,* 286f., 319–325.

20. Harnack, *Dogmengeschichte,* 3:123-134. On this criticism, see Geerlings, "Die Christologie Augustins," 221.

21. Harnack, *Dogmengeschichte,* 3:127f., 235.

22. See ibid., 3:128, with the critique of Scheel. See Loofs, *Dogmengeschichte,* 316f.

23. Harnack, *Dogmengeschichte,* 3:132f.

24. See ibid., 3:223ff., 233f., and what Loofs has to say, *Dogmengeschichte,* 317ff.

25. Seeberg, *Dogmengeschichte,* 250f.

26. Ibid., 253.

27. Ibid., 424–428.

28. O. Du Roy, *L'intelligence de la foi en la Trinité selon saint Augustin* (Paris, 1966). On this work see Madec, *La patrie et la voie,* 47f.

29. See especially the works of P. Courcelle. On the subject, see J. T. Newton, *Neoplatonism and Augustine's Doctrine of the Person and Work of Christ,* dissertation (Atlanta, 1969); W. Mallard, "The Incarnation in Augustine's Conversion," *RechAug* 15 (1980) 80–98.

30. T. van Bavel, *Recherches sur la christologie de saint Augustin,* Paradosis 10 (Fribourg, 1954). *

31. See van Bavel, *Recherches,* especially 57–73. The accuracy of this claim is demonstrated in my studies, *"Consubstantialis Patri—consubstantialis matri:* Une antithèse christologique chez Léon le Grand," *REAug* 18 (1972) 87–115, especially 112ff., and *"Una persona in Christo:* Ein augustinisches Thema bei Leo dem Grossen," *Aug* 15 (1985) 453–487.

32. Van Bavel, *Recherches,* 119–145: "La vie affective du Christ."

33. Ibid., 149–175.

34. On this point, see P. Agaësse, "Humanité du Christ I/B, 3: S. Augustin," *DSp* 7/1 (1969) 1043–1053.

35. See E. Mersch, *The Whole Christ: The Development of the Doctrine of the Mystical Body in Scripture and Tradition,* trans. J. R. Kelly (Milwaukee, 1938; French original: Louvain, 1933); H. U. von Balthasar, *Augustinus: Das Antlitz der Kirche,* 2nd ed. (Einsiedeln, 1956); E. Franz, *Totus Christus: Studien über Christus und die Kirche bei Augustin,* dissertation in the Evangelical faculty (Bonn, 1956); R. Bernard, "La prédestination du Christ total selon s. Augustin," *RechAug* 3 (1965) 1–58; P. Borgomeo, *L'église de ce temps dans la prédication de saint Augustin* (Paris, 1972).

36. But see Seeberg, *Dogmengeschichte,* 463–472.

37. See Loofs, *Dogmengeschichte,* 330–334, and especially Seeberg, *Dogmengeschichte,* 472–487.

38. See Geerlings, *Christus Exemplum,* 7; and J. A. Jungmann, *The Place of Christ in Liturgical Prayer,* trans. A. Peeler (Staten Island, 1965; German original: Münster, 1925).

39. See especially K. Baus, "Die Stellung Christi im Beten des hl. Augustinus," *TTZ* 63 (1954) 321–339; K. Baus, "Ostern in der Verkündigung des hl. Augustinus," *Festschrift J. A. Jungmann* (Freiburg, 1959) 57–67. See also B. Studer, "Zum *Triduum Sacrum* bei Augustin von Hippo," Congresso Internazionale di Liturgia, *La celebrazione del Triduo pasquale: Anamnesis e mimesis,* Studia Anselmiana 102 (Rome, 1990) 273–286, with the literature on *Ep.* 55, and W. Marreves, *The Ascension of Christ in the Works of Saint Augustine* (Ottawa, 1967).

40. See below.

41. On Augustinian exegesis, see G. Strauss, *Schriftgebrauch, Schriftauslegung und Schriftbeweis bei Augustin,* Beiträge zur Geschichte der biblischen Hermeneutik 1 (Tübingen, 1959).

42. See M. Comeau, *S. Augustin, exégète du quatrième évangile* (Paris, 1930), along with *RSR* 40 (1951–1952) 80–89.

43. See M. Réveillaud, "Le Christ-Homme, tête de l'Eglise," *RechAug* 5 (1968) 67–94.

44. BA, vols. 71–73B. See also R. P. Hardy, *Actualité de la révélation divine: Une étude des "Tractatus in Ioannis evangelium" de saint Augustin,* Théologie historique 28 (Paris, 1974).

45. A. Verwilghen, *Christologie et spiritualité selon saint Augustin: L'hymne aux Philippiens,* Théologie historique 72 (Paris, 1985). See Geerlings, "Die Christologie Augustins," 227.

46. P.C.J. Eijkenboom, *Het Christus-Medicusmotief in de preken van sint Augustinus* (Assen, 1960); M. F. Berrouard in BA 71:854f. with bibliography.

47. T. van Bavel, "L'humanité du Christ comme *lac parvulorum* et comme *via* dans la spiritualité de saint Augustin," *Augustiniana* 7 (1957) 245–281.

48. P.C.J. Eijkenboom, *"Christus Redemptor* in the Sermons of St. Augustine," *Festschrift C. Mohrmann* (Utrecht, 1963) 233–239.

49. S. Poque, *"Christus mercator,"* *RSR* 48 (1960) 564–577.

50. S. Poque, "Le Christ *iurisperitus* et la procédure *per rescriptum* dans la prédication d'Augustin d'Hippone," *RHDF* 57 (1979) 331–344.

51. B. Muzungu, *Le médiateur entre Dieu et les hommes selon saint Augustin* (Fribourg, 1973); G. Remy, *Le Christ médiateur dans l'oeuvre de saint Augustin* (Paris, 1979); P. Ciarlantini, *"Mediator:* Paganismo y Cristianismo en *De civitate Dei* VIII,12—XI,2 de San Augustín," *RAE* 14 (1983) 9–62; G. Remy, "La théologie de la médiation selon s. Augustin: Son actualité," *RThom* 91 (1991) 580–623.

52. B. Studer, "Jésus-Christ, notre justice, selon saint Augustin," *RechAug* 15 (1980) 99–143.

53. See C. Mohrmann, *Etudes sur le latin des chrétiens* (Rome, 1961–1965); S. Poque, *Le langage symbolique dans la prédication d'Augustin d'Hippone* (Paris, 1984).

54. See now the balanced presentation in A. Adam, *Lehrbuch der Dogmengeschichte,* vol. 1: *Die Zeit der Alten Kirche* (Gütersloh, 1965) 284–290 ("Christologie und Soteriologie").

55. Some typical treatments of soteriology in isolation: J. Tixeront, *History of Dogmas,* 5th ed., vol. 2: *From St. Athanasius to St. Augustine (318–430),* trans. H. L. B. (St. Louis, 1914) 373–381, and J. Rivière, *Le dogme de la rédemption chez s. Augustin* (Paris, 1933). In contrast, see Geerlings, *Christus Exemplum,* especially 9ff.; B. Studer, *Soteriologie,* especially 58f. In the overview of the history of dogma which I give in my *Trinity and Incarnation,* I have considered the doctrine of the Trinity as well; see especially 13–19. And see E. TeSelle, *Augustine the Theologian* (New York, 1970) 132–182.

56. G. Bavaud, "Un thème augustinien, le mystère de l'incarnation à la lumière de la distinction entre le verbe intérieur et le verbe proféré," *REAug* 9 (1963) 95–101; E. Bailleux, "La christologie de saint Augustin dans le *De Trinitate,*" *RechAug* 7 (1971) 219–243; J. Verhees, "Heiliger Geist und Inkarnation in der Theologie des Augustinus von Hippo," *REAug* 22 (1976) 234–253.

57. See, for example, A. Sage, "De la grâce du Christ, modèle et principe de la grâce," *REAug* 7 (1961) 17–34. On this subject, see the introductions and notes in BA, vols. 21–24.

58. O. Schaffner, *Christliche Demut: Des heiligen Augustinus Lehre von der Humilitas* (Würzburg, 1959).

59. O. Brabant, *Le Christ, centre et source de la vie morale chez saint Augustin* (Gembloux, 1971).

60. See Geerlings, "Die Christologie Augustins," 229, with the reference to his *Christus Exemplum,* 241–258; See also J. Ries, "Jésus-Christ dans la religion de Mani," *Augustiniana* 14 (1964) 437–444; E. Feldmann, "Christus-Frömmigkeit des Manijünger," *Pietas: Festschrift B. Kötting* (Münster, 1980) 196–216.

61. See Madec, *La patrie et la voie,* with his now generally accepted nuances.

62. See Geerlings, "Die Christologie Augustins," 228.

63. K. H. Lütcke, *"Auctoritas" bei Augustin* (Stuttgart, 1968).

64. C. P. Mayer, *Die Zeichen in der geistigen Entwicklung und in der Theologie Augustins,* vols. 1–2 (Würzburg, 1969, 1974).

65. P. de Luis Vizcaíno, *Los hechos de Jesús en la predicación de Agustín* (Rome, 1983).

66. H. Drobner, *Person-Exegese und Christologie bei Augustinus* (Leiden, 1986).

67. B. Studer, *"Sacramentum* et *Exemplum* chez saint Augustin," *RechAug* 10 (1975) 87–141; Studer, *"Delectare et prodesse:* Zu einem Schlüsselwort der patristischen Exegese," *Mémorial J. Gribomont* (Rome, 1988) 555–581, especially 557–579.

68. Harnack, *Dogmengeschichte,* 3:99.

Part I, Chapter 1

1. See *Serm.* 4.1; 144.1.1; 184.1.1; *Io. ev. tr.* 3.1; 14.1; 17.1; 79.1.

2. See the details in *Thesaurus Augustinianus,* Series A — Formae (= Cetedoc; Turnhout, 1989) 91: *Christus* (singular), 20,607 times; 307: *Jesus,* 4,645 times. The newly discovered sermons would also have to be taken into account.

3. See *Civ.* 18.23.1; On this, see BA 72:727f.

4. See C. Eichenseer, *Das Symbolum apostolicum beim heiligen Augustinus: Mit Berücksichtigung des dogmengeschichtlichen Zusammenhangs,* Kirchengeschichtliche Quellen und Studien 4 (St. Ottilien, 1960) 204–210. G. Madec, *La patrie et la voie: Le Christ dans la vie et la pensée de saint Augustin,* Jésus et Jésus-Christ 36 (Paris, 1989) 138ff.

5. *En. Ps.* 103.3.13.

6. See *Cons. ev.* 1.13.20; *Civ.* 17.6.2, with 1 Kgs 24:7; *Nupt. et conc.* 1.32.37; *En. Ps.* 108.26; *Fide invis.* 3.5. On the subject, see BA 23:708ff., with the reference to E. Lamirande, "L'idée d'onction dans l'ecclésiologie de saint Augustin," *RUnivOtt* 35 (1965) 103*–126*.

7. See *C. litt. Pet.* 2.104.239: "For Christ himself derives his name from 'chrism,' that is, from anointing. The Hebrews call this 'messiah,' a word that has its cognate in the Punic language, as do many other and indeed almost all Hebrew words." See *C. Faust.* 5.1.

8. *Trin.* 15.26.46.

9. *En. Ps.* 44.19. See *En. Ps.* 104.4.18.

10. *Serm.* 229.6 (Hill 8:232). See *Trin.* 13.10.14.; *Civ.* 22.22.4; *Serm.* 174.6.7.

11. *Ep. Io. tr.* 3.6. See *Civ.* 16.38.2; *C. Faust.* 12.26.

12. See *En. Ps.* 108.26, where Christ is explained symbolically as "lamb" and "lion."

13. *Io. ev. tr.* 73.3.

14. See *En. Ps.* 26.2.2; 44.19; 149.6.

15. *Civ.* 17.10. See *En. Ps.* 26.2.2; 104.10. And see Madec, *La patrie et la voie,* 100f.

16. *En. Ps.* 26.2.2. See *Civ.* 20.10: "We call all Christians 'Christs' in virtue of their sacramental anointing" (Bettenson, 919); *Io. ev. tr.* 21.8; *Ep.* 76.2f. On this, see Madec, *La patrie et la voie,* 101, note 35, with further texts. It is to be noted, however, that catechumens, too, are called "Christs" and are no longer pagans, since they believe in Christ. See *En. Ps.* 32.1.29; *Serm.* 17.6.6: "A heathen is one who does not believe in Christ" (Hill 1:370); 150.3.4 (the catechumens have placed themselves under Christ's name: see *Serm.* 302.4.3f.) and therefore belong to Christ (*Serm.* 130.4; 140.3). On the subject, see E. Lamirande, "La signification de *christianus* dans la théologie de S. Augustin et la tradition ancienne," *REAug* 9 (1963) 221–234; but he does not take into account the sociological opposition between "Christians" and "Gentiles/pagans."

17. See *Io. ev. tr.* 7.13; 15.27.

18. See Eichenseer, *Das Symbolum apostolicum,* 200–235, especially 204, with the reference to Christ as a proper name in Paul; T. van Bavel, *Recherches sur la christologie de saint Augustin,* Paradosis 10 (Fribourg, 1964) 69.

19. *Io. ev. tr.* 19.15. In the same context, the preacher speaks also of "Son of God" and "Human One" *(filius hominis).* See *Io. ev. tr.* 36.2; 78.2f.; *Ep. Io. tr.* 10.8; *Serm.* 242.2.

20. *Io. ev. tr.* 3.3f.: "Who is the physician? Our Lord Jesus Christ. Who is the Lord Jesus Christ? He who was seen even by those who crucified him. He who was arrested, struck, flogged, smeared with spittle, crowned with thorns, hung on a cross; who died, was

pierced by a lance, taken down from the cross, laid in the tomb. He is the very Lord Jesus Christ; he is clearly the Lord, and in his totality he is the physician of our wounds. Is he not this in his totality? He is indeed, but what the Jews saw is not the whole of him; that is not the whole of Christ. What is, then? *In the beginning was the Word.* In what beginning? *And the Word was with God.* What kind of Word? *And the Word was God."* See other passages cited in van Bavel, *Recherches,* 15 and 67: *En. Ps.* 9.35; *Div. qu.* 75.2; *Serm.* 214.3; *C. Faust.* 12.35; *Ep.* 164.514; *Io. ev. tr.* 43.9.

21. See, for example, *Io. ev. tr.* 8.2; *En. Ps.* 70.2.10; *Io. ev. tr.* 19.15.

22. See *Serm.* 213.2.2; 214.5ff.; 215.3ff.

23. See *Serm.* 113A.5.

24. See, for example, *Serm.* 12.1.5.

25. *Serm.* 194.1.1: "Christ is born: God from the Father, [human being] from his mother" (Hill 6:53).

26. *Io. ev. tr.,* 78.1; 78.2f.; *Ep.* 187.3.10.

27. See *Serm.* 130.3; *Agon.* 20.22.

28. See *Serm.* 214.6; 215.7; *Ep. Io. tr.* 10.7f.; *Serm.* 123.1.1; 160.2f.; 238.2.

29. *Ep.* 140.4.12: "Thus, the number of Persons is not increased when the human being is added to the Word to form the one Christ." See *En Ps.* 44.19: "Christ was made"; *C. Max.* 1.19: "Christ appeared in the human being"; *Serm.* 265B.2; *En Ps.* 30.1.3: "[Christ] came."

30. *Io. ev. tr.* 108.5: "In whom the true [Human One, *filius hominis*] was sanctified from the beginning of his creation, when the Word was made flesh, because the Word and the human being became one person. At that time, then, the [human being] sanctified [himself] in himself, that is, the human himself in the Word itself, because the one Christ is Word and human being, sanctifying the human being in the Word."

31. See van Bavel, *Recherches,* 110–118.

32. *En. Ps.* 90.2.1; *Serm.* 341.1.1. See Madec, *La patrie et la voie,* 141.

33. *En. Ps.* 100.3: "before us, for us, in us."

34. See *C. Faust.* 12.32f.

35. See *En. Ps.* 33.2.7; *Io. ev. tr.* 27.11; *En. Ps.* 33.10: "Christ was carried in his own hands, when, entrusting his body, he said: *This is my body."*

36. *Trin.* 13.19.24. On this point see van Bavel, *Recherches,* 23.

37. See *Beata v.; Sol.; Imm. an.; Dial.; Gramm.; Rhet.*

38. *Conf.* 9.4.7.

39. *Ep.* 6.1. Compare *Conf.* 7.19.25, and see Madec, *La patrie et la voie,* 75–78.

40. *Acad.,* 3.20.43.

41. *Mag.* 11.38. See *Ord.* 1.10.28; *Lib. arb.* (eight times).

42. Especially *Doct. chr.* 4.

43. Ibid., 1.11.11–13.12.

44. Ibid., 1.14.13–21.19.

45. See especially *Serm.* 52. Also, *Serm.* 117–120 (on John 1:1-3); *Serm.* 126–127; 135; 139ff.; *Ep.* 170; 171A; 173A.

46. *C. Max.* 1.1; 3.6f.; 11; 14.5-8; etc.

47. *Agon.* 22.24–33.35.

48. *Ver. rel.* 4; 6–9; 24f.; 31ff.

49. See *C. Litt. Pet.* 1; *Brevic.; Emer.; Bapt.* 1–6.

50. *Perf. iust.,* with Rom 7:25; *Nat. et grat.; Gest. Pel.; Spir. et litt.*

51. *C. Iul.* 3.6.13–16.30; 3.19.36–21.45; 4.1.1–2.13; 4.8.41–16.83.

52. See *Serm.* 187; 222; 223; 223E-K, as well as *Serm.* 3; 11; 16; 20; 22A; 29; 29A; 33; 35; 42; 48; 69; 70; 107A–110; 148; 151; 159; 207; 208; 223; 282.

53. See *En. Ps.* 108.1; 138.2; 142.2.

54. *En. Ps.* 14; 15; 23.10 (only Rom 8:39); 30.1; 93.1-30. "Christ" is also missing from a whole series of sections of *En. Ps.* 118 (1, 5, 11 and 14).

55. *En. Ps.* 22 and 24.

56. See *En. Ps.* 105.5; 118.20.1.

57. *En. Ps.* 118.32.5.

58. See *En. Ps.* 26.2.11: "rock"; 29.2.2f. (against Apollinarism); 105.36.

59. See *En. Ps.* 138.2, and 143.3, with the theory of this exegesis.

60. See *En. Ps.* 61; 139; 140; 142.

61. See *En. Ps.* 30.2.1; 33.1 and 2; 36.2; 59; 63; 68.1 and 2; 69.2; 81; 84; 85; 87; 108; 138; 143.

62. See especially *En. Ps.* 39.1; 57; 73; 79; 147.18ff.

63. *En. Ps.* 21; 44; 109.

64. See *En. Ps.* 3.1; 82.2; 137.15f.; 140.24; 144.2.

65. *Io. ev. tr.* 70 (trinitarian); 85; 90.

66. *Div. qu. 83* 25; 43–56; 70; 73f.

67. *Civ.* 7f.; 11f.; 19.

68. *Civ.* 6.

69. *Ep.* 1–14, except for 6.1; 37f.; 41–45; 57; 59; 65; 70f.; 74; 77; 110f.; 113ff.; 207; 210; 229; 239ff.; 246; 249; 267.

70. *Ench.* 1.6; 18.68. See 33.132.

71. *Conf.* 1.11.17: "I was already a believer. . . . prevent my believing in Christ" (Chadwick, 14).

72. *Conf.* 7.5.7: "There was a firm place in my heart for the faith, within the Catholic Church, in your Christ, 'our Lord and Saviour' (2 Pet. 2:20). In many respects this faith was still unformed. . . ." (Chadwick, 116).

73. *Conf.* 7.18.24, with 1 Tim 2:5; Rom 9:5; and John 14:6.

74. The preceding survey is not meant to explain the so-called conversion of Augustine but to show the variety of ways in which he uses the word "Christ" in the *Confessions.*

75. *Exp. prop. Rm.; Ep. Rm. inch.; Exp. Gal.; Serm.* 152–178, except for 159, 171ff., and 178; *Div. qu.* 66–76; *Simpl.* 1.1.1 (Rom 7:7-25); *Simpl.* 1.2 (Rom 9:10-29); *Ep.* 149; 194; *Doct. chr.* 3 and 4 (exegetical examples).

76. See. *Serm.* 16A; 23; 26; 54; 64A; 94A (with 2 Tim 3:12); 301.

77. *En. Ps.* 38; 42 (except for the introduction); 110; 114; etc.

78. See *Mor.* (six citations of seven passages); *Vera rel.* (Pauline language in nine passages); *Mend.* (with 1 Cor 15:15); *Op. mon.* (except for 25.33 to the end, citations almost exclusively from Paul); *Trin.* 5–7; *Cont.* (citations from Paul explaining the antithesis of flesh and spirit).

79. See BA 23:770-778.

80. See *Gest. Pel.* 6.20; 8.21; 15.61f.

81. *Pecc. mer.* 1.17.40-52.

82. *Spir. et litt.* 1.17.3.

83. See A. Verwilghen, *Christologie et spiritualité selon saint Augustin: L'hymne aux Philippiens,* Théologie historique 72 (Paris, 1985) 71f., 83.

84. See *Trin.* 12f.; 15; *Ench.* 9.31; 10.42.

85. *Civ.* 19–22, especially 20.15-20; 22.12-20.

86. *Ep.* 55, especially 2.3–6.11; 14.25f.

87. *Conf.* 11.8.10–9.11 (on Gen 1:1); 9.1.1 (where Ps 18:15 is addressed to Christ); 9.8.17 (citing Ps 5:8: "the branch of your Christ").

88. See *Serm.* 71; 78; 89; 122f.; 130; 229N; 279 (conversion of Paul); 287–293 (on John the Baptist); 295–299C (on Peter; "to deny Christ," frequently); 308A. In addition, see *S. dom. m.*

89. See *Div. qu.* ("Christ" 50 times); *Serm.* 133; 149; 183 (where 1 John 4:2 triggers an antiheretical excursus).

90. See above, p. 18.

91. *Ep. Rm. inch.* 4; *Serm.* 78.5.

92. See *C. Faust.* 19.11: "showing nothing else in those [books] but Christ prophesied," and *Civ.* 18.32: "I should be inclined to take it as standing for the profundity of the inspired Scriptures in which Christ is prophesied" (Bettenson, 801); *C. Sec.* 21; *Cat. rud.* 21.38; 27.53; *En. Ps.* 58.1.22; *Serm.* 201.3.

93. See *Serm.* 4–8; 16B; 17ff.; 45f.

94. *Civ.* 17.8-19.

95. See A. Corticelli in NBA 25: xix–xl.

96. See, for example, *En. Ps.* 54.1; 55.1; 58.1f.; 96.2f.; 142.1ff. (David-Goliath = Christ-devil); 144.2.

97. See especially *En. Ps.* 37.6; 90.12.2; 138.2; 142.2f. On this point, see Madec, *La patrie et la voie,* 179ff.

98. *En. Ps.* 84.9; 118.13.1; 131.27.

99. Ibid., 66.5.

100. Ibid., 118.9.2.

101. Ibid., 118.21.2.

102. Ibid., 26.2.11, and frequently.

103. See, for example, *En. Ps.* 37; 40; 58 (anti-Jewish in tone); 81; 84; 87; 103.3; 130; 138; 140; 143; 147.18-28.

104. Ibid., 2.44; 108, especially 18; 109.

105. See *C. Faust.* 12.33 (with Col 1:26f.), and, in addition, *Ep.* 149.2.24: "to know the mystery of God, which is Christ," and *En. Ps.* 140.1, where Augustine asks, with the Apostle (Col 4:2-4), for the disclosure of the mystery of Christ. On this subject, see NBA 22:483, n. 11, on *Ep.* 149; Madec, *La patrie et la voie,* 115, 127.

106. *C. Faust.* 22.94. See *Ep. Io. tr.* 2.1.

107. *Serm.* 46.14.33 (Hill 2:285). See *En. Ps.* 17.2; 59.1; *Serm.* 6.6.8; *C. Faust.* 12.27; *Gn. litt.* 1.1.1; *Ep.* 137.415f.

108. *Ep.* 149.2; 149.3; *En. Ps.* 103.1.9.

109. *En. Ps.* 98.1.

110. *Cat. rud.* 4.8.

111. *C. Adim.* 13.3. See *Io. ev. tr.* 4.2.

112. *C. Adim.* 9.1. See *Serm.* 2.5. But Augustine does not like to call Christ himself a "prophet." See *Io. ev. tr.* 24.7. On the subject, see BA 72:779f.

113. *Io. ev. tr.* 24.2.

114. See *Serm.* 53A.2.6; 57.13.13; 59.2.3; 132.1.1; 136.6 in the context; 134.5.6; 135.1.2; 144.1.1; 184.4.7; *En. Ps.* 109.3; etc.

115. See *Serm.* 130.1; *C. Faust.* 22.46.66; *Ep.* 137.4.15.

116. See also the passages that deal in general with symbolic speech about Christ: *Serm.* 4.24.25; *En. Ps.* 103.1.13; 103.3.22f.

117. See especially *En. Ps.* 140.1. On the subject, see *Cat. rud.* 8.12–9.13; *En. Ps.* 46.1; 103.2.1; 118.22.7; *C. Faust.* 12.12; 12.39f.

118. See *Gn. adv. Man.* 2.3.7.

119. See *Io. ev. tr.* 9.3; *Serm.* 2.2.2; *Util cred.* 9; *Gn. adv. Man.* 1.33; *En. Ps.* 7.1; *C. Faust.* 12.4; *Io. ev. tr.* 24.5; etc.

120. See *Serm. dom. m.* 1.40; 1.41; 1.78; 2.25.

121. See *F. et op.* 6.9; 17.31; 26.48.

122. *Serm.* 144.2.2 (with an explanation of the expression); 150.3.3; *Lib. arb.* 1.3.7; *Ep. Io. tr.* 1.12; *Ep.* 82.2.8-12 (several times); *Ep.* 157.2.6; 217.1.3; and often.

123. *En. Ps.* 48.2.1.

124. See, for example, *En. Ps.* 32/2.2.13; 48.2.2; *Ep. Io. tr.* 5.7; *Serm.* 301A.8.

125. *Serm.* 301A.8.

126. *Ep. Io. tr.* 7.6.

127. *Serm.* 228B.3 (Hill 6:262).

128. *Serm.* 229B.2 (Hill 6:274).

129. *Ep.* 98.9.

130. See Eichenseer, *Das Symbolum apostolicum,* 200–235; Madec, *La patrie et la voie,* 197, n. 12.

131. *Serm.* 22.1; 52.4.8-13; 110.4.4; 113A.7; 121.5; 214.7; *Cat. rud.* 27.54; *Ep. Io. tr.* 1.4, and especially 4.7.

132. *Ep.* 78.

133. *Ep.* 82.

134. *Ep.* 86. See *Ep.* 97; 99; 130; 153; 155; 157; 167; 186; 188; 191.2; 193; 200; 206; 214f.; 215A; 217; 220; 229; 231; 244.2; 248; 261; 264f.; 266; 267; 21*; 19*.

135. *Ep.* 72.2.3.

136. *Ep.* 100.1.

137. *Ep.* 63.4.

138. *Ep.* 26.1; 40.6.9; 48.1; 122.1; 134.2; 209.9; 213.5; 214.2 (with 1 Cor 1:10). Add *Ep.* 133.1.

139. *Ep.* 96.3. See also *Ep.* 51.5; 53.3.7; 99.3; 127.9; 132; 139.4; 148.5.18; 153.6.26: "Dear son, may you live happily in Christ"; 224.3; 256; 10*, but especially *Ep.* 64.4, and 137.5.20.

140. *Ep.* 228.

141. See *Ep.* 25.75; 94; and 121 among the letters of Augustine.

142. See *Ep.* 258 and 243. On this, see Madec, *La patrie et la voie,* 222–228.

143. See further on.

144. See *Trin.* 3, prol. 1: "By the part of bishop which I play in Christ's service" (Hill, 127); *Ep.* 130.1.1: "I should have paid my debt and served your pious desire in the love of Christ."

145. See *B. vid.* 1.1; 3.4; 11.12; etc.

146. *Op. mon.* 25.33–33.41. See *En. Ps.* 132.6: "soldiers of Christ, soldiers of the devil" (and see *Serm.* 4.36 for the concept); *Ep.* 123.11: "servants of God, monks hastening to the perfection of the commandments of Christ"; *Ep.* 243.1: "Novice of Christ"; *Ep.* 130.16.29ff.: "widow of Christ" and "family of Christ"; *Ep.* 48: "rest in Christ," "fragrance of Christ due to a holy way of life"; *Ep.* 211.16: "emitting the good fragrance of Christ by a holy way of life"; as well as *Ep.* 27.2; *Ep.* 26.5: "yoke of Christ."

147. *Serm.* 49.11 (Hill 2:340).

148. *Serm.* 53.1 (Hill 3:66).

149. *Serm.* 299F.2; 299E.2.

150. *Serm.* 274.1 (Hill 8:23).

151. See Madec, *La patrie et la voie,* 227f.

152. See *Conf.,* 3.6.

153. *Ep.* 236.2.

154. *Retr.* 2.7.1.

155. See *Serm.* 16.8ff.; *C. ep. Man.* 8.9; *C. Faust.* 29 and 30.

156. *Gn. adv. Man.* 2.37. See *Serm.* 12.12; *Ep.* 236.2; *Agon.* 22.24; *C. Faust.* 5.2-5.

157. *C. Adim.* 21, with Gal 3:13.

158. *Cont.* 10.24f., especially: "How can there be truth in their teaching when they preach that the flesh of Christ was illusory? How could there have been no wickedness in Christ if he was guilty of such a great deception? . . . In every sin against Christ concupiscence is doubtless at work; but when [Christ] who heals all our illnesses has brought the Church to the promised healing of illness, then there will be no slightest stain or wrinkle in any of [Christ's] members."

159. *Serm.* 182.2.2 (Hill 5:332). See *Serm.* 183.1.1.

160. *Serm.* 182.3.4. See *C. Faust.* 11.1-8, with 1 Cor 5:16f.

161. *Serm.* 182.6.6: "Believe, acknowledge that Christ has come in the flesh, that he received what he was not, and did not lose what he was" (Hill 5:335).

162. The theme of "prophecy of Christ" is not found, however, only in writings formally directed against the Manichees. Augustine took it up elsewhere, as, for example, in *Civ.;* see 20.1-2. But in the defense presented here, he moderated to some extent the allegorical exegesis developed against the Manichees and took a more critical attitude toward the Christological interpretation of the Old Testament; see *Civ.* 20.31.1, and see BA 37:783.

163. See also *Gn. adv. Man.* 2.27.

164. *C. Faust.* 12.2-6, with 2 Cor 3:15f., and Luke 22:44. See also *C. Faust.* 16.27-31.

165. See the teaching on the "ages" *(aetates)* in *C. Faust.* 12.8.

166. See *C. Faust.* 13.4: ". . . that entire people and entire kingdom became a prophet of Christ and the Christian kingdom"; 12.23. On the subject, see Madec, *La patrie et la voie,* 245f.

167. *C. Faust.* 12.7: "But who can. . . . enumerate all the oracles of the Hebrew prophets concerning our Lord and Savior Jesus Christ, since everything contained in those books is spoken either about [Christ] or for [Christ's] sake?" See 12.22; 12.27; 16.9; *C. Adim.* 12.5.

168. See especially *C. Faust.* 12.9-13, with the comparison of Cain to the unbelieving Jews.

169. *C. Faust.* 12.6-36.

170. See *C. Faust.* 22.24; 22.40; 22.46: "All these, then, speak of Christ: the head that has already ascended to heaven and this body of [Christ] that labors to the end on earth"; *C. Adim.* 16.2; *C. Sec.* 21; *F. invis.* 5.8; 7.10.

171. *C. Faust.* 12.29; 12.37.

172. *C. Faust.* 12.14: "Who is not moved to seek and understand Christ in those books, even omitting those passages which require longer explanation, although there is greater sweetness in contemplating what is derived from more obscure texts?"

173. *C. Faust.* 12.39.

174. Ibid., 12.40.

175. Ibid., 13.1; see, earlier, 12.45f.

176. See ibid., 13.7; 13.10; 13.23.

177. Ibid., 13.14: "When this pagan sees that in these and similar testimonies of the prophets predictions were made and have now been fulfilled regarding persecution by kings and peoples, the faith of kings and peoples, the destruction of idols, the blindness of the Jews, the evidence of codexes preserved by them, the madness of heretics, the excellence of the holy Church of true and authentic Christians, what would this pagan find more worthy of belief than those prophets, and whom should this one choose to believe when it comes to the divinity of Christ?" See also 13.7, with the most important prophecies.

178. *C. Faust.* 13.15.

179. Ibid., 13.2.

180. See ibid., 12.45, with Rom 10:14f.; 13.5; 13.17. On the subject, see *F. invis.* 3.5: "They are greatly deceived who think that we believe in Christ without any proofs of him. For what proofs are clearer than the things we see predicted and fulfilled?"

181. *C. Faust.* 12.46.

182. Ibid., 13.14.

183. Ibid., 13.18.

184. Ibid., 13.15.

185. Ibid., 13.4; 16.9.

186. Ibid., 13.4ff.

187. Ibid., 33.9: "I briefly exhort, you who are held fast by so impious and detestable an error, that if you wish to follow the authority of the Scriptures as preferable to every other, you would follow it in the form in which it has been preserved, commended, and made clearly known throughout the world, coming down from the time of Christ present on earth, through the ministry of the apostles and the indisputable succession of bishops in their sees, to the present time. For there you will see the obscurities even of the Old Testament explained and its prophecies fulfilled."

188. But see ibid., 13.5 (citing John 5:39f.; 8:18; 10:38; Luke 16:29, 31); and *C. Faust.* 13.16. See *C. Faust.* 28.2: "the Church begun by Christ and carried on by the apostles."

189. See *C. Faust.* 13.1.

190. *C. Adim.* 9.1; 13.2.

191. See 2 Cor 3:15f. in *En. Ps.* 7.1; *Util. cred.* 3.9; *Gn. adv. Man.* 1.33; see also *Serm.* 2.2.

192. *Util. cred.* 14.32. See ibid., 14:31 (even the heretics demanded faith in Christ).

193. Ibid., 15.33.

194. See Madec, *La patrie et la voie,* 248–253.

195. *C. Faust.* 12.46.

196. See M.-F. Berrouard, "La permanence à travers le temps de la foi dans le Christ selon saint Augustin," *Signum pietatis: Festschrift C. P. Mayer* (Würzburg, 1989) 303–324; Madec, *La patrie et la voie,* 255, with *C. Faust.* 16.28 and 22.84.

197. See, for example, *C. Adim.,* in which Augustine speaks of "Jesus" fifteen times and "Christ" thirty-nine times.

198. See Madec, *La patrie et la voie,* 28–31 (bibliography); W. Geerlings, *Christus Exemplum: Studien zur Christologie und Christusverkündigung Augustins,* Tübinger Theologische Studien 13 (Mainz, 1978) 241–258.

199. See *C. Fel.* 1; *C. Sec.* 25; *C. ep. Man.* 5–8. In addition, see E. Feldmann, *Die epistula fundamenti der nordafrikanischen Manichäer* (Altenberge, 1987) 24ff.

200. See *C. Faust.* 20.12; *En. Ps.* 140.10-12: "He, they say, is Christ who is crucified throughout the world. In the gospel, I learned of Christ the Savior; but you in your books are the saviors of Christ. Obviously, you blaspheme against Christ and therefore are not to be saved by Christ." See Feldmann, *Die epistula fundamenti,* 61f. See also *En. Ps.* 95.15; 37.6.

201. See *C. Fort.* 16ff. On this, see Feldmann, *Die epistula fundamenti,* 97ff.

202. Geerlings, *Christus Exemplum,* 249.

203. *C. Faust.* 20.2. See a similar confession in *C. Sec.* 1, which speaks of "the firstborn king of all lights." There are a number of references to Christ in *C. Sec.*

204. See *Conf.* 3.4.8; 7.9.13.

205. See, for example, *Serm.* 105.6.8–8.11; 113A; 196.4.4; 296.5.6–10.11; *En. Ps.* 101.2.7; 136.9f.; *Exc. urb.* 8.9 (Christ as model for all who suffer). On the subject, see F. van der Meer, *Augustine the Bishop: Church and Society at the Dawn of the Middle Ages,* trans. B. Battershaw and G. R. Lamb (New York: Sheed & Ward, 1961; rev. ed., New York: Harper Torchbooks, 1965) 46–75.

206. See, for example, *En. Ps.* 40, especially 9; 141.

207. See F. Dolbeau, "Nouveaux sermons de saint Augustin pour la conversion des païens et des donatistes," *REAug* 37 (1991) 37–78, especially 58–77, with the text of *Serm. Mainz* 61: "a sermon of St. Augustine when pagans came in." See also *Serm. Mainz* 60 (Dolbeau 42–52).

208. *Ep.* 137. See *Ep.* 135, where Augustine speaks not of Christ but of Christianity (*christianitas*).

209. *Ep.* 118.2.12.

210. *Ep.* 118.3.21: "From this we see that even the philosophers of the Platonic breed, once they have changed a few things which Christian teaching rejects, ought to bend their necks devoutly to the one unconquered king, Christ, and recognize that the Word of God, clothed in human nature, who commands and is believed, is the Word which they feared even to utter."

211. *Ep.* 118.4.23.

212. *Ep.* 118.5.33.

213. *Ep.* 233; 234.3; 235.1. See Madec, *La patrie et la voie,* 280f.

214. *Ep.* 102.2-7, 8-15, 30-37.

215. *Ep.* 232 (ca. 400), especially 2; see *Ep.* 235.1.

216. *Civ.* 1.1.

217. See especially *Civ.* 2.1-4.

218. See ibid., 12.21; 22.5, 9f.

219. See ibid., especially 15.26f.; 16.41.

220. Ibid., 21.20-25.

221. Ibid., 16.

222. Ibid., 17.

223. Ibid., 20.1-20.

224. Ibid., 22.12-20.

225. See ibid., 1.1; 1.10; 2.29.1; 19.22f.(where "Christianity" *[christianismus]* also occurs in a citation from Porphyry); *Ep.* 91.10 ("Christians," "pagans"); *Serm.* 105.8.11; *Serm.* 196.4.4 ("You're Christians, you're members of Christ" [Hill 6:62]); *Serm.* 296.7.8 ("pagans," "Christians," "Christ"); *En. Ps.* 40.14; ibid., 101.2.7 ("pagans," "Christians," "Christ"); ibid., 138.9 (same).

226. See *Civ.* 1.7: "This is to be attributed to the name of Christ and the influence of Christianity" (Bettenson, 13)

227. See *Civ.* 2.21: "But true justice is found only in that commonwealth whose founder and ruler is Christ. . . . 'Glorious things are said about you, City of God'" (Bettenson, 75); 1.35; 15.8; 15.20.1; 17.4.2; 17.15; 20.11 (with the opposition between "city of God" and "city of the devil").

228. *Civ.* 10.29.2 (Bettenson, 416); see the entire context. See also *Civ.* 9.20 (demons); 13.1.

229. *En. Ps.* 141.9.

230. *Civ.* 10, especially 10.6.

231. Ibid., 3.31; 5.22; *Vera rel.* 3.3; *Ep.* 118.3.21; see *Civ.* 2.3.

232. *Civ.* 1.1; 1.7; 12.21; *Serm.* 113A.11.13; *Serm.* 105.6.7; *Serm.* 296.6.7. See Madec, *La patrie et la voie,* 283ff.

233. See *Civ.* 11.3; 13.21; 15.57. On the point, see *Cat. rud.* 6.10 (5).

234. *Civ.* 7.32; compare 22.5: the belief, everywhere in the world, in the resurrection of Christ as proof of Christianity and its hope of everlasting life.

235. See *Civ.* 10.32.1.

236. See *Civ.* 10.32.3: "Porphyry, however, says that the universal way for the soul's salvation has never come to his knowledge in his study of history. Yet what could be found more striking than this historical record, which has taken possession of the whole world by its towering authority; or what more worthy of belief, seeing that in this record the events of the past are so narrated as to be also prophecies of the future? Many of these prophecies we see to have been fulfilled, and we confidently expect the fulfillment of the rest" (Bettenson, 424). See *Civ.* 11.1, and B. Studer, "Zum Aufbau von Augustins *De civitate Dei,*" *Mélanges T. J. van Bavel* (Leuven, 1990) 937–951.

237. See especially *Cons. ev.* 1.7.11.

238. See, for example, ibid., 1.10.15f.

239. Ibid., 1.10.15.

240. Ibid., 1.15.23.

241. Ibid., 1.16.24.

242. Ibid., 1.31.47.

243. See ibid., 1.16.24; 1.26.40; and, above all, 1.33.51.

244. See ibid., 1.30.47.

245. See ibid., 1.35.53f.

246. See *Conf.* 7.5.7: "faith . . . in your Christ. . . . in many respects . . . still unformed" (Chadwick, 116).

247. Ibid., 7.18.24f.

248. See especially the later *In Joannis evangelium tractatus* (20–22; 55–124).

249. See, for example, *En. Ps.* 29.2.2f.; 80.13f.

250. See *Serm.* 37.12.17 (citing Gal 3:27); 136 (on John 9); 139 (on John 10:30); 140 (on John 12:44-50); 183 (on 1 John 4:2).

251. *F. et sumb.; Serm.* 212–216; *Ench.* 10.34–12.41.

252. See *Conl. Max.; C. Max.; C. s. Arrian.*

253. See *Ep.* 219, and Madec, *La patrie et la voie,* 234–237.

254. *Haer.* 49–55; *Serm.* 92.33; *Persev.* 24.66; etc. See the anti-Arian excursus in *Praed. sanct.* 15.30f., as well as the exposition of the Apollinarist errors in *Div. qu.* 83.80. For the complete extent of the dogmatic range, see van Bavel, *Recherches,* where the various

Christological themes are systematically presented with the central texts; to this add the summary of this exposition in A. Grillmeier, *Jesus Christus im Glauben der Kirche,* vol. 1: *Von der Apostolischen Zeit bis zum Konzil von Chalkedon (451)* (Freiburg, 1979) 594–604. See further the general index of the Maurists in PL 46:144-148.

255. See the properly dogmatic books, *Trin.* 5–7, where the name of Christ occurs rarely.

256. See van Bavel, *Recherches,* 69, with the texts adduced (58–67); Verwilghen, *Christologie,* 148ff.

257. *Serm.* 92.3.3: *Homo verus, Deus verus: Deus et homo totus Christus. Haec est catholica fides.* See *En. Ps.* 80.13: "Our Christ, just recently a human being, but God ever-lasting"; 84:9; 80:5: "One Christ, God and human being"; *Serm.* 37.12.17; 217.1: "The Lord Jesus Christ, who listens to us with the Father, was also quite ready to pray for us to the Father. . . . Christ, you see, is [a human being] and God; he prays as [a human], he gives what he prays for as God" (Hill 6:177); 123.3.3; 142.7.7; 174.1.1; 175.3.3; 293.7; 261.6.7.

258. *C. Faust.* 23.5. See ibid., 2.4 (against the myth of the Son of the Primal Human); 5.4; *Serm.* 121.5; 196.3.3; 214.6; *Cat. rud.* 17.19f.; *Ench.* 35.10: "The one Son of God is likewise the Human One *[hominis filius]*; the unique [Human One] is likewise the Son of God; there are not two sons of God, one God and one a human being, but one Son; God without beginning, human being with a certain beginning; our Lord Jesus Christ"; *C. s. Arrian.* 11.9. See Hilary, *Trin.* 10.19.

259. See *Serm.* 194.1.1; *En. Ps.* 54.20; 123.2; *C. Max.* 2.18.1f.

260. *Serm.* 44.3.6; 184.2.3; 189.4.4; 195.2.2; 196.1.1.

261. See *C. Sec.* 5: "therefore, since the divine oracles attest [Christ] to be both only-begotten and first-born: only-begotten because he has no brothers or sisters; first-born, be-cause he has brothers and sisters . . ." (with the relevant references to the Bible; see *C. Sec.* 7).

262. See *C. Faust.* 3.3; *Serm.* 183.4.5.

263. *C. s. Arrian.,* 11.9; *C. Max.* 1.5; *Ench.* 35.10.

264. See *Io. ev. tr.* 99.1: "One person consisting of two substances, one divine and one human"; *Serm.* 130.3; *Trin.* 13.17.22; *Ench.* 12.38; *Serm.* 294.9.9: ". . . to indicate one person in both natures" (Hill 8:186); *Ep.* 140.4.10; *C. s. Arrian.* 8.6; *Persev.* 23.67.

265. See, for example, *Io. ev. tr.* 18.2: "Who, then is Christ? (I am speaking to Catholics, for you have indeed believed.) He is not the Word only nor flesh only, but the Word made flesh in order to dwell among us"; 183.4.5: "[Christ] emptied himself and took the form of a slave in such a way that he did not lose the form of God. The form of a slave came, the form of God did not depart. That is what it means to confess that Christ came in the flesh."

266. See Verwilghen, *Christologie,* 61–96.

267. See, for example, *Serm.* 117.2-5; 119.3.3; 120.2f.; 188.1.1; *Io. ev. tr.* 1.8f.; 23.8.

268. See *Ep.* 164.7.19. The subject will be taken up further on.

269. See already in *Div. qu.* 69.1: "The rule of the Catholic faith is that when statements are made in the Scriptures to the effect that [Christ] is less than the Father, they are to be understood as applying to the human being; but when statements are made showing that [Christ] is equal, they are to be understood as applying to [Christ] as God." Further: *Io. ev. tr.* 18.2. On the subject, see Verwilghen, *Christologie,* 334–400, and Hilary, *En. Ps.* 54.

270. See BA 72:731f, with *Trin.* 2.1.1–2.4.

271. Augustine himself regards the denial of a human soul in Christ as both Apollinarist and Arian.

272. *En. Ps.* 85.4. See *Div. qu.* 80.1; *Serm.* 242.2 (ca. 410); 242.2 (412–413); 261.7.7 (410 or 411) (with scripture texts for all three elements); 265B.2; 265D.3; 374B.7.

273. See the detailed demonstration in *Div. qu.* 80.3; *Serm.* 214.7.

274. See *Div. qu.* 80.4; *En. Ps.* 87.3: "Why then do we say that the human soul of Christ was filled, not with human sins, but nonetheless with human ills?"; 90.1.1 (on the tempting of Jesus); *Io. ev, tr.* 49.18 (of Christ's free acceptance of the affections); *Ench.* 41.13 (God made Christ to be sin, that is, a sacrifice for sins); the same in *Serm.* 152.10f.; *Io. ev. tr.* 41.5f.; and *C. litt. Pet.* 3.6.16.

275. *Serm.* 238.2 (ca. 400) (Hill 7:56) (citing John 1:1f.; 19:30; and Luke 24:38-47).

276. See Ambrose, *En Ps.* 61.5; Jerome, *Ep.* 120.9. On the subject, see Grillmeier, *Jesus Christus,* 1: 559, 594.

277. Critics disagree on the dating of these sermons. See the details on the relevant sermons in P.-P. Verbraken, *Etudes critiques sur les sermons authentiques de saint Augustin* (Steenbrugge, 1976) 85 etc.

278. *Serm.* 130.34 (ca. 400). See *Io. ev. tr.* 19.15; *Ench.* 35:10: "Not two sons of God but one Son of God"; *Ep.* 269.2.8; 219.1 (no "quaternity").

279. See *Serm.* 174.2.2 (411–413); 265D.

280. *Ep.* 137.11.

281. See Grillmeier, *Jesus der Christus,* 1:599-602.

282. See, earlier, *F. symb.* 4.10; also *Ep.* 140.4.12.

283. See below in Part 1, Chapter 2.

284. See van Bavel, *Recherches,* 21.

285. *Serm.* 186.1.1; 261.6.7; *En. Ps.* 44.19.

286. *C. Sec.* 5; *Agon.* 22.24; *Vera rel.* 16.30; *Corrept.* 11.30; *Iul. imp.* 4.84; *Serm.* 119.7; 174.2.2.

287. *C. Faust.* 5.4; See *C. Fel.* 2.9: "The Word became flesh: it assumed flesh but was not changed into flesh, for it assumed the humanity but did not lose the divinity"; *Agon.* 11.12; *Cons. ev.* 1.35,53; *Serm.* 88.15.14. See also *C. Max.* 19 (where various verbs are used: *sumere, suscipere, accipere*).

288. *Serm.* 121.5: "The Word came near to what it was not, without losing what it was; it became the Human One *[filius hominis],* but did not cease to be the Son of God." See *Serm.* 119.7.7: "The Word . . . went out into the flesh" (Hill 4:230).

289. *Ep.* 137.3.11: "The person of Christ is a mixture *(mixtura)* of God and human being" (the words *permixtio* and *mixtio* are also used); *Serm.* 195.2.2: "he was tempered to us *(contemperatus nobis).*"

290. See *Io. ev. tr.* 82.4; *Persev.* 23.67.

291. See *Trin.* 13.17.22; 15.26.46; *Corrept,* 11.30; *Ep.* 137.3.11. See Geerlings, *Christus Exemplum,* 118–125; B. Studer, "*Una Persona in Christo:* Ein augustinisches Thema bei Leo dem Grossen," *Aug* 15 (1985) 453–487, especially 483f.; H. Drobner, *Person-Exegese und Christologie bei Augustinus* (Leiden, 1986), passim.

292. *Conf.* 6.4.5 (Chadwick 94).

293. Ibid., 7.5.7 (Chadwick 116).

294. See *Bapt.* 1–5.

295. See especially *Ep.* 43; 93; 141 (a synodal letter). In addition, see *Ep.* 23; 33; 49.3; 51; 52; 53; 76; 87; 89; 97; 105; 108; 128; 129; 142; 185 (includes all the themes); 204; *Epd.* 28.

296. See *Serm.* 46f. (on the true shepherd); 62; 90 (on Matt 22:1-14); 129; 137; 138; 146; 164; 218B.

297. See especially *En. Ps.* 21.2.30ff. On the subject, see Madec, *La patrie et la voie,* 258–264 ("L'honneur du Christ en son Eglise"); and *En. Ps.* 39.1; 57; 119; 145; 147.18ff.; 149.

298. *Io. ev. tr.* 1–16 (winter, 406–407), especially 6.21. See also *Ep. Io. tr.* 10.

299. See BA 30:46, with the corresponding texts on the imitation of Christ by the martyrs and the persecuted community of the Donatists. On the Christological background of Augustine's answer, see Madec, *La patrie et la voie,* 255–264, with *En. Ps.* 21.2.

300. BA 28:77. See *Cath. fr.* 2.2: "The question is certainly discussed among us: Where is the Church? With us or with them?"

301. See *En. Ps.* 145.16.

302. On these three themes, see BA 30:82-91.

303. *Ep.* 105.4.14–5.17; see *Serm.* 49.1; 129.5f. (with anti-Donatist testimonia).

304. *Cath. fr.* 2.2 (with a proof from Scripture). See *En. Ps.* 57.6: "From the mouth of truth I come to recognize Christ as Truth itself; from the mouth of truth I come to recognize the Church as sharer in the truth" (with the entire context); *C. litt. Pet.* 3.8.9; *Ep.* 89.4; *Agon.* 29.31; *Serm.* 4.24; 46.33; *Ep.* 185.12f.

305. *En. Ps.* 21.2.31. See *Agon.* 29.31; *En. Ps.* 117.12.

306. See *Serm.* 137.12.15: "In the name of Christ you are the people of God, you are the Catholic people, you are members of Christ" (Hill 4:382). Add *En. Ps.* 149.7: "The whole world is already Christ's chorus."

307. *C. litt. Pet.* 1.2.2f.; *Ep.* 23.2; 76.1; *Serm.* 129.4.5.

308. See *C. litt. Pet.* 2.9.19; 2.31.71; *C. ep. Parm.* 2.5.10; *Ep.* 49.3; 23.1; 43.24; 52.4; 53.3.6; 69.1: "the Catholic mother who devoutly received you into Christ's inheritance when you fled after being cut off from your inheritance"; *Ep.* 76.6-8; 87.6.9; *En. Ps.* 60.2; 119.7; 122.2. See J. Fellermayr, *Tradition und Sukzession im Lichte des römisch-antiken Erbdenkens: Untersuchungen zu den lateinischen Vätern bis zu Leo dem Grossen* (Munich, 1979) 116–130.

309. See *Ep.* 43.8.21: "they break up the unity of Christ"; 52.3; 141.13; 185.4.15; *Io. ev. tr.* 6.21; *En. Ps.* 130.1; 147.20.

310. See *En. Ps.* 119.9: "Love Christ, love peace"; *Ep.* 51.2.5; 105.2.5; 129.5: "Let the unity of Christ live in peace"; *Serm.* 47.22. See BA 28:711-713, where other passages are cited.

311. See *Ep. Io. tr.* 9.11: "Let us cling fast to the unity of the Church, let us cling fast to Christ, let us cling fast to charity"; *Ep.* 61.1f.; 105.1.1. Relevant here is the theme of the law of Christ (Gal 6:1f.), along with charity and peace, in *C. ep. Parm.* 3.2.5, and elsewhere.

312. *En. Ps.* 147.18; *Serm.* 90.6.

313. *Serm.* 138.8.8–9.9.

314. *Serm.* 313C.2.

315. See *Ep.* 33.5: "They are in disagreement with the altar of Christ"; 43.2.4; 43.8.21.

316. *Serm.* 164.7.11.

317. *Ep.* 185.6.14: "The banquet of the Lord is the unity of the body of Christ not only in the sacrament of the altar but also in the bond of peace."

318. See *Serm.* 227; 228B.3: "Therefore receive and eat the body of Christ, yes, you that have become members of Christ in the body of Christ; receive and drink the blood of Christ. . . . You turn into the body of Christ" (Hill 6:262).

319. See *Serm.* 62, passim; 90; 129.3.4; 137.1.1–3.3; 138.5.5; *Agon.* 26.28; *Cath. fr.* 4.7: "The whole Christ is head and body: the head is the only-begotten Son of God and the body is his Church"; 2.2.

320. See J. Ratzinger, "Beobtachtungen zum Kirchenbegriff des Tyconius im *Liber Regularum,*" *REAug* 2 (1956) 173–185.

321. M. Rondeau, *Les commentaires patristiques du psautier (IIIᵉ–Vᵉ siècles),* vol. 2: *Exégèse prosopologique et théologie,* OCA 220 (Rome, 1985); Drobner, *Person-Exegese,* 11–126.

322. BA 30:82ff., with *C. litt. Pet.* 2.24.57.

323. BA 30:78ff., with *C. litt. Pet.* 2.30.69; 2.105.241. See *C. ep. Parm.* 2.5.10.

324. See *C. litt. Parm.* 1.2.2; 1.4.5f.

325. This is a fundamental theme in the controversy with the Donatists. See *C. litt. Pet.* 3.42.51f.; 3.52.64: "Petilian subsequently grants me that Christ is the origin and root of those who are regenerated, and head of the Church, and not just any human being who gives and administers baptism"; *Cresc.* 3.5.6; 3.11.12; 3.37.41; 3.77.88; 4.19.22–21.26. On the subject, see BA 28:55-64.

326. See especially *Io. ev. tr.* 4.14; 5.18 (with the entire context); 6; *Bapt.* 3.4.6; *C. litt. Pet.* 3.49.59. On the subject, see BA 71:869ff.

327. See, for example, *Ep.* 54.5.10; 61.1f. On the subject, see BA 28:616ff.

328. *C. litt. Pet.* 3.49.59.

329. See *Serm.* 352.1.3: "Because baptism, that is to say the water of salvation, has no power to save unless it has been consecrated by the name of Christ, who shed his blood for us, the water is signed with his cross" (Hill 10:139); *Ep.* 23.4; *Bapt.* 6.25.47: "The baptism of Christ, that which is consecrated by the words of the gospel, is everywhere the same" (see the context); *Io. ev. tr.* 80.3: "The word is added to the element, and there is a sacrament" (citing Rom 10:8-10: confession of faith in Christ).

330. *Ep.* 141.13: "If . . . you come into harmony with the peace and unity of Christ, we shall rejoice at your amendment; and the sacraments of Christ, which you now possess in sacrilegious schism, will be useful and salutary to you once you have Christ as your head in the Catholic peace in which charity covers a multitude of sins." Augustine develops his teaching on the "character," the "sign of Christ," to explain sacramental incorporation into the Church. See, for example, *Ep.* 204.2: "It is our desire that all who bear the sign of Christ, though they are in opposition to Christ, . . . should abandon their perversity and rejoice with us in [Christ's] unity."

331. See *Serm.* 229A.1: "Come the consecration, and that bread will be the body of Christ, and that wine will be the blood of Christ. This is brought about by the name of Christ, brought about by the grace of Christ" (Hill 6:269); 227: "That bread . . . sanctified by the word of God. . . . That cup . . . sanctified by the word of God" (Hill 6:254); 229.3; 234.2: "Christ's blessing" (Hill 7:37). On the subject, see M. Klöckener, "Das eucharistische Hochgebet bei Augustinus," *Signum pietatis: Festschrift C. P. Mayer* (Würzburg, 1989) 461–495, especially 485–489 ("Die Konsekrationsworte").

332. *Io. ev. tr.* 27.11.

333. See *Serm.* 164.7.11.

334. *Ep.* 89.9.33.

335. See especially *Conf.* 5.9.16; 7.21.27.

336. See *Persev.* 20.53. On the subject, see Madec, *La patrie et la voie,* 265.

337. *Haer.* 88.

338. See the important citation of 1 Cor 1:17 ("so that the cross of Christ will not be made void") in *Nat. et gr.* 7.7; *C. Iul.* 6.11.36; *C. Iul. imp.* 3.56; On the subject: NBA 17, pt. 1: xxvii–xxviii.

339. See *C. Iul.* 4.3.17; 5.4.18; *C. Iul. imp.* 2.198.

340. See *Ep.* 177.1; 178.1; 179.10f., *Serm.* 131.9.9; *Nupt. et conc.* 2.2.5; *C. ep. Pel.* 1.1.2; 2.2.3; *C. Iul.* 2.10.37. On the subject, see BA 22:711-715 and NBA 17, pt. 1: xxix–xxx.

341. Romans 7:24f. no doubt has first place among the preferred Pauline texts; see further on. See also *C. Iul.* 2.10.34: "to preach against the Catholic faith and against the grace of Christ"; *Gr. et pecc. or.* 2.24.28. On the subject, see Madec, *La patrie et la voie,* 271.

342. *En. Ps.* 105.36.

343. *Gr. et pecc. or.* 1. See also *Serm.* 49.

344. *Serm.* 26; 49f.; 131; 158; 168ff.; 174; 176; 181; *En. Ps.* 105.36.

345. *Ep.* 157; 166; 177ff.; 186; 189; 190; 194.

346. See, for example, *Ep.* 186; 194; *Serm.* 26; *Perf. iust.* 8.17–21.44; *C. Iul.* 1.3.5–7.35; *C. Iul. imp.* 6.31-41, with 1 Cor 15. See above, pp. 17f.

347. See, for example, *C. Iul.* 6.4.8fff.; 6.24.79; *Trin.* 13.10.14. On the verse, see A.-M. La Bonnardière, "Le verset paulinien Rom 5,5 dans l'oeuvre de s. Augustin," *AugMag* (Paris, 1954) 2:657-665.

348. See the earlier *Vera rel.* 53.163; *Div. qu.* 66.5; *Simpl.* 1; *C. Faust.* 1.123.1. Then, *Nat. et gr.* 53.61; 64.72–70.84; *Gest. Pel.* 6.20; 8.21; 15.61f.; *Perf. iust.* 1.1–81.6 (Rom 7:25 as answer to the propositions *[Definitiones]* of Caelestius); *Corrept.* 2.3; 11.32; *Persev.* 12.31; *Serm.* 26.5.10 and 12; 151.8.8. See BA 23:770-778.

349. *Serm.* 183.8.12; *C. Iul.* 6.5.13f.

350. *Ep.* 186.7.25.

351. *Nat. et gr.* 8.9; *Ep.* 177.2.8ff.; 186.1.2; 190.2.7.

352. *Trin.* 12.7.12.

353. *Div. qu.* 71, and very frequently.

354. *Ep.* 186.11.37. See A. Trapè in NBA 17, pt. 1: xxvii–xxviii.

355. *Ep.* 186.9.33.

356. *Ep.* 140.24.61.

357. The passage embodies the central idea of *Pecc. mer.* 2.23.26–41.47. See BA 22:729-732. See, further, *Ep.* 190.2.5; *Serm.* 193.7 and 8. See also Du Roy, *L'intelligence de la foi,* 88–95; G. Remy, "La théologie de la médiation selon saint Augustin: Son actualité," *RThom* 91 (1991) 580–623, especially 588ff.

358. See, for example, *Gr. et pecc. or.* 1.38.42; 2.18.20; *An. et or.* 1.9.10; 2.9.13; 3.10.13f.; *C. ep. Pel.* 2.4.8–6.11; *C. Iul.* 2–3; 5.10.41; 6.2.3; 6.7.18; *C. Iul. imp.* 1.50.64; *Persev.* 12.30.

359. *An. et or.* 1.13.16; *C. Iul. imp.* 2.115.

360. *Ep.* 167.1.1; *Gr. et pecc. or.* 2.23.26; *Nupt. et conc.* 1.20.22; *C. Iul.* 6.3.6; 6.22.69; *C. Iul. imp.* 1.64; 2.1; 2.101; 2.236; 4.13; and often.

361. The discussion was primarily of Rom 5:12-19 and 1 Cor 15:21f.; see, for example, *Nupt. et conc.* 2.27.46; *C. Iul. imp.* 2.68f. (Julian comments on *Nupt. et conc.*).

362. *C. Iul. imp.* 2.177; 2.190; 2.194ff.; *C. Iul.* 2.10.33; 6.24.80; *Ep.* 187.9.30. See *En. Ps.* 95.5 (Adam stands for scattering, Christ for unification).

363. See *C. Iul.* 1.3.9; 5.15.52; *C. Iul. imp.* 4.45-49 (the name of Christ occurs very frequently); 6.22.

364. *C. Iul. imp.* 6.23 and 27. See *C. Iul. imp.* 4.57 (Christ fulfilled the entire Law).

365. See *Pecc. mer.* 1.14.18f.; *C. Iul. imp.* 2.146; 2.189-196. In this last passage, Augustine says that the words "Adam, a type of the one who was to come" (Rom 5:14) refer not to sin and justice but to birth and rebirth. Also to be considered are texts in which

Augustine insists that Christ is not only an example, but also a gift, a help, and a sacrament; see the early *Serm.* 101.5.6, and later on, for instance, *C. Iul. imp.* 1.140: "example of grace, example of life"; *C. Iul. imp.* 4.86. On the subject, see B. Studer, *"Sacramentum et Exemplum* chez saint Augustin," *RechAug* 10 (1975) 87–141. See also the summarizing passage in *Gr. et lib. arb.* 14.27: "For the grace that is given through Jesus Christ our Lord is neither knowledge of the divine law nor nature nor simply the forgiveness of sins, but rather causes the law to be fulfilled and nature to be set free and prevents sin from gaining control." Also *Pecc. mer.* 1.28.56 (expiation by Christ).

366. See, for example, *C. ep. Pel.* 3.4.11; *C. Iul. imp.* 1.124; *Serm.* 19.3; *Ep.* 157.3.14; *Ench.* 31.118. See below.

367. See *C. Iul. imp.* 3.112.

368. See *Nat. et gr.* 70.84: "[Charity] is not poured out in our hearts from the resources of either nature or the will, but by the Holy Spirit. . . . It is the grace of God through Jesus Christ our Lord"; *Perf. iust.* 9.21 (Rom 7:25 with 5:5); *C. Iul.* 4.31; 6.22.71; *C. Iul. imp.* 2.119; 6.13.

369. *Spir. et litt.* 29.51; *C. Iul.* 4.23; 4.25; 4.51.

370. See *Io. ev. tr.* 26.4: "How much more forcibly must we not say that a human being who delights in truth, delights in justice, delights in everlasting life is being drawn to Christ, since Christ is all these things?" See also *Corrept.* 2.4; *Serm.* 159.3.3–4.5; 335.1.1; *Ench.* 22.81; 31.118.

371. *Praed. sanct.* 8.15: "Therefore, to be drawn to Christ by the Father and to hear and learn from the Father that we must come to Christ—this is nothing else but to receive the gift by which we believe in Christ." See *Io. ev. tr.* 26.2-9; *Gr. et pecc. or.* 1.10.11; *C. ep. Pel.* 1.3.6.

372. *Ep.* 186 (citing 1 Tim 2:5; Gal 2:21; Rom 7:25); and especially *Ep.* 186.4.11: "It is a much greater kindness and undoubtedly a greater gift that the grace of God through Jesus Christ our Lord should be given to infants so that their birth from Adam may not hinder them and their rebirth in Christ may be of profit to them." See, further, *Ep.* 177, to Innocent I (416); 190 (418); and 194, to Sixtus of Rome (418).

373. See especially the anti-Arian semantic field in, for example, *Ep.* 238, and the hagiographic semantic field in, for example, *En. Ps.* 40, but also in *Ep.* 147f., with the citations from Ambrose.

374. See *Conf.* 9.1.1; *En. Ps.* 140.24.

375. *Ep.* 137, and Madec, *La patrie et la voie,* 226.

376. *Ep.* 187.

377. *Io. ev. tr.* 100.3; *Serm.* 186; 187. On this point, see BA 24:835ff. See also *Agon.* 22.24–33.35, with Madec, *La patrie et la voie,* 204; *Io. ev. tr.* 66.2; *Serm.* 92.3.3.

378. See *Io. ev. tr.* 100.3: "The Holy Spirit did not glorify [Christ] with authentic glory except in the holy Catholic Church."

Part I, Chapter 2

1. *Io. ev. tr.* 26.4. See *Io. ev. tr.* 13.5: "God [the Word] becomes everything for you because [the Word] is for you the totality of the things you love"; 60.2-5.

2. *Virg.* 27.27. On this see G. Madec, *La patrie et la voie: Le Christ dans la vie et la pensée de saint Augustin,* Jésus et Jésus-Christ 36 (Paris, 1989) 207ff. See also Augustine's praise of St. Cyprian in *Serm.* 313C.2.

3. *Io. ev. tr.* 10.13. See ibid., 7.7; *Serm.* 136.5.

4. *En. Ps.* 85.1.

5. The expression *Christus omnia* occurs once in Augustine. See *En. Ps.* 131.3: "Since the body of Christ is a house and a city, [Christ], who is head of the body, dwells in the house and sanctifies the temple and is king of the city. As the Church is all those things, so Christ is all these *(Christus omnia ista).*" See *C. Faust.* 16.42: "Everything belongs to Christ."

6. See, earlier, *Acad.* 2.1.1, and *Mor.* 16.26f.

7. See Madec, *La patrie et la voie,* 21–82: "La conversion."

8. See *Ench.* 1.6; 18.68.

9. See *Cat. rud.* 4.8; *Io. ev. tr.* 9.3f., and similar texts. See also above. In addition, see Madec, *La patrie et la voie,* 89–92, on the reading of Scripture in the liturgy.

10. *Io. ev. tr.* 18.2. See ibid., 3.2f.; 19.4; *En. Ps.* 70.2.10; 102.3.20; *Serm.* 261.8. See BA 73A:1910.

11. *Io. ev. tr.* 36.2. See *C. Faust.* 16.15.

12. *Io. ev. tr.* 19.15. See *Serm.* 23A.3; 218C.1; 225.1.1. On the subject, see BA 73A:19f. and note 10, where other texts are given in which John 1:1 and 1:14 are combined.

13. *Io. ev. tr.* 108.5.

14. See A. Verwilghen, *Christologie et spiritualité selon saint Augustin: L'hymne aux Philippiens,* Théologie historique 72 (Paris, 1985) 230f.

15. *Io. ev. tr.* 47.13. See ibid., 26.19; 78.2f.

16. *Serm.* 312.6.6.

17. *Io. ev. tr.* 15.6; *En. Ps.* 103.3.20 ("made—re-made"); *Serm.* 114.1; *En. Ps.* 45.14; 94.10.

18. See *Io. ev. tr.* 38.8: ". . . for I am the former and re-former, the creator and re-creator, the maker and re-maker of human beings"; *En. Ps.* 32.2.16.

19. *Serm.* 156.2.2.

20. *Io. ev. tr.* 3.15; see *En. Ps.* 119.1.

21. *Serm.* 217.1 (Hill 6:177). See *Io. ev. tr.* 102.4; *Serm.* 175.3.3.

22. See B. Studer, with the collaboration of B. Daley, *Soteriologie: In der Schrift und Patristik,* HDG 3/2a (Freiburg, 1978) 155f.

23. See above.

24. *Vera rel.* 16.30; *Cons. ev.* 1.35.53.

25. *Io. ev. tr.* 49.18. See *Serm.* 174.2.2.

26. See *Exp. Gal.* 27; *Cons. ev.* 1.35.53, with Madec, *La patrie et la voie,* 304ff.; *C. ep. Man.* 6.7. Note, moreover, that the predominant emphasis on the divine also received philosophical support from the Neoplatonically tinged comparison of the incarnation with the joining of soul and body in human beings. See J. T. Newton, *Neoplatonism and Augustine's Doctrine of the Person and Work of Christ,* dissertation (Atlanta, 1969) 53–135, as well as M.-F. Berrouard in BA 72:764f. and the bibliography given there.

27. See especially *Conf.* 7. On the subject, see Madec, *La patrie et la voie,* 39–50, especially 47f., where O. Du Roy's thesis is discussed.

28. See especially the dogmatic passage in *Ench.* 10.34–11.37.

29. See *Serm.* 294.9.9, on John 3:13: "In each of these there are not two Christs, two Sons of God, but one person, one Christ the Son of God, and the same one Christ, not an-other, being the [Human One *(filius hominis)*]; but the Son of God in his divinity, the Human One in his flesh" (Hill 8:186); *Io. ev. tr.* 19.15.

30. See especially *Io. ev. tr.* 19.15: "For since the Human One *[filius hominis]* clings to the Son of God in the unity of the person, the result is one person, and the Son of God is the same person as the Human One." This is followed by the comparison with the human being, which is not made of two persons. See also *Io. ev. tr.* 49.3.

31. See *Ep.* 137.3.11: "Therefore the person of the human being is a combination of soul and body; but the person of Christ is a combination of God and human being." On the *persona* terminology, see H. Drobner, *Person-Exegese und Christologie bei Augustinus* (Leiden, 1986) 241–253. See *Civ.* 10.29.2; *Serm.* 218C.3; 261.6.7; and 265D.3, where *persona* does not occur.

32. *Ep.* 187.3.10.

33. *Serm.* 214.7.

34. Ibid. (many assign a very early date for this sermon); *An. et or.* 1.17.28; *Io. ev. tr.* 47.13; 69.3; 78.2f.; *C. Iul. imp.* 2.178.

35. See T. van Bavel, *Recherches sur la christologie de saint Augustin,* Paradosis 10 (Fribourg, 1954) 57–63; W. Geerlings, *Christus Exemplum: Studien zur Christologie und Christusverkündigung Augustins,* Tübinger theologische Studien 13 (Mainz, 1978) 125–131; Drobner, *Person-Exegeses,* 258.

36. See, for example, *Serm.* 80.5 (delivered in 410): "God died, to strike a balance in a kind of celestial bargain, to prevent humanity seeing death. Christ, you see, is God, but he didn't die in that aspect in which he was God. It's the same person who is God and who is [human being], since Christ is one person, God and [human being]" (Hill 3:353); *Io. ev. tr.* 27.4 (414); van Bavel, *Recherches,* 57, where other passages are given.

37. *Serm.* 265B.3: "Each substance or nature, you see, shares with the other the names that are proper to itself, both divine names with the human nature, and human names with the divine nature, so that on the one hand the Son of God can be called a [human being], and on the other the [Human One] can be called God, while each, all the same, is identical with Christ himself" (Hill 7:250). See almost the same statement in *C. s. Arrian.* 8.6.

38. See *Trin.* 1.4.7, with Madec, *La patrie et la voie,* 209f.; *Serm.* 52.9.22 (410–412); *Io. ev. tr.* 99.1; *Persev.* 23.67. On the controversy over the formula *Unus ex Trinitate passus* ("One of the Trinity suffered") that occupied the theologians of both West and East in the first half of the sixth century and in which the issue was the communication of idioms as understood by Cyril of Alexandria, see A. Grillmeier, *Jesus der Christus im Glauben der Kirche,* vol. 2, pt. 2: *Die Kirche von Konstantinopel im 6. Jahrhundert* (Freiburg, 1989) 333–359, as well as B. Studer, *Trinity and Incarnation: The Faith of the Early Church,* trans. M. Westerhoff, ed. A. Louth (Collegeville, 1993), passim.

39. *Io. ev. tr.* 23.6.

40. See Studer, *Soteriologie,* 160ff, with the references to the dissertations of B. Muzungu and G. Remy. See also G. Remy, "La théologie de la médiation selon saint Augustin: Son actualité," *Rthom* 91 (1991) 580–623.

41. On this point, see *Ench.* 10.33ff.; 14.48; 23.92; 28.108.

42. See *Civ.* 9.15f.; *Ep.* 137.3.12; *Serm.* 47.12; 121.5.

43. See especially *Trin.* 4.7.11–12.15.

44. See, for example, *Exp. Gal.* 24; *Trin.* 1.7.14; *En. Ps.* 29.2.1 (as human being Christ is mediator between the Trinity and humanity); *Serm.* 174.2.2; 293.7. See also *En. Ps.* 109.10: "through the mediation of his flesh [Christ] called us to eternity."

45. *Conf.* 7.18.24 (Chadwick, 128).

46. See the more biblical perspective at work in the summation of the "sacrament of the mediator" in *Ench.* 28.108. See BA 22:729-732 on the influence of the Pelagian controversy.

47. See *Civ.* 10.22: "And so the [hostile] power is conquered in the name of [the one] who assumed human nature and whose life was without sin, so that in him, who was both priest and sacrifice, remission of sins might be effected, that is, through the 'mediator between God and [humankind], the [human being] Christ Jesus,' through whom we are purified from our sins and reconciled to God" (Bettenson, 402–403).; 10.20; *Pecc. mer.* 1.28.56; *Serm.* 293.8.

48. See *Io. ev. tr.* 41.4.

49. See *Civ.* 4.31.1; 10.22.

50. See *Trin.* 4.9.12–13.18; *Ench.* 28.108.

51. *Conf.* 10.43.68. See *Spir. et litt.* 27.47f. on the mediator and the justifying grace of Christ. For the connection between reconciliation, victory over the devil, and justification through the justice of Christ, see *Trin.* 13.11.15–14.18, where, however, the word "mediator" does not occur.

52. In addition to the passages already cited, see *Serm.* 174.2.2, where in explaining the gospel text Augustine says that Jesus had a truly human but sinless nature; he did not, however, merit the incarnation; rather his human nature was assumed by the Word, the only Son of God.

53. See BA 71:848ff.; O. Du Roy, *L'intelligence de la foi en la Trinité selon saint Augustin* (Paris, 1966) 96–106; Madec, *La patrie et la voie,* 35–50.

54. See the details in CCL 36:699; 40:2238. On the subject, see M.-F. Berrouard, "S. Augustin et le mystère du Christ: Chemin, Vérité et Vie," *Mélanges T. J. van Bavel* (Leuven, 1990) 431–449.

55. See *Conf.* 7.18.24, with 1 Tim 2:5; Rom 9:5; John 14:6 and John 1:14 (cited above).

56. *Civ.* 11.2 (Bettenson, 430).

57. *Conf.* 7.9.13ff., with 7.18.24 (see above); 7.20.26: ". . . unless I had sought your way in Christ our Saviour" (Chadwick, 130); and 7.21.27: "It is one thing from a wooded summit to catch a glimpse of the homeland of peace and not to find a way to it, but vainly to attempt the journey along an impracticable route surrounded by the ambushes and assaults of fugitive deserters with their chief, 'the lion and the dragon' (Ps. 90:13). It is another thing to hold on to the way that leads there, defended by the protection of the heavenly emperor. There are no deserters from the heavenly army waiting to attack. For this way they hate like a torture" (Chadwick, 131–132). See Madec, *La patrie et la voie,* 35–50. See *Doct. chr.* 1.10.10f., where the eternal and incarnate Wisdom is said to be both way and home country.

58. *Civ.* 10.29.1. See *Civ.* 11.1 and *En. Ps.* 29.2.1 (Christ, mediator between the Trinity and humanity).

59. See especially *Trin.* 13.19.24, and Madec, *La patrie et la voie,* 306f. See also *Cons. ev.* 1.5.8, where Augustine describes the two "virtues," the "active" and the "contemplative," as, respectively, "that by which we travel" and "that by which we arrive."

60. *Ord.* 2.5.6.

61. See *Acad.* 3.19.42–20.43; *Util. cred.* 14.31–16.34; and, from a later period, *Ep.* 137.3.12. On the subject, see K. H. Lütcke, *"Auctoritas" bei Augustin* (Stuttgart, 1968) 123–128, especially 127.

62. *Mag.* 11.38.

63. *C. ep. Man.* 36.41: "One true teacher teaches, who is himself the incorruptible truth; [this one] alone is the interior teacher; [this one] also became exterior, in order to call

us from exterior things to interior." See M. Löhrer, *Der Glaubensbegriff des heiligen Augustinus in seinen ersten Schriften bis zu den Confessiones* (Einsiedeln, 1955) 133–137 and especially 175, with its conclusion that the Augustinian dualism of believing and understanding corresponds to the duality of natures in Christ.

64. *Cons. ev.* 1.35.53. See Madec, *La patrie et la voie,* 304–306, with *Trin.* 4.18.24 and 13.19.24.

65. See *Io. ev. tr.* 2.4.

66. *Io. ev. tr.* 2.3. See ibid. 2.4 and *Serm.* 141 (explanation of John 14:6).

67. *Io. ev. tr.* 13.4. On the theme of the bread of angels, see Madec, *La patrie et la voie,* 150–160. See *Serm.* 9.13.21: "Christ has made himself into a broad road and highway which leads us straight home" (Hill 1:278); 92.3; 123.3.3: "That's the way; proceed along humility, in order to come to eternity. Christ as God is the home country we are going to; Christ as [human being] is the way we are going by. It's to him we are going, by him we are going; why are we afraid of going wrong?" (Hill 4:245); 375C.5.

68. *Serm.* 189 (Frangipane 4) (Hill 6:36). See Madec, *La patrie et la voie,* 130.

69. *Serm.* 141.4.4 (Hill 4:411).

70. *En. Ps.* 123.2.

71. *Serm.* 92.3.3 (Hill 3:467-468) (citing John 1:1, 14, and Phil 2:6).

72. *Serm.* 144.2 (Hill 4:431).

73. See *Ench.* 7.21 (with allusions to 2 Cor 5:7; Gal 5:6). The expression "way of faith" occurs again in *En. Ps.* 146.14 (without a reference to Christ); *En. Ps.* 106.4: "When in this temptation the wearied person cries out to God, [that one] is led to the way of faith, on which [one] begins to make [one's way] to the city of rest. The person is therefore led to Christ, who said: *I am the way*"; *Serm.* 27.6: "At the moment we are still on the road. What is the road? It's faith. For the sake of your faith Christ became deformed, yet Christ remains 'sightly'" (Hill 2:107); *Retr.* 1.14.26.

74. See, for example, *Io. ev. tr.* 22.8 (with the verbs "walking, going, crossing, believing"); 2.2-4 ("crossing the sea").

75. *Trin.* 15.27.49 (Hill, 434).

76. *En. Ps.* 123.2. See *En. Ps.* 106.4: "[One] is led to the way of faith. . . . [One] is therefore led to Christ"; 106.13; 134.20: "If one believes, the way lies open, and Christ himself is the way; but if one does not believe in God, the way is closed"; *Serm.* 27.6: "What is the road? It's faith. For the sake of your faith Christ became deformed, yet Christ remains 'sightly'. . . . Let us hold to the way, and we shall arrive at the sight" (Hill 2:107).

77. See *Vera rel.* 8.14; *Serm.* 113A.5. But it is to be noted how Augustine describes orthodoxy as the virginal integrity of the Church; see *Serm.* 72A.8.

78. *An. et or.* 24.28.

79. See *En. Ps.* 101.2.7: "The faith of Christians is not to be praised because they believe that Christ died, but because they believe that Christ rose"; *Serm.* 141.1.1: "The proper object of Christian faith is the resurrection of the dead"; *En. Ps.* 120.6, and *Trin.* 13.20.25.

80. *Io. ev. tr.* 53.10.

81. *Civ.* 11.2 (Bettenson, 430–431). See *Cons. ev.* 1.35.53: "Since those who contemplate the truth enjoy things eternal while the faith of believers is owed to things that have a beginning, human beings are purified by faith in things temporal so that they may come to know the truth of things eternal. . . . Those two things are above, namely, eternity and truth, and these other two are below, namely, things that have a beginning and faith. In order, then, that we may be called from the lowest to the highest and that what has a beginning

may receive eternity, we must come through faith to truth" (with the entire context, in which Augustine speaks of the incarnation and the mediatorship of Christ).

82. *Serm.* 141.1.

83. See *Acad.* 3.20.43; *Util cred.* 15.33–17.35. See what was said earlier on the subject.

84. See Madec, *La patrie et la voie,* 155–185.

85. See *En. Ps.* 130.13; *Serm.* 126.1.1.

86. *Io. ev. tr.* 13.4: "Through Christ as human being to Christ as God; through the Word made flesh to the Word that was in the beginning, God with God; from that which human beings ate to that which the angels eat daily." See *Conf.* 7.18.24; *Io. ev. tr.* 98.2-6; *Ep. Io. tr.* 3.1; *En. Ps.* 130.9-14. On the subject, see Madec, *La patrie et la voie,* 187f., with texts on the bread of angels.

87. See *Vera rel.* 8.14: "For [the mysteries of Christ] are not only believed but are also judged to belong to the mercy which God shows to the human race."

88. See *Io. ev. tr.* 15.6ff.; 49.18f.; *En. Ps.* 85.1.

89. See *Div. qu.* 80.2: "The evangelist wants therefore to commend to us a love of the humility of God who humbled [the divine self]"; *Pecc. mer.* 2.27; *Civ.* 14.13; *C. ep. Pel.* 4.8; *C. Iul.* 6.8f.; 6.77; *Ench.* 20.76. This fundamental, but often only hinted at, theme of the love of God as commended to us (that is, to our remembrance) by the abasement of Christ is based on Rom 5:8. See *C. Adim.* 21; *Exp. Gal.* 36; *Nat. b.* 31; *Cat. rud.* 4.7f.; *Trin.* 4.1.2; 13.10.13f.; 13.16.21; *C. ep. Pel.* 4.6; *En. Ps.* 146.4. For an understanding of the theme, the connection between commending and memory must be kept in mind (see *Mor.* 1.71; *Cons. ev.* 2.69; 3.73) as must the circumstance that the commending occurs in time (*Div. qu.* 57.2), that is, in the New Testament (see *C. Adim.* 17; *Doctr. chr.* 3.34.48), and is reported in the "history," that is, in the Scriptures (*Vera. rel.* 46; *C. Faust.* 16.11; *Civ.* 10.16.1; *Doctr. chr.* 1.31.34). On the theme of the love of God that has appeared in the humanity of Christ, see R. Strauss, *Der neue Mensch innerhalb der Theologie Augustins* (Zurich, 1967) 26ff.

90. *Serm.* 143.1.1 (Hill 4:425). See *Serm.* 143.2.2.

91. *Serm.* 161.1.1 (Hill 5:135) (on 1 Cor 6:15).

92. *Serm.* 33A.4 (Hill 2:164); see *Serm.* 301A.2. On the subject, see below.

93. See *Io. ev. tr.* 22.1, with no reference to Christ; but see ibid. 22.3: "For we have Christ within as teacher . . . who teaches me what to say and distributes to you as he deigns" (that is, for the understanding of the Nicene faith); *Serm.* 179.7.7 ("the Word as teacher").

94. *Ep.* 166.4.9; *Serm.* 23.1; 270.1; 301A.2; *Ep. Io. tr.* 3.13. See also *Conf.* 9.8.10; *En. Ps.* 131.1, as well as especially *Retr.* 1.12, with the reference to *Mag.*

95. See *Io. ev. tr.* 59:1: at the washing of the feet "Christ was teacher of humility by both word and example"; *Serm.* 98.3.3 (the significance of miracles in "the school of Christ"). See also *Serm.* 264.4 (on Christ who speaks exteriorly and interiorly).

96. See *Mag.* 11.38: "[The one] who is consulted and who is said to 'dwell in the inner [human being],' [This one] it is who teaches us, namely, Christ, that is to say. 'the unchangeable Power of God and everlasting Wisdom.' This is the Wisdom which every rational soul does indeed consult, but it reveals itself to each according to [that person's] capacity to grasp it by reason of the good or evil dispositions of the will" (trans. R. Russell, in Fathers of the Church 59 [New York, 1968] 51), along with *Ep.* 66.1: "I know that you can hear many things if you lend an ear to Christ, and that by your very possession of [Christ] you are admonished about how wickedly you speak of Christ"; *Ep.* 112.3; 133.1.

97. *Io. ev. tr.* 96.4 (on John 16:12f.).

98. See, earlier, *Lib. arb.* 3.9.28, as well as 3.10.30 (citing John 1:3, 14, but without mentioning Christ).

99. See *Civ.* 10.29.1: "And yet you refuse to recognize the incarnation of the unchanging Son of God, which brings us salvation, so that we can arrive at those realities in which we believe, and which we can in some small measure comprehend. Thus you see, to some extent, though from afar off and with clouded vision, the country in which we must find our home, but you do not keep to the road along which we must travel" (Bettenson, 414). On the subject, see *Ep.* 118.3.17 and 21; 118.4.23.

100. *Ep.* 118.3.22. See *Civ.* 10.29.2; *C. ep. Parm.* 3.2.5 (on the pride of Adam as the beginning of human pride).

101. *Conf.* 7.9.14; 7.18.24.

102. *Serm.* 68.5.6 (Mai 127.6) (Hill 3:227). See *Virg.* 33.33: "Since, therefore, all Christians must safeguard humility, inasmuch as their name 'Christian' is from Christ, whose gospel no one examines closely who does not find [Christ] in it as teacher of humility . . ."; and *Serm.* 68.11 (Mai 126.11): "In [Christ] is to be found the standard of humility" (Hill 3:230).

103. *Serm.* 50.8.11 (Hill 2:350) (citing 2 Cor 10:17 and Matt 11:29). See *Io. ev. tr.* 51.3.

104. *Serm.* 304.3.3 (Hill 8:317).

105. *En. Ps.* 31.2.18. See *En. Ps.* 33.10; 90.1.1; *Io. ev. tr.* 5.3 (where the way of humility is linked to the baptism of Jesus).

106. *Serm.* 142.2.2 (Hill 4:413-414). See *Serm.* 123.3.3, and especially the very important passage in *Cat. rud.* 48, in which, at the end, reference is made to Christ as "sign of divine love for us" and "example of human humility among us."

107. *Ep.* 11.4. See *Vera rel.* 16.30ff., especially 32: "Therefore his whole life on earth, through the human being whom he had deigned to assume, was a lesson in morals" (without mention of the name Christ); *Div. qu.* 43, which should be compared with *Perf. iust.* 20.43; *En. Ps.* 32.2.2; *Io. ev. tr.* 15.2; *Cons. ev.* 1.35.53 ("example of the return").

108. See especially *C. Iul. imp.* 4.189: "With regard to the example of Christ, I answered you earlier that on the one hand we may not deny his excellence, due to which as perfect human being, but one born of the Spirit and not conceived by the lusting flesh, he lived a life of righteousness beyond that of any other human being; on the other hand, we may not, on account of this excellence, excuse ourselves from endeavoring to imitate him as far as this is possible. . . . We imitate him when we commit no sin, which means not that we do not have the desire of sinning but that we do not consent to this desire. Although we imitate this Saint of saints by living a holy life, there remains reason for us to say in our prayer, 'Forgive us our debts.'" Similarly, in *C. Iul. imp.* 4.57. On the entire subject, see Studer, *Soteriologie,* 169ff., and Studer, "Jésus-Christ, notre justice, selon Saint Augustin," *RechAug* 15 (1980) 99–143.

109. See *Trin.* 13.13.17–14.18; 13.16.20.

110. *Virg.* 35.35.

111. See *Virg.* 31.31; 36.36–37.38. See Madec, *La patrie et la voie,* 205ff.

112. *Serm.* 144.2.2 (Hill 4:43). See *Serm.* 158.6.6; *En. Ps.* 90.1; on the connection between faith, hope, and love, see especially *Ench.* 31.117f., as well as *Trin.* 8.4.6.

113. *Serm.* 156.5.5 (Hill 5:99). See *Serm.* 158.6.6 (same idea), as well as *Gr. et lib. arb.* 7.18 (on faith without works).

114. See, for example, *Serm.* 168.2.2; 183.9.13; 234.3; *En. Ps.* 130.1; *Io. ev. tr.* 22.7; 83.3.

115. See *Ench.* 31.117, and the scriptural index in CCL 36:703 and 40:2253.

116. See *En. Ps.* 90.1. See also *Serm.* 81.8 (on trust in the midst of an aging world); *En. Ps.* 104.4.4 (Christ our hope and trust in the tempest of life).

117. See *En. Ps.* 101.2.7: "To believe that Christ rose and to hope that you will rise through Christ: this is praiseworthy faith"; *Serm.* 241.1.1; *En. Ps.* 120.6.

118. *Serm.* 156.5.5: "The faith to be admired, the true faith of grace, is the sort that works through love" (Hill 5:99).

119. See *C. ep. Pel.* 4.5.10; *Praed. sanct.* 8.15 (citing John 6:44); *En. Ps.* 118.22.1 (citing Phil 3:9).

120. *Praed. sanct.* 2.3-6; *Persev.* 21.54ff. (with the reference to *Corrept.* 6.10).

121. See *Ench.* 31.117.

122. *Serm.* 71.12.19; 156.5.5; 271.1; *Io. ev. tr.* 102.5; *Ep.* 157.2.4; *Pecc. mer.* 1.17.27; *Spir. et litt.* 3.5; *Perf. iust.* 20.43; *C. ep. Pel.* 4.5.10. See above.

123. *En. Ps.* 118.10.6: "Delight in righteousness expands the heart. This is God's gift, that in following [God's] precepts we are not constricted by fear of punishment but expanded by love and delight in righteousness"; see *En. Ps.* 127.8; *Spir. et litt.* 3.5.

124. See *Civ.* 13.5: "Genuine righteousness is never so beloved, never gives such delight, without the help of God's grace" (Bettenson, 514); *Spir. et litt.* 30.52.

125. See *Persev.* 7.13ff.

126. See *Serm.* 210.2.3; *Cons. ev.* 1.35.53: "By saying and doing, suffering and enduring what was in keeping with our salvation, [Christ] became an example of the return for human beings here below."

127. *Ep.* 137.3.12.

128. *Serm.* 101.5.6 (Hill 4:68). See *Div. qu.* 61.2, and other passages in B. Studer, "*Sacramentum et Exemplum* chez saint Augustin," *RechAug* 10 (1975) 129f.

129. See Studer, "*Sacramentum et Exemplum,* 125–133.

130. *Trin.* 4.3.6.

131. See Studer, "*Sacramentum et Exemplum,*" 89f. On the theme, see *Civ.* 10.23; 18.49.

132. See *Persev.* 21.55, and *Retr.* 2.1, on the discovery of the full doctrine of grace. See *Serm.* 156.11.12f.: explanation of the absolute necessity of the "help" *(adiutorium)* of Christ. The extent to which, after 412, Augustine was simply developing earlier approaches may be seen in the theme of Christ the physician. See R. P. Hardy, *Actualité de la révélation divine: Une étude des "Tractatus in Ioannis evangelium" de saint Augustin,* Théologie historique 28 (Paris, 1974) 112–116, with bibliography. See above on the anti-Pelagian development of the mediator theme.

133. *Nat. et gr.* 79.84. See also ibid. 53.62; 60.70 (continual prayer for the forgiveness of sins and hope in Christ).

134. *C. Iul. imp.* 2.14.6: "This is the hidden and terrible virus of your heresy, that you want the grace of Christ to consist in his example and not in his gift, saying that people become just by imitating him and not through the sending of the Holy Spirit so that they may be led to imitate him. . . . If, then, righteousness comes through imitation of righteous persons, Christ died for no reason, since even before him there were righteous persons who could be imitated by those who wanted to be righteous."

135. *C. Iul. imp.* 1.140. See *Pecc. mer.* 1.15.19 (imitation, and grace that regenerates through the Spirit); *Nat. et. gr.* 40.47; *Gr. et pecc. or.* 1.39.43 (citing Rom 7:25 on "help for virtue" and "example for imitation"); *Perf. iust.* 20.43: "The grace of God through our Lord Jesus Christ acts with us not only through precepts, sacraments, and examples, but also

through the Holy Spirit"; *C. Iul. imp.* 5.15.58: "In Christ [there were] both example and the protection of the grace that filled him"; *Io. ev. tr.* 98.3 (the cross as source of grace and as example). In *Serm.* 37.11.16, the antithesis is inverted: it is necessary to put on Christ "not only in the celebration of the sacrament but also in acting out the role" (Hill 2:193). See *C. litt. Pet.* 3.56.68 (celebration of the sacrament and works of righteousness).

136. Ephesians 3:17 is already cited in *Mag.* 11.38. See *En. Ps.* 54.10; 74.4; 120.7. On the theme, see A. Manrique, "Presencia de Cristo en los corazones por la fe según Agustín," *RAE* 14 (1973) 41–61.

137. *Io. ev. tr.* 49.19. See *En. Ps.* 103.4.4.

138. *En. Ps.* 120.7; see *Serm.* 81.8.

139. *En. Ps.* 138.16.

140. See above. On the topic, see *Ep. Io. tr.* 8.1, where it is said that Christ, who dwells in the inner self through faith, also, like the leader of an army, uses the virtues as servants.

141. *Io. ev. tr.* 49.19.

142. *Serm.* 63 (on Matt 8:23-27).

143. *Serm.* 38.8.10f.

144. *Serm.* 174.4.5 (Hill 5:260) (an anti-Pelagian explanation of Luke 19:1-10).

145. *Serm.* 165.2.2 (Hill 5:202) (citing Eph 3:16-19). See *Ep.* 140.25.62f. (citing Eph 3:14-19, on the grace of the New Testament); *Ep.* 237.8 (citing 1 Cor 3:16).

146. *Ep.* 140.26.63.

147. See *Serm.* 63, as well as *Ep.* 131, in which Augustine addresses those who have faith in their hearts.

148. *En. Ps.* 108.32.

149. See *Serm.* 46f., especially 46.13.20.

150. See Madec, *La patrie et la voie,* 85–92.

151. On what follows, see F. Schnitzler, *Zur Theologie der Verkündigung in den Predigten des hl. Augustinus* (Freiburg, 1968), especially 115–122, where many passages are cited.

152. *Disc. chr.* 1.1. See *Serm.* 134.1.1: "It's the one who dwells in all of us that's the Teacher of us all. [This Teacher] was talking to all of us just now in the gospel, and saying to us what I am also saying to you; [the Teacher] says it, though, about us, about both you and me" (Hill 4:341).

153. *Disc. chr.* 14.15. See *Serm.* 33A.3: "This is what is learned in the school of Christ the Teacher"; *En. Ps.* 79.1; 98.1; 98.3; 107.2.

154. See G. Madec in BA 63:545-548.

155. *En. Ps.* 126.3. See *Serm.* 261.2.2: "In this school . . . we are all fellow students; heaven is our professor's chair. So listen to what sort of God Christ is" (Hill 7:209); *Serm.* 134.1.1.

156. See *Corrept.* 9.22: "We call ourselves therefore elect and disciples of Christ and children of God"; *Serm.* 301A.2; 129.2.2: "The Lord . . . used to speak to his disciples; and of course, what he had to say to them, he was also saying to us who came after them" (Hill 4:303).

157. See above, pp. 21–24, 27.

158. *Serm.* 17.1: "[Christ] did not keep silent through the patriarchs, . . . did not keep silent through the prophets, . . . did not keep silent through the mouth of his own body. And if [Christ] were silent now, he would still be speaking through the scriptures, wouldn't he? The reader goes to the lectern, but it is Christ who is not silent. The preacher explains the text; if [the preacher] says what is true, it is Christ speaking. If Christ were silent, I myself

would not be saying all this to you. Nor has [Christ] been keeping silent through your mouths. When you were singing, [Christ] was speaking" (Hill 1:366).

159. *Io. ev. tr.* 47.3 (with the entire context, 1–3).

160. See the explanation of this basic principle in *Doct. chr.,* prol. 5. On the theme see *En. Ps.* 125, where Augustine explains that through preachers Christ is building the house.

161. See Madec, *La patrie et la voie,* 117f.

162. See *Ep.* 54.1 (in the sacramental order of the New Testament Christ has laid a light yoke on his followers).

163. See above, p. 35.

164. See above, pp. 35f.

165. See *Serm.* 229.2. See what is said above about the "blessing" and the "Eucharistic Prayer."

166. *Civ.* 10.6 (Bettenson, 380). See *Serm.* 227. On the subject, see Madec, *La patrie et la voie,* 112f.

167. See *Serm.* 272, especially: "If it's you that are the body of Christ and its members, it's the mystery meaning you that has been placed on the Lord's table; what you receive is the mystery that means you. It is to what you are that you reply *Amen*" (Hill 7:300). See also *Serm.* 229A; *Io. ev. tr.* 26.13; *Ep.* 187.6.20f. See also Madec, *La patrie et la voie,* 98–110, with other passages.

168. *En. Ps.* 119.7. See *En. Ps* 29.2.5; 39.28; 61.4; 74.4; 85.1; 103.1.2; 122.2; 123.7; 130.1; *Serm.* 91.7f.

169. On the opposition between birth in Adam and rebirth in Christ, see above, p. 37.

170. *En. Ps.* 74.4.

171. Ibid., 85.1.

172. See Madec, *La patrie et la voie,* 92–98 (on *Ep.* 54 and 55).

173. *Serm.* 9.17.21 (Hill 1:278). See *Serm.* 18.4; 25.8; 32.20; 39.4.6; 123.4f.; 197.5; *En. Ps.* 146.17; 147.13. On the subject, see Madec, *La patrie et la voie,* 111, with many other passages, but *Serm. Denis* 7, with its words "let us feed Christ in the poor," is regarded as spurious by Verbraken.

174. *Serm.* 25.8.8. See *Serm.* 41.7 (on Prov 22:28: to possess the faith along with Christ and the poor).

175. *Ep. Io. tr.* 10.3.

176. *En. Ps.* 61.4. See *En. Ps.* 85.19; 86.5; 87.15 ("the whole day"); *Io. ev. tr.* 108.5 (citing Col 1:24).

177. *En. Ps.* 90.1.1f.; 90.2.1; 60.3; 94.14; *Io. ev. tr.* 60.2-5; 103.3.

178. *En. Ps.* 40.1. See *En. Ps.* 63.3 (Christ, prototype of the martyrs).

179. *Serm.* 263.1. See *Serm.* 91.7f.; 137.1f.; 144.5f.; *En. Ps.* 123.1ff.

180. See *Ep.* 187, especially 3.10 (Christ is there whence he will come, that is, [Christ] is not everywhere, even though it is possible to say, by reason of the communication of idioms, that [Christ] is everywhere) and 5.17 ("presence according to likeness"); *Serm.* 137.1.1 (on the intercession of Christ in heaven).

181. See Augustine's theology of Easter in *Ep.* 55, especially 2.3–3.5. See also *Serm.* 179.6.6, and on the subject, B. Studer, "Zum *Triduum Sacrum* bei Augustin von Hippo," Congresso Internazionale di Liturgia, *La celebrazione del Triduo pasquale: Anamnesis e mimesis,* Studia Anselmiana 102 (Rome, 1990) 273–286.

182. See *En. Ps.* 142.2. On the theme, see Y. Congar, *"Ecclesia ab Abel," Festschrift K. Adam* (Düsseldorf, 1952) 79–108, and *Serm.* 300.1-5 (on the martyrs who preceded Christ).

183. See, for example, *En. Ps.* 143.3 and 12.

184. See *En. Ps.* 64.2; 98.4; *Gn. litt.* 11.15.20; *Civ.* 14.28.

185. See, for example, *En. Ps.* 61.5ff. On the theme, see J. van Oort, *Jerusalem and Babylon: A Study in Augustine's City of God and the Sources of His Doctrine of the Two Cities* (Leiden, 1991), trans. from the Dutch, *Jeruzalem en Babylon* ('s-Gravenhage, 1986).

186. See *Cat. rud.* 20.36. On the theme, see Madec, *La patrie et la voie,* 123–127. See also the description of Christ as "emperor" in, for example, *Serm.* 74.5.

187. See especially *Civ.* 17.16 and 20.

188. See *Civ.* 1, prol; 22.1.1.

189. See *Cat. rud.* 4.6.

190. *Civ.* 10.32.1.

191. See *Civ.* 10.32.2; 11.2. On the theme, see B. Studer, "Zum Aufbau von Augustins *De civitate Dei,*" *Mélanges T. J. van Bavel* (Leuven, 1990), especially 943–950.

192. See Madec, *La patrie et la voie,* 283ff. (citing *Vera rel.* 3.3, and *Ep.* 118.21). See also *Cons. ev.* 1.16.24; 1.26.40.

193. See *Serm.* 81.8 (with the objections of the pagans to the "Christian times"). See also *Serm. Mainz* 61.25f., with the allusion to the visit of Emperor Honorius to Rome in 404; see F. Dolbeau, "Nouveaux sermons de saint Augustine pour la conversion des païens et des donatistes," *REAug* 37 (1991) 55f.

194. See *En. Ps.* 30.2.4; 61.4; 142.3.

195. See ibid., 36.3.4; 41.1; 67.7-12; *Serm.* 341.9.11.

196. See *Serm.* 180.3, and 191.3.4; 192.2.

197. See *En. Ps.* 90.2.1.

198. See, for example, *Serm.* 13.2; *C. Iul. imp.* 140, and the biblical indexes in CCL 36:702 and 40:2248.

199. See *Serm.* 26.2-9, with the anti-Pelagian distinction between the grace of creation and the grace of redemption.

200. See *Spir. et litt.* 27.47: "By which grace the righteousness erased by sin is written again in the renewed interior self; and this mercy on the human race comes through Christ Jesus our Lord."

201. See Studer, *Soteriologie,* 168f.

202. See above, p. 57.

203. *En. Ps.* 49.31.

204. See above, pp. 52–55.

205. *Praed. sanct.* 15.31.

206. *Trin.* 13.14.18; *Ench.* 13.41.

207. See *Ep.* 140.4.10; *C. ep Pel.* 2.6.11. See, even earlier, *C. Faust.* 3.3.

208. *C. Iul. imp.* 1.138. See ibid., 1.140.

209. *Praed. sanct.* 15.31.

210. Ibid. See *Serm.* 174.2.2; 265D.7; *Trin.* 13.17.22; *Io. ev. tr.* 82.4; *Ench.* 12.36; *Corrept.* 11.30. See BA 24:819f., where further passages are given.

211. *Praed. sanct.* 15.30; *Persev.* 24.67.

212. *Serm.* 67.4.7 (Hill 3:218).

213. *Civ.* 10.29.1 (Bettenson, 414–415).

214. See M.-F. Berrouard, "La permanence à travers le temps de la foi en Christ selon saint Augustin," *Signum pietatis: Festschrift C. P. Mayer* (Würzburg, 1989) 303–324.

215. *Ep.* 195.2.6. See *Ep.* 157.3.14; *C. ep. Pel.* 3.4.11; *Nupt. et conc.* 2.11.24; *Gr. et pecc. or.* 2.24.28; 2.26.30; *En. Ps.* 36.3.4; *Serm.* 19.3.

216. See *En. Ps.* 72.1; 104.10; *Trin.* 2–4, and B. Studer, *Zur Theophanie-Exegese Augustins: Untersuchungen zu einem Ambrosius-Zitat in der Schrift "De videndo Deo" (ep. 147),* Studia Anselmiana 59 (Rome, 1971).

217. *Serm.* 300.2.

218. See above, p. 58.

219. See Eph. 2:18. Augustine cites this verse in *C. Fort.* 16f.; *Pecc. mer.* 1.27.46; *Serm.* 204.2; *C. adv. leg.* 2.5. His interest, however, is not in the trinitarian aspect of the verse but in the connected statement about the unity of Jews and pagans. Nevertheless, the triadic formula in Eph. 2:18 may be taken as a good summation of his thinking about the trinitarian way of salvation.

220. *Praed. sanct.* 8.13.

221. See *Conf.* 1.1.1: "My faith, Lord, calls upon you. It is your gift to me. You breathed it into me by the humanity of your Son, by the ministry of your preacher" (Chadwick, 3). See, further, *Conf.* 7.9.13; 10.43.68; 3.6.10; 12.15.19; 13.4.5; 13.5.6.

222. *Conf.* 1.11.17.

223. Ibid., 3.4.8. See ibid., 7.7.11; 7.18.24; 9.1.1 (here it is Christ Jesus who is addressed); 9.4.7.

224. See *Serm.* 217.1 (after 418, on John 17:24): "What you have to grasp is that [Christ] assigns everything to the Father for the simple reason that the Father is not from [Christ], but [Christ] is from the Father. [Christ] gives everything to the fount from which he is derived" (Hill 6:177); *Io. ev. tr.* (with the somewhat hesitant trinitarian interpretation of "I live because of the Father").

225. See also *Haer.* 88, with its trinitarian adaptation of the doctrine of grace.

226. See above, p. 15.

227. See *Cat. rud.* 26.52; *Io. ev. tr.* 21.17; 36.7; 40.6; 42.8; *En. Ps.* 103.4.18: "[Christ] spoke himself to you. How did [Christ] speak himself to you? Through the Word. What Word? Christ. [Christ] both spoke to you and spoke himself. By sending Christ, [Christ] spoke himself."

228. *C. Max.* 2.16.3.

229. *Io. ev. tr.* 21.9. Augustine is here explaining an explicitly anti-Arian text, John 5:20.

230. *Praed. sanct.* 8.15.

231. *En. Ps.* 85.15 (citing Isa 53:1); *Serm.* 131.2.

232. *Io. ev. tr.* 26.5.

233. See *Serm.* 71.16.26: "The Holy Spirit proceeds primarily from [the one] of whom the Son is born" (Hill 3:262), as well as *Serm.* 156.5.5 (Rom 5:5 with 1 John 4:16); *Ep.* 140.18.25 (Rom 5:5, with scriptural passages having to do with the vision of the Father and the worship of God).

234. See, for example, *En. Ps.* 48.1.10: "We who may still be toiling here on earth do not have life in that way; that will not be our lot hereafter, for Christ will be our life through eternity." See also *En. Ps.* 42.4; 122.2; *Io. ev. tr.* 69 (explanation of John 14:4-6).

235. See *Serm.* 96.3.3: "Who wouldn't want to follow Christ there, where total happiness reigns, total peace, perpetual security?" (Hill 4:31).

236. *En. Ps.* 33.2.6.

237. Ibid., 46.10. See A.-M. La Bonnardière, *"Anima iusti sedes sapientiae* dans l'oeuvre de saint Augustin," *Mélanges J. Daniélou* (Paris, 1972) 111–120.

238. *En. Ps.* 36.1.6; 77.17; 127.10. Other passages in Madec, *La patrie et la voie,* 187f.

239. *En. Ps.* 36.3.4.

240. See *En. Ps.* 60.4.

241. *Io. ev. tr.* 13.4. See also ibid., 69.1-3, where John 16:10, "I am going to the Father," is explained.

242. *En. Ps.* 42.14.

243. See *En. Ps.* 146.4: "Seeing God, all the citizens of that city rejoice within that great and broad and heavenly city; what they see is God's very self."

244. *En. Ps.* 145.18.

245. Ibid., 37.38.

246. Ibid., 29.2.1.

247. *Io. ev. tr.* 47.3 (on John 10:14-21). See *En. Ps.* 103.4.10, as well as *Serm.* 144.2.3 (John 16:10) and 155.5.5 (John 13:1).

248. See B. Studer, *"Credo in Deum Patrem omnipotentem:* Zum Gottesbegriff des heiligen Augustinus," *Atti: Congresso internazionale su S. Agostino nel XVI Centenario della Conversione,* Studia Ephemeridis "Augustinianum" 24 (1987) 173–178.

249. See M. Klöckener, "Das eucharistische Hochgebet bei Augustinus," *Signum pietatis: Festschrift C. P. Mayer* (Würzburg, 1989) 461–495.

250. See *En. Ps.* 21.2.23; 82.3; 91.11; 140.3.24; *Io. ev. tr.* 52.1f.; *Virg.* 35.35.

251. See K. Baus, "Die Stellung Christi im Beten des hl. Augustinus," *TTZ* 63 (1954) 323ff.; B. Fischer, *Die Psalmen als Stimme der Kirche* (Trier, 1982), especially 87f.

252. See, for example, *Serm.* 264.5: "So the provision of the flesh of Christ is necessary for the faithful in this life, so that by it they may wend their way to the Lord; but when you come to the sight of that Word, no more fleshly provision will be needed. And that's why [Christ's] presence in the flesh among them for forty days after the resurrection was necessary; it was to demonstrate that faith in the incarnation of Christ is necessary as long as the ark is being taught in this life how to float on the waters of the flood" (Hill 7:231).

253. On the appearance of the Human One for judgment, see, for example, *Io. ev. tr.* 19.15f.; 21.13; *Civ.* 20.30.4.

254. See *Io. ev. tr.* 105.6f. On the theme, see van Bavel, *Recherches,* 54f.

255. See *En. Ps.* 27.2. On the theme, see Studer, *Soteriologie,* 174.

256. *Civ.* 22.30.4 (Bettenson, 1090).

257. See *En. Ps.* 45.15: "We shall have leisure amid tranquillity, so that we may know God as the author of all [God's] gifts"; *Pecc. mer.* 1.17.27.

258. *Civ.* 22.30.4 (Bettenson, 1090). And see *En. Ps.* 118.13.4: "'Law' is to be understood as the one of which the Apostle speaks when he says that love is the fulfillment of the law. For it is this law that will be observed by the saints, from whose mouths the word of truth shall not be taken, that is, by the Church of Christ, not only in this world, that is, until this world ends, but also in the other world, which is called 'world without end.'"

Part II, Introduction

1. On what follows, see B. Studer, *"Credo in Deum Patrem omnipotentem:* Zum Gottesbegriff des heiligen Augustinus," *Atti: Congresso internazionale su S. Agostino nel XVI Centenario della Conversione,* Studia Ephemeridis "Augustinianum" 24 (1987) 163-188, with bibliography.

2. See especially A. von Harnack, *Lehrbuch der Dogmengeschichte,* 4th ed., vol. 3: *Die Entwickelung des kirchlichen Dogmas,* pts. 2-3 (Tübingen, 1910, rpt. Darmstadt, 1964) 3, 64f., 100 ("He loved God, he loved his Church, and he was truthful"), 106ff. (citing *Sol.* 1.2.7); R. Seeberg, *Lehrbuch der Dogmengeschichte,* 3rd ed., vol. 2: *Die Dogmenbildung in der Alten Kirche* (1923; rpt. Darmstadt, 1953); E. Przywara, *Augustinus: Die Gestalt als Gefüge* (Leipzig, 1934), especially 30-34, 191-296; R. Guardini, *Die Bekehrung des Aurelius Augustinus,* 2nd ed. (Munich, 1950) 94-107; ET: *The Conversion of Augustine,* trans. E. Briefs (Westminster, MD, 1960) 71-84 ("The Blissful Life and the God-Value"); H. Urs von Balthasar, *Herrlichkeit,* vol. 2: *Fächer des Stils* (Einsiedeln, 1962) 97-108; ET: *The Glory of the Lord: A Theological Aesthetics,* vol. 2: *Studies in Theological Styles: Clerical Styles,* trans. A. Louth et al. (San Francisco, 1984) 95-143; L. Boros, *Aurelius Augustinus: Gotteserfahrung und Weg in die Welt* (Olten, 1982) 71-135.

3. See B. Studer, *La riflessione teologica nella Chiesa imperiale (sec. IV e V)* (Rome, 1989) 48f.

4. See B. Studer, "Zum Aufbau von Augustins *De civitate Dei,*" *Mélanges T. J. van Bavel* (Leuven, 1990) 937-951.

5. See *Sol.* 1.2.7.

6. *Conf.* 1.1.1 (Chadwick, 3).

7. Extensive bibliographical references, especially on the question of God, are given in the bibliography of A. Schindler, "Augustinus," *TRE* 4 (1979) 689-698. Further references are in my own articles: *"Credo in Deum Patrem omnipotentem"* (note 1, above); "Agostino d'Ippona e il Dio dei Libri sapienziali: Letture cristiane dei Libri sapienziali," Incontro di Studiosi dell'Antichita cristiana, *Letture cristiane dei Libri sapienziali,* Studia Ephemeridis "Augustinianum" 37 (1992) 115-125; *"Deus, Pater et Dominus* bei Augustinus von Hippo," *Festschrift C. Stead* (Leiden, 1993).

8. It is not possible to enter here into the discussion of the relationship between theology and philosophy in Augustine, a discussion that was already under way in the Middle Ages and has continued until today. See C. Stead, *Philosophie und Theologie,* vol. 1: *Die Zeit der Alten Kirche* (Stuttgart, 1990), and see *TRev* 88 (1992) 119-123.

9. See Schindler, "Augustinus," 660ff.: excursus on Augustine's development according to the scholarship of the last ninety years.

10. A. von Harnack, *Augustins "Confessionen"* (Giessen, 1988).

11. See F. Loofs, *Leitfaden zum Studium der Dogmengeschichte,* 1st ed. (Tübingen, 1889), no. 47.; W. Thimme, *Augustins geistige Entwicklung in den ersten Jahren nach seiner "Bekehrung," 386-391* (Berlin, 1908).

12. P. Courcelle, *Recherches sur les Confessions de saint Augustin* (Paris, 1950; 2nd ed., 1968).

13. See especially J. J. O'Meara, *The Young Augustine: The Growth of St. Augustine's Mind up to His Conversion* (London, 1954).

14. R. Holte. *Béatitude et Sagesse: St. Augustin et le problème de la fin de l'homme dans la philosophie ancienne* (Paris, 1962).

15. See Schindler, "Augustinus," 661f.

16. For judgments on the historicity of the *Confessions,* see A. Solignac in BA 13:55-84 (1962). On the question of the Platonism of the Church Fathers and of Augustine in particular, see R. Arnou, "Platonisme (des Pères)," *DTC* 12 (1935) 2258-2392; R. J. O'Connell, *St. Augustine's Platonism* (Villanova, 1984); W. Beierwaltes, *Denken des Einen: Studien zur neuplatonischen Philosophie und ihrer Wirkungsgeschichte* (Frankfurt, 1985); W.

Pannenberg, "Christentum und Platonismus: Die kritische Platonrezeption Augustins und ihre Bedeutung für das gegenwärtige christliche Denken," *ZKG* 96 (1985) 147-161; G. Madec, "Platonisme," *Catholicisme* 11 (1986) 491-507; A. Solignac, "Platonisme," *DSp* 12/2 (1986) 1803-1811.

17. See especially G. Madec, *S. Ambroise et la Philosophie* (Paris, 1974); F. Regen, "Zu Augustins Darstellung des Platonismus am Anfang des 8. Buches der *Civitas Dei*," *Festschrift H. Dörrie* (Münster, 1983) 208-227.

18. See, for example, O. Du Roy, *L'intelligence de la foi en la Trinité selon saint Augustin* (Paris, 1966); Schindler, "Augustinus," 685-687 (teaching on God and Christology).

19. A selection of studies on this point are J. Hausleiter, "*Deus internus* c.xv, Augustinus," *RAC* 3 (1957) 834-838; B. Aland, "*Cogitare Deum* in den *Confessiones* Augustins," *Pietas: Festschrift B. Kötting* (Münster, 1980) 93-104; H. J. Horn, "Gottesbeweis," *RAC* 11 (1981) 951-977, especially 97 ff.; K. Flasch, *Augustin: Einführung in sein Denken* (Stuttgart, 1980); I. Bochet, *Désir de Dieu* (Paris, 1982); B. Studer, "God," *EECh* 1:354-356; G. Bonner, "Christ, God and Man, in the Thought of Saint Augustine," *Angelicum* 61 (1984) 268-294.

20. See K. Flasch, *Die Logik des Schreckens: Augustinus von Hippo, Die Gnadenlehre von 397* (Mainz, 1990) especially, 10, 31, 40ff., 46, 88f., 92, 96.

21. P. Alfaric, *L'évolution intellectuelle de saint Augustin,* vol. 1: *Du manichéisme au néoplatonisme* (Paris, 1918).

22. See Schindler, "Augustinus," 660.

23. G. Quispel, "Mani the Apostle of Jesus Christ," *Mélanges J. Daniélou* (Paris, 1972) 667-672, especially 672.

24. See Schindler, "Augustinus," 658.

25. See *Util. cred.* 1.2.

26. On the subject generally, see Schindler, "Augustinus," 694. Further, see especially A. Adam, "Das Fortwirken des Manichäismus bei Augustin," *ZKG* 69 (1958) 1-25 (as well as his *Lehrbuch der Dogmengeschichte,* vol. 1: *Die Zeit der Alten Kirche* [Gütersloh, 1965]); F. Decret, *Aspects du manichéisme dans l'Afrique romaine* (Paris, 1970); W. Geerlings, "Zur Frage des Nachwirkens des Manichäismus in der Theologie Augustins," *ZKT* 93 (1971) 45-60 (and see his *Christus Exemplum: Studien zur Christologie und Christusverkündigung Augustins,* Tübinger Theologische Studien 13 [Mainz, 1978]); E. Feldmann, *Der Einfluss des Hortensius und des Manichäismus auf das Denken des jungen Augustinus von 373* (Münster, 1975) (and "Christus-Frömmigkeit des Manijünger," *Pietas: Festschrift B. Kötting* [Münster, 1980] 196-216, with bibliography); G. Wenning, "Der Einfluss des Manichäismus und des Ambrosius auf die Hermeneutik Augustins," *REAug* 36 (1990) 80-90; R. A. Markus, "Augustine's *Confessions* and the Controversy with Julian of Eclanum: Manicheism Revisited," *Mélanges T. J. van Bavel* (Leuven, 1990) 913-925; J. van Oort, *Jerusalem and Babylon: A Study in Augustine's City of God and the Sources of His Doctrine of the Two Cities* (London, 1991); M. G. Mara, "Agostino e la polemica antimanichea: Il ruolo di Paolo e del suo epistolario," *Aug* 32 (1992) 119-143.

27. Przywara, *Augustinus,* 91f.

28. It is worth noting, however, that this outline of a teaching on God is already announced in Cicero's *De natura deorum* 2.3: "In general the philosophers of our school [the Stoics] divide the whole theological question into four parts. First, we teach that divine beings exist. Second, we explain their nature. Third, we describe their government of the

world. And last, we show how they care for [humankind]" (Cicero, *The Nature of the Gods,* trans. H.C.P. McGregor [Penguin Books; New York, 1972] 123-124).

29. See E. Portalié, "Augustin," *DTC* 1 (1902) 2268-2472; ET: *A Guide to the Thought of St. Augustine,* trans. R. J. Bastian (Chicago, 1960); X. Le Bachelet, "Dieu," *DTC* 4 (1911) 1023-1152.

30. E. Gilson, *Introduction à l'étude de saint Augustin* (Paris, 1929; 4th ed., 1969); ET: *The Christian Philosophy of Saint Augustine,* trans. L. E. M. Lynch (New York, 1960). See also F. Cayré, *Initiation à la philosophie de s. Augustin* (Paris, 1947); Cayré, *Dieu présent dans la vie de l'esprit* (Paris, 1951).

31. See, among others, S. J. Grabowsky, *The All-Present God: A Study in St. Augustine* (St. Louis, 1954); A. D. R. Polman, *De leer van God bij Augustinus* (Kampen, 1965); E. TeSelle, *Augustine the Theologian* (New York, 1970). See also M. Schmaus, *Die psychologische Trinitätslehre des hl. Augustinus,* 2nd ed. (Münster, 1927; rpt. 1967).

32. G. Pelland, *Cinq études d'Augustin sur le début de la Genèse* (Paris, 1972); A. Solignac, in P. Vignaux, ed., *In Principio: Interprétation des premiers versets de la Genèse* (Paris, 1973) 153-171. See also B. Studer, *Zur Theophanie-Exegese Augustins: Untersuchungen zu einem Ambrosius-Zitat in der Schrift "De videndo Deo" (ep. 147),* Studia Anselmiana 59 (Rome, 1971).

33. G. Knauer, *Die Psalmenzitate in den Konfessionen Augustins* (Göttingen, 1955); M. Vincent, *S. Augustin, Maître de prière d'après les Enarrationes in Psalmos,* Théologie historique 84 (Paris, 1990). See also G. Madec, "Connaissance de Dieu et action de grâce: Essai sur les citations de l'Epître aux Romains 1,18-25 dans l'oeuvre de saint Augustin," *RechAug* 2 (1962) 273-309; D. Dideberg, *St. Augustin et la Première Epître de s. Jean,* Théologie historique 34 (Paris, 1975).

34. See B. Studer, "Zum Aufbau von Augustins *De civitate Dei*" (note 4, above) 937-951 (bibliography).

35. See C. Eichenseer, *Das Symbolum Apostolicum beim hl. Augustinus: Mit Berücksichtigung des dogmengeschichtlichen Zusammenhanges,* Kirchengeschichtliche Quellen und Studien 4 (St. Ottilien, 1960).

36. Schindler, "Augustinus," 685. See, earlier, H. Weinand, *Die Gottesidee, der Grundzug der Weltanschauung des heiligen Augustinus* (Paderborn, 1910).

37. See the conclusions reached by L. Wittmann, *Ascensus: Der Aufstieg zur Transzendenz in der Metaphysik Augustins* (Munich, 1980), and some pages in Flasch, *Augustin,* and especially Flasch's *Die Logik des Schreckens.*

38. See Schindler, "Augustinus," 662, with reasons for a similar approach.

39. See Studer, *La riflessione teologica,* especially 142-193.

40. It is not an exaggeration to say that the well-known observations of K. Rahner, in his "*Theos* in the New Testament," *Theological Investigations,* vol. 1, trans. C. Ernst (Baltimore, 1961) 79-148, also apply to a great extent to the writings of Augustine. See especially 147, where, referring to Th. de Regnon, *Etudes de théologie positive sur la Trinité,* vol. 1, 495-499, Rahner says: "In the official prayers of the liturgy, it is the Father to whom we pray through the Son, and this Father is simply called *Deus.*"

Part II, Chapter 1

1. See A. Solignac, *Augustin, Les Confessions,* BA 13 (Paris, 1962) 181. On the subject, see B. Aland, "*Cogitare Deum* in den *Confessiones* Augustinus," *Pietas: Festschrift B.*

Kötting (Münster, 1980) 93–104, especially 94; L. Sánchez Navarro, "La noción de Dios en las *Confessiones*," *Aug* 34 (1989) 347–354; G. Madec, *La patrie et la voie: Le Christ dans la vie et la pensée de saint Augustin,* Jésus et Jésus-Christ 36 (Paris, 1989) 21–82 ("La conversion").

2. In addition to Solignac's introduction in BA 13:9-233, see A. Trapè, *Agostino, Le Confessioni,* 3rd ed., NBA 1 (Rome, 1975), Introduction; A. Schindler, "Augustinus," *TRE* 4 (1979) 660–662 (Excursus on scholarship in this area). See also C. Quillen, "Consensius as a Reader of Augustine's *Confessions,*" *REAug* 37 (191) 87–109; J. Fontaine, "Introduzione generale," in *Sant'Agostino: Confessioni,* vol. 1 (Rome: Fondazione L. Valla, 1992) ix–cxxxiv.

3. A. Trapè, "Saint Augustine," A. Di Berardino, ed., *Patrology,* vol. 4: *The Golden Age of Latin Patristic Literature from the Council of Nicea to the Council of Chalcedon,* trans. P. Solari (Westminster, Md., 1992) 343. See also E. Feldmann, *"Et inde rediens fecerat sibi Deum (Conf.* 7.20): Beobachtungen zur Genese des augustinischen Gottesbegriffes und zu dessen Funktion in den *Confessiones,*" *Mélanges T. J. van Bavel* (Leuven, 1990) 881–904, especially 385: "The accounts given in the *Confessions* for the periods prior to and in Milan are reliable, but they are to be interpreted as a story that has been reflected on."

4. See *Conf.* 1.1.1.

5. See *Conf.* 8.12.29 (citing Rom 13:13f.). On the subject, see Solignac, BA 13:252-255: "V. La scène du jardin et le Tolle, lege" (with bibliography to 1962).

6. See G. Madec, "Notes sur l'intelligence de la foi," *REAug* 17 (1971) 119–142; Madec, "Pour l'interprétation de *Contra Academicos* II,II,5," *REAug* 17 (1971) 322–328, especially 324 (Augustine looks back to the faith of his childhood, and this leads him to read Paul).

7. See Solignac, BA 13:113-163 (with earlier literature); A. Mandouze, *S. Augustin: L'aventure de la raison et de la grâce* (Paris, 1968) 83–119; Schindler, "Augustinus," 646–650, 656–662; K. Flasch, *Augustin: Einführung in sein Denken* (Stuttgart, 1980) 229–262; G. Bonner, "(Aurelius) Augustinus," *AugLex,* vol. 1, fasc. 4 (1990) 519–550. For problems concerning the history of philosophy and the history of literature, see P. Courcelle, *Recherches sur les Confessions de saint Augustin* (Paris, 1950). On the subject, see G. Madec, "Dieu dans la conversion d'Augustin," *Didaskalia* 19 (1989) 1–19.

8. See, for example, *Conf.* 3.2.2ff. (criticism of the theater).

9. On what follows, see also W. Geerlings, "Bekehrung durch Belehrung," *TTZ* 167 (1987) 195–208. And see the observations of Madec, "Dieu dans la conversion d'Augustin," 1ff.

10. See Solignac, BA 13:130, and Flasch, *Augustin,* 17–20, 28–35.

11. See R. J. Teske, "Immortality," *The Modern Schoolman* 63 (1986) 233–249: on the surmounting of Manicheism and the encounter with Platonism according to *Conf.* 7.

12. On this phase of Augustine's intellectual development, see Solignac, BA 14:550ff. ("Idipsum"); B. Studer, *"Credo in Deum Patrem omnipotentem:* Zum Gottesbegriff des heiligen Augustinus," *Atti: Congresso internazionale su S. Agostino nel XVI Centenario della Conversione,* Studia Ephemeridis "Augustinianum" 24 (Rome, 1987) 165–171, and especially Feldmann, *"Et inde rediens . . .,"* 888ff. (according to whom, *Conf.* 7.14.20 represents a turning point in Augustine's development of his philosophical concept of God).

13. See especially the schematic summary in Feldmann, *"Et inde rediens . . .,"* 889, note 33.

14. See Solignac, BA 13:9-54, 207–233. On the subject, see J. Fontaine, "Une révolution littéraire dans l'Occident latin: Les Confessions de s. Augustin," *BLE* 88 (1987) 173–193.

15. See Solignac, BA 13:9-12; M. Vincent, "Le vocabulaire de la prière chez s. Augustin," *Mélanges T. J. van Bavel* (Leuven, 1990) 783–804, especially 803f.

16. See Solignac, BA 13:36-40, where this aspect is inadequately treated; Flasch, *Augustin,* says nothing at all about it; S. Poque, "L'invocation de Dieu dans les *Confessions,"* *Mélanges T. J. van Bavel* (Leuven, 1990) 927–935, does not go into the sources.

17. See G. N. Knauer, *Die Psalmenzitate in den Konfessionen Augustins* (Göttingen, 1955), especially 31–74 ("Zitate bei Anrufungen Gottes"). See also S. Poque, "Les Psaumes dans les *Confessions,"* *Saint Augustin et la Bible,* ed. A.-M. La Bonnardière (Paris, 1986) 155–166; K. Kienzler, "Der Aufbau der *Confessiones* des Augustin im Spiegel der Bibelzitate," *RechAug* 24 (1989) 123–164.

18. See Solignac, BA 13:12-15 ("Un dialogue avec Dieu"), 223f.; A. Mandouze, *S. Augustin,* 665–714 ("Rencontre avec Dieu").

19. See *Ep.* 3.1.

20. See Mandouze, *S. Augustin,* 677: "God is not just in charge of the intellectual work but is the main character in the *Confessions.*"

21. See *Conf.* 11.2.2-4, where Augustine renews his dialogue with God. Solignac, BA 13:19ff., along with Pl. Landsberg, distinguishes three major themes in the *Confessions:* memory (1–9), contemplation (10), and expectation (11–13); we may add that in all three parts, Augustine is speaking with God.

22. See, further, *Conf.* 1.7.12; 1.8.13; 1.9.14; 1.13.21; 1.15.24; 1.18.28.

23. See *Conf.* 1.11.17; 7.9.14 (with a paraphrase of Phil 2:6-11); and especially 9.4.7ff. with the words, "You subjected Alypius . . . to the name of your only-begotten Son, our Lord and Saviour Jesus Christ" (no. 7) (Chadwick, 160), and the prayer, largely made up of words from the psalms, that is addressed to the Lord and the Father (nos. 8f.). On the whole question, see the conclusion reached by Poque, "L'invocation de Dieu dans les Confessions," 932f.: "While the trinitarian God is formally invoked, 'God, one trinity and triune unity,' and while we find, though rarely, an invocation of Christ, 'Lord Jesus, Christ Jesus,' it is upon the Father that Augustine most often calls, 'Father, good Father' *(pater bone* or *bone pater)."* In his footnotes, Poque cites a whole series of passages, including *Conf.* 10.31.46; 11.17.22; 11.22.28. The question of whether "God" means the Father in particular is not raised.

24. The question of the extent to which such expressions as "gentle Father," "good Father," and especially "Father of piety" echo not only the Bible but the language of antiquity is taken up in H. Stirnimann, *Grund und Gründer des Alls: Augustins Gebet in den Selbstgesprächen* (Freiburg, 1992) 74f.; in his commentary on *Sol.* 1.1.2, he gives references to the name "father" in Plato and Plotinus.

25. See Stirnimann, *Grund und Gründer,* 18f., with the reference to W. Beierwaltes, *Denken des Einen: Studien zur neuplatonischen Philosophie und ihrer Wirkungsgeschichte* (Frankfurt, 1985).

26. See M.-A. Vannier, *"Creatio," "conversio," "formatio" chez s. Augustin,* Paradosis 31 (Fribourg, 1991), where, with references to the studies of J. Pépin and E. R. Dodds, the author brings out the difference between Plotinus and Augustine in regard to a personal God and thus between Greek and biblical anthropology.

27. See Feldmann, *"Et inde rediens . . .,"* 901, with the reference to W. Simon, "Von Gott reden, Beobachtungen und Bemerkungen zu Augustins *Conf.* I,4," *WissWeis* 45 (1982) 130–157.

28. See BA 13:652-657.

29. See A. Trapè, *Patrologia,* ed. A. Di Berardino, vol. 3 (Casale, 1978) 388.

30. See Solignac, BA 13:182 (transcendence and immanence in Augustine).

31. See the entire context of *Conf.* 6.3.4. Add *Conf.* 3.8.16: "God most high and most gentle" (Chadwick, 47).

32. On God as creator, see *Conf.* 11.12.14–13.16 (on eternity and time, without which there is no creation); 11.31.41; 12.11.11 and 12.15.19 (on the eternity of the creator); 13.5.6 (the Trinity as creator of the entire creation).

33. See especially *Conf.* 7.10.16; 7.12.18; 12.15.18. On the theme, see Feldmann, *"Et inde rediens . . .,"* 899, and *Conf.* 10.2.2: "Now however my groaning is witness that I am displeased with myself. You are radiant and give delight and are . . . an object of love and longing" (Chadwick, 179). Consequently, in his conversion, Augustine became aware that God is his creator. See also Vannier, *"Creatio,"* 20–43 (on Augustine and Neoplatonism, with the most important passsages from the *Conf.;* according to Vannier, the Neoplatonic return into the self was an experience of creation).

34. See *Conf.* 1.3.3: "Or have you, who contain all things, no need to be contained by anything because what you will you fill by containing it? We cannot think you are given coherence by vessels full of you, because even if they were to be broken, you would not be spilt. When you are 'poured out' (Joel 2:28) upon us, you are not wasted on the ground. You raise us upright. You are not scattered but reassemble us" (Chadwick, 4). *Conf.* 3.11.19 (conclusion of the account of Monica's vision): "You are good and all-powerful, caring for each one of us as though the only one in your care, and yet for all as for each individual" (Chadwick, 50). See Solignac, BA 13:181-186, on the presence and providence of God, with further texts; see especially 183: "God acts in all things and through all things, but in wonderful and hidden ways" (citing *Conf.* 4.4.7; 5.6.10; 5.7.13; 7.21.27).

35. See Feldmann, *"Et inde rediens . . .,"* 900f.

36. Ibid., 891ff. (citing *Conf.* 7.14.20).

37. See *Retr.* 2.1.1, with its judgment on the *Quaestiones ad Simplicianum.*

38. See Solignac, BA 13:181 (on the two poles, God and sin); 184ff.: "As I became unhappier, you came closer" (*Conf.* 6.16.26) (Chadwick, 109).

39. See *Conf.* 7.10.16 and 2.10.18, with the explanation of Solignac, BA 13:664f., as well as *Conf.* 1.18.28: "The younger son . . . went to live in a far country and prodigally dissipated what you, his gentle father, had given him on setting out (Luke 15:11-32), showing yourself even gentler on his return as a bankrupt. To live there in lustful passion is to live in darkness and to be far from your face" (Chadwick, 20), with the explanation in BA 13:662f.

40. *Conf.* 10.28.38 (Chadwick, 201), with BA 16:569ff.

41. *Conf.* 7.10.16. See *Conf.* 10.45.65, as well as *Beata v.* 1.4, with allusions to Cicero and Plotinus. See also Feldmann, *"Et inde rediens . . .,"* 885f. on the significance of *Conf.* 7 (with the literature on the subject).

42. See *Conf.* 3.4.7f. (philosophy as love of wisdom), as well as *Conf.* 6.11.18; 8.7.17. See Solignac, BA 13:667f., and Holte, *Béatitude et Sagesse: St. Augustin et le problème de la fin de l'homme dans la philosophie ancienne* (Paris, 1962) 17f.

43. See *Conf.* 3.4.7 (although nothing is said here of truth). A comparison with *Util. cred.* 1.1 shows, however, that Cicero in fact laid a great emphasis on truth. See also *Conf.*

3.6.10, according to which the Manichees promised truth. On the entire question, see O. Du Roy, *L'intelligence de la foi en la Trinité selon saint Augustin* (Paris, 1966) 25–29, especially 27 and note 4; Flasch, *Augustin,* 58; Madec, *S. Augustin, Dialogues philosophiques,* pt. 3: *De magistro—De Libero arbitrio,* BA 6, 3rd ed. (Paris, 1976) 172, note 39, and 554–557, with the reference to M. Testard, *S. Augustin et Cicéron,* 67.

44. See *Conf.* 9.10.23; 10.23.33; 10.45.60; 12.25.34. See Feldmann, *"Et inde rediens . . .,"* 902, with the reference to E. König, *Augustinus Philosophus* (Munich, 1970) 77–86, where passages of the *Confessions* are cited in which God and the truth are identified. See also Geerlings, "Bekehrung durch Belehrung," 195–207; G. Cavacoli, "Dio come verità eterna in S. Agostino," *Sacra Doctrina* 32 (Bologna, 1987) 665–687.

45. See *Conf.* 6.4.6, and Flasch, *Augustin,* 55–66, as well as F. Decret, *L'Afrique manichéenne (IVᵉ–Vᵉ siècles)* (Paris, 1978) 243f.

46. See *Conf.* 10.40.65: "Without you [truth] I could discern none of these things, and I found that none of these things was you" (Chadwick, 217), as well as *Conf.* 1.1.1, together with *Beata v.* 1.4. On the subject, see Flasch, *Augustin,* 225, and BA 14:566. See also R. A. Markus, "Augustine's Confessions and the Controversy with Julian of Eclanum," *Mélanges T. J. van Bavel* (Leuven, 1990) 915f., concerning the influence of the new vision of 396 on the necessity of grace as seen in the *Confessions.*

47. See *Conf.* 7.17.23; 8.10.16. See Solignac, BA 13:104f. and 682–689, with the reference to texts of Plotinus, especially *Enneads* 6.1; also Poque, "L'invocation de Dieu," 931f., with passages in which God is invoked as light.

48. See Schindler, "Augustinus," 665f. (excursus, with bibliography); E. Gilson, *The Christian Philosophy of St. Augustine,* trans. L.E.M. Lynch (New York, 1960) 96–105; Holte, *Béatitude et Sagesse,* 352f.

49. See D. Doucet, "L'*ars memoriae* dans les *Confessiones,*" *REAug* 33 (1987) 49–69. See also A. Trapè, NBA 1:xv, and Solignac, BA 14:557-567 and *DSp* 10 (1980) 994–999.

50. See *Conf.* 2.1.1 (remembrance of his sinful past); 9.3.6 (God is mindful of us); 10.8.12 (description of memory); 9.7.16: "'Thanks be to you, my God' (Luke 18:11). From what starting-point and to what end have you led my memory to include even these events in my confession to you, when I have passed over much that I have forgotten?" (Chadwick, 166); 13.1.1 (God has never forgotten Augustine): "You made me and, when I forgot you, you did not forget me" (Chadwick, 273). See *En. Ps.* 24.6.

51. See *Conf.* 10.17.26: "Memory . . . this is mind, this is I myself" (Chadwick, 194). See BA 14:557-567, especially 560. In this context, Augustine explains: "I will also ascend beyond memory to touch [God]. . . . As I rise above memory, where am I to find you? . . . And how shall I find you if I am not mindful of you?" (Chadwick, 195).

52. See *Conf.* 13.34.49, on predestination, especially: "All these things we see, and they are very good, because you see them in us, having given us the Spirit by which we see you and love you in them" (Chadwick, 304). See Flasch, *Augustin,* 258f., 229–232, and R. Lorenz, "Gnade und Erkenntnis bei Augustinus," *ZKG* 75 (1964) 21–78.

53. See NBA 3, pt. 1 (1970), for the writings composed before Augustine's baptism—*Contra Academicos, De beata vita, De ordine, Soliloquia, De immortalitate animae, Libri de disciplinis*—and NBA 3, pt. 2 (1976) for those composed after his baptism—*De animae quantitate, De libero arbitrio, De musica, De magistro.*

54. On these questions, see the relevant articles in the various lexikons, especially the *Augustinus-Lexikon (AugLex),* and the introductions to modern editions of the writings in question. On the "philosophy" of Augustine see Gilson, *Christian Philosophy of St.*

Augustine; Holte, *Béatitude et Sagesse;* Du Roy, *L'intelligence de la foi;* J. Verhees, "Augustins Trinitätsverständnis in den Schriften aus Cassiciacum," *RechAug* 10 (1975) 45–75, which provides correctives to some views of Du Roy.

55. See Studer, *La riflessione teologica nella Chiesa imperiale (sec. IV e V)* (Rome, 1989) 117ff.; C. Stead, *Philosophie und Theologie,* vol. 1: *Die Zeit der Alten Kirche* (Stuttgart, 1990).

56. See D. Gentili, NBA 3, pt. 1, xxxixff.; Verhees, "Augustins Trinitätsverständnis," 61; E. Mühlenberg, "Über die Ordnung *(De ordine),*" *Augustinus: Philosophische Frühdialoge,* ed. C. Andresen (Zurich, 1972) 217f. It is to be noted how often in these writings reference is made to the authority of the Scriptures and to the faith of the Catholic Church. Observe especially the fact that Augustine represents his mother, a woman of faith, as a friend of wisdom; see *Ord.* 1.11.31ff.; 2.20.52; *Conf.* 6.1.1; 1.11.17 (Monica linked to Mother Church). On the subject, see M. More O'Ferrall, "Monica, the Mother of Augustine," *RechAug* 10 (1975) 23–43, especially 40–43, with the reference to A. Mandouze, "Monique à Cassiciacum," *RELat* 47bis (1969) 131–141.

57. *Sol.* 1.1.1.

58. The point was already made by A. von Harnack, *Lehrbuch der Dogmengeschichte,* 4th ed., vol. 3 (Tübingen, 1909) 107ff.

59. See Gentili, NBA 3. pt. 1, xxxvii, and Mühlenberg, "Über die Ordnung," 217f.

60. See Gentili, NBA 3, pt. 1, xxxviii, with *Acad.* 2.19.42, and *Ord.* 2.5.16.

61. See B. R. Voss, "*Academicis,*" *AugLex* vol. 1, fascs. 1–2 (1986) 45–51; Du Roy, *L'intelligence de la foi,* 114–123 and passim; Flasch, *Augustin,* 55–66.

62. See *Retr.* 1.1.1-4.

63. See Voss, "*Academicis,*" 45f.

64. See *Retr.* 1.1.2: ("to live not according to reason but according to God"); 1.1.3 (God the Creator is in the divine self "the region of origin of the soul's blessedness").

65. On the concept of *exercitatio,* see *Mag.* 8.21, and H.-I. Marrou, *Saint Augustin et la fin de la culture antique,* 4th ed. (Paris, 1958) 304f., 486ff.

66. See *Retr.* 1.1.1; *Ench.* 7.20. On the subject, see Voss, "*Academicis,*" 49f.

67. *Acad.* 3.19.42. See 2.2.5, with the reference to the reading of Paul.

68. See Mühlenberg, "Über die Ordnung," 238. For the trinitarian background of the passage, see Verhees, "Augustins Trinitätsverständnis," 50ff.

69. See J. Doignon, "*Beata vita (De),*" *AugLex,* vol. 1, fasc. 4 (1990) 618–624, with extensive bibliographical references. Among the latter is the same author's new edition of the work in BA 4, pt. 1 (1986), with Introduction, 7–46. See also BA 13:79ff.; NBA 3, pt. 1, 169–225; Du Roy, *L'intelligence de la foi,* 149–168 (commentary on *Beat v.* 4.34f., with references to Cicero and Plotinus); I. Schwarz-Kirchenbauer and W. Schwarz, "Über das Glück *(De beata vita),*" *Augustinus: Philosophische Frühdialoge,* ed. C. Andresen (Zurich, 1972) 149–179; M. E. Miotti, "*De beata vita di Agostino: Rapporto con il V libro delle Tusculanae Disputationes* di Cicerone," *Scritti offerti a R. Iacoangeli,* ed. S. Felici, Biblioteca delle Scienze Religiose 10 (Rome, 1992) 203–225.

70. *Beata v.* 2.8f.

71. *Retr.* 1.2.

72. *Beata v.* 4.32: "Measure, then, is the soul's wisdom."

73. Ibid., 4.33.

74. See Du Roy, *L'intelligence de la foi,* 154–161, with references to Plotinus.

75. See Doignon, BA 4, pt. 1, 148, with the reference to Cicero.

76. See *Beata v.* 4.34.

77. *Retr.* 1.2.4.

78. *Beata v.* 4.26-30.

79. Ibid., 3.17; 4.33f. See J. Hausleiter, *"Fruitio Dei,* Augustinus," *RAC* 8 (1972) 551–555, with references to the sources and to relevant studies.

80. *Beata v.* 4.35: "'A certain admonition, flowing from the very foundation of truth, urges us to remember God, to seek [God], and to thirst after [God] tirelessly. . . . This, then, is the full satisfaction of souls, this the happy life: to recognize piously and completely the One through whom you are led into the truth, the nature of the truth you enjoy, and the bond that connects you with the supreme measure. These three show to the intelligent [person] the one God, the one Substance excluding the variety of all vain and superstitious images.' Our mother, recalling here these words that still deeply adhered in her memory, awoke to her faith, as it were, and, inflamed with joy, uttered this verse of our priest: 'Help, O Trinity, those that pray.' Then she added: 'Indeed, this is undoubtedly the happy life, that is, the perfect life which we must assume that we can attain soon by a well-founded faith, a joyful hope, and an ardent love'" (trans. L. Schopp, Fathers of the Church 1 [New York, 1948]). See NBA 3, pt. 1, 224, with the references to Plotinus; and Du Roy, *L'intelligence de la foi,* 165f.

81. See *Beata v.* 4.36, and Verhees, "Augustins Trinitätsverständnis," 59f.

82. See *Sol.* 1.1.4; *An. quant.* 2.3. On the subject, see G. O'Daly, *"Anima, animus,"* *AugLex* vol. 1, fascs. 1–3 (1986, 1988) 315–340.

83. See the Introductions in BA 5:7-21 and NBA 3, pt. 1, 363–376; Du Roy, *L'intelligence de la foi,* 143–147 (knowledge), 168–183 (passages on the Trinity), 196–206 (the great prayer).

84. See *Ep.* 3 (to Nebridius); *Retr.* 1.4.1.

85. *Sol.* 2.7.14.

86. Ibid., 1.2.7; see 1.12.20; 1.15.27.

87. Ibid., 2.1.1.

88. Ibid., 2.13.23; 2.15.27; 2.19.33.

89. Ibid., 2.18.32.

90. Ibid., 1.1.2-6. See the commentaries of Du Roy, *L'intelligence de la foi,* 196–206, and Stirnimann, *Grund und Gründer des Alls,* as well as G. Raeithel, "Das Gebet in den Soliloquien Augustins," *ZRG* 20 (1969) 139–153.

91. Du Roy, *L'intelligence de la foi,* 196.

92. *Sol.* 1.1.3, with the New Testament passages cited. For the Neoplatonic background, see Du Roy, *L'intelligence de la foi,* 196–203, and NBA 3, pt. 1, 384–391 (the notes).

93. See Solignac, BA 13:80f., and Du Roy, *L'intelligence de la foi,* 196f.

94. *Sol.* 1.1.2.

95. Ibid., 1.1.3.

96. Ibid., 1.1.3f.

97. Ibid., 1.1.4.

98. Ibid., 1.1.5f.

99. Verhees, "Augustins Trinitätsverständis," 60–70, where the author questions the trinitarian structure of the prayer. Elsewhere, Verhees seems more open to the hypothesis that the passage has a trinitarian meaning. He speaks there of a "certain stimulus" that reaches the point of a "sweet lingering"; see Verhees, "Die Bedeutung des Geistes Gottes

im Leben des Menschen nach Augustins frühester Pneumatologie (bis 391)," *ZKG* 88 (1977) 161–189, especially 172ff.

100. *Sol.* 1.1.4.

101. Ibid., 1.4.3.

102. In this supposition, we would be dealing with a kind of prayer which, according to Du Roy, *L'intelligence de la foi,* 206, note 2, occurs only here and in *Trin.* 15.27.51. However, see also *Ench.* 3.9.

103. *Sol.* 1.15.30.

104. See NBA 3, pt. 1, 491–547; Du Roy, *L'intelligence de la foi,* 183–196.

105. *Imm. an.* 8.14–11.18.

106. Ibid., 13.22.

107. NBA 3, pt. 1, 491–547; Du Roy, *L'intelligence de la foi,* 183–196; K.-H. Lütcke, "*Animae quantitate (De),*" *AugLex* 1, fasc. 3 (1988) 350–356.

108. *An. quant.* 7.12.

109. Ibid., 34.76.

110. Ibid., 2.3.

111. Ibid., 28.54f.

112. Ibid., 33.76: "If we hold with great constancy to the course which God has commanded us and which we undertook to hold, we will come by the power and wisdom of God to that supreme cause or supreme author or supreme origin of things, or whatever other name may be more suitably given to so great a reality." On the Neoplatonic background of the seven-stage ascent in *An. quant.* 33, 70–76, see Lütcke, "*Animae quantitate (De),*" 353.

113. *An. quant.* 34.77: "To sum up briefly: just as it must be admitted that the human soul is not what God is, so it must be taken for granted that nothing among all the things [God] has created is nearer to God than the soul. Therefore by divine revelation and in a special way in the Catholic Church it is handed down that no creature is to be worshiped by the soul . . . but only the creator of everything that is, the one from whom all things are, through whom all things are, in whom all things are; that is, the immutable source, the immutable wisdom, the immutable love, the one true and perfect God, who never was not, never will not be, never was different, never will be different; than whom nothing is more hidden, nothing more present . . . and anything else we humans can say that is more incredible but at the same time more suitable and fitting."

114. See *Civ.* 8.4. On the subject, see P. Alfaric, *L'évolution intellectuelle de saint Augustin,* vol. 1: *Du manichéisme au néoplatonisme* (Paris, 1918) 483, note 1, with *Mus.* 6.56; *Vera rel.* 55.113; and *Civ.* 8.4.

115. See *Conf.* 9.6.14.

116. See especially G. Madec, "Analyse du *De magistro,*" *REAug* 21 (1975) 63–71, as well as his introduction and commentary in BA 6, 3rd ed. See also NBA 3, pt. 1, 3–133; Du Roy, *L'intelligence de la foi,* 256–267.

117. *Mag.* 1.1-2.

118. Ibid., 2.3–11.37.

119. On the meaning of *docere* as "communicate," see Madec, BA 6, 3rd ed., 535f.

120. See especially *Mag.* 10.31.

121. See ibid., 10.33f.

122. See *Mag.* 11.36, especially: "It is a very valid argument and true saying that, when words are spoken, we either know or do not know what they mean; if we know, we are

remembering rather than learning; if we do not know, we do not even remember but are perhaps urged to seek the meaning."

123. See *Mag.* 14.46: "For the present, I have cautioned you that we must not ascribe more importance to words than is their due. Accordingly, we should no longer merely believe, but also begin to understand the truth of those words based on divine authority, that we should not call any [person] on earth a teacher, seeing that 'there is One in heaven who is the Teacher of all.' What is meant by 'in heaven' is something that will be taught us by [the one] who directs us even through human agencies and external signs to turn inwardly to [the one] for our instruction" (trans. R. Russell, The Fathers of the Church 59 [New York, 1968] 60). On the subject, see Du Roy, *L'intelligence de la foi,* 214.

124. See the note on *foris admonet, intus docet,* in Madec, BA 6, 3rd ed., 540–543, with the reference to *Serm.* 264.4. Also connected with the same idea are *credere* and *intelligere* in *Mag.* 11.37; see Madec, BA 6, 3rd ed., 549–551.

125. See *Beata v.* 4.35; *Sol.* 1.1.2f. See BA 6:477-479 (with bibliography); Du Roy, *L'intelligence de la foi,* 161–171; BA 6, 3rd ed., 543ff; Stirnimann, *Grund und Gründer,* 84ff.

126. See *Mag.* 11.38, especially: "But as for all those things which we 'understand,' it is not the outward sounds of the speaker's words that we consult, but the truth which presides over the mind itself from within, though we have been led to consult it because of the words. [The one] who is consulted and who is said to 'dwell in the inner [human being]' [that one] it is who teaches us, namely, Christ, that is to say, 'the unchangeable Power of God and everlasting Wisdom.' This is the wisdom which every rational soul does indeed consult, but it reveals itself to each according to [each one's] capacity to grasp it by reason of the good or evil dispositions of the will" (trans. Russell, 51). Especially to be noted is the parallel: to consult the truth, to consult Christ, who is "the unchangeable Power of God and everlasting Wisdom." See Du Roy, *L'intelligence de la foi,* 164, note 4 (on the theme of "consultation of the truth," which Augustine subsequently uses frequently); 214, note 3 (on the role of the external words by which persons are urged to enter into themselves and obtain the counsel of the Teacher).

127. See ibid., 11.36: "[The one] who is consulted and who is said to 'dwell in the inner [human being]' [that one] it is who teaches us, namely, Christ, that is to say, 'the unchangeable Power of God and everlasting Wisdom.'" (trans. Russell, 51). See also ibid., 12.40: "God disclosing it interiorly." On the subject, see W. Beierwaltes, "*Deus est veritas:* Zur Rezeption des griechischen Wahrheitsbegriffes in der frühchristlichen Theologie," *Pietas: Festschrift B. Kötting* (Münster, 1980) 15–29, especially 26–29.

128. *Civ.* 11.25.

129. See Madec, BA 6, 3rd ed., 34f.

130. See Vannier, *"Creatio,"* 34–38.

131. See *Mag.* 12.39. See BA 6:475ff.; Madec, BA 6, 3rd ed., 536ff. (on *commemoratio*).

132. See *Conf.* 10, and the commentaries on it, for example, BA 14:557-567.

133. See *Trin.* 15.7.12, as well as *Trin.* 9.7.12. See below, Chapter 2, Section 1, on "God" in *The Trinity.*

134. See NBA 3, pt. 1, 227–359; Mühlenberg, "Über die Ordnung," 213–243, especially 239–243, with the plan of the work, and especially J. Rief, *Der Ordobegriff des jungen Augustinus* (Paderborn, 1962).

135. See *Ord.* 1.3.6f.

136. See ibid., 1.4.10.

137. See the state of the question in ibid., 1.1.1–2.3.

138. See ibid., 1.7.17.

139. See ibid., 1.1.2 (comparison with a mosaic, from which one must stand back in order to view it).

140. See Rief, *Der Ordobegriff,* 251, according to whom the concept of evil as a deficiency makes its first appearance in *Ord.*

141. *Ord.* 1.7.18.

142. Ibid., 1.7.19.

143. See ibid., 1.9.27-10.30, especially 1.10.28: "Order is that by which all the things that God has established are set in motion," but also 9.27: "Order is that which if held to in this life will lead us to God, and if we do not hold to it, we will not reach God."

144. I. Hadot, *Arts libéraux et philosophie dans la pensée antique* (Paris, 1984) 101-136; W. Hübner, "Der *ordo* der Realien in Augustins Frühdialog *De ordine,*" *REAug* 33 (1987) 25-48.

145. See *Ord.* 2.5.17, with the references to the Neoplatonic background in Hadot, *Arts libéraux,* 131. See also the remark of Mühlenberg, "Über die Ordnung," 232: "The way to the vision of order, that is, to the certainty that God rules everything through the order God imposes, thus underlies this very order itself." For the trinitarian background of the passage, see Verhees, "Trinitätsverständnis," 60-64 and 64ff., with *Ord.* 1.9.26.

146. See Rief, *Der Ordobegriff,* 80-86 ("Das Gottesbild des jungen Augustinus"), where passages on the "well-disposed God" *(Deus propitius)* and on the "clemency of God" are given, for example, *Ord.* 1.10.29; 2.5.16 (goodness and incarnation).

147. See *Ord.* 2.9.16. I must mention at least Mühlenberg, "Über die Ordnung," 233ff., who speaks, with reference to this passage, of the three criteria of truth in the Christian religion and, with reference to the third, namely, the distinction between the divine authority and the phenomenal world, remarks that "Christ dies to the world and thereby points to reality, which is a world of the spirit and distinct from the world of the senses" (235).

148. See Hübner, "Der *ordo* der Realien," 48 (summary).

149. See NBA 3, pt. 2, 623-707.

150. *Mus.* 6.17.55-59.

151. Ibid., 6.14.45f., with the commentary of Holte, *Béatitude et Sagesse,* 165f. See also *Mus.* 6.5.14, on the difficulties the soul has in overcoming sin, with Rom 7:24f.

152. See *Beata v.* 1.4 and *Acad* 1.5. See Flasch, *Augustin,* 39f., with the reference to the influence of Ambrose.

153. See Flasch, *Augustin,* 67-73, where, with an eye on *Acad.* 3.17.37, he explains how Augustine understands the correspondence between God and the soul: the soul is seen as the source of knowledge and thereby of life, while God is the source of the intelligible world and thereby of unity; for God embraces all laws, while the soul with its dignity is able to live according to these laws.

154. See ibid., 78ff., on the optimism of the early writings.

155. See Flasch, *Die Logik des Schreckens,* 67-73, where he refers to *Sol.* 2.14.25, and *Acad.* 3.20.43, but also speaks of a decrease in Augustine's Platonism.

156. On *C. Fortunatum, C. Faustum,* and *C. Felicem,* see F. Decret, *Aspects du manichéisme dans l'Afrique romaine* (Paris, 1970) 39-89; for the other writings, see Decret, *L'Afrique,* 17-157. See also R. Jolivet and M. Jourjon, eds., *S. Augustin, Six traités anti-manichéennes,* BA 17 (Paris, 1961).

157. Decret, *L'Afrique,* 81. See J. Ries, "Dieux cosmiques et Dieu biblique dans la religion de Mani," *Mélanges T. J. van Bavel* (Leuven, 1990) 757-772, especially 763, where the author compares the two societies. See *Nat. b.* (399), which is a "second edition" of *Mor.*

158. See *Vera rel.* 9.17: "In this work I explain as best I can, with the arguments God deigns to give me, how secure the Catholic faith is against them [the Manichees], and how the considerations that move people to accept their opinions need not disturb the mind."

159. See Du Roy, *L'intelligence de la foi,* 310-317, with an analysis of the entire work.

160. See *Vera rel.* 9.16: "I believe that God will assist me so that this work . . . may be effective, not against one false and bad opinion only but against all. Mainly, however, it is aimed at those who think that there are two natures or substances, each with its own principle, that are in rebellion against one another." See *Retr.* 1.13 (12).1: "This book is, however, directed chiefly against the two natures of the Manichees."

161. Decret, *L'Afrique,* 81.

162. In addition to Decret, *Aspects,* see A.-M. La Bonnardière, "Ecrits manichéens transmis par le seul Augustin," *S. Augustin et la Bible,* ed. A.-M. La Bonnardière (Paris, 1986) 331f.

163. See Decret, *Aspects,* 39-89, especially 62, with the extensive footnote on the literary genre of the *capitulum.* See also Decret, *L'Afrique,* 217-220, with the description of the historical context of both disputations.

164. See Decret, *L'Afrique,* 281f., on the historical value of what Augustine has to say about African Manicheism; see also, much earlier, Alfaric, *L'évolution intellectuelle de saint Augustin,* 215-219.

165. See G. Bonner, *St. Augustine of Hippo* (London, 1963) 193-236.

166. See *Ep.* 236.2; *Util. cred.* 18.36; *Vera rel.* 9.16, as well the late and very polemical passage in *Haer.* 36. In these passages, reference is also made to Christological Docetism, but this is not our concern here.

167. See BA 17:12ff., and above all, Decret, *L'Afrique,* 235-246 ("3. Aspects intérieurs du manichéisme en Afrique"), where the author outlines Manichean teachings in the area of knowledge and of theodicy and anthropology.

168. See BA 17:14: "Augustine always ends up showing how unworthy of God is a teaching that dares to represent God in this way."

169. See *C. Sec.* 2 (BA 17:512ff.), with the objection that Augustine had abandoned the truth out of fear, and where Augustine says in his defense that he had abandoned the sect out of fear of God.

170. In addition to Decret, numerous authors, J. Ries foremost among them, have in various studies dealt with African Manicheism in Augustine's time. However, these studies rely in great measure on H.-Ch. Puech, *Le manichéisme: Son fondateur, sa doctrine* (Paris, 1949).

171. See Decret, *L'Afrique,* 285-289 (the entrance into the self leads to knowledge of the kinship of human beings with God); 323ff. (on the two souls, one of which emanates from God).

172. See ibid., 239-289 (the paths of knowledge), especially 265 (on enlightenment) and 268 (on the role of the community).

173. See A. Adam, "Der manichäische Ursprung der Lehre von den zwei Reichen bei Augustin," *TLZ* 77 (1952) 385-390; Adam, "Das Fortwirken des Manichäismus bei Augustin," *ZKG* 69 (1958) 1-25. See also Decret, *L'Afrique,* 348f., where the author, despite all his reservations regarding the supposed traces of Manicheism in Augustine, establishes

that the separation between Manichees and Christians in the Africa of 400 was not as great as the ancient and medieval heresiologists claimed. See also J. van Oort, *Jerusalem and Babylon: A Study of Augustine's City of God and the Sources of His Doctrine of the Two Cities* (Leiden, 1991).

174. W. Geerlings, "Zur Frage des Nachwirkens des Manichäismus in der Theologie Augustins," *ZKT* 93 (1971) 45-60.

175. See Vannier, *"Creatio,"* 44-62.

176. See the passages in which Augustine prays for the Manichees or urges them to conversion: *Duab. an.* 15.24; *C. ep. Man.* 1.1-2.2; *C. Sec.* 24. On these, see Decret, *L'Afrique,* 155f.

177. In connection with the following expositions, see especially Madec, BA 6, 3rd ed.

178. See *Lib. arb.* 1.2.4, as well as what was said earlier about *Ord.* See also Madec, BA 6, 3rd ed., 171-173, on the origin of the problem according to the stories of Augustine's own experiences which he relates in the *Confessions.*

179. The *De libero arbitrio* is not explicitly presented as a piece of anti-Manichean polemics, but *Ep.* 166.3.7, and *Retr.* 1.9.1 and 6, as well as parallel passages from the same period, leave no doubt on the point. See Madec, BA 6, 3rd ed., 174f., as well as F. De Capitani, *Il De libero arbitrio di S. Agostino: Studio introduttivo, testo, traduzione e commento* (Milan, 1987); R. J. O'Connell, "'Involuntary Sin' in *Libero arbitrio*," *REAug* 37 (1991) 23-36.

180. *Lib. arb.* 1.4. See 2.6, and *Vera rel.* 9.17.

181. On the influence of Plotinus and Porphyry, see Madec, BA 6, 3rd ed., 175-178 and especially 557-561. Unfortunately, Madec does not go into the differences between Augustine and the Neoplatonists in their concept of sin.

182. In addition to Madec, see the critical edition by W. M. Green in CSEL 74 (1956), reprinted in CCL 29 (1970) 205-321; F. J. Thonnard (ed.), *S. Augustin, Dialogues philosophiques: De magistro—De libero arbitrio,* BA 6 (Paris, 1952); Du Roy, *L'intelligence de la foi,* 241-254; Decret, *L'Afrique,* 51-63.

183. It is to be noted that from *Lib. arb.* 3.12 onward, the text gives a discourse of Augustine.

184. See Madec, BA 6, 3rd ed., 551-554, on the *lex aeterna,* with references to the Ciceronian origin of the concept. See Cicero, *De re publica* 3.22.33: "True law is right reason in agreement with nature; it is of universal application, unchanging and everlasting. . . . There will be one master and ruler, that is, God, over us all, for [God] is the author of this law, its promulgator, and its enforcing judge. Whoever is disobedient is fleeing from [oneself] and denying [one's] human nature, and by reason of this very fact will suffer the worst penalties, even if [one] escapes what is commonly considered punishment" (trans. C. W. Keyes, Loeb Library [New York, 1928] 211).

185. On the implications for moral theology of these reflections of Augustine, see Holte, *Béatitude et Sagesse,* 229 and 248, with various parallel passages.

186. See Madec, BA 6, 3rd ed., 561-566, on *Lib. arb.* 2.3.7-15.39; H. J. Horn, "Gottesbeweis," *RAC* 11 (1981) 951-977, especially 971ff., on Augustine; W. M. Neumann, *Die Stellung des Gottesbeweises in Augustins De libero arbitrio* (Hildesheim, 1986). In fact, this proof of God's existence is not regarded as apodictic even by Augustine himself (see *Ep.* 162.2). It is rather a kind of *intellectus fidei.* See Holte, *Béatitude et Sagesse,* 357-360.

187. See especially *Lib. arb.* 2.19.53.

188. See BA 6:134, and especially *Lib. arb.* 1.2.5, with the principle that underlies the conversation between Augustine and Evodius: "To think well of God is the truest source of piety."

189. See *Retr.* 1.9 (8).3-6, with the defense of the views presented in *Lib. arb.* On this point, see Madec, BA 6, 3rd ed., 179f.

190. See Madec, BA 6, 3rd ed., 174f.

191. See *Duab. an.* 1.1 and 2.2 (all souls are created by God); *C. Sec.* 4-7; *C. Fel.* 17 (explanation of the phrase "come from God"); *Nat. b.* 1.1-3.3.

192. See *Mor.* 2.3; *Div. qu.* 83.21; *Duab. an.* 6.6-9 (the vices do not come from God); *C. Fort.* 9.22. It is to be noted, above all, that Augustine explains the possibility of sinning by the fact that as creatures human beings are changeable, while, contrary to what the Manichees think, God is absolutely unchangeable. See *C. Sec.* 8 and 20; *C. ep. Man.* 38.44: "Insofar as they are natures, God made them; insofar, however, as they are corruptible, God did not make them, for corruption is not from [God] who alone is incorruptible," with the entire context.

193. See especially *C. ep. Man.* 41.47: "Why then, you say, does corruption take away what God gave to nature? It does not take it away except when God allows; [God] allows it, however, in cases in which [God] judges it most just and in keeping with order, according to the gradation of being and the merits of souls [there follows a comparison with a speech, the words of which come one after another and are understood only in the context of the entire speech]. . . . So too, the beauty of temporal things, lowest in rank as it is, is pierced by the passing of things and marked by the death of what has been born. If sense and memory could capture the order and modalities of this beauty, it would so please us that we would not dare give the name 'corruptions' to the defects that mark it. Because, however, we toil in that sector of this beauty in which the passing temporal things that we love desert us, we suffer the punishments for sin and are warned to love what is eternal." See also *C. ep. Man.* 37.42; *C. Fort.* 23 (no one can harm God); *C. Adim.* 20.3 (God loves peace but without abandoning justice); *C. Faust.* 26.3; *C. Fel.* 2.8 (God is described as "just avenger of free will, supreme physician, good caretaker, merciful creator"); *Nat. b.* 7.7-18.18.

194. See Madec, BA 6, 3rd ed., 173f., with *An. quant.* 36.80.

195. *Vera rel.* 23.44.

196. See Decret, *L'Afrique,* 302f., citing the passages in which, with an eye on the tendency of the Manichees to place the two principles on the same level, Augustine rejects their dualism; and see 305-322, on the materialism which Augustine ascribes to the Manichees.

197. See *Lib. arb.* 3.4.11 (on the just avenger); 3.9.26 (on the just punishment for sins).

198. See ibid., 3.20.55.

199. See the rejection of dualism in *C. Faust.* 21.

200. See *C. ep. Man.* 2.2, with the note in BA 17:780; *C. Faust.* 22.9.

201. In addition to Decret, *L'Afrique,* see E. Feldmann, *Die Epistula Fundamenti der nordafrikanischen Manichäer* (Altenberge, 1987) 39 (monotheistic piety); Ries, "Dieux cosmiques et Dieu biblique" (note 157, above), 770f.

202. See K.-H. Lütcke, *"Auctoritas," AugLex* vol. 1, fasc. 4 (1990) 498-510, where he summarize his study, *"Auctoritas" bei Augustin* (Stuttgart, 1969); Madec, BA 6, 3rd ed., 549-551 ("croire pour comprendre"); Studer, *La riflessione teologica,* 168ff. On the subject, see Holte, *Béatitude et Sagesse,* 303-396, especially 329-334, as well as W. Beierwaltes, *"Deus est veritas,"* especially 26-29 (on Augustine).

203. For the following explanations, see G. Strauss, *Schriftgebrauch, Schriftauslegung und Schriftbeweis bei Augustin,* Beiträge zur Geschichte der biblischen Hermeneutik 1 (Tübingen, 1959) 1-73.

204. See above, p. 87.

205. *Ord.* 2.5.16, and 2.9.27. See the commentary in Holte, *Béatitude et Sagesse,* 321-327. See also *Acad.* 3.19.42.

206. *Ep.* 120, especially 1.2-2.10 and 3.13: "It is no small beginning of the knowledge of God if before we can know what God is, we already begin to know what God is not. But have a great love of understanding because unless you correctly understand those holy writings that persuade you to believe great things before you understand them, they cannot be useful to you." See also *Ench.* 1.4, and the note in BA 9:332f.

207. See *Gn. litt.* 1.19.38f., and the commentary of E. Cavalcanti, "Il significato dell'e-segesi litterale in Basilio e in Agostino," *ASE* 4 (1987) 119-142, especially 141.

208. See Strauss, *Schriftgebrauch,* 67.

209. See *Mor.* 2.55; *Util cred.* 1.2; 8.20. On Augustine's disappointment at not receiving from the Manichees the desired proof of the truth, see Decret, *L'Afrique,* 242-254; here the author refers, among other passages, to *C. ep. Man.,* 12.14f., which deals with the apologetic methods of the Manichees, but he underscores the point that the latter had a different ideal of knowledge *(cognitio manifesta)* than did Augustine.

210. *C. ep. Man.* 5.6, and the note in BA 17:783.

211. *Vera rel.* 24.45-36.67, especially 24.25: "Authority calls for faith and prepares the human being for reason. Reason leads to knowledge and understanding. And yet reason is not completely inactive when authority is at work since thought is given to the one who is being believed, and the authority of truth already known and clearly visible is certainly supreme"; 25.46 (criteria of credibility), and 31.57f. (where it is said that one must judge "according to God" who is the "supreme law," and "with God," that is, in purity and out of love for that which we know). See also *Vera rel.* 10.19 (on the necessity of the temporal dispensation for the passage to eternity); 16.30ff. (on the necessity of the incarnation and the *disciplina morum* for the attainment of truth).

212. See M. Löhrer, *Der Glaubensbegriff des heiligen Augustinus in seinen ersten Schriften bis zu den Confessiones* (Einsiedeln, 1955), especially 160-164; W. Geerlings, "Jesaja 7,9b bei Augustinus," *WissWeis* 50 (1987) 5-12, with a good survey of the Augustinian theology of faith.

213. See *Lib. arb.* 1.2.4; 2.2.6; *Mag.* 11.39, with the commentary of Du Roy, *L'intelligence de la foi,* 213f. See also *Ep.* 120.1.3. See, in addition, Geerlings, "Jesaja 7,9b," 9, with the reference especially to *Util. cred.* 12.26; Mandouze, *S. Augustin,* 265-268, with note 2 on 267; Madec, BA 6, 3rd ed., 549.

214. See Studer, *La riflessione teologica,* 199, with the bibliography given there.

215. See *C. Faust.* 13.1.

216. See especially *Util. cred.* 13.28-17.35. See also *C. ep. Man.* 14.17f. (critique of Mani, who demands a faith without any knowledge), and see the note in BA 17:282f.

217. See Decret, *L'Afrique,* 260, citing *C. Sec.* 5, and see entire context of this passage in BA 17:520f.

218. See especially *C. Faust.* 33.6f., with its whole program of historical criticism.

219. See *Doctr. chr.* 2.27.42ff., and the important references in Marrou, *Saint Augustin,* passim.

220. See *C. Faust.* 33.9; also 33.19-22; 32.22.

221. See above, with the reference to Feldmann in note 46. In addition, see Decret, *L'Afrique,* 295, who cites *C. Faust.* 21.1 and 9.1, according to which philosophical dualism leads to the rejection of the Old Testament; Vannier, *"Creatio,"* 59.

222. See, earlier, *Ord.* 2.27.

223. See *Vera rel.* 10.20: "Almighty God . . . demonstrating through [the divine self] the things that are true and helping people of good will to consider and perceive them through agency of the good angels and some human beings."

224. See Lütcke, *Auctoritas bei Augustin,* 123-146.

225. See *C. Faust.* 26.3: "God, the creator of all natures, does nothing that is contrary to nature; for whatever is done by [God] from whom all measure, number, and order come, will be natural to each thing"; and also 22.9, where Augustine describes God as the sun of spirits and creator of the visible sun.

226. See Strauss, *Schriftgebrauch,* 30f., with *C. Faust.* 4.2: "Let us suppose, since you so wish, that perfect faith has these two parts: one consists of words, that is, the confession that Christ was born, and the other of deeds, that is, the observance of the commandments." On the moral presuppositions of religious knowledge, see Holte, *Béatitude et Sagesse,* 382-385, and especially 265f., where the author speaks of sin as a perversion of love and a refusal to acknowledge God.

227. For this distinction, see *Doctr. chr.* 2.28.44: "While it is in historical narratives that we are told about human institutions of the past, history itself must not be counted among human inventions, because what has been done in the past cannot now become undone; it has to be held in the succession of times, which have been established and are being controlled by God" (trans. E. Hill, *On Teaching Christianity,* 72, The Works of St. Augustine 11 (Brooklyn, N.Y.: New City Press, 1995). Compare this with 2.28.42: "Everything therefore that we are told about the past by what is called history is of the greatest help to us in understanding the holy books" (trans. ibid., 71).

228. See Strauss, *Schriftgebrauch,* 68.

229. See F. Decret, *"Adimantus," AugLex* vol. 1, fascs. 1-2 (1986) 94f.

230. See F. Decret, *"Adimantum Manichaei discipulum (Contra)," AugLex* vol. 1, fascs. 1-2 (1986) 90-94, where he summarizes his book, *L'Afrique.*

231. See especially *C. Adim.* 3 and 7.

232. See ibid., 3: "People who accepted the Old Testament were held imprisoned by certain shadows and figures of the true realities before the Lord came in accordance with a wonderful and most orderly distribution of times; and yet in that Testament there is a great foretelling and advance announcement of the New Testament."

233. See ibid., 2.

234. See ibid.

235. See ibid., 2.2; 3.4; 12.5.

236. See ibid., 13.

237. See ibid., 12.1f.

238. Ibid., 17.7 and 22.

239. See Decret, *Aspects,* 97-104, and Strauss, *Schriftgebrauch,* 68-72. See also P. Cantaloup, *L'harmonie des deux Testaments dans le "Contra Faustum Manichaeum" de saint Augustin,* dissertation (Toulouse, 1955), which is frequently cited in C. P. Mayer, *Die Zeichen in der geistigen Entwicklung und in der Theologie Augustins,* 2 vols. (Würzburg, 1969-1974).

240. See especially *C. Faust.* 31.3. Also ibid., 16.28: "Therefore there is a difference of time, not of teaching," with the entire context; 6, 8: "For that was the time for signs, this is the time for manifestation"; 8.2, with the distinction between Jewish servitude and Christian freedom; 32.9.

241. See ibid., 6.2; 32.9, citing Col 2:16f.

242 See ibid., 16.6: "Christ, by whose blood we are redeemed and cleansed, is the truth to which those figures point"; 4.2; 22.51 (citing Gal 4:22ff.); 22.85; 22.94; 32.9 (citing 1 Cor 10:11); etc.

243. See ibid., 6.2, with its distinction between "precepts for the living of life" and "precepts that signify life." Similarly in 10.2. See Mayer, *Die Zeichen,* 2:367-373.

244. *C. Faust.* 12.27. See 12.5; 16.26; 18.6. Especially noteworthy are the references to Christ's own testimony regarding the value of the Old Testament (13.5, and the whole of book 16), and the idea of true teaching about the incarnation as a criterion of authority (32.22).

245. See ibid., 14 (with its detailed exegesis of Deut 21:23); 17.19 (with its explanation of Matt 5:17); 22.23-98 (with its long-winded explanation of the immorality of the patriarchs and other Old Testament personalities). On the claims of immorality in the Old Testament, see Decret, *Aspects,* 146f.; Mayer, *Die Zeichen,* 2:373-392 ("Die *crimina Patrum*").

246. See *C. Faust.* 19.16: the Manichees think that "when signs and sacraments are changed, the realities too are different." And see 6.8.

247. See Mayer, *Die Zeichen* 2, especially 88-104.

248. See *C. Adim.* 13.2: "Because nothing can be said of God, these people reached the point of thinking that since they cannot avoid learning [in the Old Testament] things they as human beings deem unworthy of God, therefore even what they think might suitably be said of the ineffable divine excellence is likewise unworthy of God's majesty. But since [God's] wisdom was to come down into a human body, it first came down into human words." On the same subject see 7.4, and 7.11: "For the Holy Spirit, who instills into human minds the realization of how ineffable the supreme divine attributes are, also willed to use even the words which human beings usually misuse. . . . A respectful silence before God would be more fitting than any human words."

249. See Flasch, *Logik.* This study contains the Latin text (from CCL 44:24-56) with a German translation, and in its introduction and commentary goes into all the literary, historical, and theological questions. In *REAug* 37 (1991) 387-390 G. Madec presents the work in an understandably polemical way, but he pays too little attention to factual questions and especially to the question of God.

250. For the literary characteristics of *Div. qu.* 1.2, see Flasch, *Logik,* 97f.

251. See especially ibid., 96 ("Dokument der Ablösung der augustinischen Position von 386 bis 395"), 25-30, 132f., 270-296 ("Augustins Wandlungen"), especially 270f. with bibliography, and the summary on 295f.

252. See ibid., 48-51 (citing *Retr.* 2.1.3; *Praed. sanct.* 4.7f.; *Persev.* 20.52 and 21.55).

253. See ibid., 270-276.

254. In addition to ibid., 97-105, see M. G. Mara, "Agostino e la polemica antimanichea: il ruolo di Paolo e del suo epistolario," *Aug* 32 (1992) 119-143, citing texts written before 397 and further literature.

255. Flasch himself explicitly refers to the anti-Manichean context of *Div. qu.* 1.2. See Flash, *Logik,* 55, 106f., 123.

256. Ibid., 59f., with the reference to *Div. qu.* 1.2.18 (CCL 44:44-46, ll. 535-616)

257. Flasch, repeatedly goes into the question of God, though in a way that is to some extent one-sided. See *Logik,* 114f., 240, 257ff.

258. See ibid., 128.

259. See ibid., 63ff.

260. See ibid., 257.

261. Flasch does touch on the question of damnation (see *Logik,* 11, 86, 92), but he does not take sufficient account of the extent to which this question goes beyond the earlier problems of evil and sin, and especially of the fact that the reality of hell, which Augustine and his contemporaries (Ambrose, for example) presuppose, is a dreadful question for them.

262. See ibid., 66-71.

263. On the novelty of Augustine's teaching on original sin, see ibid., 72-78, 86, 277-285, 294. But see also G. Madec, *REAug* 37 (1991) 388, with the reference to A. Sage, "Péché originel: Naissance d'un dogme," *REAug* 13 (1967) 211-248.

264. On this question, see also A. Sage, "La volonté salvifique universelle de Dieu dans la pensée de saint Augustin," *RechAug* 3 (1965) 107-131, especially 109 and 122.

265. According to Flasch, *Logik,* 65-71, the main problem for Augustine is to maintain God's justice.

266. See ibid., 65-71, especially 70; see also 243, 257f.

267. Flasch rightly stresses the point that Augustine reads his ideas and theories into the biblical text. See *Logik,* 97-105, 248, 259-262, and especially 296f., with the very biting remarks there. But Flasch himself completely neglects the question of the extent to which, in the light of the Bible, Augustine has modified the ideas he had taken over from contemporary culture. For all of Flasch's claim to take the entire context of *Div. qu.* into account, he does not go into the contemporaneous expositions of the Bible in *En. Ps.* and the sermons.

268. See *Div. qu.* 1.2.6, and above all the fundamental passage in 1.2.1: "The Apostle and all the justified through whom we have gained an understanding of grace have no other aim than this: that anyone who boasts should boast in the Lord. That free will has great power is certainly true. But what power has it in those sold into the power of sin?"

269. See Flasch, *Logik,* 92f., 292f.

270. See *Div. qu.* 1.2.21 (CCL 44:53, ll. 740f.).

271. See especially ibid., 1.2.21 (CCL 44:53, ll. 750-758); 1.2.22 (CCL 44:55, ll. 794-803), with the example of Paul's conversion.

272. According to Augustine, grace "is victorious" and does not work together with human freedom, as Flasch repeatedly insists; see especially *Logik,* 291ff.

273. See ibid., 81ff.

274. See ibid., 121-124.

275. See ibid., 283f., with the references to inconsistent phraseology in Augustine. But the justifiable criticism of the inconsistency could be more benevolent. See the uncompromising but measured criticism of Augustine's overly refined logic in A. Solignac, "Les excès de l'*intellectus fidei* dans la doctrine d'Augustin sur la grâce," *NRT* 110 (1988) 825-849, especially 827f. (citing the explanation of the *massa damnata* in *Div. qu.* 1.2), and 845-849 (summary).

276. See Flasch, *Logik,* 268ff., where the tone is intensely polemical.

277. See *Conf.* 11.2.2: "But when shall I be capable of proclaiming by 'the tongue of my pen' (Ps 44:2) all your exhortations and all your terrors and consolations and directives, by which you brought me to preach your word and dispense your sacrament to your people?" (Chadwick, 221). See Flasch's commentary on this passage in *Logik,* 117f., where he cites another text, *Ep.* 93.1, in which Augustine speaks of "the Father's whips" *(flagella Patris).* The passage is understood quite differently by S. Poque, *Le langage symbolique dans la prédication d'Augustin d'Ippone* (Paris, 1984) 193-224 ("La loi du Père"). See also

B. Studer, *"Deus, Pater et Dominus* bei Augustinus von Hippo," *Festschrift C. Stead* (Leiden, 1993).

278. See *En. Ps.* 7.5.

279. See *Div. qu.* 1.2.4 (CCL 44:29, ll. 130-137) (the connection between creation and election); 1.2.8 (CCL 44:32, ll. 230-241); 1.2.18 (CCL 44:45, ll. 542-560, and 44:46, l. 575). See Flasch, *Logik,* 63ff., with the references to Augustine's teaching on creation. Precisely at this point, it would be interesting to make a comparison with sermons from the same period, for example, *Serm.* 223A (Denis 2), in which, in explaining the creation story, Augustine presupposes a very personalist concept of God.

280. See Flasch, *Logik,* 42-48, especially 43; 115.

281. See B. Studer, *"Credo in Deum,"* 425ff., where references are given to E. Benz, *Marius Victorinus und die Entwicklung der abendländischen Willensmetaphysik* (Stuttgart, 1932), and F. Szabckl *Le Christ Créateur chez saint Ambroise* (Rome, 1968). See, further, Vannier, *"Creatio."*

Part II, Chapter 2

1. On what follows, see especially A. Schindler, *Wort und Analogie in Augustins Trinitätslehre* (Tübingen, 1965). See also M. Schmaus, *Die psychologische Trinitätslehre des heiligen Augustinus,* 2nd ed. (Münster, 1927; rpt., Münster, 1967), and the introductions and notes to the editions in BA 13, pt. 4 and NBA 4.

2. See especially *Serm.* 52; 117; *Io. ev. tr.* 99.

3. *Ep.* 120; 169.

4. *Trin.* 1.3.5 (Hill, 68); 1.2.4.

5. See ibid., 1.2.4: "That is why, with the help of the Lord our God, we shall undertake to the best of our ability to give them the reasons they clamor for, and to account for the one and only and true God being a trinity, and for the rightness of saying, believing, understanding that the Father and the Son and the Holy Spirit are of one and the same substance or essence" (Hill, 67).

6. See ibid., 1.4.7; 1.3.5.

7. See ibid., 1.2.4; 15.3.5.

8. See ibid., 5.11.12 (spirit); 6.1.1–5.7 (wisdom, charity); 7.1.1–4.7 (wisdom); 15.17.30f.; 15.19.37.

9. See ibid., 5.11.12.

10. See ibid., 4.202.28: "the Father is from no one"; 4.20.29: "thereby [God] indicated that the source of all godhead, or if you prefer it, of all deity, is the Father." See also the anti-Arian passages in *Serm.* 140.2; *C. Max.* 3; 9; 23.

11. See *Trin.* 1.1.1, where Augustine speaks of the three errors about God. See also Schindler, *Wort und Analogie,* 122f.

12. The interpretation of the third error causes some difficulties. The text says that one must not imagine "God" to be something that has no parallel in either the corporeal or the spiritual world. This seems to refer to a divinity who begets itself.

13. See *Trin.* 8.1-4. Augustine thus provides the beginning of a treatise *De Deo uno.* This is denied by A.D.R. Polman, *De leer van God bij Augustinus* (Kampen, 1965), but on insufficient grounds. In fact, he himself, in ch. 4 of his excellent study, gives a kind of

synthesis of Augustinian teaching about God in the narrow sense, in which he takes as his starting point (as E. Gilson had earlier done) the two names for God ("He who is," and "The God of the Fathers").

14. See the opening of *Trin.* 1.4.7, and the summary in 4.21.32, as well as the list of contents in 15.3.5: "In the first book the unity and equality of that supreme trinity is demonstrated from the scriptures. The same point is made in the second, third and fourth books, but a thorough treatment of the question of the mission of the Son and the Holy Spirit produced three books. . . ." (Hill, 397). See also *Ep.* 147.

15. See Schindler, *Wort und Analogie,* 119.

16. See *Trin.,* bks. 1 and 2, with the discussion of the traditional texts of Scripture, especially 1.6.9; 1.6.13.

17. See ibid., 1.5.8.

18. See the summary of Augustine's plan in 2.7.13; 3.prol.3

19. Ibid., 1.6.11.

20. See ibid., 2.8.14–9.16, and the explanations of the individual theophanies in 2.10.17–18.35.

21. See ibid., 3.1.4.

22. Ibid., 3.11.22-27.

23. See especially the summary in ibid., 3.11.27.

24. See ibid., 4.20.30ff.

25. Ibid., 3.2.7.

26. Ibid., 3.4.9.

27. Ibid., 3.4.10.

28. Ibid., 3.5-6 and 11.

29. Ibid., 3.7.12–9.19.

30. Ibid., 2.5.9f.

31. Ibid., 4.21.30f.

32. Ibid., 2.7.12.

33. Ibid., 4.20.27ff.

34. See ibid., 5.1.1f.; 7.4.7.

35. Ibid., 5.2.3. See Ibid., 5.8.10f.; 7.5.10; as well as 3.11.21; *Ep.* 120.17; *C. s. Arrian.* 36.34.

36. See *Trin.* 5.1.2–2.3; 7.5.10.

37. See ibid., 5.5.6–6.17, especially 5.8.9: "The chief point then that we must maintain is that whatever that supreme and divine majesty is called with reference to itself is said substance-wise; whatever it is called with reference to another is said not substance- but relationship-wise; and that such is the force of the expression 'of the same substance' in Father and Son and Holy Spirit, that whatever is said with reference to self about each of them is to be taken as adding up in all three to a singular and not to a plural. Thus the Father is God and the Son is God and the Holy Spirit is God, and no one denies that this is said substance-wise; and yet we say that this supreme triad is not three Gods but one God" (Hill, 195). See also 5.1.2–2.3 and BA 15:584, with *Civ.* 11.10.1.

38. See *Trin.* 5.11.12.

39. See ibid., 6.7.8; 6.10.12: "So they are each in each and all in each, and each in all and all in all, and all are one" (Hill, 214).

40. Ibid., 7.1.1–3.6.

41. See ibid., 5.9.10.

42. Ibid., 7.4.7f.

43. Ibid., 7.4.9.

44. Ibid., 7.4.7.

45. See ibid., 7.6.11, especially: "It is not one thing for God to be and another for [God] to be person, but altogether the same" (Hill, 228).

46. See ibid., 5.1.2f.; 5.8.9; 7.6.10f., where the category of "substance," too, is excluded from God. See Schindler, *Wort und Analogie,* 149–156, on Augustine's teaching on the categories and on the sources of this teaching, and also 167.

47. See *Trin.* 8.1.1f.

48. See ibid., 1.2.4, on the distinction between the methods used in the first and second parts of the work; also 8.1.1, where Augustine describes the method used in the second part as being "in a more inward manner" (Hill, 242).

49. Ibid., 8.2.3–3.5.

50. Ibid., 8.6.9.

51. Ibid., 8.3.5.

52. See ibid., 8.9.13.

53. On *mens—imago,* see Schindler, *Wort und Analogie,* 180f.

54. See *Trin.* 8.10.14, as well as 9.2.2.

55. Ibid., 14.12.15: "This trinity of the mind is not really the image of God because the mind remembers and understands and loves itself, but because it is also able to remember and understand and love [God] by whom it was made. And when it does this it becomes wise. If it does not do it, then even though it remembers and understands and loves itself, it is foolish. Let it then remember its God to whose image it was made, and understand and love [God]" (Hill, 383). See 14.14.18 (on the image of wisdom). See also BA 16:635ff., and Schindler, *Wort und Analogie,* 212ff.

56. On this point, see the important explanations in *Ep.* 120.3.13-16, in which Augustine virtually excludes a divinity that is prior to the three persons, and emphasizes that the Father, who is the originating God, does not have a divinity different from that which belongs in common to the Father, the Son, and the Spirit.

57. *Trin.* 15.4.6–5.7.

58. See ibid., 15.5.7, as well as 15.3.5, with the summary of the eighth book.

59. Ibid., 14.1.1.

60. Ibid., 14.14.18.

61. See ibid., 15.3.5; 15.14.23 (The Son is "being from being"); 15.26.47 ("The Father alone is not from another, and therefore [the Father] alone is called unbegotten" [Hill, 432]); *C. s. Arrian.* 4.4.

62. See ibid., 8.4.6–7.8.

63. See ibid., 15.4.6; 15.7.13; 8.2.3–3.5. On the subject, see Schindler, *Wort und Analogie,* 121f.

64. *Trin.* 15.7.13.

65. Ibid., 15.2.2.

66. Ibid., 8.7.12.

67. See ibid., 15.26.45ff.; 4.20.29.

68. In connection with the following presentation of Augustine's theology of creation, see E. Gilson, *The Christian Philosophy of Saint Augustine,* trans. L.E.M. Lynch (New York, 1960) 187–224.; L. Scheffczyk, *Schöpfung und Vorsehung,* HDG, vol. 2, fasc. 2a (Freiburg, 1963) 61–66. E. TeSelle, *Augustine the Theologian* (New York, 1970) 197–223;

BA 48–49; K. Flasch, *Augustin: Einführung in sein Denken* (Stuttgart, 1980) 263–286; and, above all, M. Vannier, *"Creatio," "conversio," "formatio" chez s. Augustin,* Paradosis 31 (Fribourg, 1991).

69. *Gn. adv. Man.* (388); *Gn. litt. imp.* (393); *Conf.* 11–13 (397–401).

70. *Civ.* 11–12 (ca. 417). On the whole subject, see G. Pelland, *Cinq études d'Augustin sur le début de la Genèse* (Paris, 1972). See also Vannier, *"Creatio,"* 83–94, who, however, supposes a different chronology and in addition refers also to *Serm. Denis* 2 (*Serm.* 223A), from the year 399.

71. See Vannier, *"Creatio,"* 64–82.

72. See ibid., 89–94.

73. See BA 48:32-50, with texts on the figurative sense, such as *Gn. litt.* 1.1.1; 4.28.45.

74. See BA 48:39-45 ("metaphorical sense"), citing *Gn. adv. Man.* 1.2.4; *Gn. litt.* 1.2.6; 1.14.20; 1.20.40 (on the caution in interpretation that this mystery calls for); 5.16.34; 5.38.45 (light in the true sense).

75. See Vannier, *"Creatio,"* 176f.

76. See *Gn. litt.* 1.9.15; 1.14.29; 1.17.32; 1.18.36; 2.6.11; 2.8.19; etc.

77. Ibid., 1.18.36; 2.8.19.

78. See ibid., 1.6.12 (Taylor 1, 25).

79. Ibid., 8.19.38 (Taylor 259–260). See ibid., 9.15.26, as well as *Serm.* 223A (*Serm. Denis* 2).3, with its similar explanation of Gen 1:1: that God created through the Word. See also Vannier, *"Creatio,"* 114–122, on the trinitarian interpretation of the beginning of Genesis.

80. On what follows, see—in addition to Vannier, *"Creatio"*—Gilson, *Christian Philosophy of St. Augustine,* 187–224; Scheffczyk, *Schöpfung,* 61–66; TeSelle, *Augustine the Theologian,* 197–223; BA 48–49; Flasch, *Augustin,* 263–286 ("Die Zeit").

81. See especially BA 48:653-668, and in particular 661 (where *Gn. litt.* 5.20.40–23.46 is cited).

82. Cicero, *De natura deorum* 2.75. On this, see TeSelle, *Augustine the Theologian,* 210. See also *Civ.* 7.30, where Augustine still follows the cited passage of Cicero.

83. Tertullian, *Spectac.* 2.4 (CCL 1:228): "No one denies that God is the maker of the universe and that this universe is both good and made over to human beings. . . . But because they have no deep knowledge of God . . . they are inevitably ignorant of how [God] commands or forbids [God's] world to be administered"; 2.11 (CCL 1:229): "Even though these same works are administered by things [God] has made." See René Braun, *Deus Christianorum: Recherches sur le vocabulaire doctrinal de Tertullien* (Paris, 1962) 354–357 (on *conditor*), 390–395 (on *instituere, institutor,* etc.). But Braun does not go into the theme of *administratio.* See also Cyprian, *Ep.* 5.8: *administrationes divinae* in the ecclesial sense.

84. See Seneca, *Prov.* 5.8: "Although the great creator and ruler of the universe himself wrote the decrees of Fate, yet he follows them. He obeys for ever, he decreed but once. 'Why, however,' you ask, 'was God so unjust in his allotment of destiny as to assign to good men poverty, wounds, and painful death?' It is impossible for the moulder to alter matter" (Seneca, *Moral Essays,* trans. J. Basore, Loeb Library [New York, 1928] 1:39).

85. See, for example, *Civ.* 7.30f.: "[God] has created, and [God] directs . . . creator and regulator of all the waters. . . . [God] directs the whole of [God's] creation. . . . The benefits which God lavishes on good and bad alike in accordance with [God's] government of the natural order" (Bettenson, 291–92).

86. See *Gn. litt.* 4.10.20–13.244; 5.17.35; 5.20.41f.

87. See ibid., 4.11.21, where Gen 2:2 and John 5:17 are both cited.

88. In addition to BA 48:653-668, see G. Sfameni Gasparro, "Double Creation," *EECh* 1:251-252.

89. *Gn. litt.* 5.11.27 (Taylor 1, 162). See 5.4.11; 5.20.40; 5.29.46.

90. See BA 48:645-53.

91. See *Gn. litt.* 4.18.31–35.56, and especially the summary in 4.35.56. On the subject, see G. Madec, *"Angelus,"* *AugLex* 1:307, on the knowledge of the angels.

92. See especially *Gn. litt.* 5.29.46.

93. Ibid., 5.17.35 (Taylor 1, 168). See also 6.10.17.

94. See ibid., 6.5.12, and BA 48:659f.

95. See *Gn. litt.* 5.5.12; 4.32.49; 6.10.17 (the "reasons": in the Word, in the elements of the world, in things, in seeds).

96. See ibid., 5.23.46.

97. Ibid., 5.20.41.

98. See ibid., 4.33.51f.; 5.20.41; 6.14.25f. (creation of the human being).

99. Ibid., 5.23.46 (Taylor 1, 176). See Gilson, *Christian Philosophy of St. Augustine*, 217–224.

100. *Gn. litt.* 5.12.28–14.33; 6.10.17. On the subject, see BA 48:672ff. (the life which creatures have in the Word).

101. *Gn. litt.* 4.3.7–7.14: on the "six" days of creation. See BA 48:635-639, with further literature.

102. *Gn. litt.* 5.14.31f.

103. Ibid., 5.15.33–16.34.

104. See ibid., 1.5.11; 1.7.13: ". . . so that God may be thought of as loving the work to be produced not out of any need or necessity, but solely out of the largeness of [the divine] bounty" (Taylor 1, 26). See BA 8:584ff., on the creative goodness of God and on the Holy Spirit, with the reference to H. Cousineau, "Creation and Freedom: An Augustinian Problem, *'quia voluit?'* and/or *'quia bonus?'"* *RechAug* 2 (1962) 253–271.

105. *Gn. litt.* 1.8.14 (Taylor 1, 27).

106. Ibid. (Taylor 1, 27).

107. See ibid., 5.20.41.

108. See ibid., 5.22.43f.

109. Ibid., 4.12.22: "The power and might of the Creator, who rules and embraces all, makes every creature abide; and if this power ever ceased to govern creatures, their essences would pass away and all nature would perish" (Taylor 1, 117).

110. On what follows, see BA 48:676-680.

111. *Gn. litt.* 5.20.41: "God moves [God's] whole creation by a hidden power, and all creatures are subject to this movement: the angels carry out [God's] commands, the stars move in their courses. . . . They would not be sent forth to run their course if [God] who made creatures ceased to exercise [God's] provident rule over them" (Taylor 1, 171–172).

112. Ibid., 5.21.42f. See *Civ.* 10.14, where Augustine attributes this universalist conception to Plotinus (*Provid.* 1.13.23 [ed. Harder V^a.72ff.]), but is in all likelihood relying on a commentary by Porphyry.

113. See *Gn. litt.* 1.18.36; 4.5.12.

114. Ibid., 8.18.37–27.50, especially 23.44: "The nature of the Trinity is absolutely immutable and hence so perfectly eternal that nothing can be coeternal with It. Dwelling by Itself and in Itself beyond all time and space It nevertheless moves through time and space

the creatures dependent on It. It creates beings by Its goodness, and It rules wills by Its power, so that there is no being not from It, and as far as wills are concerned there is no good will that It does not assist and no evil will that It cannot use for a good purpose" (Taylor 2, 63). On the subject, see BA 49:510-516. See also *Gn. litt.* 8.25.46–26.48 and 8.9.17f. See TeSelle, *Augustine the Theologian,* 219f.

115. See the continuation of the passage just cited, *Gn. litt.* 8.24.45: "Hence it is that God by the twofold working of [God's] providence is over all creatures, that is, over natures that they may have existence, and over wills that they may do nothing without either [God's] command or [God's] permission" (Taylor 2, 65).

116. See ibid., 3.24.37: "God is the all-good Creator of beings, but [God] is the all-just Ruler of creatures who sin" (Taylor 1, 102). And see Vannier, *"Creatio,"* 133–137: "La conversion constitutive du sujet."

117. See BA 49:512f., citing *Gn. litt.* 8.10.23, a passage that was perhaps added later.

118. On the problems with this conception of order, see BA 49:513. See also *Gn. litt.* 3.24.37; 8.23.44.

119. See *Gn. litt.* 6.11.19; 7.28.42.

120. See ibid., 5.20.41: "Hence God moves [God's] whole creation by a hidden power, and all creatures are subject to this movement. . . . It is thus that God unfolds the generations which [God] laid up in creation when first [God] founded it; and they would not be sent forth to run their course if [God] who made creatures ceased to exercise [God's] provident rule over them" (Taylor 1, 171–172).

121. See ibid., 5.23.44f., especially 45: "In the seed, then, there was invisibly present all that would develop in time into a tree. And in this same way we must picture the world, when God made all things together, as having had all things together which were made in it and with it" (Taylor 1, 175). See BA 48:677f. On the theme of the world-tree, see also Plotinus, *Provid.* 2.7.9-24 (59–62) (ed. Harder V^a.114), with the note on 7.14 (V^b.366).

122. See *En. Ps.* 91.8, on Ps 91:6: "Your thoughts are exceedingly deep."

123. *Gn. litt.* 1.8.14 (Taylor 1, 27). See ibid., 3.16.25; 4.1.1.

124. Ibid., 5.5.12. See BA 48:659f., citing *Conf.* 11.13.15f.; *Civ.* 11.6.

125. See especially *Gn. litt.* 6.8.13; 6.10.17; 9.1.1: "The first creation of creatures [was] accomplished in the six days, when all were perfected in their causal principles and were begun in such a way that the causes would be brought subsequently to their effects" (Taylor 2, 70).

126. See ibid., 8.26.48: "Without any distance or unit of time, by [God's] immutable eternity [God] is more ancient than all things because [God] is before them all, and newer than all things because {God} is also after them all" (Taylor 2, 67). The theme of God as goal of the creation is less to the fore in *Gn. litt.* See, however, 8.25.47, on the praise offered by the angels, and the summary description of the "two loves" in 12.15.20.

127. See ibid., 8.20.39; 8.22.43; 8.26.48. See also ibid., 8.19.38: there is no change in the substance of God.

128. Ibid., 8.21.40–22.43.

129. Ibid., 8.21.40 (Taylor 1, 61). See ibid., 8.22.43, on the difficulty human beings have in thinking without using temporal and spatial notions.

130. See the references to the philosophical background and especially to Plotinus in BA 48:664f. and 48:678ff., with the reference to *Civ.* 10.14, where Augustine puts Plotinus down as a defender of providence.

131. *Gn. litt.* 4.8.15–17.30. And see BA 48:639-644.

132. *Gn. litt.,* 6.13.23–18.29. And see 9.17.32f., on the formation of Eve.

133. See BA 48:685-690.

134. See *Gn. litt.* 6.13.23: "By [the divine] power [God] has given numbers to [God's] creation, but [God] has not bound [the divine] power by these numbers" (Taylor 1, 194); and 6.17.28: "But if they are also in the foreknowledge of God as things that are going to be, they are truly going to be. But if they are there as determined otherwise, then they will come about as they are in the foreknowledge of [God] who cannot be deceived" (Taylor 1, 198). See also 6.18.29 (on the creation of Adam): "To suppose that God made him contrary to the cause which [God] undoubtedly had freely predetermined is as unthinkable as to say that [God] created him against [God's] own divine will. If God, however, did not place all causes in the original creation but kept some in [God's] own will, those which [God] kept in [God's] own will are not dependent on the necessity of the causes [God] created. Nevertheless, those which [God] kept in [God's] own will cannot be contrary to those which [God] predetermined by [God's] own will" (Taylor 1, 199).

135. Ibid., 9.18.33: "God, therefore, has in [the divine self] the hidden causes of certain things which [God] has not placed in creatures, and [God] makes them operative not in the work of [God's] ordinary providence by which [God] brings things into being, but in that work by which [God] administers according to [the divine] will the things that [God] has created as [God] has willed. In this sphere of God's action is the grace by which sinners are saved. For nature corrupted by its own evil will is unable to return to God through its own efforts, but it can do so by the grace of God, by which it is helped and renewed" (Taylor 2, 93–94).

136. Ibid., 9.18.34: "Hence St. Paul has said that the mystery of this grace was hidden, not in the world, in which the causal reasons of all things destined to come forth in the processes of nature have been hidden, as Levi was hidden in the loins of Abraham when he paid tithes, but in God who created all" (Taylor 2, 94).

137. Ibid., 8.18.37–27.50. See BA 49:510-516, with references to the philosophical sources.

138. See *Gn. litt.* 8.18.37; 8.27.49; 9.2.4; 1.33.43 (on Gen 3:8).

139. See ibid., 5.20.40.

140. See ibid., 5.23.46, cited above; also 5.21.42 (order subject to the divine command).

141. See the main focus of Vannier, *"Creatio."*

142. See *Retr.* 2.69; *Civ.,* praef. (CCL 47:3). In the citations that follow, the book and chapter, but also the lines in the CCL edition (vols. 47–48), are given so that anyone desiring to look up the Latin text may do so more easily, especially in chapters that are quite lengthy; for example, *Civ.* 15.8.18 = bk. 15, ch. 8, l. 18 in the CCL edition.

143. See especially *Cat. rud.* 19.31–24.45 (and 19.31, in particular); 20.36f. Also *Vera. rel.* 27.50. On the history of the theme of the two cities, see BA 33:52-92, and especially J. van Oort, *Jerusalem and Babylon: A Study of Augustine's City of God and the Sources of His Doctrine of the Two Cities* (Leiden, 1991).

144. *Cat. rud.* 19.33; 20.36.

145. See *Civ.* 15.8.16; 15.20.6f.; 17.4.65 (with the entire context); 18.1.5.

146. See *Civ.* 1.prol.1-8: "Here, my dear Marcellinus, is the fulfillment of my promise, a book in which I have taken upon myself the task of defending the glorious City of God against those who prefer their own gods to the Founder of that City. . . . The task is long and arduous; but God is our helper" and 1.prol.12-16: "The King and Founder of this City . . . has revealed in the Scripture of [God's] people this statement of the divine law, 'God

resists the proud, but [God] gives grace to the humble'" (Bettenson, 5); 11.1.1-16 (with various psalm verses); 18.54.89ff.: "The other city, the Heavenly City on pilgrimage in this world, does not create false gods. [It itself] is the creation of the true God, and [it itself] is to be [God's] true sacrifice" (Bettenson, 842). See also 10.6.

147. See ibid., 5.11.1-4: "Thus God is the supreme reality, with God's Word and the Holy Spirit—three who are one. [God] is the God omnipotent, creator and maker of every soul and body; participation in [God] brings happiness to all who are happy in truth" (Bettenson, 196); 10.29.28-31: "The grace of God could not be commanded in a way more likely to evoke a grateful response, than the way by which the only Son of God, while re- maining unchangeably in [the Son's] own proper being, clothed [the Son's self] in human- ity and gave to [human beings] the spirit of [the Son's] love by the mediation of a [human being], so that by this love [humans] might come to [the Son]" (Bettenson, 414–15).

148. See ibid., 10.30.20-28; 19.23.134-37): "Porphyry certainly did well in thus pro- claiming God the Father, and in telling of the conduct by which [the Father] is to be wor- shipped; and the prophetic books of the Hebrews are full of such precepts, when the life of holiness is commanded or praised" (Bettenson, 888), with the entire context, especially 19.22.17-20.

149. See B. Studer, "Zum Aufbau von Augustins *De civitate Dei,*" *Mélanges T. J. van Bavel* (Leuven, 1990) 943–950.

150. See *Civ.* 15.1.25-28.

151. See ibid., 15.8.1; 15.8.8; 15.12.53; and especially 15.9.38-41: "Nevertheless we should not for that reason [the longevity of individuals] call in question the reliability of the sacred narrative *[sacra historia]*. Our impudence in doubting the sacred record is measured by the certainty of the fulfillment of its prophecies, which we see before our eyes" (Bettenson, 610). Other passages using "sacred history" or "sacred narrative" are 15.15.66; 15.16.90. The Latin expression *historia divina* (divine or inspired history) also occurs in 17.8.59. Note, in this connection, that Jerome, too, speaks of "sacred history"; see *In Isaiam* 92A; 380D; 551B. On this subject, see P. Jay, *L'exégèse de saint Jérôme d'après son "Commentaire sur Isaïe"* (Paris, 1985) 135–142 (reference to three meanings of "history": the events that make up history, the narrative of events, the exegetical sense). See also Jerome, *In Hieremiam* 6.50.4.

152. See *Civ.* 10.32.133-139. See the comment on this passage, below. It is worth not- ing that elsewhere, too, in his antipagan polemics Augustine makes use of the record of the past, the history of events *(historia narrans): Civ.* 4.1.13; 12.10.8.

153. *Civ.* 1.8.10-13: "Yet the patience of God still invites the wicked to penitence, just as God's chastisement trains the good in patient endurance. God's mercy embraces the good for their cherishing, just as [God's] severity chastens the wicked for their punishment" (Bettenson, 13). And see 1.29.1-6: "The whole family of the servants of the supreme and true God has its consolation, which never disappoints, which does not depend on hope in shifting and transitory things; and those servants have no reason to regret even this life of time, for in it they are schooled for eternity. They enjoy their earthly blessing in the manner of pilgrims and they are not attached to them, while these earthly misfortunes serve for test- ing and correction" (Bettenson, 41).

154. Ibid., 1.10.1-5 and 95–99.

155. Ibid., 1.29.10ff., with the formula: "My God is present everywhere, and wholly present everywhere. No limits confine [God]. [God] can be present without showing [the divine self]: [God] can depart without moving" (Bettenson, 41). See 1.28.5-7: "The provi-

dence of the Creator and Governor of the universe is a profound mystery" (Bettenson, 39), citing Rom 11:33; 1.14 (Christians can find their God everywhere).

156. See ibid., 2.3.1-17 (on historical events), and see 3.1.14-26.

157. On this historical and cultural background, see Studer, "Zum Aufbau," 940f., with the literature cited there.

158. See *Civ.* 2, especially chs. 16 and 27ff.

159. This is the main thesis of the third book; see 3.1.10-26.

160. See especially ibid., 5.12.1-3: "Let us go on to examine for what moral qualities and for what reason the true God deigned to help the Romans in the extension of their empire; for in [God's] control are all the kingdoms of the earth" (Bettenson, 196). The "moral qualities" are analyzed in detail in the remainder of this chapter.

161. This is the main thesis of bk. 5. See especially 5.21.1-4: "This being so, we must ascribe to the true God alone the power to grant kingdoms and empires. [God] it is who gives happiness in the kingdom of heaven only to the good, but grants earthly kingdoms both to the good and to the evil, in accordance with [God's] pleasure, which can never be unjust" (Bettenson, 215).

162. Ibid., 4.2.45-51, citing Matt 5:45.

163. Ibid., 4.33f., especially 4.33.1-9: "It is therefore this God, the author and giver of felicity, who, being the one true God, gives earthly dominion both to good [human beings] and to evil. And he does this not at random or, as one may say, fortuitously, because [God] is God, not Fortune. Rather [God] gives in accordance with the order of events in history, an order completely hidden from us, but perfectly known to [the divine self]. Yet God is not bound in subjection to this order of events; God is . . . in control, as the master of events, and arranges the order of things as a governor. As for felicity, [God] grants that only to the good. [Humans] may have this happiness—or not have it—when they are slaves, or when they are rulers. But it can only be enjoyed in its fullness in that life where no one is any longer a slave" (Bettenson, 176–177). The imperfect happiness found on earth is "the sacrament, the hidden meaning of the Old Testament," in which earthly prosperity prefigured the blessedness of eternity.

164. See ibid., 5.9, especially 5.9.138f.

165. Ibid., 5.10.21ff.: "[God] is rightly called 'all-powerful,' although [God] has not the power to die, or to be mistaken. 'All-powerful' means that [God] does what [God] wills, and does not suffer what [God] does not will" (Bettenson, 194).

166. See especially ibid., 5.15, in particular ll. 15-19; 5.19.48-56: "I have now sufficiently explained, as far as I can, the reason why the one true and just God has assisted the Romans, who are good according to the standards of the earthly city, to the attainment of the glory of so great an empire. But it may be that there is another more hidden cause on account of the diverse merits of [humankind], which are better known to God than to us. However, it is the conviction of all those who are truly religious, that no one can have true virtue without true piety" (Bettenson, 213).

167. See ibid., 5.23.37f.

168. See ibid., 5.11.1-7: "Thus God is the supreme reality, with God's Word and the Holy Spirit—three who are one. [God] is the God omnipotent, creator and maker of every soul and every body; participation in [God] brings happiness to all who are happy in truth and not in illusion; [God] has made [the human being] a rational animal, consisting of soul and body; and when [a person] sins [God] does not let [that person] go unpunished, nor does [God] abandon [that person] without pity" (Bettenson, 196).

169. Ibid., 6–10.

170. See ibid., 6.1.7-22, and Studer, "Zum Aufbau," 941ff.

171. See *Civ.* 7.29f., and especially 7.30.31-37: "These are without doubt the works which Varro, shrewdest of scholars, has endeavoured to parcel out among his select gods, by some kind of 'natural' interpretation, whether he took over the principle from elsewhere or conjured it up out of his own imagination. But it is the one true God who is active and operative in all those things, but acting always as God, that is, present everywhere in [the divine] totality, free from all spatial confinement, completely untrammelled, absolutely indivisible, utterly unchangeable, and filling heaven and earth with [God's] ubiquitous power which is independent of anything in the natural order" (Bettenson, 292).

172. See ibid., 8.1-3, and especially 8.1.25-34: "Such philosophers certainly go far beyond Varro's ideas and come much nearer to the truth. For Varro could extend his 'natural' theology as far as the visible world, or the World-Soul, but no further. But these thinkers acknowledge a God who transcends any kind of soul, being the maker not only of this visible world—heaven and earth, in the familiar phrase—but also of every soul whatsoever, a God who gives blessedness to the rational and intelligent soul—the class to which the human soul belongs—by giving it a share in [God's] unchangeable and immaterial light" (Bettenson, 298–99).

173. See especially ibid., 8.10.46-54; 13.1-14.

174. Ibid., 8.4-9, especially 8.9.1-4: "Thus there are philosophers who have conceived of God, the supreme and true God, as the author of all created things, the light of knowledge, the Final Good of all activity, and who have recognized [God] as being for us the origin of existence, the truth of doctrine and the blessedness of life" (Bettenson, 311)

175. See ibid., 8.9f., and especially ll.37-52.

176. Ibid., bks. 6–7. See the titles given to these books in W. Thimme's German translation: bk. 6: "The Gods of the Poets' Tales and of the Civic Cult Cannot Give Everlasting Life"; bk. 7: "Even the Select Gods Do Not Bestow Everlasting Life."

177. Ibid., bk. 8. Thimme's title: "The Platonists and Their Teaching on Gods and Demons."

178. Ibid., bk. 9. Thimme's title: "Demons Are Not Suitable Mediators."

179. Ibid., bk. 10, which reaches its high point in ch. 6. See B. Studer, "Das Opfer Christi nach Augustins *De civitate Dei* X, 5-6: *Lex orandi—lex credendi*," *Miscellanea C. Vaggagini,* Studia Anselmiana 79 (Rome, 1980) 93–107, with the further literature listed there. See also *Civ.* 9.15, especially ll. 41–50.

180. See *Civ.* 10.11, where Augustine discusses Porphyry's letter to Anebo.

181. Ibid., 11.1.

182. See BA 34:34ff., on *Civ.* 10, chs. 18, 21, 25, and 32.

183. *Civ.* 10.12-15.

184. Ibid., 10.20.7-13: "[Christ] intended the daily sacrifice of the Church to be the sacramental symbol of this; for the Church, being the body of which [Christ] is the head, learns to offer itself through [Christ]. . . . This one sacrifice was prefigured by many rites, just as many words are used to refer to one thing, to emphasize a point without inducing boredom" (Bettenson, 401).

185. Ibid., 10.29.1-37.

186. Ibid., 10.6.53ff.; 10.20.7ff.

187. Ibid., 10.32, especially ll. 132-139: "Porphyry, however, says that the universal way for the soul's liberation has never come to his knowledge in his study of history. Yet what

could be found more striking than this historical record, which has taken possession of the whole world by its towering authority; or what more worthy of belief, seeing that in this record the events of the past are so narrated as also to be prophecies of the future? Many of these prophecies we see to have been fulfilled, and we confidently expect the fulfilment of the rest" (Bettenson, 424). See Studer, "Zum Aufbau," 945f.

188. *Civ.* 10.32.139-144.

189. See the overview in 18.1.1-17 (summary of the first seventeen books).

190. See Studer, "Zum Aufbau," 943–950.

191. See *Civ.* 11.1, with references to the biblical testimony regarding the city of God, especially ll. 13–16; "From such testimonies as these—and it would take too long to quote them all—we have learnt that there is a City of God: and we have longed to become citizens of that City, with a love inspired by its founder" (Bettenson, 429). See Studer, "Zum Aufbau," 947–50.

192. See *Civ.* 1, prol; 10.32.175-187; 11.1.27-35; 18.1.1-8.

193. See Studer, "Zum Aufbau," 946f.

194. *Cat. rud.* 4.8, and 6.10. See Van Oort, *Jerusalem and Babylon,* 179f., with further passages; and P. Siniscalco, *"Christum narrare et dilectionem monere,"* Aug 14 (1974) 605–623.

195. See below, Chapter 3, Sections 3d and 3e.

196. *Civ.* 11.2-3.

197. Ibid., 11.2-8, especially 11.5, with the questions concerning the endless time before the world began and the endless space outside the world.

198. Ibid., 11.10.

199. Ibid., 11.10.1-24.

200. Ibid., 11.10.68-83; see 11.29.26-32 (on the "reasons" in the Word).

201. Ibid., 11.16-19, especially 11.17.8ff.: "But God, who is supremely good in [God's] creation of natures that are good, is also completely just in [God's] employment of evil choices in [God's] design" (Bettenson, 448).

202. Ibid., 11.21.17-27.

203. Ibid., 11.21ff., especially 11.21.47ff.: "There can be no better author than God, no more effective skill than [God's] word, no better cause than that a good product should be created by God, who is good" (Bettenson, 453), with the reference to Plato. See also 11.17.7-10: "That is why the *choice* of evil is an impressive proof that the *nature* is good. But God, who is supremely good in [God's] creation of natures that are good, is also completely just in [God's] employment of evil choices in [God's] design" (Bettenson, 448).

204. See ibid., 11.24-28, with the comparison between the Trinity and the tripartite division of philosophy.

205. Ibid., 12.1-9.

206. Ibid., 12.1.11ff.

207. Ibid., 12.2.19ff.: "It follows that no existence is contrary to God, that is to the supreme existence and the author of all existence whatsoever" (Bettenson, 473); 12.5.11-117.

208. Ibid., 12.7.1-4; 12.9.1-34.

209. Ibid., 12.3-4.

210. Ibid., 12.15-17, especially 12.15.8-13: "Who could plumb this unplumbable depth of God's counsel, and scrutinize [God's] inscrutable design? This is the design by which God made [the human being] as a being in time, when no [human being] had existed before

[that person], making [that person] in time with no change of purpose, and multiplying the whole human race from that one person" (Bettenson, 489).

211. Ibid., 12.12-14; 12.18; 12.21.56-74.

212. Ibid., 12.19.35-41: "In fact [God's] wisdom is multiple in its simplicity, and multiform in uniformity. It comprehends all incomprehensible things with such incomprehensible comprehension that if [God] wished always to create new things of every possible kind, each of them unlike its predecessor, none of them could be for [God] undesigned and unforeseen, nor would it be that [God] foresaw each just before it came into being; God's wisdom would contain each and all of them in [God's] eternal prescience" (Bettenson, 497).

213. Ibid., 12.26.11-18: "By [God's] divine power, by what we may call [God's] 'effective' power, which cannot be made, but can only make, the round sky and the round sun received that form, when the world was made; and from the same 'effective' power of God, which cannot be made but can only make, came the roundness of the eye and the apple, and the other natural shapes which we observe as given to all things in nature, not externally, but by the power of the Creator working within" (Bettenson, 505).

214. Ibid., 14.11, and especially 14.26ff.

215. See especially ibid., 14.26.44-54: "But despite what has happened, God almighty, the supreme and supremely good creator of all beings, who assists and rewards good wills, while [God] abandons and condemns the bad (and yet [God] controls both good and bad) surely did not fail to have a plan whereby [God] might complete the fixed number of citizens predestined in [the divine] wisdom, even out of the condemned human race. [God] does not now choose them for their merits, seeing that the whole mass of [humankind] has been condemned as it were in its infected root; [God] selects them by grace and shows the extent of [the divine] generosity to those who have been set free not only in [God's] dealings with them but also in [God's] treatment of those who have not been freed" (Bettenson, 591–92).

216. Ibid., 14.27.9-14.

217. Ibid., 14.28.23-27: "In the Heavenly City, on the other hand, [humanity's] only wisdom is the devotion which rightly worships the true God, and looks for its reward in the fellowship of the saints, not only holy [persons] but also holy angels, 'so that God may be all in all'" (Bettenson, 594), with the entire context.

218. Ibid., 15.1.21-28.

219. See ibid., 18.1, with its look back at the preceding books.

220. See ibid., 15.8.1-20 (on the credibility of the history told in the books inspired by God).

221. See ibid., 16.16; 16.17 (the three world-wide kingdoms since Abraham's time); especially 18.2-8; 18.15-26.

222. Ibid., 18.41.1-4: "Again, to pass on from the question of historical knowledge, the philosophers themselves—from whom we digressed to discuss these points—do not seem to have had any other aim in their laborious pursuits than to discover how we should regulate our lives towards the attainment of happiness" (Bettenson, 815).

223. Ibid., 18.54.91-94 (Bettenson, 842).

224. Ibid., 18.2.13-16: "The result has been—though under the providence of God, in whose power it rests to order conquest or subjugation in each case—that some nations have been entrusted with empire, while others have been subdued to alien domination" (Bettenson, 762).

225. Ibid., 18.47.1-11.

226. See ibid., 15.1-3, especially 15.1.16-20: "I also call these two classes the two cities, speaking allegorically . . . one of which is destined to reign with God for all eternity, the other doomed to undergo eternal punishment with the Devil" (Bettenson, 594), as well as 15.3.7-13 (on wisdom as artisan); 15.6.24-27 (on the interior working of grace); 15.18.27ff.; 16.35.10-13 (with an allusion to Rom 9:11f.).

227. See ibid., bk. 15, chs. 16, 18, 24, 26, 37; bk. 16, chs. 12, 16, 18, 21, 26, 28f., 38.

228. See ibid., bk. 15, chs. 18, 21, 26ff.; bk. 16, chs. 2, 31, 37, 39, 41ff.; and especially 17.1.1-5: "We have learned that it is from the line of Abraham that the Israelite race derives its origin, in respect of physical descent; while, in respect of faith, all nations have issued from him; and this is according to God's promise. And the history of the City of God, as it develops through succeeding periods, will show how the promises made to Abraham are being fulfilled" (Bettenson, 711).

229. See especially ibid., 17.3.1-16 (on the threefold meaning of the prophetic oracles); also 17.3-20 (application of this principle to various biblical texts, especially those of the Psalms); also 17.23.

230. Ibid., 18.48-51.

231. See ibid., 18.51.16-41 (providence—discipline, consolation, training).

232. Ibid., 18.40-41, especially 41.81ff.: "[Any] who followed them [the genuine authors of sacred writings] in [their] thinking and in [their] manner of life [were] guided in [their] thinking and [their] living not by mere [human beings], but by God who spoke through these [writers]" (Bettenson, 818). In 18.40.12-16, Augustine also sets down the principle that the "inspired history" is more to be trusted than the "historians" (Bettenson, 815).

233. Ibid., 15.25. See J. M. Hallman, "The Emotions of God in the Theology of St. Augustine," *RTAM* 51 (1984) 5–19, with important bibliographical data.

234. *Civ.* 16.5.

235. Ibid., 16.6.19-27.

236. See ibid., 19.1.2-9: "I must first explain . . . the arguments advanced by mortal [human beings]. . . . My purpose is to make clear the great difference between their hollow realities and our hope, the hope given us by God, together with the realization—that is, the true bliss—which [God] will give us; and to do this not merely by appealing to divine authority but also by employing such powers of reason as we can apply for the benefit of unbelievers" (Bettenson, 843).

237. Ibid., 19.4; 19.10.12ff.: "This [peace] is indeed the ultimate bliss, the end of ultimate fulfilment that knows no destructive end" (Bettenson 864); 19.11.24ff.: ". . . The end of this City, whereby it will possess its Supreme Good, may be called either 'peace in life everlasting' or 'life everlasting in peace'" (Bettenson, 865–66).

238. Ibid., 19.13.10f.

239. Ibid., 19.13.61-75 (Bettenson, 872).

240. Ibid., 19.14.23-41.

241. Ibid., 19.17.66-70: "This peace the Heavenly City possesses in faith while on its pilgrimage, and it lives a life of righteousness, based on this faith, having the attainment of that peace in view in every good action it performs in relation to God, and in relation to a neighbour, since the life of a city is inevitably a social life" (Bettenson, 878–79)

242. See ibid., 19.4.6-10: "That is why the Scripture says, 'The just [person] lives on the basis of faith.' For we do not yet see our good, and hence we have to seek it by believing; and it is not in our power to live rightly, unless while we believe and pray we receive help

from [God] who has given us the faith to believe that we must be helped by [God]."
(Bettenson, 852); 19.13.59ff.; 19.27.31-46 (it is said here that righteousness consists in the
God-given subordination of the person to God and of the body to the soul; the same is true
in everlasting peace, but sustained then by "delight and facility in obeying" [Bettenson,
893]).

243. Ibid., 19.20.15f.: "that ultimate state in which God will be all in all, in the assur-
ance of eternity and the perfection of grace" (Bettenson, 881).

244. See ibid., 19.17: "Thus even the Heavenly City in [its] pilgrimage here on earth
makes use of the earthly peace and defends and seeks the compromise between human wills
in respect of the provisions relevant to the mortal nature of [humanity], so far as may be permitted without detriment to true religion and piety. In fact, that City relates the earthly peace
to the heavenly peace, which is so truly peaceful that it should be regarded as the only peace
deserving the name, at least in respect of the rational creation; for this peace is the perfectly
ordered and completely harmonious fellowship in the enjoyment of God, and of each other
in God" (Bettenson, 878).

245. Ibid., 19.21.

246. Ibid., 19.22. See BA 37:145ff.

247. *Civ.* 19.23.1-105.

248. Ibid., 19.23, especially ll. 134–137. See 22.25.11-15.

249. Ibid., 19.23.29-41; 19.23.134-163.

250. See ibid., 19.23.128-133, where Porphyry is cited: "For God, as being the father of
all, has indeed no lack of anything, but it is well for us when we adore [God] by means of
justice, chastity, and other virtues, making our life itself a prayer to [God] by imitating
[God] and seeking to know [God]. For seeking to know [God] purifies us, while imitation
of [God] deifies us by bringing our disposition in line with [God's]" (Bettenson, 888).

251. Ibid.: "And yet it is we ourselves—we, [God's] City—who are [God's] best, [God's]
most glorious sacrifice. The mystic symbol of this sacrifice we celebrate in our oblations,
familiar to the faithful. . . . It follows that justice is found where God, the one supreme
God, rules an obedient City according to [God's] grace, forbidding sacrifice to any being
save to [the divine self] alone; and where in consequence the soul rules the body in all [per-
sons] who belong to this City and obey God, and the reason faithfully rules the vices in a
lawful system of subordination; so that just as the individual righteous [person] lives on the
basis of faith which is active in love, so the association, or people, of righteous [persons]
lives on the same basis of faith, active in love, the love with which a [person] loves God as
God ought to be loved, and loves [the] neighbour as [oneself]. But where this justice does
not exist, there is certainly no 'association of [persons] united by a common sense of right
and by a community of interest'" (Bettenson, 890).

252. See ibid., 19.23.181-85.

253. Ibid., 20.1.

254. Ibid., 20.2-5.

255. Ibid., 20.5-17.

256. Ibid., 20.18-29. See especially 20.28.28 (on the justice of God).

257. See *Io. ev. tr.* 19.7-10; 21.12f.; 22.3.

258. *Civ.* 20.20.

259. Ibid., 20.30.108-112, with the entire context.

260. See ibid., 21.1.1-13, where Augustine justifies this order.

261. See especially ibid., 21.3.

262. See BA 37:795-801 and 825–831.

263. See *Civ.* 20.30.175-187, where, in announcing the final two books, the "truth and omnipotence of God" are said to be the "strongest proof" of things that seem incredible (Bettenson, 963).

264. Ibid., 21.9.45-54. See also the passages on the beauty of creation and especially those on the beauty of the human being: 22.24.171-220.

265. Ibid., 22.5.

266. Ibid., 21.6.54-78; 21.8.2.

267. Ibid., 22.19.24-37 (on the almighty artisan).

268. See ibid., 21.7.31-44; 21.8.104-128. And see *Ep.* 205.1.4.

269. *Civ.* 22.1.16-57. And see 22.1.1-38; 22.24.1-67.

270. See, provisionally, ibid., 21.12; 21.15f.; 21.24.163-185; 22.24.79-120. And see BA 37:851ff., with the references to passages on predestination.

271. *Civ.* 22.29: "The Kind of Vision with Which the Saints Will See God in the World to Come" (Bettenson's title, 1081).

272. Ibid., 21.17-27. And see BA 37:806-809.

273. *Civ.* 21.23.

274. Ibid., 21.24.1-67.

275. Ibid., 21.24.67 to 27.204.

276. See ibid., 21.12.19-22: "If this due punishment were imposed on all, no one would have the right to criticize the justice of God in that retribution; but the fact that so many are released from it is the ground for heart-felt thanksgiving for the free bounty of our Deliverer" (Bettenson, 989). See BA 37:801f.

277. See *Civ.* 22.2.35-39: "According to [God's] own will, which, along with [God's] foreknowledge, is eternal, God assuredly made all things in heaven and earth; [God] has made whatever [God] willed to make, and not only things past and present. [God] has already made things that are yet to be" (Bettenson, 1024).

278. Ibid., 22.30, especially ll. 95-100: "If they were to lose the knowledge of their past misery how will they, as the psalm says, 'sing the mercies of the Lord for all eternity'? Nothing will give more joy to that City than this song to the glory of the grace of Christ by whose blood we have been set free. There that precept will find fulfilment: 'Be still, and know that I am God'" (Bettenson, 1090).

279. Ibid., 22.30.205: "There we shall be still and see; we shall see and we shall love; we shall love and we shall praise. Behold what will be, in the end, without end!" (Bettenson, 1091).

Part II, Chapter 3

1. See *Ep.* 147.5.13f.; 147.6.17f.

2. See ibid., 6.18 (a "great question"); *Ep.* 187.2.3; 7.22.

3. For Augustine's dependence on Ambrose, see E. Dassmann, "Ambrosius," *AugLex,* vol. 1, fascs. 1–2 (1986) 270–285, especially 277–281.

4. See *Ep.* 147.2.7; 147.5.12 (citing 1 John 3:2 and 11:26); *Ep.* 187.5.17; 187.8.29.

5. *Retr.* 2.41.

6. *Ep.* 147.1.14.17; see also *Ep.* 147.16.36–19.46.

7. See *Ep.* 147.5.15 (we know that God can be seen even though we have not seen God; we believe it on the basis of the Scriptures; citing 1 John 3:2: "we know"); *Ep.* 147.19.39 (with the relevant passages of the Bible).

8. *Ep.* 147.2.7.

9. See ibid., 147.1.3, and especially 18.45.

10. Ibid., 147.15.37.

11. Ibid., 147.1.3.

12. Ibid., 147.5.37. See also 8.9.21 (God's plenitude is inconceivable).

13. See ibid., 147.5.16; 147.8.20; 147.10.23 (if the powers and the seraphim are invisible, then much more so the Trinity).

14. See ibid., 147.15.37; 147.6.18 (citation from Ambrose with the formula, "to be seen with the aid of a likeness which [God's] will chooses, not one formed by nature"); 147.7.19f., 147.11.26; 147.19.47.

15. Ibid., 147.8.20; 147.10.23; 147.11.26; 147.14.35 (contemplation); 147.15.37; etc.

16. Ibid., 147.11.28: "like these visible things that are seen by bodily sight."

17. Ibid., 147.15.37: "But the only-begotten Son, who is in the bosom of the Father, narrates, without the aid of sound, the nature and substance of the deity and thus, again invisibly, shows it to those who are worthy of and fitted for such a vision." See ibid., 147.9.22.

18. Ibid., 147.12.29: "an image becoming known to the mind, that it may shine there with its interior and indescribable light." See ibid., 147.23.54.

19. Ibid., 147.12.29.

20. Ibid., 147.14.35: "It is certainly clear that when [Paul] said 'we know' (2 Cor 5:16), he was speaking of the knowledge that comes from the faith by which the just now live, and not from the sight by which we will see God as [God] is." In the context, the knowledge of Christ is connected with knowledge of the Father.

21. Ibid., 147.14.34, especially: "in the depths, the unsearchable judgments of God whence this grace comes to human beings." See also *Ep.* 140.25.62f.

22. See *Ep.* 147.7.19.

23. Ibid., 147.7.19f.

24. See ibid., 147.25.37 (citing 1 Tim 1:17); 147.19.46 (citing Jas 1:17 and 1 Tim 6:16); 147.9.47 (no citation).

25. On this subject, see B. Studer, *Zur Theophanie-Exegese Augustins: Untersuchungen zu einer Ambrosius-Zitat in der Schrift "De videndo Deo" (ep. 147),* Studia Anselmiana 59 (Rome, 1971) 72–82, on the prehistory of the distinction between essence and form.

26. *Ep.* 147.6.17f., citing Ambrose, *Exp. Ev. Lc.* 1.24-27; 8.20.

27. See Studer, *Zur Theophanie-Exegese,* 82–98, especially 94f.

28. *Ep.* 147.11.26; see 147.17.44.

29. Ibid., 147.11.16, citing Ex 33:13 and Ps 16:15.

30. Ibid., 147.24.27; 147.20.48 (with reference to Ambrose); and frequently.

31. Ibid., 147.23.53 (following Eph 3:19); see 147.15.36, where the idea that a human being can become wholly like God is excluded.

32. Ibid., 147.23.53. See also 147.1.2.

33. Ibid., 147.5.15; 147.11.25.

34. Ibid., 147.9.22; 147.11.27; 147.20.48 (with the reference to *Ep.* 92.3: even in the resurrection human beings will not be able to see God with their bodily eyes); 147.23.54 (with the anticipation of *Civ.* 22.29). In *Ep.* 148 (especially 3), this rejection of a bodily vision of God is grounded more particularly in the nonspatiality and incorporeality of the

divine substance and is confirmed by passages from the Fathers. According to *Ep.* 148.3.11 and 5.17 God can be seen with the eyes of the heart.

35. *Ep.* 147.12.30.

36. Ibid., 147.13.31.

37. Ibid., 147.13.32 (citing Num 12:8).

38. *Retr.* 2.49.

39. *Ep.* 187.2.5f.

40. Ibid., 187.2.4; 187.3.8f.

41. Ibid., 187.13.41.

42. Ibid., 187.5.16; 187.12.35; 187.13.38.

43. Ibid., 187.5.17: "[God] is said to be everywhere because [God] is not absent from any part of things; [God] is said to be wholly present because [God] does not make a part of [the divine self] present to a part of things, and another part of [the divine self] to another part, but is wholly present to each part in the same way."

44. Ibid., 187.6.18: "[God] is everywhere because [God] is nowhere absent. 'In [the divine self],' because [God] is not contained by the things to which [God] is present as though [God] cannot exist without them."

45. See ibid., 187.4.1.

46. See ibid., 187.6.19, as well as 187.3.7 (citing John 1:5).

47. See ibid., 187.4.11f. (great wisdom or immortality in more or less great human beings); 187.4.13 (health as a quality of bodies).

48. See ibid., 187.4.13f.

49. Ibid., 187.4.14: "God is 'spread abroad' through all things, not in the sense that [God] is a quality of the world, but in the sense that [God] is the substance that creates the world, governing it without effort and containing the world without it being onerous to [God]." See also ibid., 187.12.36, where miracles are ascribed to the omnipresent God.

50. Ibid., 187.4.15.

51. Ibid., 187.5.16: "Therefore we must confess that God is everywhere by the presence of the divinity but not everywhere by the grace of the indwelling."

52. Ibid., 187.12.35. See 187.5.16; 187.6.20.

53. Ibid., 187.5.17: "Just as [God] who is everywhere does not dwell in all, so [God] does not dwell equally in those in whom [God] dwells. . . . Why is it that among the saints some are holier than others, if not because they have God dwelling more fully in them?. . . . Those who have become unlike [God] by sinning are said to be distant from [God], and those who receive the likeness to [God] by a devout life are said to draw near to [God]."

54. See ibid., 187.13.38: "God, then, is everywhere present and everywhere wholly present; [God] does not dwell everywhere but in [God's] temple, to which [God] shows kindness and mercy through grace; [God] is received as dweller, more by some, less by others." See, further, 187.6.19: ". . . although those in whom [God] dwells possess [God] according to their varying capacities, some more, others less; these [God] builds up into the most beloved temple of [God's] gracious goodness." See 187.6.18.

55. Ibid., 187.12.37.

56. Ibid., 187.6.21; 187.8.26. See 187.9.31ff. (on the necessity of baptism).

57. Ibid., 187.8.29, especially: ". . . they exert themselves in walking, that is, in advancing, asking, and receiving transparent understanding through a devout faith."

58. Ibid., 187.8.27; see 187.8.29.

59. See ibid., 187.8.27.

60. Ibid., 187.13.41.

61. Ibid., 187.6.19; 187.13.38.

62. See ibid., 187.6.19; 187.8.27.

63. Ibid., 187.13.39f. (with the development of Col 2:9).

64. Ibid., 187.3.8.

65. Ibid., 187.3.10.

66. See ibid., 187.11.34 (the necessity of faith in Christ).

67. See ibid., 187.9.22; 187.15.37.

68. See the explanation of *clementia* in R. Holte, *Béatitude et sagesse: St. Augustin et le problème de la fin de l'homme dans la philosophie ancienne* (Paris, 1962) 314–318.

69. See CCL 49:69-73 and DS 222–230.

70. See, above all, Pelagius' *De natura,* which is refuted in *Nat. et gr.*

71. See *Praed. sanct.* 3.74.8 (with the references to *Simp.* 1.2) and *Persev.* 20.52ff. (with the details of the doctrine of predestination).

72. See the distinction between nature and vice in *Nat. et gr.* (415) 3.3; *Gest. Pel* (417) 3.7.

73. See *Spir. et litt.* 3.5: ". . . in order that, because of this free gift given as a pledge, [one] may burn with desire to cling to the creator and may passionately long to attain to a share in that true light, so that [one] may have the fullness of being from [God] from whom [one] has [one's] being." See also *Nat. et gr.* 43.50; *Perf. iust.* 3.7f.; 4.10. See also the passages in which the concept of "the grace of the creator" is explained, in BA 22:722, especially *Ep.* 177.7.

74. *Nat. et gr.* 34.39.

75. See *C. ep. Pel.* (421) 3.8.24f., especially 25: "In being born, human beings refute the Manichees and praise the creator since they are good insofar as they are human beings; insofar, however, as they contract original sin, they refute the Pelagians and need a savior." See also 4.3.3–4.4.

76. See *Pecc. mer.* 2.21.35: "[Adam and Eve] therefore served God as long as they cultivated a devout obedience, by which God is worshipped. How important obedience is and how it is alone enough to keep the rational creature subject to the creator could not be better conveyed than by a prohibition from a tree that was not bad."

77. *Spir. et litt.* 9.15; 8.31; 32.56; *Gr. et pecc. or.* 1.47.52. Also *C. ep. Pel.* 3.17.20f. In connection with this point, see also *Nat. et gr.* 33.37, where any change in the substance of God is excluded.

78. See, for example, *Pecc. mer.* 1.14.18–15.19; *Nat. et gr.* 1.1; *Perf. iust.* 7.16 (citing Gal 2:21); *Gr. et pecc. or.* 2.23.26; 2.24.28.

79. See *Nat. et gr.* 53.61f., and the many passages that cite the formula from Rom 7:25: "the grace of God through Jesus Christ our Lord." See above, p. 36.

80. *Pecc. mer.* 1.14.18.

81. See the frequent use of 2 Cor 5:21, for example in *Pecc. mer.* 1.28.55; 1.33.62. See further *C. Iul.* 6.24.78.

82. See *Gr. et pecc. or.* 1.14.15 (citing John 6:45); also *Praed. sanct.* 8.13f.

83. *Pecc. mer.* 2.1.1.

84. See *Spirit. et litt.* 5.7; *Gr. et pecc. or.* 1.5.6 (citing Phil 2:12f.); 1.13.14; etc. But one should observe that Augustine also gives biblical texts a dogmatic reinterpretation. For

example, he turns the New Testament "Father" into "the Trinity." See *C. ep. Pel.* 3.7.18 (on Matt 18:10): "The angels of God are endowed with the perfection of this justice; they always see the face of the Father and thereby of the entire Trinity because they see through the Son in the Holy Spirit."

85. See *Gr. et pecc. or.* 1.5.6 (citing Phil 2:12f.): "and in order that they may know that not only in what they can do . . . but also in what they actually do they are helped by God, [Paul] does not say: 'For it is God who effects in you the capacity,' as though they already had of themselves the power to will and to do and did not need his help in these two areas; but he says 'For it is God who works in you, enabling you to will and to do.'" See also ibid., 1.13.14; 1.47.52.

86. *Spir. et litt.* 34.60.

87. *Gr. et pecc. or.* 1.3.3.

88. *Spir. et litt.* 3.5: "By which [a person's] soul experiences the delight in and love of that supreme and immutable good that is God."

89. See *Pecc. mer.* 2.19.32. On the subject, see BA 24:15-18.

90. *Pecc. mer.* 1.39.70.

91. See M. Vincent, *S. Augustin, Maître de prière d'après les Enarrationes in Psalmos,* Théologie historique 84 (Paris, 1990) 261–295: on grace and prayer, with special attention to *En. Ps.* 118.

92. See *En. Ps.* 118.17.1; 84.15.

93. See ibid., 139.11.

94. See *Nat. et gr.* 69.83; *Perf. iust.* 10.22.

95. See *Pecc. mer.* 2.29.47; *Perf. iust.* 20.43; *Gest. Pel.* 3.7. See also *Spir. et litt.* 24.40 (God does what God promises).

96. See *Retr.* 2.1. On the subject, see K. Flasch, *Die Logik des Schreckens: Augustinus von Hippo, Die Gnadenlehre von 397* (Mainz, 1990) 48–51.

97. See *C. ep. Pel.* 2.1.1; *C. Iul.* 1.1.3; *C. Iul. imp.* 3.124.

98. *C. Iul. imp.* 3.124; 3.136: "[Children] are by nature good, because God creates them; but due to sin they are wicked and therefore God heals them"; 3.159.

99. *C. ep. Pel.* 2.1.1. See also *An. et or.* 2.3.5: "Every nature is either God, who has no author, or is from God because it has [God] as its author." By "God" here is meant God the Father, as is clear from the trinitarian context. See BA 22:807-810.

100. *C. Iul. imp.* 3.155; see *C. Iul.* 3.23.52.

101. See *C. Iul.* 3.21.46f., and the entire third book.

102. *C. Iul. imp.* 6.16. See, earlier, *Perf. iust.* 14.32.

103. *C. Iul. imp.* 1.100f.

104. Ibid., 4.124.

105. Ibid., 4.125.

106. *Gr. et lib. arb.* 21.42f.

107. Ibid., 23. 45.

108. See ibid., 20.41–23.45.

109. *C. Iul. imp.* 5.60.

110. *Gr. et lib. arb.* 6.15.

111. Ibid., 8.20.

112. Ibid., 18.37f.

113. See *Corrept.* 12.38, and BA 24:784ff.

114. *C. Iul.* 4.8.44.

115. See *Gr. et lib. arb.* 21.42f., especially: "These and other testimonies . . . make it clear that God acts in the hearts of human beings to incline their wills in whatever direction [God] decides, whether to good or to evil depending on their merits; [God's] decision is sometimes clear, sometimes hidden, but is always just." On the passage, see BA 24:779ff., with the explanation of "incline to sin" as meaning that God permits sin. See also *Persev.* 8.19, and *Spir. et litt.* 8.14, where God is called "examiner of the heart and inmost will."

116. See *Gr. et pecc. or.* 1.47.52.

117. See *Gr. et lib. arb.* 22.44 (citing Rom 11:30-33), and *An. et or.* 2.13.18.

118. See *Corrept.* 8.17ff. (citing Rom 9:20 and 11:33).

119. See ibid., 13.42, as well as *Gr. et lib. arb.* 20.41–23.45, on the mysterious action of God in the human heart.

120. *Praed. sanct.* 16.41.

121. See *Persev.* 22.57-62. Add *Persev.* 8.19 (citing 1 Cor 10:12) and *Corrept.* 13.40 (citing Rom 11:20).

122. *Corrept.* 8.18.

123. See *Ep.* 103.3.9-12; *An. et or.* 2.13.18 (and BA 22:828ff.); *C. Iul.* 4.8.45; 5.4.14; *Corrept.* 8.19; *Praed. sanct.* 8.14. See also, earlier, *Nat. et gr.* 25.28.

124. See *Praed. sanct.* 10.19, and *Corrept.* 11.20. On the question of the divine foreknowledge of what will never happen, see *An. et or.* 1.8.8; 1.12.15 (BA 22:792-795), as well as *Praed. sanct.* 14.26 (and BA 24:818, on the knowledge of the those things that could happen in the future *[futuribilia]*).

125. See *An. et or.* 4.11.16: ". . . those predestined to everlasting life by the most merciful giver of grace who is also the most just dispenser of punishment to those whom [God] has predestined to everlasting death." See BA 22:828ff.

126. See especially Rom 8:28ff. and 9:9-21. See BA 24:19.

127. See BA 24:20f., 806f.

128. See BA 24:11f. and the various passages cited there, especially *C. Iul.* 4.8.42ff.

129. See the harsh criticism of Flasch, *Die Logik des Schreckens,* 60f., 268ff. But see also A. Sage, "La volonté salvifique universelle dans la pensée de saint Augustin," *RechAug* 3 (1965) 107–131; A. Solignac, "Les excès de l'*intellectus fidei* dans la doctrine d'Augustin sur la grâce," *NRT* 110 (1988) 825–849.

130. *Corrept.* 10.27. See *Ep.* 190.3.10; *Gr. et lib. arb.* 20.41f. (on the mysterious power which God exercises over the human will) and 23.45 (the source of righteousness and wisdom is in God). There is also no mistaking the fact that Augustine believed, on the basis of his experience, that many human beings, even Christians, are actually lost.

131. See *Praed. sanct.* 15.31; *Persev.* 24.67.

132. See Studer, *Zur Theophanie-Exegese,* 82–85. See also M.-A. Vannier, *"Creatio," "conversio," "formatio" chez s. Augustin,* Paradosis 31 (Fribourg, 1991) 111f. ("Quia voluit").

133. See H.-I. Marrou, *Saint Augustin et l'augustinisme* (Paris, 1955) 150f. On this subject, see also the still worthwhile study of J. Sirmond, *Historia predestinatiana,* printed in PL 53:673-692.

134. The extent to which Augustine carried his logic too far is also clear from the fact that he did not succeed in applying his concept of the all-transcendent God in the same way to Adam and prelapsarian humanity. On this subject, see G. Greshake, *Gnade als konkrete Freiheit: Eine Untersuchung zur Gnadenlehre des Pelagius* (Mainz, 1972) 261–264.

135. See *Gest. Pel.* 14.34; *En. Ps.* 18.2.3; 134.10 (citing Ps 134:6); *Corrept.* 14.45; *En. Ps.* 99.15 (applied to Christ).

136. See G. N. Knauer, *Die Psalmenzitate in den Konfessionen Augustins* (Göttingen, 1955); Vincent, *S. Augustin, Maître de prière,* 10–15. See above, pp. 81f.

137. See M. Pontet, *Exégèse de saint Augustin prédicateur,* Théologie 7 (Paris, n.d.); H. Urs von Balthasar, *Aurelius Augustinus: Über die Psalmen* (Leipzig, 1936); Vincent, *S. Augustin, Maître de prière,* 10–30.

138. For the chronology of the *En. Ps.,* see NBA 25, 2nd ed. (Rome, 1982) xliv–xlvii (chronological table and bibliography)

139. *En. Ps.* 101.2.12; 103.1.1.7 (God created everything easily).

140. Ibid., 99.5: "We observe creation as a whole, the land and sea and sky and everything that is in them; we observe that each thing has its origin and cause, the vigor of its seeds, the order in which it arises, the way in which it lasts, its decline and passing. . . ."; 103.1.1: "From the greatness and beauty of the building we are led to love the incalculable greatness and beauty of the builder, even though we do not see [the builder]"; 94.10; 118.27.1.

141. Ibid., 103.4.2: "Whatever God made was made in wisdom and was made by wisdom."

142. Ibid., 134.10: "The cause of all things that [God] made is [the divine] will. . . . God created out of goodness, [God] needed nothing that [God] made; therefore [God] created everything that [God] wanted."

143. See the entire exposition of Ps 93. On the subject, see S. Poque, *Le langage symbolique dans la prédication d'Augustin d'Ippone* (Paris, 1984) 193–224 ("La loi du Père").

144. See *En. Ps.* 87.12: "Like forgotten land is the person who has forgotten God, for [such a one] can be unbelieving to the point of sinking into such darkness that one foolishly says in one's heart: 'There is no God.'" But according to Augustine, there are few human beings who deny the existence of God. On this subject, see A.D.R. Polman, *De leer van God bij Augustinus* (Kampen, 1965) 48. See also the attack on the idols of the pagans in *En. Ps.* 94.6; 113.2.1.

145. See *En. Ps.* 73.25.

146. Ibid., 74.9; 93.2.

147. See ibid., 48.1.1: "We commonly hear people murmuring against God because the wicked prosper in this life while the good toil," with the entire context; 93.1f.

148. See ibid., 88.2.2 (do not reject the discipline imposed by God); 93.13 (comparison of God, who educates the nations, with the teacher who demands an accounting from the teacher's pupils); 93.18; 94.9; 118.17.3f.: "God teaches discipline, then, by tempering affliction . . .; teach me discipline while giving me patience."

149. See ibid., 102.5f.; 84:1: "By giving [the divine] salvation, [God] heals in us the power to see what [God] shows. [God] does not heal as human physician[s do] when the latter seek to show this [earthly] light to those whom [they have] healed. The light that [physicians] seek to show is other than [themselves]; different too [are] the physician[s] who heal the eyes to which [they] show a light that is not [themselves]. It is not thus that the Lord our God acts, for [God] is a physician who cures the power that enables us to see, and [God's own self] is the light that we are able to see."

150. See *En. Ps.* 124.2.

151. Ibid., 31.2.16; 50.15; 91.3.

152. Ibid., 32.2.1.1; 48.1.1.

153. Ibid., 32.2.1.2: "Who are the upright? Those who direct their hearts according to God's will; if human weakness troubles them, divine justice strengthens them. For although they may desire one thing within their mortal hearts, something befitting their momentary situation or business or present need, yet when they understand and realize that God wills something else, they give precedence to the will of their superior over their own will, and the will of the almighty over the will of a weakling, and the will of God over the will of a human being." See ibid., 99.6 (because Christ is both a slave and a free human being, he does not murmur against God).

154. Ibid., 93.18: "Do not try to twist God's will to match your will, but correct your will according to God's will. Thus God's will serves as a ruler. . . . The ruler in this case, however, remains unaffected by anything, for it is an unchangeable ruler." See ibid., 44.17f. (the *rectitudo* or "straightness" of God); 86.1.12; 100.6; 118.1.1 (the law of God as the way to blessedness); 124.6: "Those who desire to follow God, do so with [God] going before and them following, not them going before and [God] following; and in all things, they find [God] good, whether [God] is correcting them or consoling or training or crowning or purifying or illuminating."

155. See ibid., 118.31.3: "The Father's judgments, then, are praised even in affliction, if [the Father's] promises are loved in time of reward"; 134.1.1 (the just praise God even in time of distress; they look to God for nothing but the God alone).

156. Ibid., 41.6.

157. Ibid., 41.10. See 37.14; 41.14; 126.1.

158. See ibid., 32.2.1.10f., especially: "Consider mercy and justice in themselves. The time for mercy is now, the time for judgment will be later. . . . [God] now calls those who have turned away, forgives the sins of those who turn back, is patient with sinners until they are converted, . . . exhorts the sluggish, consoles the afflicted. . . . Judgment will come; then there will be repentance, but it will be fruitless"; 70.1.1: "Love and fear of God have great power to move: fear of God because [God] is just; love because [God] is merciful"; 118.19.6: "Mercy and truth are so recommended in the divine utterances that while they are to be found in many places, especially in the psalms, in one place we read even this, 'All the ways of the Lord are mercy and truth.' Here [God] gave first place to truth, by which we are humbled in death, under the judgment of [the one] whose judgments are justice; then comes mercy, by which we are restored to life, in accordance with the promise of [the one] whose blessing is freely given." See the entire section in 100.1-3, especially: "Let no one rashly delude oneself about the mercy of God, since there is also judgment; and let no one who has changed for the better be terrified at God's judgment, because mercy has gone before it" (1) and "[Paul] finds [God] a giver in time of mercy, he has [God] as a debtor in the time of judgment" (2). In addition, see 110.2: "According to these (justifications), mercy fails no one who confesses, and no one's wickedness goes unpunished"; 88.1.3 ("truthfulness" in the fulfillment of the promises to the Jews, "mercy" toward the pagans); 88.1.25.

159. See Vincent, *S. Augustin, Maître de prière,* 297–433.

160. *En. Ps.* 44.9: ". . . the supreme work of human beings is naught else than to praise God"; 72.34.

161. See ibid., 39.4; 103.1.3. On the subject, see Vincent, *S. Augustin, Maître de prière,* 302ff.

162. *En. Ps.* 144.1; 62.2.

163. This theme is often discussed. See, most recently, Vincent, *S. Augustin, Maître de prière,* 438–447, with its survey of the relevant passages.

164. *En. Ps.* 110.6. See also 7.19; 94.4; 95.7ff.; 105.2; 117.1: "Confession is either confession in praise of [God] or confession of our sins"; 117.2, as well as *Serm.* 67.1.1.

165. See *En. Ps.* 91.6: "When you see that you are acting properly, confess to God"; 49.21 (explanation of the "sacrifice of praise": thanksgiving for all blessings and for the forgiveness of sins; see Vincent, *S. Augustin, Maître de prière,* 71ff.); 106.2: "If you have tasted how sweet the Lord is, then *Give praise to the Lord because [the Lord] is sweet;* if you have tasted with ardent desire, then break forth in eager praise. For [God's] mercy endures forever"; 118.17.7; 137.5.

166. See ibid., 104.1: "The meaning of this word [alleluia], or rather of these two words, is 'Praise God.' That is why [the psalmist] begins: *Give praise to the Lord and call upon [the Lord's] name*"; 106.1.

167. Ibid., 146.2. See 144.2; 148.1.

168. Ibid., 83.8: "*They shall praise you for ever and ever.* This will be our entire business: unending alleluia. . . . Let us be sure then, brothers and sisters: we will never grow tired of the praise of God, the love of God. If you fail in love, you will fail in praise; but if love is everlasting, because the beauty that can never cloy will be there, then do not be afraid that you will not be able always to praise [the one] whom you will always be able to love"; see 86.9.

169. See ibid., 55.19: "*There is within you something to vow and to pay.* From the coffer of the heart bring forth the incense of praise; from the storeroom of a good conscience bring forth the sacrifice of praise. Whatever you bring forth, set it on fire with love. Make vows to praise God, and pay them"; 104.1 (praise and love); 105.3 (praise God who does good works in us); 106.1 (praise of God must be ever in our hearts); 115.8: "Let each one carefully think of what they may vow to God and what vows they may pay: let them vow themselves, let them pay themselves." See Vincent, *S. Augustin, Maître de prière,* 371 (citing *En. Ps.* 146.1; 32.2.1.8; 146.1).

170. See *En. Ps.* 32.2.1.3 (with the image of the father of the family, who disciplines and consoles); 48.2.9.

171. Ibid., 90.1.2; 30.2.3.12.

172. Ibid., 31.2.25.

173. See ibid., 148.8: "Happy those whose business is to praise God. . . . We reflect: Will we be among them? Come, let us sigh with yearning, let us sigh and groan." And see ibid., 147.6.

174. Ibid., 148.3; 144, especially 13; 145.

175. See ibid., 70.1.15: "God is praised in all that [God] has made, in all [God's] creatures, in everything that [God] has established, in [God's] governance and rule of the ages. . . . To this praise be added the resurrection of our Lord Jesus Christ." In addition, see 103.4.2; 144.10.

176. Ibid., 117.2: "The praise of God could not be explained with greater brevity than by saying: *Because [God] is good.* I see nothing more sublime than this brief phrase, since it is a property of God that [God] is good" (citing Mark 10:17f.); 134.4.

177. Ibid., 96.12 (God alone is to be worshipped); 103.1.3 (God's unchangeable greatness is to be praised); 134.4; 144.5-8 (God's greatness is unlimited, especially 7: God is to be praised because God has made all things).

178. See ibid., 110.1: "Be present in spirit, singers of [God] who is good, children who praise and glorify the true and changeless God"; 38.7; 89.15; 101.2.10; 146.11, together with 101.27f.

179. See 92.1: ". . . because God works in repose, [God] always acts and is always at rest."

180. Ibid., 121.12: "The fullness of delights and sufficiency of riches is . . . [God's] very self, [God] in whom the city together shares; [God] will be our wealth, too"; see 121.5f.; 38.7 (explanation of "make known to me what the number of my days is").

181. See 134.4: "Ignoring all the names [God] might be given, God replies that [the divine] name is Pure Being (Ex 3:14). . . . You see, [God] is such that by comparison with [God] created things are not. When not compared with [God], they are, because they are from [God]; but when compared with [God], they are not, because authentic being is unchangeable being, and [God] alone is this"; 127.15; 146.11: "What does 'in the same' mean, if not that [God] cannot change? Other things, which are created, can be thus or so; but [God] who created them cannot be thus or so. You may change them, and they will be changed; but you are yourself, and your years shall not fail."

182. See ibid., 34.1.6: "I shall look for no other salvation but the Lord my God"; 34.1.12; 89.3: ". . . implying that God's substance is utterly unchangeable; in [God] there is no 'is, was, and will be,' but only 'is' (Ex 3:13)"; 101.27f.: "See how this eternity has been made our refuge, so that, since we are to abide in it, we may take refuge in it from this changeable time"; 118.12.2 (everlasting salvation consists in the everlasting good, which is God's very self).

183. See especially the passages that speak of predestination, such as *En. Ps.* 87.13; see also 102.7 (God will crown the divine gifts).

184. See ibid., 109.1: "God is faithful who has made [the divine self] our debtor, not by receiving something from us but by making us such great promises" 88.1.3; 72.32.

185. Ibid., 101.2.14 (God's eternity as the basis of our hope of resurrection).

186. Ibid., 110.9. See 102.7: "The reward is that you may for eternity praise God without ceasing."

187. Ibid., 144.5.

188. See Vincent, *S. Augustin, Maître de prière,* 307ff.

189. See *En. Ps.,* 85.12: "[The psalmist] says: *Lord, there is no one like you among the gods.* But how God is unlike all the others [the psalmist] did not say, because it cannot be said. Pay attention, beloved: God is ineffable. We more easily say what [God] is not than what [God] is"; 144.11.

190. Ibid., 85.12.

191. Ibid., 134.11.

192. See ibid., 32.2.1.8. "Sing with jubilation. Singing well, you see, means singing with jubilation. And what does it mean to sing with jubilation? It means to understand that the heart's song cannot be explained in words. . . . And who is rightly to receive this jubilation if not the ineffable God? [God] is ineffable, that is, you cannot express [God] in words. But if [God] cannot be expressed in words, and yet you may not remain silent, what is left except to jubilate? Then the heart rejoices without words, and the measureless breadth of joy is not limited by syllables."

193. Ibid., 145.4: "*Praise the Lord* the psalm says. Try with feelings of devotion; you will fall short in praising [God]. It is better to fall short in praising God than to advance by praising yourself. For when you praise God and do not explain what you intend, your thought is extended into your interior self, and this extension makes you more capable of [the one] whom you praise."

194. See ibid., 134.4: "Again, when I enter into [God] as far as I can, I find that [God] is both within me and above me, because God is good in such a way that [God] does not

need these things in order to be good. Finally, I do not praise [God] without [the divine] help; I find that [God] is perfect without these things, in need of nothing, changeless, not seeking any good by which [God] may be increased, not fearing any evil by which [God] may be diminished"; 74.9: "Even though [God] is closer to you than you are to yourself, there is no place to which you can flee from God when [God] is angry, except to God who is appeased; there is absolutely no place to which you may flee. . . . But because God, and not a human being, is the judge, do not look for [God] in places. You will be [God's] place if you are good, if you call upon [God] with praise."

195. See ibid., 118.18.4: "By [God's] very self, because [God] is light, God illumines devout minds to understand the divine things that are said or shown to them" (with the entire context). See Vincent, *S. Augustin, Maître de prière*, 62–91 (on prayer of the heart).

196. *En. Ps.* 55.7.

197. Ibid., 144.1: "I venture to assert, beloved, that [God] praised [the divine self] so that God might be praised by human beings; and because [God] deigned to praise [the divine self], human beings find the way to praise [God]. . . . For human beings to praise themselves is arrogance; for God to praise [the divine self] is an act of mercy."

198. Ibid., 72.32.

199. Ibid., 110.1 (on the forty days as expression of a longing for the everlasting praise of Easter); 110.9 (the praise of God and the divine wisdom will endure forever).

200. Ibid., 89.3.

201. Ibid., 34.1.12; 118.16.1 ("my portion" as participation in the only true God).

202. Ibid., 79.14; 134.11.

203. Ibid., 5.1.

204. Ibid., 35.5; 41.2; 143.3.

205. Ibid., 96.12 ("commanding officer" of the angels).

206. Ibid., 136.12; 92.6; 44.23.

207. Ibid., 32.2.2.17: "[God] is our inheritance, our possession. Are we perhaps speaking rashly when we make God our possession, since [God] is after all the Lord, since [God] is the creator? This is not rashness; it is the affection produced by desire and the sweetness that hope gives"; 32.2.2.18: "[God] possesses, then, and is possessed, and all for our sake. For it is not possible that as we possess [God] in order to be happy in [God], so [God] would have to possess us in order to be happy. [God] both possesses and is possessed for no other reason than that we might be happy."

208. See ibid., 2.4; 3.6; 112.4, and 131.22 (on "rest").

209. See, for example, ibid., 122.3 (on the ascent to God).

210. See ibid., 127.15 (on the "king of Jerusalem, who is").

211. This theme has been often studied. See Vincent, *S. Augustin, Maître de prière*, 34–61 ("Prayer of Christ, Prayer of the Church"). See the references in the first part of the present book, especially pp. 57f.

212. See *En. Ps.* 46.1-10, together with the observations made above.

213. Ibid., 85.1.

214. Ibid., 85.21. See also 29.2.1, where the question is asked, "What does it mean to be mediator between God and human beings?" and the answer is given, "Not between the Father and human beings, but between God and human beings. What is 'God'? Father and Son and Holy Spirit."

215. Ibid., 81.2. Augustine himself answers the question by referring to Christ. See, further, *En. Ps.* 32.2.2.5: "This Trinity, then, is one God"; 37.27; 49.1f.; 135.6.

216. See especially ibid., 100.1: "First, reflect on God, so that you too may imitate the Father to the extent that [the Father] grants you. Nor is it arrogance of our part to say that we ought to imitate our Father, for the Lord himself, the only Son of God, exhorts us to do so." In addition, 49.18 (God has knowledge of creatures in the Word); 61.18f. (God "has spoken once for all" in the Word). Especially to be noted is the approach to God in 146.1 (the almighty Lord is praised because the Lord is the Father); 146.4 (God sent God's Son as redeemer); 146.6 (through Jesus Christ and the indwelling of the Holy Spirit, God heals the contrite of heart); 146.9 (God regards human beings and joins them to the "body of the Only-begotten"). On the subject, see also M. Neusch in his introduction to Vincent, *S. Augustin, Maître de prière,* vii (on the theocentrism of prayer in Augustine).

217. Interesting in this regard is *En. Ps.* 71.2, where Augustine is explaining the words, "Give to the king your judgment, O God, and to the king's son your justice"; following a tradition that goes back to the beginning, he distinguishes between the Father and the Son and relates the word "God" unambiguously to the Father. See especially: "This king is also the son of a king, since God the Father is a king. . . . It is made sufficiently clear why the Father who is king has given to the Son who is king [the Father's] judgment and justice."

218. *F. et symb.*

219. *Agon.* (396–397) and *Ench.* (421 or 423). See C. Eichenseer, *Das Symbolum Apostolicum beim hl. Augustinus: Mit Berücksichtigung des dogmengeschichtlichen Zusammenhanges,* Kirchengeschichtliche Quellen und Studien 4 (St. Ottilien, 1960) 146–157 (the places where this creed appears in Augustine), as well as A. Zumkeller, *"Agone christiano (De)," AugLex,* vol. 1, fascs. 1–2 (1986) 221–227.

220. See Eichenseer, *Das Symbolum Apostolicum,* 157–199, especially 157.

221. See ibid., 57–163.

222. See *En. Ps.* 77.8: "This also includes believing in God *(credere in Deum),* which is more than simply believing God *(credere Deo).* For we often have to give credence to one or other human being, but this does not mean that we must believe in [that person]. Believing in God, then, means adhering by faith to God who works for good so that we may properly cooperate with [God]."

223. See *Serm.* 56.1.1 (on the history of calling on the name of God).

224. This is also the view of Eichenseer, *Das Symbolum Apostolicum,* 169: "The Father, who revealed the divine self in the Old Testament as the God beside whom there are no other gods, is described as 'God,' a word that had become, so to speak, the Father's proper name."

225. See above, p. 117.

226. *Serm.* 213.1.2 (= Morin, *MA* 1.441) (Hill 6:136).

227. See *Serm.* 212.1: "Nor must you separate the Son of God from this absolute perfection and superiority" (Hill 6:136).

228. Ibid., especially: "This Trinity is one God, almighty, invisible, immortal, king of the ages, creator of things visible and invisible" (Hill 6:137).

229. See *Serm.* 213.4.4; 214.8; 215.7. Also: 213.9.9 (God the Father as a farmer, in the sense of John 15:1, 5), as well as 214.6 (where the formulas "equal to God" [with a citation of Phil 2:7] and "equal to the Father" are found).

230. See S. Poque (ed.), *Augustin d'Hippone: Sermons pour la Pâque,* Sources chrétiennes 116 (Paris, n.d.) 65–69.

231. See *Serm.* 56.1.1; 57.1.1; 58.1.1; 59.1.1.

232. *Serm.* 58.1.1f. (Hill 3:118). See 57.2.2 (the Son of God teaches us to pray to the Father); 59.2.3 (the same); 56.2.2: "From the Lord our God, from the Lord Jesus Christ, from God the Father of the prophets, apostles, and martyrs, from the Father of our Lord Jesus Christ, from the God who made heaven and earth and the sea and all that is in them, it's from [this one] that you must ask for anything that it is right to ask for" (Hill 3:96).

233. *S. dom. m.* 2.4.15. See, earlier, Origen, *De oratione* 22.1, and A. Hamman, *La prière,* vol. 2: *Les trois premiers siècles* (Tournai, 1963) 309.

234. *Serm.* 58.2.2–6.7. Also 56.4.5; 56.5.7 (faith in God the almighty Father, and prayer for the accomplishment of the Father's will); 56.10.14 ("God is our father, the Church our mother" [Hill 3:103]); 57.5.5 (prayer for the coming of God's reign, citing Matt 25:34).

235. But see also *Ench.* 3.9, where "the one and true God" is given priority over the Trinity: ". . . to believe in the goodness of the creator, who is the one and true God . . . and that God is a trinity, namely, the Father and the Son, who is begotten by the Father, and the Holy Spirit, who proceeds from the same Father." It is to be noted, however, that Augustine here is not expressly citing the creed and, in addition, is speaking at a more theological level.

236. See *Serm.* 215.3; 21.8 (with the entire context, in which the preacher is speaking of the fidelity of a slave to the slave's master); *Ep.* 138.1.6, together with *En. Ps.* 15.2.

237. See *Serm.* 213.1.1. See also *Serm.* 57.2.2: "Remember that our creator has agreed to be our Father" (Hill 3:110), and *S. dom. m.* 2.4.15f.

238. *C. Faust.* 3.3.

239. *Serm.* 214.5f.; 215.3. Other texts are given in Eichenseer, *Das Symbolum Apostolicum,* 173, note 69. See also *Io. ev. tr.* 19.6 ("God the creator," "Father of the Son").

240. See Eichenseer, *Das Symbolum Apostolicum,* 175.

241. *Serm.* 213.1.

242. *Serm.* 59.1.2; 58.2.2.

243. *Serm.* 59.4.7: "I'm warning you, my children in God's grace and my brothers and sisters under that Father. . . ." (Hill 3:128).

244. *Serm.* 58.2.2; see *S. dom. m.* 2.4.16.

245. Eichenseer, *Das Symbolum Apostolicum,* 174–186, where he gives the prehistory of the title.

246. *Serm.* 214.2ff.

247. See the summarizing passage in *Serm.* 214.5: "Almighty God, therefore, who has done all that ever [God] has willed, begot the one and only Word through which all things were made; but this not out of nothing, but from [the divine self]" (Hill 6:153). See *F. et symb.* 2.2 (omnipotence and creation from nothing).

248. *Ench.* 3.11–8.23; see especially 3.11: "For the omnipotent God, whom they also confess and who has supreme power over things, is supremely good and would by no means permit any evil in [the divine] works, unless [God] were so omnipotent and good that [God] could bring good out of evil"; 4.12 (all creatures are good, but not supremely and unchangeably good like the creator).

249. Ibid., 3.11.

250. Ibid., 8.23. See BA 9:1481, with the references to *Ench.* 5.16 and 4.12.

251. *Serm.* 213.2 (Guelf. 1), citing Ps 102:2f. (Hill 6:141).

252. *Serm.* 213.2.

253. See Eichenseer, *Das Symbolum Apostolicum,* 187–199.

254. *Serm.* 215.2: "[God] is indeed the almighty God who at the origin of the world made all things out of nothing, who is before the ages, and who made and governs the ages. [God] doesn't, after all, grow with time, or stretch out in space, nor is [God] shut in or bounded by any material; but [God] abides with and in [God's self] as full and perfect eternity, which neither human thought can comprehend, nor tongue describe" (Hill 6:160). See also *Serm.* 214.4: "God, you see, is willingly whatever [God] is; so [God] is willingly eternal and unchangeable and truthful and blessed and undefeatable"; *Serm.* 212 (where the additional attributes—invisible, immortal [everlasting], creator of things visible and invisible, king of all the ages—are ascribed both to the Son and to the Trinity, while at the same time three gods are excluded).

255. See W. Roetzer, *Des heiligen Augustinus Schriften als liturgiegeschichtliche Quelle* (Munich, 1930) 117–128, especially 120; M. Klöckener, "Das eucharistische Hochgebet bei Augustinus," *Signum pietatis: Festschrift C. P. Mayer* (Würzburg, 1989) 461–498.

256. *Serm.* 227 (Hill 6:255). See also ibid., (toward the end): "Let your faith be firm in God, let it be acceptable to God" (Hill 6:256).

257. See *Serm.* 229 (Denis 6).3; 53.13.14; 68.4.5 (citing Rom 1:18-22). Also *Ep.* 140.19.48.

258. See *Ep.* 217.1.2; *Serm.* 58.10.12 (with reference to the petitions of the Lord's Prayer); *Serm.* 300.2.2; *Cura. mort.* 1.3.

259. *Serm.* 272 (Hill 7:301). "Turning to the Lord," with references to various petitions, occurs in *Serm.* 67.10; 183.15; *En. Ps.* 150.8 (at the end of the entire work), while at the end of many sermons only the initial words, "turning to the Lord," are given.

260. See, for example, *Serm.* 136.6: "O Lord Jesus, suffering for us, not for yourself, being without fault and bearing the punishment, in order to undo both fault and punishment" (Hill 4:357); *Serm.* 213.5.7: "May the Trinity deliver us from the multitude of our sins" (Hill 6:144) (where the context speaks of the works done inseparably by the Trinity). See above, pp. 64, 81f.

Part II, Chapter 4

1. See, for example, the way in which Augustine speaks of God in *En. Ps.* 145.11f.: "God of Jacob" (Gen 32:28); "the Lord God" (Ps 145:6); "The father is a vinedresser" (John 15:1, 5); "one God the Father" as distinct from "one Lord Jesus Christ" (1 Cor 8:6). Likewise, see *Ep.* 118.3.14 ("Lord, God," 1 Cor 3:7; "our Father," Matt 6:9); *Ep.* 120.4.19: "[God is] justice which lives in itself . . . and lives immutably. . . . [The Son of God is] the Father's wisdom and justice" (citing 1 Cor 1:30f.).

2. See, for example, *Trin.* 15.4.6.

3. Ibid., 15.5.7 (Hill, 300).

4. See B. Studer, "Augustin et la foi de Nicée," *Dominus Salvator: Studien zur Christologie und Exegese der Kirchenväter,* Studia Anselmiana 107 (Rome, 1992) 393.

5. See especially *Ench.* 3.9; *Trin.* 15.28.51 (the prayer that concludes the *De Trinitate*).

6. The same holds for "Lord" and other biblical names for God. See, for example, the discussion of the disputed text, Deut 6:4, in *Ep.* 138.3.18.

7. See above, pp. 104f., 107f.

8. See, for example, *Serm.* 140.2 (against Maximinus); *Conl. Max.* 13. See also *Conl. Max.* 9 (only the Son praises the Father worthily).

9. *Trin.* 15.3.5; see 15.21.40.

10. Ibid., 4.19.

11. *Conl. Max.* 23.

12. On what follows, see B. Studer, *"Credo in Deum Patrem omnipotentem:* Zum Gottesbegriff der heiligen Augustinus," *Atti: Congresso internazionale su S. Agostino nel XVI Centenario della Conversione,* Studia Ephemeridis "Augustinianum" 24 (1987) 163–188, with the literature listed there.

13. See, for example, *En. Ps.* 38.7 (explanation of the verse "What is the number of my days"); 134.6 (on Exod 3:24f.).

14. See *Conf.* 7.14.20, where Augustine briefly summarizes the stages of his journey to knowledge of truth.

15. See *En. Ps.* 101.2.10; 121.5; 49.14. Also the theme of "the truest philosophy"; see B. Studer, *La riflessione teologica nella Chiesa Imperiale (sec. IV e V)* (Rome, 1989) 117ff.

16. *Trin.* 5.2.3; 15.13.22; *Io. ev. tr.* 99.4; and see *Ep.* 120.3.17.

17. See above, pp. 106f.

18. See especially *Trin.* 15.27.49, where Augustine explains that the highest "understanding of faith" about God is attained through meditation on the highest element in the human being. See above, p. 107.

19. See above, pp. 112–114. On the connection with the discussion of the Arian thesis "There was a time when the Word did not yet exist," see Studer, "Augustin et la foi de Nicée," 391.

20. See above, p. 127.

21. See *En. Ps.* 109.10; *Trin.* 2.17.32.

22. See above, p. 128.

23. On 397 as a turning point, see the excursus on *Simpl.* 1.2, above, pp. 101–103. On the roots of Augustinian voluntarism, see, in addition to E. Benz, *Marius Victorinus und die Entwicklung der abendländischen Willensmetaphysik* (Stuttgart, 1932), M. Pohlenz, *Die Stoa,* 3rd ed. (Göttingen, 1964) 448.

24. See *En. Ps.* 113.1.14; 134.10; 134.12.

25. See above, p. 134.

26. See especially *Civ.; Ep.* 118 and 137.

27. See above, pp. 119, 122f.

28. *Ep.* 118.3.15.

29. See *Civ.* 8.6ff.; *Ep.* 118.3.19. On the subject, see P. Hadot, "La présentation du platonisme par Augustin," *Festschrift C. Andresen* (Göttingen, 1979) 271–279.

30. See especially *Gn. litt.* 8.11.24: explanation of "Lord God" at the beginning of the exposition of the paradise story; God's lordship calls for human beings "to be obedient under [God's] rule" and to "serve [God] not for [God's] advantage and welfare but for ours" (Taylor 2, 49–50).

31. See *Ep.* 138.6 (citing Ps 15:2: "Lord God"); *Gn. litt.* 8.11.24 (citing Ps 15:2 and 72:28).

32. See B. Studer, *"Deus, Pater et Dominus* bei Augustinus von Hippo," *Festschrift C. Stead* (Leiden, 1993), and *Conf.* 10.31.46; 10.43.69; 13.15.17.

33. *Serm.* 213.2 (Hill 6:141). See above, p. 140.

34. See above, p. 96.

35. See Studer, *"Credo in Deum Patrem omnipotentem,"* 174f., 184f. On the subject, see M. G. Mara, "Arriani, Arrius," *AugLex,* vol. 1, fasc. 3 (1988) 450–459.

36. See, for example, *Io. ev. tr.* 21.3.

37. See Studer, *"Deus, Pater et Dominus"* (note 32, above). On the problem involved in this distinction, see also G. Greshake, *Gnade als konkrete Freiheit: Eine Untersuchung zur Gnadenlehre des Pelagius* (Mainz, 1972), who admits that for Augustine, the whole of history is subordinate to God but who, in treating of the distinction between the orders of creation and redemption, does not take sufficient account of the entire historical context of the fourth century.

38. See B. Studer, "Agostino d'Ippona et il Dio dei Libri sapienziali: Letture cristiane dei Libri sapienziali," Incontro di Studiosi dell'Antichita cristiana, *Letture cristiane dei Libri sapienziali*. Studia Ephemeridis "Augustinianum" 37 (1992) 115–125, and especially *"Deus, Pater et Dominus,"* where this theme is extensively developed.

39. On this subject, see J. Marquardt, *Das Privatleben der Römer*, 2nd ed., vol. 1 (1886; rpt. Darmstadt, 1964) 1–6; E. Sachers, "Pater familias," *PWK* 18/2 (1949) 2121–2157; J. Gaudemet, "Familie," *RAC* 7 (1969) 286–358; Gaudemet, *Le droit romain dans la littérature chrétienne occidentale du IIIe au Ve siècle* (Milan, 1978) 152–162. Further literature on the subject may be found in A. Wlosok, "Die Gottesprädikation *Pater et Dominus* bei Laktanz: Gott in Analogie zum römischen *pater familias*," *Laktanz und die philosophische Gnosis* (Heidelberg, 1960) 233–246, and in *Der Kleine Pauly* 4:545ff., with the reference there to M. Kaser, *Das römische Privatrecht*, vols. 1 and 2 (Munich, 1955, 1959), and to S. Poque, *Le langage symbolique dans la prédication d'Augustin d'Hippone* (Paris, 1984) 205–208; A. Wlosok, "Vater und Vatervorstellungen in der römischen Kultur," *Res humanae—res divinae*, ed. E. Heck and E. A. Schmidt (Heidelberg, 1990) 35–83.

40. The following may be mentioned as passages in which Augustine applies the concept of *pater familias* to God: *Serm.* 97A.4; *En. Ps.* 38.11f.; *Serm.* 61.4.4; *Qu. ev.* 2.21. On the subject, see Studer, *"Deus, Pater et Dominus."*

41. See the use of Matthew 13:24-43 in many anti-Donatist texts, such as *C. ep. Parm.* 2.23.43, and *C. litt. Pet.* 3.4.5; of Matthew 20:1-16 in *Serm.* 49.2; 87.3.4, and *C. ep. Pel.* 2.7.13; of Matthew 21:33-46 in *Serm.* 87.2.3; of Matthew 24:45-51 in *Serm.* 37.15; of Luke 14:15-24 in *Ep.* 93.2.5; 208.7; and *C. Gaud.* 1.37.50; of Matthew 10:25 in *S. dom. m.* 1.22.75; *En. Ps.* 40.8; and *C. litt. Pet.* 3.7.8.

42. See *En. Ps.* 40.8; 55.8; *Spec.* 25 (CSEL 12:163, citing Matt 10:24); *Ep.* 228.2; 199.1; *Epd.* 18.3; *Serm.* 340A.9; *Cresc.* 3.58.64; *Qu. Mt.* 15 (CCL 44B:138, citing Matt 13:51: "instructed in the Church"). And see *Ep.* 173.3 (on the duties of the bishop as a father).

43. *Cons. ev.* 2.80. Augustine here gives the usual translation of the New Testament Greek word *oikodespotēs*. See also *Loc.* 4.80. It is to be noted that this definition of *pater familias* is very like that of the Roman jurists. See H. Heumann and E. Seckel, *Handlexikon zu den Quellen des römischen Rechtes*, 11th ed. (Graz, 1971) 408f. *(pater)*, citing 1.195-2 D:50.16: "He is called 'father of the household,' who has mastery over the house . . . even if he have no child."

44. For the use of *paterfamilias* in the pre-Augustinian patristic period see Wlosok, *Laktanz und die philosophische Gnosis*, 233–246.

45. For the connection between education, family patrimony, and ancestor worship see Marquardt, *Das Privatleben der Römer*, 1:385.

46. See *En. Ps.* 70.2.10.

47. See the division of the *patria potestas* into three parts—home, state, and divine guidance of human affairs—in Cicero, *Nat. deorum* 3.85. And see W. Dürig, *"Disciplina*: Eine

Studie zum Bedeutungsumfang des Wortes in der Sprache der Liturgie und der Väter," *SE* 4 (1952) 245–297, especially 255.

48. See *Trin.* 3.4.9: "And thus God's will is the first and highest cause of all physical species and motions. For nothing happens visibly and in a manner perceptible to the senses which does not issue either as a command or as a permission from the inmost invisible and intelligible court of the supreme emperor, according to [God's] unfathomable justice of rewards and punishments, favors and retributions, in what we may call this vast and all-embracing republic of the whole creation" (Hill, 132). see also *En. Ps.* 49.15; 70.2.2; 103.1.15; 138.14.

49. See *En. Ps.* 30.2/3.2; *Conf.* 3.8; *Vera rel.* 23.46; *Civ.* 7.12; *Trin.* 12.9.

50. See *Civ.* 1.8.1, together with 1.29.

51. The preceding presentation is based especially on *Civ.* 19.16. See H. Fuchs, *Augustin und der antike Friedensgedanke* (Berlin, 1926), especially 92f., 139–154; Dürig, *"Disciplina,"* 254–262 *("Domestica disciplina")*; M. Schrama, *"Praeposito tamquam patri oboediatur:* Augustinus über Frieden und Gehorsam," *Mélanges T. J. van Bavel* (Leuven, 1990) 846–876, especially 848–860.

52. See Studer, *"Deus, Pater et Dominus"* and especially "Agostino d'Ippona e il Dio dei Libri sapienziali."

53. See *En. Ps.* 37.23. See other texts in Studer, *"Deus, Dominus et Pater"* (note 34, above). See also Poque, *Le langage symbolique,* 193–224 ("La loi du Père").

54. See *Serm.* 55.5.5; *Io. ev. tr.* 7.7; *En. Ps.* 93.17.

55. The focus is especially on Exod 3:14f. The pertinent passages in Augustine may be found in E. Zum Brunn, "L'exégèse augustinienne de *Ego sum qui sum* et la métaphysique de l'exode," *Dieu et l'Être,* ed. P. Vignaux (Paris, 1978) 141–164, especially 164, and in G. Madec, *"Ego sum qui sum* de Tertullien à Jérôme," *Dieu et l'Etre,* 121–139, especially 128. See also A. D. Polman, *De leer van God bij Augustinus* (Kampen, 1965) 248–261, who, following E. Gilson, *Philosophie et incarnation selon saint Augustin* (Montreal, 1947), brings together and explains the most important passages. Gilson himself discusses God in the divine self and God for us, 24f. and 34f., where he explains that God who is with us leads us to God who is.

56. *Serm.* 7.

57. *Serm.* 7.2.

58. *Serm.* 7.3-6.

59. *Serm.* 7.7.

60. See *Serm.* 6.3.4 (God's name as the unchangeable one); *En. Ps.* 89.3: "But [God] used a verb signifying the present and suggesting that the substance of God is utterly unchangeable, that [God] is not 'was and will be' but only 'is,' therefore, 'I am who am.'"

61. See *En. Ps.* 38.7.

62. See ibid., 101.2.10; 121.5; 89.3.

63. See ibid., 82.14.

64. *Serm.* 7.7 (Hill 1:237; but the second sentence is not in Hill's translation).

65. See *En. Ps.* 134.6: "That I am who I am has to do with me; that I am the God of Abraham and the God of Isaac and the God of Jacob has to do with you"; 149.14: "I am God (Exod 3:14) and I am your God (Exod 3:15); but even if I be not your God, I am God"; 101.2.10.

66. *Serm.* 7.7 (Hill 1:237).

67. *En. Ps.* 101.2.10.

68. *En. Ps.* 101.2.10. See *Serm.* 6.4.5; *En. Ps.* 38.22; 89.3.

69. *En. Ps.* 121.5.

70. Ibid., 134.6. See *Serm.* 9.11.

71. *Serm.* 7.7.

72. Ibid.

73. *En. Ps.* 121.5. See also ibid., 130.12, where the theme of milk and food is developed.

74. *Serm.* 7.7.

75. See *En. Ps.* 104.4.

76. See *Io. ev. tr.* 38.8.8; *En. Ps.* 104.4; and, on the subject, Gilson, *Philosophie et incarnation,* 20f.

77. See B. Aland, "*Cogitare Deum* in den *Confessiones* Augustins," *Pietas: Festschrift B. Kötting* (Münster, 1980) 93–104.

78. See above, p. 107.

79. See Polman, *De leer van God,* 261–280 (on the inexpressible God), and T. J. van Bavel, "God between Affirmation and Negation according to Augustine," *Augustine: Presbyter factus sum,* Collectanea Augustiniana, vol. 2 (New York, 1993) 75–95.

80. See *En. Ps.* 85.12; *Trin.* 5.1.2; *Ep.* 120.3.13.

81. See *En. Ps.* 146.11; 99.5; 104.3 (on the text "Seek [God's] face always").

82. See E. Przywara, *Augustinus: Die Gestalt als Gefüge* (Leipzig, 1934) 31.

83. See *En. Ps.* 41.7ff.; *Ep.* 147.178.41-44; *Trin.* 8.3.4f.; etc.

84. *Ep.* 120.3.13. And see Studer, *La riflessione teologica,* 204f.

85. See *En. Ps.* 130.12: "Unless the soul is poured out within itself, it does not attain to the vision of God and to the knowledge of that immutable substance. For now, while it is still in the flesh, they say to it: *Where is your God?* But its God is within, [God] is within spiritually, and [God] is on high spiritually."

86. On what follows see Gilson, *Philosophie et incarnation,* 44ff.

87. See Przywara, *Augustinus,* 233–235, where various texts are cited; Gilson, *Philosophie et incarnation,* 51, with the entire context (the incarnation tells human beings that Being caused the becoming from nothing in order to achieve lasting being); Aland, "*Cogitare Deum,*" 103 (only through the activity of Christ did the universal action of the creator God become effective).

88. See *Serm.* 165.7.9, and Przywara, *Augustinus,* 439f., 450–453.

89. See *En. Ps.* 110.2. According to Gilson, *Philosophie et incarnation,* 47ff., the *Confessions* should be compared with *The City of God* in regard to the relationship of God to the individual human being and to the entire human race.

90. See *Trin.* 8.5.7, and B. Studer, *Soteriologie: In der Schrift und Patristik,* HDG, vol. 3, fasc. 2a (Freiburg, 1978) 162ff.

91. In my opinion, K. Flasch, *Die Logik des Schreckens: Augustinus von Hippo, Die Gnadenlerhe von 397* (Mainz, 1990), especially 292f., takes this dialectical relationship too lightly. It is certainly correct that Augustine let his logic carry him too far and that he thereby had a negative influence on posterity. But we must not overlook the fact that the theological voluntarism, which he undoubtedly held in too incautious a manner, culminated ultimately in the Johannine "God is love." At most, therefore, we can reproach Augustine for not allowing himself to be guided more by this logic of love and as a result to rise above his pastoral experiences of the human lack of repentance.

92. See, above (p. 36), the remarks on the opponents of the absolute gratuitousness of grace, those who are said to be ashamed of the cross.

93. See Przywara, *Augustinus,* 91f.

Summary

1. See B. Studer, "*Consubstantialis Patri—consubstantialis matri*: Une antithèse chris-tologique chez Léon le Grand," *Dominus Salvator: Studien zur Christologie und Exegese der Kirchenväter,* Studia Anselmiana 107 (Rome, 1992) 29–66, especially 51–63.

2. Augustine cites 2 Cor 5:18 rather often. Apart from passages in which he is inter-ested only in explaining the idea of "world," he understands the text either theologically, as Paul himself does ("God" = the Father), or Christologically, along with the tradition ("God" = Christ). On one occasion, he even says explicitly that the text can be understood in these two senses. See *En. Ps.* 67.23: "either of the Father in Christ or of the Word in the human being." The text is interpreted theologically in *Io. ev, tr.* 110.4: "Therefore [Christ] said: *I in them and you in me,* as though he were saying: '*I in them* to whom you sent me, and *you in me,* reconciling the world to yourself through me"; 102.2; *En. Ps.* 34.2.5 (citing John 14:10); 59.8. Compare the Christological interpretations: *En. Ps.* 75.1; *Io. ev. tr.* 110.4. See also *Ench.* 9.33: "the mediator, that is, the reconciler" (citing Rom 5:10).

3. See above, especially pp. 119f., 122 on the origin and end of the city of God.

4. See above, especially pp. 104f.: the remarks on the presuppositions for an explana-tion of the mystery of the Trinity.

5. See *En. Ps.* 75.1; 34.2.5, especially: "the humanity in me addresses the divinity in me."

6. See above, especially p. 41 on "creator—re-creator," "former—re-former"; and pp. 95–97, 101 (on anti-Manichean polemics).

7. See B. Aland, "*Cogitare Deum* in den *Confessiones* Augustins," *Pietas: Festchrift B. Kötting* (Münster, 1980) 103f.

8. See above, p. 114.

9. See above, p. 122.

10. To the extent that "the grace of God" is understood as meaning the mystery of Christ by means of which God (the Father) reconciles the world to God's self in Christ (see 2 Cor 5:18f.), it is something that is in any case accessible only to faith.

11. See the conclusion already reached in my "Augustin et la foi de Nicée," *Dominus Salvator,* 400.

Bibliography

Adam, A. "Der manichäische Ursprung der Lehre von den zwei Reichen bei Augustinus." *TLZ* 77 (1952) 385–390.

_____. "Das Fortwirken des Manichäismus bei Augustin." *ZKG* 69 (1958) 1–25.

_____. *Lehrbuch der Dogmengeschichte.* Vol 1: *Die Zeit der Alten Kirche.* Gütersloh, 1965.

Agaësse, P. "Humanité du Christ, I/B,3: S. Augustin." *DSp* 7/1 (1969) 1043–1053.

Aland, B. "*Cogitare Deum* in den *Confessiones* Augustins." *Pietas: Festschrift B. Kötting.* Münster, 1980. pp. 93–104.

Alfaric, P. *L'évolution intellectuelle de saint Augustin.* Vol 1: *Du manichéisme au néoplatonisme.* Paris, 1918.

Babcock, W. S. "Sin and Punishment: The Early Augustine." *Augustine: Presbyter factus sum,* Collectanea Augustiniana. Vol. 2. New York, 1993. pp. 235–248.

Bailleux, E. "La christologie de saint Augustin dans le *De Trinitate.*" *RechAug* 7 (1971) 219–243.

Balthasar, H. U. von. *Aurelius Augustinus: Über die Psalmen.* Leipzig, 1936.

_____. *Augustinus: Das Antlitz der Kirche,* 2nd ed. Einsiedeln, 1956.

_____. *Herrlichkeit.* Vol. 2: *Fächer des Stils.* Einsiedeln, 1962. ET: *The Glory of the Lord: A Theological Aesthetics.* Vol 2: *Studies in Theological Styles: Clerical Styles.* Trans. A. Louth and others. San Francisco, 1984.

Baus, K. "Die Stellung Christi im Beten des hl. Augustinus." *TTZ* 63 (1954) 321–339.

_____. "Ostern in der Verkündigung des hl. Augustinus." *Festschrift J. A. Jungmann.* Freiburg, 1959. pp. 57–67.

Bavaud, G. "Un thème augustinien, le mystère de l'incarnation à la lumière de la distinction entre le verbe intérieur et le verbe proféré." *REAug* 9 (1963) 95–101.

Beierwaltes, W. "*Deus est veritas:* Zur Rezeption des griechischen Wahrheitsbegriffes in der frühchristlichen Theologie." *Pietas: Festschrift B. Kötting.* Münster, 1980. pp. 15–29.

_____. *Denken des Einen: Studien zur neuplatonischen Philosophie und ihrer Wirkungsgeschichte.* Frankfurt, 1985.

Benz, E. *Marius Victorinus und die Entwicklung des abendländischen Willensmetaphysik.* Stuttgart, 1932.

Bernard, R. "La prédestination du Christ total selon s. Augustin." *RechAug* 3 (1965) 1–58.

Berrouard, M.-F. "La permanence à travers le temps de la foi dans le Christ selon saint Augustin." *Signum pietatis: Festschrift C. P. Mayer.* Würzburg, 1989. pp. 303–324.

_____. "S. Augustin et le mystère du Christ: Chemin, Vérité et Vie," *Mélanges T. J. van Bavel.* Leuven, 1990. pp. 431–449.

Bochet, L. *Désir de Dieu.* Paris, 1982.

Bonner, G. *St. Augustine of Hippo.* London, 1963.

_____. "Christ, God and Man, in the Thought of St. Augustine." *Angelicum* 61 (1984) 268–294.

_____. "(Aurelius) Augustinus *(vita).*" *AugLex.* Vol. 1, fasc. 4. Basel, 1990. pp. 519–550.

Borgomeo, P. *L'Église de ce temps dans la prédication de saint Augustin.* Paris, 1972.

Boros, L. *Aurelius Augustinus: Gotteserfahrung und Weg in die Welt.* Olten, 1982.

Brabant, O. *Le Christ, centre et source de la vie morale chez saint Augustin.* Gembloux, 1971.

Braun, R. *Deus Christianorum: Recherches sur le vocabulaire doctrinal de Tertullien.* Paris, 1962.

Canaloup, P. *L'harmonie des deux Testaments dans le "Contra Faustum Manichaeum" de saint Augustin.* Dissertation. Toulouse, 1955.

Cavacoli, G. "Dio come verità eterna in S. Agostino." *Sacra Doctrina* 32 (Bologna, 1987) 665–687.

Cavalcanti, E. "Il significato dell'esegesi litterale in Basilio e in Agostino." *ASE* 4 (1987) 119–142.

Cayré, F. *Initiation à la philosophie de s. Augustin.* Paris, 1947.

_____. *Dieu présent dans la vie de l'esprit.* Paris, 1951.

Ciarlantini, P. *"Mediator:* Paganismo y Cristianismo en *De civitate Dei* VIII,12–XI,2 de San Agustín," *RAE* 14 (1983) 9–62.

Comeau, M. *S. Augustin, exégète du quatrième évangile.* Paris, 1930. See *RSR* 40 (1951–52) 80–89.

Congar, Y. *"Ecclesia ab Abel."* *Festschrift K. Adam.* Düsseldorf, 1952. pp. 79–108.

Courcelle, P. *Recherches sur les Confessions de saint Augustin.* Paris, 1950; 2nd ed., Paris, 1968.

Cousineau, H. "Creation and Freedom: An Augustinian Problem, *'quia voluit?'* and/or *'quia bonus?'"* *RechAug* 2 (1962) 253–271.

Dassmann, E. "Ambrosius." *AugLex.* Vol. 1, fascs. 1-2. Basel, 1986. pp. 270–285.

De Capitani, F. *Il De libero arbitrio di S. Agostino: Studio introduttivo, testo, traduzione e commento.* Milan, 1987.

Decret, F. *Aspects du manichéisme dans l'Afrique romaine.* Paris, 1970.

_____. *L'Afrique manichéenne (IVᵉ–Vᵉ siècles).* Paris, 1978.

_____. *"Adimantum Manichaei discipulum (Contra)."* *AugLex.* Vol. 1, fascs. 1-2. Basel, 1986. pp. 90–94.

_____. *"Adimantus."* *AugLex.* Vol. 1, fascs. 1-2. Basel, 1986. pp. 94f.

Di Berardino, A., ed. *Patrology.* Vol. 4: *The Golden Age of Latin Patristic Literature from the Council of Nicea to the Council of Chalcedon.* Trans. P. Solari. Westminster, Md., 1992.

_____. *Patrologia.* Vol. 3. Casale, 1978.

Dideberg, D. *St. Augustin et la Première Epître de s. Jean.* Théologie historique 34. Paris, 1975.

Doignon, J. *"Beata vita (De)."* *AugLex.* Vol. 1, fasc. 4. Basel, 1990. pp. 618–624.

Dolbeau, F. "Nouveaux sermons de saint Augustin pour la conversion des païens et des donatistes." *REAug* 37 (1991) 37–78, 261–306.

Doucet, D. "L'*ars memoriae* dans les *Confessiones.*" *REAug* 33 (1987) 9–69.

Drobner, H. *Person-Exegese und Christologie bei Augustinus.* Leiden, 1986.

Du Roy, P. *L'intelligence de la foi en la Trinité selon saint Augustin.* Paris, 1966.

Dürig, W. *"Disciplina:* Eine Studie zum Bedeutungsumfang des Wortes in der Sprache der Liturgie und der Väter." *SE* 4 (1952) 245–297.

Eichenseer, C. *Das Symbolum Apostolicum beim heiligen Augustinus: Mit Berücksichtigung des dogmengeschichtlichen Zusammenhanges.* Kirchengeschichtliche Quellen und Studien 4. St. Ottilien, 1960.

Eijkenboom, P. C. J. *"Christus Redemptor* in the Sermons of St. Augustine." *Festschrift C. Mohrmann.* Utrecht, 1963. pp. 233–239.

———. *Het Christus-Medicusmotief in de preken van sint Augustinus.* Assen, 1960.

Feldmann, E. *Der Einfluss der Hortensius und des Manicháismus auf das Denken des jungen Augustinus von 373.* Munster, 1975.

———. "Christus-Frömmigkeit des Manijünger." *Pietas: Festschrift B. Kötting.* Münster, 1980. pp. 196–216.

———. *Die Epistula fundamenti der nordafrikanischen Manichäer.* Altenberge, 1987.

———. *"Et inde rediens fecerat sibi Deum (Conf.* 7,20): Beobachtungen zur Genese des augustinischen Gottesbegriffes und zu dessen Funktion in den *Confessiones." Mélanges T. J. van Bavel.* Leuven, 1990. pp. 881–904.

Fellermayr, J. *Tradition und Sukzession im Lichte des römisch-antiken Erbdenkens: Untersuchungen zu den lateinischen Vätern bis zu Leo dem Grossen.* Munich, 1979.

Fischer, B. *Die Psalmen als Stimme der Kirche.* Trier, 1982.

Flasch, K. *Augustin: Einführung in sein Denken.* Stuttgart, 1980.

———. *Die Logik des Schreckens: Augustinus von Hippo, Die Gnadenlehre von 397.* Mainz, 1990.

Fontaine, J. "Une révolution littéraire dans l'Occident latin: Les Confessions de s. Augustin." *BLE* 88 (1987) 173–193.

Franz, E. *Totus Christus: Studien über Christus und die Kirche bei Augustinus.* Dissertation in the Evangelical faculty. Bonn, 1956.

Fuchs, H. *Augustin und der antike Friedensgedanke.* Berlin, 1926.

Gaudemet, J. "Familie." *RAC* 7 (1969) 286–358.

———. *Le droit romain dans la littérature chrétienne occidental du IIIe au Ve siècle.* Milan, 1978.

Geerlings, W. "Zur Frage des Nachwirkens des Manichäismus in der Theologie Augustins." *ZKT* 93 (1971) 45–60.

———. *Christus Exemplum: Studien zur Christologie und Christusverkündigung Augustins.* Tübinger Theologische Studien 13. Mainz, 1978.

———. "Bekehrung durch Belehrung." *TTQ* 167 (1987) 195–208.

———. "Jesaja 7,9b bei Augustinus." *WissWeis* 50 (1987) 5–12.

———. "Die Christologie Augustins: Zum Stand der Forschung." *Internationales Symposium über den Stand der Augustinus-Forschung.* Ed. C. Mayer and K. H. Chelius. Würzburg, 1989. pp. 219–230.

Gilson, E. *Introduction à l'étude de saint Augustin.* Paris, 1929; 4th ed., 1969. ET: *The Christian Philosophy of Saint Augustine.* Trans. L. E. M. Lynch. New York, 1960.

———. *Philosophie et incarnation selon saint Augustin.* Montreal, 1947.

Grabowsky, S. J. *The All-Present God: A Study in St. Augustine.* St. Louis, 1954.

Greshake, G. *Gnade als konkrete Freiheit: Eine Untersuchung zur Gnadenlehre des Pelagius.* Mainz, 1972.

Grillmeier, A. *Jesus Christus im Glauben der Kirche.* Vol. 1: *Von der Apostolischen Zeit bis zum Konzil von Chalkedon (451).* Freiburg, 1979.

————. *Jesus Christus im Glauben der Kirche.* Vol. 2, pt. 2: *Die Kirche von Konstantinopel im 6. Jahrhundert.* Freiburg, 1989.

Guardini, R. *Die Bekehrung des Aurelius Augustinus,* 2nd ed. Munich, 1950. ET: *The Conversion of Augustine.* Trans. E. Briefs. Westminster, Md., 1960

Hadot, I. *Arts libéraux et philosophie dans la pensée antique.* Paris, 1984.

Hadot, P. "La présentation du platonisme par Augustin." *Festschrift C. Andresen.* Göttingen, 1979. pp. 271–279.

Hallmann, J. M. "The Emotions of God in the Theology of St. Augustine." *RTAM* 51 (1984) 5–19.

Hamman, A. *La prière.* Vol. 2: *Les trois premiers siècles.* Tournai, 1963.

Hardy, R. P. *Actualité de la révélation divine: Une étude des "Tractatus in Ioannis evangelium" de saint Augustin.* Théologie historique 28. Paris, 1974.

Harnack, A. von. *Augustins "Confessionen."* Giessen, 1988 (rpt. from *Reden und Aufsätze.* Vol 1. Giessen, 1904). pp. 51–79.

————. *Lehrbuch der Dogmengeschichte,* 4th ed. Vol. 2: *Die Entwickelung des kirchlichen Dogmas,* pt. 1. Tübingen, 1909 (rpt., Darmstadt, 1964).

————. *Lehrbuch der Dogmengeschichte,* 4th ed. Vol 3: *Die Entwickelung des kirchlichen Dogmas,* pts. 2–3. Tübingen, 1910 (rpt., Darmstadt, 1964).

Hauschild, W. D. "Dogmengeschichtsschreibung." *TRE* 9 (1982) 116–125.

Hausleiter, J. "*Deus internus* b.xv: Augustinus." *RAC* 3 (1957) 834–838.

————. "*Fruitio Dei*: Augustinus." *RAC* 8 (1972) 551–555.

Heumann, E., and E. Seckel. *Handlexikon zu den Quellen des römischen Rechts,* 11th ed. Graz, 1971.

Holte, R. *Béatitude et Sagesse: St. Augustin et le problème de la fin de l'homme dans la philosophie ancienne.* Paris, 1962.

Horn, H. J. "Gottesbeweis." *RAC* 11 (1981) 951–977.

Hübner, W. "Der *Ordo* der Realien in Augustins Frühdialog *De ordine.*" *REAug* 33 (1987) 25–48.

Jay, P. *L'exégèse de saint Jérôme d'après son "Commentaire sur Isaïe."* Paris, 1985.

Jungmann, J. A. *Die Stellung Christi im liturgischen Gebet.* Münster, 1925. ET: *The Place of Christ in Liturgical Prayer.* Trans. A. Peeler. Staten Island, 1965.

Kaser, M. *Das römische Privatrecht.* Vols. 1–2. Munich, 1955, 1959.

Kelly, J.N.D. *Early Christian Doctrines,* 2nd ed. London, 1960.

Kienzler, K. "Der Aufbau der *Confessiones* des Augustin im Spiegel der Bibelzitate." *RechAug* 24 (1989) 123–164.

Klöckener, M. "Das eucharistische Hochgebet bei Augustinus." *Signum pietatis: Festschrift C. P. Mayer.* Würzburg, 1989. pp. 461–495.

Knauer, G. N. *Die Psalmenzitate in den Konfessionen Augustins.* Göttingen, 1955.

König, E. *Augustinus Philosophus.* Munich, 1970.

La Bonnardière, A.-M., ed. *S. Augustin et la Bible.* Paris, 1986.

————. "Le verset paulinien Rom 5,5 dans l'oeuvre de s. Augustin." *AugMag.* Vol. 2. Paris, 1954. pp. 657–665.

————. "*Anima iusti sedes sapientiae* dans l'oeuvre de saint Augustin." *Mélanges J. Daniélou.* Paris, 1972. pp. 111–120.

Lamirande, E. "La signification de *christianus* dans la théologie de S. Augustin et la tradition ancienne." *REAug* 9 (1963) 221–234.

_____. "L'idée d'onction dans l'ecclésiologie de saint Augustin." *RUnivOtt* 35 (1965) 103*–126*.

Le Bachelet, X. "Dieu." *DTC* 4 (1911) 1023–1152.

Liébaert, J. *Christologie: Von der Apostolischen Zeit bis zum Konzil von Chalkedon (451).* HDG. Vol. 3, fasc. 1a. Freiburg, 1965.

Löhrer, M. *Der Glaubensbegriff des heiligen Augustinus in seinen ersten Schriften bis zu den Confessiones.* Einsiedeln, 1955.

Loofs, F. *Leitfaden zum Studium der Dogmengeschichte,* 1st ed. Tübingen, 1889.

_____. *Leitfaden zum Studium der Dogmengeschichte,* 7th ed. Pts. 1 and 2.: *Alte Kirche, Mittelalter und Katholizismus bis zur Gegenwart.* Ed. K. Aland. Tübingen, 1968.

Lorenz, R. "Gnade und Erkenntnis bei Augustinus." *ZKG* 75 (1964) 21–78.

_____. "Gnade und Erkenntnis bei Augustin." *Zum Augustin-Gespräch der Gegenwart.* Vol 2. Ed. C. Andresen. Darmstadt, 1981. pp. 43–125.

Löser, W., et al., eds. *Dogmengeschichte und katholische Theologie.* Würzburg, 1985.

Luis Vizcaíno, P. de. *Los hechos de Jesús en la predicacio: Studio intro* Rome, 1983.

Lütcke, K.-H. *"Auctoritas" bei Augustin.* Stuttgart, 1968.

_____. "Auctoritas." *AugLex.* Vol. 1, fasc. 4. Basel, 1990. pp. 498–510.

_____. "Animae quantitate (De)." *AugLex.* Vol. 1, fasc. 3. Basel, 1988. pp. 350–356.

Madec, G. "Connaissance de Dieu et action de grâce: Essai sur les citations de l'Epître aux Romains 1,18-25 dans l'oeuvre de saint Augustin." *RechAug* 2 (1962) 273–309.

_____. "Notes sur l'intelligence de la foi." *REAug* 17 (1971) 119–142.

_____. "Pour l'interprétation de *Contra Academicos* II,II,5." *REAug* 17 (1971) 322–328.

_____. *S. Ambroise et la philosophie.* Paris, 1974.

_____. "Analyse du *De magistro.*" *REAug* 21 (1975) 63–71.

_____ (ed.). *S. Augustin, Dialogues philosophiques.* Pt. 3: *De magistro—De libero arbitrio,* 3rd ed. BA 6. Paris, 1976.

_____. "*Ego sum qui sum* de Tertullien à Jérôme." *Dieu et l'Être.* Ed. P. Vignaux. Paris, 1978. pp. 121–139.

_____. "Angelus." *AugLex.* Vol. 1, fascs. 1-2. Basel, 1986. pp. 303–315.

_____. "Platonisme." *Catholicisme* 11 (1986) 491–507.

_____. "Dieu dans la conversion d'Augustin." *Didaskalia* 19 (1989) 1–19.

_____. *La patrie et la voie: Le Christ dans la vie et la pensée de saint Augustin.* Jésus et Jésus-Christ 36. Paris, 1989.

Mallard, W. "The Incarnation in Augustine's Conversion." *RechAug* 15 (1980) 80–98.

Mandouze, A. *S. Augustin: L'aventure de la raison et de la grâce.* Paris, 1968.

_____. "Monique à Cassiciacum." *RELat* 47bis (1969) 131–141.

Manrique, A. "Presencia de Cristo en los corazones por la fe según Agustín." *RAE* 14 (1973) 41–61.

Mara, M. G. "Agostino e la polemica antimanichea: Il ruolo di Paolo e del suo epistolario." *Aug* 32 (1992) 119–143.

Markus, R. A. "Augustine's *Confessions* and the Controversy with Julian of Eclanum: Manicheism Revisited." *Mélanges T. J. van Bavel.* Leuven, 1990. pp. 913–925.

Marquardt, J. *Das Privatleben der Römer,* 2nd ed. 1886 (rpt., Darmstadt, 1964).

Marreves, W. *The Ascension of Christ in the Works of Saint Augustine.* Ottawa, 1967.

Marrou, H.-I. *Saint Augustin et la fin de la culture antique,* 4th ed. Paris, 1958.

_____. *Saint Augustin et l'augustinisme.* Paris, 1955.

Mayer, C. P. *Die Zeichen in der geistigen Entwicklung und in der Theologie Augustins.* Vols. 1–2. Würzburg, 1969 and 1974.

Meijering, E. P. *Theologische Urteile über die Dogmengeschichte: Ritschls Einfluss auf von Harnack.* Leiden, 1978.

Mersch, E. *Le corps mystique du Christ.* Vol. 2. Louvain, 1933. ET: *The Whole Christ: The Development of the Doctrine of the Mystical Body in Scripture and Tradition.* Trans. J. R. Kelly. Milwaukee, 1938.

Miotti, M. E. "*De beata vita* di Agostino: Rapporto con il V libro delle *Tusculanae Disputationes* di Cicerone." *Scritti offerti a R. Iacoangeli.* Ed. S. Felici. Bibliotheca di Scienze Religiose 10. Rome, 1992. pp. 203–225.

Mohrmann, C. *Études sur le latin des chrétiens.* Rome, 1961–1965.

More O'Ferrall, M. "Monica, the Mother of Augustine." *RechAug* 10 (1975) 23–43.

Mühlenberg, E. "Über die Ordnung *(De ordine)*." *Augustinus: Philosophische Frühdialoge.* Ed. C. Andresen. Zurich, 1972.

_____. "Augustin—Die schöpferische Grundlage der Tradition." *Handbuch der Dogmen- und Theologiegeschichte.* Vol. 1: *Die Lehrentwicklung im Rahmen der Katholizität.* Ed. C. Andresen. Göttingen, 1982. pp. 406–463.

Muzungu, B. *Le médiateur entre Dieu et les hommes selon saint Augustin.* Fribourg, 1973.

Neumann, W. M. *Die Stellung des Gottebeweises in Augustins De libero arbitrio.* Hildesheim, 1986.

Newton, J. T. *Neoplatonism and Augustine's Doctrine of the Person and Work of Christ.* Dissertation. Atlanta, 1969.

O'Connell, R.J.S. *Augustine's Platonism.* Villanova, 1984.

_____. "'Involuntary Sin' in *De libero arbitrio*." *REAug* 37 (1991) 23–36.

O'Daly, G. "*Anima, animus.*" *AugLex.* Vol. 1, fascs. 1-2. Basel, 1986. pp. 315–320. Vol. 1, fasc. 3. Basel, 1988. pp. 321–340.

O'Meara, J. *The Young Augustine: The Growth of St. Augustine's Mind up to His Conversion.* London, 1954.

Pannenberg, W. "Christentum und Platonismus: Die kritische Platonrezeption Augustins und ihre Bedeutung für das gegenwärtige christliche Denken." *ZKG* 96 (1985) 147–161.

Pascal, B. *Pensées.* Trans. A. J. Krailsheimer. Baltimore: Penguin Classics, 1966.

Pelikan, J. *The Christian Tradition: A History of the Development of Doctrine.* Vol. 1: *The Emergence of the Catholc Tradition (100–600).* Chicago, 1971.

Pelland, G. *Cinq études d'Augustin sur le début de la Genèse.* Paris, 1972.

Plagnieux, J. "L'influence de la lutte antipélagienne sur le *De Trinitate* ou le christo-centrisme de saint Augustin." *AugMag.* Vol 2. Paris, 1954. pp. 817–826.

Pohlenz, M. *Die Stoa,* 3rd ed. Göttingen, 1964.

Polman, A. D. R. *De leer van God bij Augustinus.* Kampen, 1965.

Pontet, M. *Exégèse de saint Augustin prédicateur.* Théologie 7. Paris, n.d.

Poque, S. "*Christus mercator.*" *RSR* 48 (1960) 564–577.

_____. "Le Christ *iurisperitus* et la procédure *per rescriptum* dans la prédication d'Augustin d'Hippone." *RHDF* 57 (1979) 331–344.

————. *Le langage symbolique dans la prédication d'Augustin d'Hippone.* Paris, 1984.

————. "Les Psaumes dans les *Confessions.*" *Saint Augustin et la Bible.* Ed. A.-M. La Bonnardière. Paris, 1986. pp. 155–166.

————. "L'invocation de Dieu dans les *Confessions.*" *Mélanges T. J. van Bavel.* Leuven, 1990. pp. 927–935.

————, ed. *Augustin d'Hippone: Sermons pour la Pâque,* Sources chrétiennes 116 (Paris, n.d.)

Portalié, E. "Augustin." *DTC* 1 (1902) 2268–2472. ET: *A Guide to the Thought of St. Augustine.* Trans. R. J. Bastian. Chicago, 1960.

Przywara, E. *Augustinus: Die Gestalt als Gefüge.* Leipzig, 1934.

Puech, H.-Ch. *Le manichéisme: Son fondateur, sa doctrine.* Paris, 1949.

Quillen, C. "Consentius as a Reader of Augustine's *Confessions.*" *REAug* 37 (1991) 87–109.

Quispel, G. "Mani the Apostle of Jesus Christ." *Mélanges J. Daniélou.* Paris, 1972. pp. 667–672.

Raeithel, G. "Das Gebet in den Soliloquien Augustins." *ZRG* 20 (1969) 139–153.

Rahner, K. "*Theos* in the New Testament." *Theological Investigations.* Vol. 1. Trans. C. Ernst. Baltimore, 1961.

Ratzinger, J. "Beobachtungen zum Kirchenbegriff des Tyconius im *Liber Regularum.*" *REAug* 2 (1956) 173–185.

Regen, F. "Zu Augustins Darstellung des Platonismus am Anfang des 8. Buches der *Civitas Dei.*" *Festschrift H. Dörrie.* Münster, 1983. pp. 208–227.

Remy, G. *Le Christ médiateur dans l'oeuvre de saint Augustin.* Paris, 1979.

————. "La théologie de la médiation selon saint Augustin: Son actualité." *RThom* 91 (1991) 580–623.

Réveillaud, M. "Le Christ-Homme, tête de l'Église." *RechAug* 5 (1968) 67–94.

Rief, J. *Der Ordobegriff des jungen Augustinus.* Paderborn, 1962.

Ries, J. "Jésus-Christ dans la religion de Mani." *Augustiniana* 14 (1964) 437–444.

————. "Dieux cosmiques et Dieu biblique dans la religion de Mani." *Mélanges T. J. van Bavel.* Leuven, 1990. pp. 757–772.

Rivière, J. *Le dogme de la rédemption chez s. Augustin.* Paris, 1933.

Roetzer, W. *Des heiligen Augustinus Schriften als liturgiegeschichtliche Quelle.* Munich, 1930.

Rondeau, M. J. *Les commentaires patristiques du psautier (IIIᵉ–Vᵉ siècles).* Vol 2: *Exégèse prosopologique et théologie.* Orientalia Christiana Analecta 220. Rome, 1985.

Sachers, E. "*Pater familias.*" *PWK* 18/2 (1949) 2121–2157.

Sage, A. "De la grâce du Christ, modèle et principe de la grâce." *REAug* 7 (1961) 17–34.

————. "La volonté salvifique universelle de Dieu dans la pensée de saint Augustin." *RechAug* 3 (1965) 107–131.

————. "Péché originel: Naissance d'un dogme." *REAug* 13 (1967) 211–248.

Sánchez Navarro, L. "La nocnoción de Dios en las *Confessiones* de san Agustín." *Aug* 34 (1989) 347–354.

Schaffner, O. *Christliche Demut: Des heiligen Augustinus Lehre von der Humilitas.* Würzburg, 1959.

Scheel, O. *Die Anschauung Augustins über Christi Person und Werk unter besonderer Berücksichtigung ihrer verschiedenen Entwicklungstufen und ihrer dogmengeschichtlichen Stellung.* Tübingen, 1901.

Scheffczyk, L. *Schöpfung und Vorsehung.* HDG. Vol. 2, fasc. 2a. Freiburg, 1963.

Schindler, A. *Wort und Analogie in Augustins Trinitätslehre.* Tübingen, 1965.

––––––. "Augustinus." *TRE* 4 (1979) 648–698.

Schmaus, M. *Die psychologische Trinitätslehre des heiligen Augustinus,* 2nd ed. Münster, 1927 (rpt., Münster, 1967).

Schnitzler, F. *Zur Theologie der Verkündigung in den Predigten des hl. Augustinus.* Freiburg, 1968.

Schrama, M. *"Praeposito tamquam patri oboediatur:* Augustinus über Frieden und Gehorsam." *Mélanges T. J. van Bavel.* Leuven, 1990. pp. 846–876.

Schwarz-Kirchenbauer, I., and W. Schwarz. "Über das Glück *(De beata vita).*" *Augustinus: Philosophische Frühdialoge.* Ed. C. Andresen. Zurich, 1972. pp. 145–213.

Seeberg, R. *Lehrbuch der Dogmengeschichte,* 3rd ed. Vol. 2: *Die Dogmenbildung in der Alten Kirche.* 1923 (rpt., Darmstadt, 1953).

Sfameni Gasparo, G. "Double Creation." *EECh.* 1:251-252.

Simon, S. "Von Gott reden, Beobachtungen und Anmerkungen zu Augustinus *Conf.* I,4." *WissWeis* 45 (1982) 130–157.

Siniscalco, P. *"Christum narrare et dilectionem monere." Aug* 14 (1974) 605–623.

Solignac, A. in P. Vignaux, ed. *In Principio: Interprétation des premiers versets de la Genèse.* Paris, 1973. pp. 153–171.

––––––. "Platonisme." *DSp* 12/2 (1986) 1803–1811.

––––––. "Les excès de l'*intellectus fidei* dans la doctrine d'Augustin sur la grâce." *NRT* 110 (1988) 825–849.

Stead, C. *Philosophie und Theologie.* Vol. 1: *Die Zeit der Alten Kirche.* Stuttgart, 1990.

Stirnimann, H. *Grund und Gründer des Alls: Augustins Gebet in den Selbstgesprächen.* Freiburg, 1992.

Strauss, G. *Schriftgebrauch, Schristauslegung and Schriftbeweis bei Augustin.* Beiträge zur Geschichte der biblischen Hermeneutik 1. Tübingen, 1959.

Strauss, R. *Der neue Mensch innerhalb der Theologie Augustins.* Zurich, 1967.

Studer, B. *Zur Theophanie-Exegese Augustins: Untersuchungen zu einem Ambrosius-Zitat in der Schrift "De videndo Deo" (ep. 147).* Studia Anselmiana 59. Rome, 1971.

––––––. *"Consubstantialis Patri—consubstantialis matri:* Une antithèse christologique chez Léon le Grand." *REAug* 18 (1972) 87–115. (*Dominus Salvator,* 29–66.)

––––––. *"Sacramentum et Exemplum* chez saint Augustin." *RechAug* 10 (1975) 87–141. (*Dominus Salvator,* 141–212.)

––––––. In collaboration with B. Daley. *Soteriologie: In der Schrift und Patristik.* HDG. Vol. 3, fasc. 2a. Freiburg, 1978.

––––––. "Jésus-Christ, notre justice, selon saint Augustin." *RechAug* 15 (1980) 99–143. (*Dominus Salvator,* 269–325.)

––––––. "Das Opfer Christi nach Augustins *De civitate Dei* X,5-6: *Lex orandi—lex credendi." Miscellanea C. Vaggagini.* Studia Anselmiana 79. Rome, 1980. pp. 93–107.

_____. "God." *EECh* 1:354-356.

_____. "Augustin et la foi de Nicée." *RechAug* 19 (1984) 133–154. (*Dominus Salvator,* 369–400.)

_____. *Trinity and Incarnation: The Faith of the Early Church.* Trans. M. Westerhoff. Ed. A. Louth. Collegeville, 1993.

_____. "*Una Persona in Christo:* Ein augustinisches Thema bei Leo dem Grossen." *Aug* 15 (1985) 453–487.

_____. "*Credo in Deum Patrem omnipotentem:* Zum Gottesbegriff des heiligen Augustinus." *Atti: Congresso internazionale su S. Agostino nel XVI Centenario della Conversione.* Studia Ephemeridis "Augustinianum" 24. Rome, 1987. pp. 163–188. (*Dominus Salvator,* 401–430).

_____. "*Delectare et prodesse:* Zu einem Schlüsselwort der patristischen Exegese." *Mémorial J. Gribomont.* Rome, 1988. pp. 555–581. (*Dominus Salvator,* 431–461).

_____. *La riflessione teologica nella Chiesa Imperiale (sec. IV e V).* Rome, 1989.

_____. "Zum Aufbau von Augustins *De civitate Dei.*" *Mélanges T. J. van Bavel.* Leuven, 1990. pp. 937–951.

_____. "Zum *Triduum Sacrum* bei Augustin von Hippo." Congresso Internazionale di Liturgia. *La celebrazione del Triduo pasquale: Anamnesis e mimesis.* Studia Anselmiana 102. Rome, 1990. pp. 273–286.

_____. "Agostino d'Ippona e il Dio dei Libri sapienziali: Letture cristiane dei Libri sapienziali." Incontro di Studiosi dell'Antichita cristiana. *Letture cristiane dei Libri sapienziali.* Studia Ephemeridis "Augustinianum" 37. Rome, 1992. pp. 115–125.

_____. *Dominus Salvator: Studien zur Christologie und Exegese der Kirchenväter.* Studia Anselmiana 107. Rome, 1992.

_____. "*Deus, Pater et Dominus* bei Augustinua von Hippo." *Festschrift C. Stead.* Leiden, 1993.

Szabó, F. *Le Christ Créateur chez saint Ambroise.* Rome, 1968.

TeSelle, E. *Augustine the Theologian.* New York, 1970.

Teske, R. "Immortality." *Modern Schoolman* 63 (1986) 233–249.

Thimme, W. *Augustins geistige Entwicklung in den ersten Jahren nach seiner "Bekehrung," 386–391.* Berlin, 1908.

Thonnard, F. J., ed. *S. Augustin: Dialogues philosophiques: De magistro—De libero arbitrio.* BA 6. Paris, 1952.

Tixeront, J. *Histoire des dogmes.* Vol. 2: *De saint Athanase à saint Augustin (318–430),* 9th ed. Paris, 1931. ET: *History of Dogmas,* 5th ed. Vol 2: *From St. Athanasius to St. Augustine (318–430).* Trans. H. L. B. St. Louis, 1914.

Van Bavel, T. *Recherches sur la christologie de saint Augustin.* Paradosis 10. Fribourg, 1954.

_____. "L'humanité du Christ comme *lac parvulorum* et comme *via* dans la spiritualité de saint Augustin." *Augustiniana* 7 (1957) 245–281.

_____. "God between Affirmation and Negation according to Augustine." *Augustine: Presbyter factus sum.* Collectanea Augustiniana. Vol. 2. New York, 1993. pp. 75–95.

Van der Meer, F. *Augustine the Bishop: Church and Society at the Dawn of the Middle Ages.* Trans. B. Battershaw and G. R. Lamb. New York: Sheed & Ward, 1961. Rev. ed., New York: Harper Torchbooks, 1965.

Van Oort, J. *Jerusalem and Babylon: A Study in Augustine's City of God and the Sources of His Doctrine of the Two Cities.* Leiden, 1991. Trans. from Dutch: *Jeruzalem en Babylon.* s' Gravenhage, 1986.

Vannier, M.-A. *"Creatio," "conversio," "formatio" chez s. Augustin.* Paradosis 31. Fribourg, 1991.

Verbraken, P.-P. *Etudes critiques sur les sermons authentiques de saint Augustin.* Steenbrugge, 1976.

Verhees, J. "Augustins Trinitätsverständnis in den Schriften aus Cassiciacum." *RechAug* 10 (1975) 45–75.

_____. "Heilier Geist und Inkarnation in der Theologie des Augustinus von Hippo." *REAug* 22 (1976) 234–253.

_____. "Die Bedeutung des Geistes Gottes im Leben des Menschen nach Augustins frühester Pneumatologie (bis 391)." *ZKG* 88 (1977) 161–189.

Verwilghen, A. *Christologie et spiritualité chez saint Augustin: L'hymne aux Philippiens.* Théologie historique 72. Paris, 1985.

Vincent, M. *S. Augustin, Maître de prière d'après les Enarrationes in Psalmos.* Théologie historique 84. Paris, 1990.

_____. "Le vocabulaire de la prière chez s. Augustin." *Mélanges T. J. van Bavel.* Leuven, 1990. pp. 783–804.

Voss, B. R. *"Academicis." AugLex.* Vol. 1, fascs. 1-2. Basel, 1986. pp. 45–51.

Weinand, W. *Die Gottesidee, der Grundzug der Weltanschauung des heiligen Augustinus.* Paderborn, 1910.

Wenning, G. "Der Einfluss des Manichäismus und des Ambrosius auf die Hermeneutik Augustins." *REAug* 36 (1990) 80–90.

Wittmann, L. *Ascensus: Der Aufstieg zur Tranzendenz in der Metaphysik Augustins.* Munich, 1980.

Wlosok, A. "Die Gottesprädikation *Pater et Dominus* bei Laktanz: Gott in Analogie zum römischen *pater familias." Laktanz und die philosophische Gnosis.* Heidelberg, 1960. pp. 233–246.

_____. "Vater und Vatervorstellungen in der römischen Kultur." *Res humanae—res divinae.* Ed E. Heck and E. A. Schmidt. Heidelberg, 1990. pp. 35–83.

Zum Brunn, E. "L'exégèse augustinienne de *Ego sum qui sum* et la métaphysique de l'exode." *Dieu et l'Être.* Ed. P. Vignaux. Paris, 1978. pp. 141–164.

Zumkeller, A. *"Agone christiano (De)." AugLex.* Vol. 1, fascs. 1-2. Basel, 1986. pp. 221–227.

Index of Scriptural Texts

Index of Persons

Index of Subjects and Concepts